CALGARY PUBLIC LIBRARY

MAR — 2008

The Knights of Winter

The History of British Columbia Hockey from 1895 to 1911

by Craig H. Bowlsby

Privately printed in Canada
2006

copyright Craig H. Bowlsby 2006

All rights reserved. No part of this work may be reproduced or used in any manner, whether electronic or mechanical, whether in print or broadcast, or for oral or visual presentation without the express written permission of Craig Bowlsby, except for short excerpts used for review purposes.

Published by Craig H. Bowlsby in Vancouver British Columbia Canada.

Canadian Cataloging in Publication Data to be announced.

ISBN 0-9691705-4-8

Contact Craig H. Bowlsby at epic@intergate.ca

Table of contents

	page
Acknowledgements	4
Introduction	5
Prologue: The Real, True History of Hockey (Maybe)	7
The First B.C. Beginning	19
1895 Season	23
1896 Season	27
1897 Season	29
1898 Season	35
1899 Season	43
1900 Season	53
1901 Season	63
1902 Season	81
1903 Season	91
1904 Season	107
1905 Season	129
1906 Season	145
1907 Season	167
1908 Season — Lester Patrick arrives	191
1909 Season — Frank Patrick arrives	216
1910 Season — The Patricks leave	241
1911 Season — The Patricks return	267
Epilogue	294
Appendix One to Prologue:	299
Appendix Two to Prologue:	301
Appendix Three to Prologue:	304
Appendix Four to Prologue:	306
Appendix Five: List of Individual Players, Men, 1895-1911	307
Appendix Six: List of Individual Players, Ladies, 1895-1911	369
Appendix Seven: List of Men's teams	374
Appendix Eight: List of Women's Teams	380
Appendix Nine: Goal Leaders, year by year, (men)	381
Appendix Ten: Overall Goal Leaders	387
Appendix Eleven: Top Goal Scoring Averages	392
Appendix Twelve: Multiple Goal Games	393
Appendix Thirteen: Goaltenders Records, Year by Year	394
Appendix Fourteen: Goaltenders Records Individual	400
Appendix Fifteen: Trophy Winners	403
Appendix Sixteen: List of Illustrations	408
Appendix Seventeen: List of Sources	408

Acknowledgements

Many thanks to the following: (In alphabetical order of first name)

Bill Fitsell
Irene Robinson
Jason Beck and The British Columbia Sports Hall of Fame
Joan Payzant
Joyce Austin and The Rossland Museum
Lynda Williams
Mavis Garrison
Morey Holzman
National Gallery of Art, Washington, for John Toole's "Skating Scene", a gift of Edgar William and Bernice Chrysler Garbisch
Ori Kowarsky
Patty Moran, USGA
Royal Ontario Museum
Sara Benson and the The Trail Museum
Shawn Lamb and The Nelson Museum
Sheelah Castle
Ted Pappas
The Bata Shoe Museum in Toronto
Wanda Mizner and the Boundary Museum

Introduction

This book should have been written twenty years ago. Alas it was not. All of the players listed have apparently died, as have the spectators. If any eye-witnesses to this golden age of hockey are still alive, they have not been found by this author.

Few statistics were kept in these pioneer days, or at least, most cannot be found.

Nevertheless, every game found reported during the period covered in this book has been chronicled here, and every player listed. However, this compilation is necessarily incomplete. Newspaper reports are the primary source, and they were often found to be deficient, erroneous or simply missing. Cross-referencing different towns' reports was necessary to achieve a reasonably accurate overview.

Names of players were often not given, or given only by last name, or, if one were lucky, with an initial. I have kept most of these listings the way they were reported, unless I was certain of the player's name from other sources. There were many brothers who played on the same teams, intermittently, and one could often not be a hundred per cent certain who the player was, even if the initial was the same. There were many players whose first names were never given. If the score or the rosters are not reported below, then they simply were not available.

Still, this glimpse into the forgotten past was exciting and full of gleaming veins of raw data, which have been surveyed and mapped out into something of a recognizable shape.

Please dig in.

PROLOGUE:

The real, true, history of hockey (Maybe)

One hundred million years ago, the great single continent of Earth, Pangea, cracked along the Atlantic fault trench, splitting the Americas away from Europe and Africa, thus making the sport of North American ice hockey possible.

The Earth's climate changed in various ways for several more million years, including the ebb and flow of several ice ages. The last ice age receded about ten thousand years ago, leaving a vast playground of lakes and rivers in North America where hockey could, and would, be played. A short period of cold, when the lakes freeze up, was provided by the slight, rhythmic wobble of the earth on its rotational axis, which still creates the seasons.

Then the earth waited while humans began multiplying, hunting, gathering, farming and fighting.

Finally, Frederick The Great of Prussia attacked Austria in 1740 A.D. and started the war of the Austrian Succession.

The great powers of Europe reluctantly chose up sides, including France and England in 1744. The conflict sputtered out in 1745, (officially ending in 1748), but remained smoldering until 1754 when it broke out again over the same basic issues, but in North America, it became the French and Indian Wars, or the Seven Years War.[1] Finally England gained the upper hand, principally with the capture of the fortresses at Louisberg, Montreal and Quebec.

But it was not these captures so much as the high price of cane sugar which then laid the foundation for the development of North American hockey. At the Treaty of Paris conference in 1763, France was given the choice of keeping their vast dominions of the North, or the tiny West Indies islands of Martinique and Guadalupe, where the cane sugar crop was worth a small fortune every year.

France chose the tiny islands.

So where England had dominated the central coast of North America, they now inherited vast, cold dominions, devoid of cane sugar, but filled with countless lakes of all sizes. Technically, they already had some of these dominions, including the vast Rupert's Land around Hudson's Bay, the peninsula of Nova Scotia, and the island of Newfoundland. But there had been few attempts to seriously colonize these places. With the capitulation of the French, the English now had control of the Saint Lawrence and of the complete, undisputed development of what became Canada. At the same time, unlike the

---

[1] The War of the Spanish Succession, from 1701-1713, had already begun pitting the French against the English in North America, but not much fighting actually took place in North America. The main North American result, won from battlefields elsewhere, was that France had to give England the peninsula of Nova Scotia at the treaty of Utrecht, (although keeping Cape Breton.) There had been many centuries of warfare between France and England, but the War of the Austrian Succession crystallized its continuance, through treaties of alternating conquest and loss, so that it seemed never to go out, even in periods of peace.

French, in the late seventeen hundreds the English became ball crazy. Any way an English boy could hit a ball with a stick was used and abused, along with other more traditional ball games. Any surface, including mud, dirt, grass or ice was used to whack at a ball made of wood, cork, cloth, rock, dung, and if they were really lucky, rubber. The streets of English towns were alive with children racing after each other and thrashing at their "cat" as it was sometimes called. Although some of these games had been known in ancient times, eventually they became refined with rules of sorts, and became known variously as hurley, bandy, shinty, rounders, cricket, field or ground hockey, or just hockey. There were of course other games with "balls" such as tennis, badminton, billiards etc. The French played some of these games, but in France they were primarily for the upper gentry, not the middle and lower classes, as was common in England, and it was in England that batting the ball along the ground was the common pastime. The Dutch had invented a game on ice of hitting a small ball into a hole which they called Kolf. This was taken up by the Scots, who didn't have as much ice, so became a dry land game called Golf, not to be confused with hockey.[2]

In England, as Napoleon Bonaparte was ravaging continental Europe, the game of Bandy was being played on the superb ice surfaces of the fen district, a lowland area in the middle of England. This was the first, true, organized game of ice hockey, employing all the necessary elements of skates, a stick, and a ball. It was natural that the fen folk would develop this game because they skated more than anyone else in the country. (See Appendix One).

William Leeland, from Bury Fen, was Captain of some of the strongest teams during the first half of the 19th century. The earliest game he personally remembered took place in the 1813-14 season, when he was eleven years old. But the tradition spoke of organized games going back into the seventeen hundreds. Bandy was also called Hockey on the ice, and the players were encouraged to play "land" hockey during the summer to develop their stick-handling skills. Generally, however, with their short, light sticks, the players used only one hand to guide the ball. They also played with eleven men a side.

In 1853 a game of hockey on the ice was organized in front of Windsor Castle. The Queen attended and Albert, the Prince Consort, defended one of the goals. (See Astley's "Fifty Years of my Life in the World of Sport.") There was no mention of Bandy per se in the source material, so it's hard to determine if it

---

[2] The Society of North American Hockey Historians and Researchers, or SONAHHR, not to be confused with the Society for International Hockey Research, or SIHR, has done an excellent job of compiling historical references to hockey, and indeed, chronicling the game in all its forms. However, they have made the mistake of referring to the game of Kolven, as played by the Dutch settlers in America, as the forerunner of ice hockey in the American colonies. Unfortunately this is one of the versions of Kolf, or Kelven, or Kolven, as stated, which has been shown by golf historians to be how golf originated. There are many references to this in books published throughout the 1800's, and several recent books have chronicled it, including, "Golf, History & Tradition 1500-1945," by David Stirk, Excellent Press, Palmers' House, Shropshire England, 1998; and "Golf & Kolf, Seven Centuries of History," by Jacques Temmerman, Martial & Snoeck, Belgium, 1994.

If one actually views paintings of the Dutch playing Kolven one would see that it is being played by only a few men, one or two in many cases; they are trying to hit a ball into a small round hole in the ice, and usually they are not wearing skates.

Plate 01. Bandy illustration from Badminton Library, Skating, 1892.

was played according to that tradition, but likely not. The game was organized by the First Light Guards, and the military intended to simply use their field hockey sticks on the ice rather than specially made "bandies." Another game, organized by bandy players, this time, did take place at the Crystal Palace in 1860.

In any case, a very organized series of tournaments was taking place in England all through the Victorian era, largely according to Bandy rules. Meanwhile, back in North America, the British Empire split apart in 1783. The United Empire Loyalists poured into Nova Scotia, and the Canadian territories, and the population burgeoned with tradesmen and farmers, who helped to form chains of towns all along the waterways.

Then the Americans invaded Canada in 1812, which didn't help the development of hockey.

But there was a greater impediment to the development of Canadian hockey, which accounted largely for its long gestation period in North America. Few people had skates![3] In Nova Scotia, there appears to be very few references before the 1820's to skating, but most luxury items like skates had been imported from England, and there were few, if any, manufacturers of skates in North America. Besides, the average Canadian had few possessions, and life in the wilderness certainly was not enhanced by lugging around skates. The travel literature and diary accounts of the time make very little mention of skates, including those involving military outposts. As indicated in Appendix One, the games of hockey played on the ice mentioned by soldiers in their

---

[3] Several authors explain that many people were skating in the late seventeen hundreds, and early eighteen hundreds, in Canada. However, beyond the Kings Edgehill School references, which seem to go back to 1810; an 1807 skating reference from the Ridout Letters, referring to Cornwall; an 1807 reference by George Heriot in a book of travels; and the supposed 1790's quote from Raddall's book, (see Appendix One), this author has seen no other actual references, until the 1820's. It is said that the Scots carried their skates with them to Nova Scotia. No doubt some of them did. But, as seen in Appendix One, there were very few Scots in Canada before the 1790's. Martin Jones in his book, "Hockey's Home," reports on a ferry service between Halifax and Dartmouth started in 1752, and then quotes a passage from the Payzant's book, "Like a Weaver's Shuttle, a History of the Halifax-Dartmouth Ferries," where they say, "The minutes of the Steam Boat Company record that a flag was to be hoisted at the Halifax Station when there was good skating in Dartmouth." Was this, finally, a reference to the 1700's? Unfortunately not. I called Joan Payzant in Dartmouth, and she informed me that the reference was from 1874.

Garth Vaughn states, on page 75 of, "The Puck Stops Here," that in the late 1700's skating was very popular in Nova Scotia. Unfortunately, he gives no references for this conclusion. I have made extensive forays into published diaries and accounts of life in Canada, and yet no reference to skating has shown up, other than those four stated, until the late 1820's. Furthermore, extensive research has been done of the pictorial representations of Canadian life. There have been no pictures found of skating by this author before the 1830's. None by George Heriot; none by Robert Field, Cockburn, Dartnell, Fowler, Griffiths, Hamel, Kreighoff, Kane, Legare, Palmer, Plamondon, or Thomas Davies; none in the Royal Ontario Museum; none in Halifax museums, etc. No doubt there must be some, somewhere. But not in Garth Vaughn's book. Not in any hockey book known to me. Where are the references for these conclusions and assumptions? I would be happy to be inundated with them, but until then, I must conclude, from the actual evidence, that skating in Canada before the 1820's was a rare thing.

diaries had little influence on the civilian population. The places where enough stability and wealth could allow skates to be bought by many and used at will by civilians were largely in Nova Scotia, the most developed of the Canadian colonies, particularly at the upper class schools like Kings-Edgehill.

But then, a couple of things happened.

First, the War of 1812 ended in 1815.

Then the Erie Canal was built.

And then the Welland Canal started construction.[4]

The Erie Canal was a long stretch of water constructed between lake Erie and the Hudson river, allowing Atlantic access to the Great Lakes for the Americans. It was begun in 1817 and ended construction in 1825. The Welland Canal was cut between Lake Ontario and Lake Erie, finally connecting the St Lawrence Seaway directly to the rest of the Great Lakes. It was started in 1824 and finished in 1829. Both projects spawned offshoots and upgrades that continued for decades. These two canals caused huge amounts of commerce and industry to explode into life. But the Welland Canal required more skilled labour than Canada could muster, and a great call went out to the mother country. In Liverpool, the papers were full of advertisements pleading for emigrants. It was the same in all the coastal communities of the United Kingdom.

So they came. Thousands upon thousands of men, who had once been boys, who still loved to play their stick games of shinty, hurley and bandy.

And finally, finally, they brought their skates.

This was especially true of the men from the fens, who were natural bargemen and river workers. Two of these men, the brothers William and John Large, were members of the famous Bury Fen team, which was renowned for never being defeated.

William Leeland, the Captain of this team from the early 1820's to 1850, (and who died in 1891 at the age of 90), said that these two young men, the Large's, emigrated to "America," which at that time also meant Canada. He didn't say exactly when, but it would have been, very roughly, circa the 1830's.

Could William and John have resisted teaching others in America their sport? It's far more likely that they continued to play it with a passion. Indeed, according to a 1929 article by Thomas K. Fischer, who just happened to have published the first hardcover manual on ice hockey in 1926, in New York, bandy was the, "parent game," in the U.S. and Canada, but that it has since followed "the genius of its own development." He describes the various changes in rules, equipment and technique from bandy to ice hockey.

The historical literature of the 1830's explodes with exuberant references to skating. It replaces all other winter sports in popularity, where a decade previous there was very little. The canals themselves become a favorite cavorting ground and young men often skated for miles as their normal exercise. The average worker's economic wellbeing also appeared to increase, which would have allowed more skates to be bought, during the 1820's and 1830's.

As for hockey, it is still slow to develop. In 1829, According to Bill Fitsell, the eminent hockey historian from Kingston Ontario, the first written

---

[4] The Shubenacadie Canal, in the Dartmouth area was also built, over a long period from 1826 to 1861. See "Hockey's Home."

account, published at the time of the event, of civilian hockey in Nova Scotia is from the Pictou Colonial Herald, when one man was found not guilty of a charge which involved skating on Sunday: "Every idler who feels disposed to profane the lords day may now turn out with skates on feet, hurley in hand and play the delectable game of break-shins, without any regard to the laws."[5] Break-shins was played with the ball usually being hit along the ice, not up in the air as hurley usually was, which shows that the sport of hockey was being molded in its infancy. Hurley sticks, or sticks that looked like hurley sticks were often being used to play the new hybrid game.

Later Halifax newspapers refer to games played with hurley sticks on the ice with names like wicket or ricket. (Bill Fitsell)

It appears that two main forms of hockey, shinny, which was essentially the new hybrid game, with "rickets" as goals, and sticks resembling hurley sticks, and bandy, tended to be split along the border, with bandy primarily in the south. The earliest known visual representation of ice hockey known to this author in North America is a painting by John Toole, circa 1835 of several skating men battling over a ball with crooked sticks on a pond, somewhere, according to curators, in the Shenandoah Valley. (This was presented at an exhibition called, "The Artist and the Sportsman," at the National Art Museum of Sport, Madison Square Garden, New York, in 1968, catalogued by Martha B.Scott. An oil on canvas, it usually resides at the National Gallery of Art, Washington D.C.) There is also a Currier and Ives print, in two versions, from 1855, showing two young boys on skates batting at a ball on a small pond, possibly depicting life in New York State. In the Currier and Ives print, both boys are using the one-handed style, while one of the men in the Toole painting is guiding the ball with one hand, which is the hall-mark of bandy.

But the Nova Scotia hybrid game was not spreading into the rest of Canada. One can postulate this by looking at negative newspaper and literary references. In other words, there does not appear to be any references in Ontario to ricket or wicket, which was one of the dominant names for ice hockey in Nova Scotia from the 1820's to the 1850's. This is a glaring anomaly. There was no hockey reported being played in Quebec until the 1870's, as if it were a buffer zone, between Nova Scotia and Ontario, and outside of Nova Scotia, in the Canadas or the Maritimes, there are no references at all to hockey-like games, known to this author, until about 1840, and they do not speak of rickets, wickets or hurley. (The known Ontario written references, as seen in Appendix Four, are, 1): The Kingston Whig-Standard, about 1839; 2): The Freeling Diary, probably from Kingston, in 1843; 3): The George Stanley book, "Life In the Woods," describing Toronto about 1844; and 4): the Horsey Diary, speaking of Kingston in 1847.) So where did this new hockey come from? It could be merely a coincidence that hockey in Ontario developed primarily after the Welland Canal and its offshoots had been built, and around the same time, probably, that William and John Large, the famous bandy players emigrated to America, along with the influx of English, Scottish and Irish canal workers, but there is no better simple explanation for why there was no hockey reported in

---

[5] An 1827 reference, as a poem, has since been found, in the Acadian Magazine, with the line, "Now at ricket with hurlies some dozens of boys/ Chase the ball o'er ice with a deafening noise." I don't know who first discovered this. My reference was from the Nova Scotia History website.

Plate 02. John Toole's "Skating Scene", circa 1835, National Gallery of Art, Washington. Notice the man on the far right, holding a "Kolf" or "Kelven" stick, in contrast to the other four men with bandies or hockies.

Plate 03. Currier and Ives Lithograph, Winter Pastime, 1855 Author's collection.

Ontario, and then there *was* hockey being reported. In any case, it had to come from somewhere. (See Appendix Two).

It's true that there are no newspaper reports or diaries speaking of bandy in Ontario, but two early authorities, J.M. Oxley, who was playing in Nova Scotia, between the 1860's to the 1880's, and Thomas Fisher, who played in New England around the turn of the twentieth century, both believed that bandy was the original influence on the sport which developed in North America, and Arthur Farrell believed that English sports, (at one point describing a bandy-like game), were the direct influence on ice hockey in Canada. (See Appendix Three).

The earliest pictorial rendering of ice hockey in Canada known to this author is William Armstrong's 1852 painting titled: "Steamer, Chief Justice Robinson, Landing Passengers on the ice in Toronto Bay." Eight skaters are clearly playing a pickup game of hockey, or bandy, with crooked sticks, some of which are held up, and some down. [6]

The most developed province in Canada at the time was Nova Scotia, where scholastic institutions allowed a kind of stability of tradition to develop amongst its young students. The earliest civilian reference in Canada to hockey may be two written accounts of school life in Kings-Edgehill school near Windsor. One, apparently referring to about 1810, although written as fiction, about 1844, by Thomas Haliburton in an English magazine called Attache, says, "the boys let out racin', yellin', hollerin', and whoopin' like mad with pleasure, and the playground, and the game at bass in the fields, or hurley on the long pond on the ice, or campin' out at night at Chester Lakes to fish."[7]

The other, referring to the period 1816-18, and published in 1876 in the Windsor Mail, states, "The Devils' Punch bowl and Long Pond, back of the college, were favorite resorts, and we used to skate in winter, on moonlight nights, on the ponds....I recollect John Cunard, [brother of Sir Samuel of steamship fame] having his teeth knocked out with a hurley by Pete Delancey of Annapolis." [8]

Unfortunately, these three references talk of skating and hurley, but not in the same sentence, which leaves the maddening technical question of whether a form of hockey, or hurley, on the ice was actually played at that time. An oral tradition around the school, however, talks of a type of very early hockey being played on Long Pond, (which is apparently now called Steel Pond, and is on the property of Howard Dill, who speaks of this oral tradition), and it is generally accepted by this author, as well as other scholars, that a form of hockey was being played here at that time. It appears that initially hurley sticks were used, because that is what the students were used to, but in time the games began to resemble Shinty, and then a new hybrid all its own. (See Appendix Two).

So, shinny from the East, which might have started as hurley on the ice, but quickly became a hybrid, played with or without rickets, or goals, with hurley sticks, or sticks resembling hurley sticks, was bubbling and coagulating

---

[6] First reference in relation to hockey published by Craig Bowlsby in 1996. The painting is found in the Royal Ontario Museum, in Toronto.
[7] This reference was first published by J.P. Martin, about 1954.
[8] Reference revived around 1988 by Leslie Loomer. It is from a series called, "Early Sketches of Windsor," to be found in an anonymous scrapbook in the PANS (Skins Collection), MG9, Vol 28, P. 81.

Plate 04. William Armstrong's painting, Toronto Bay, 1852, Royal Ontario Museum. It is difficult to see in the scan, but in the original painting there is a small object being batted by the players.

Plate 05. Thames Skating engraving 1855, Illustrated London News. (This exact same image was reprinted in this publication well into the 1860's.) Author's collection.

in its isolated Nova Scotian pot, while bandy from the South, and a mingling of other British stick and ball games were tried on the ice, rather aimlessly, in New England and Ontario.

Finally, after decades of unorganized play of all types, rules began to be formulated in Nova Scotia for a few of the variants, and then J.G.A. Creighton, who had been living in Halifax, moved to Montreal in 1872, or 1873, and brought with him the newly written rules, with some of his own changes. Thus, he became the father of organized hockey outside of Nova Scotia. (See "Hockey's Captains Colonels and Kings" by Bill Fitsell.) The disorganized games being played in Quebec and Ontario were provided a focus and began to coalesce.

Creighton, and others after him, opened the flood gates. With a definite, organized game, leagues could be formed, teams could challenge others, boys who had read Horatio Alger's stories could quantify their prowess, and men could finally make wagers.

There would never be any laws that could stop it; no mothers could prevent their children from playing it, and the hockey infection could never more be contained.

The infection spread to Manitoba in 1889.

Then to the North West Territories, (Alberta and Saskatchewan) about 1893.

And then, finally, following its own course like a winding river, to the far flung, mountain stronghold of British Columbia, in 1895.

However, before that river found its true course, there was one earlier moment of B.C. hockey, now frozen in time, as seen in the next chapter.

The First B.C. Beginning

In January of 1862, the lower delta of the Fraser River, in Southwestern B.C., froze over. This happened very rarely and it was a magical event to the three hundred inhabitants of New Westminster. The townspeople immediately took advantage of this and stopped everything else they were doing and rushed onto the ice to skate and play hockey, as if they'd been waiting for just such an opportunity for decades. But to play hockey they first had to run out of their ramshackle townsite, and up, over the hills which had been previously denuded, to find trees in the surrounding forest with appropriate branches, and then hack away as fast as they could, and shape them into something approximating a hockey stick.

Those lucky enough to have skates strapped them on and cavorted as long as they could, and began to play hockey.

We know all this happened because of two references. The first is a diary of the Reverend John Sheepshanks, who was appointed temporary chaplain to the Royal Engineers in 1859. His life and diary were incorporated into a book called, "A Bishop in the Rough," published in 1909. (See, "A Bishop in the Rough," edited by D.W. Duthie, London, 1909.)[9] The second is a page in the British Columbian, a New Westminster newspaper, on January 16, 1862.[10]

The editor Duthie, of Sheepshank's memoirs, wrote, "In January, 1862, winter set in with a severity unusual even in British Columbia…The frost brought with it opportunities which no Englishman can resist. For the first time since the Creation skating began on the hardened surface of the river. Early one morning the young Siwash rushed into Mr. Sheepshanks' room to tell him, in much excitement, that a Boston man, (that is, American), was moving about in a very quick and surprising way upon the ice." Then he quotes Sheepshank, "It being then apparent that we were in for a spell of wintry weather, various preparations were made, notably by the Canadian portion of the population for winter amusements. Sleighs were rapidly made, and presently the ladies were being driven about in the rough equipages, made smart with skins, and jingling with bells. Hockey sticks were cut from the forest, and the male portion of the population, officials, parsons, storekeepers, woodmen, and Indians, were engaged in this exciting game upon the broad river. This has continued now for some weeks. Occasionally carts come down the river upon the ice, and cattle are driven across to the other side. Business is at a standstill, and sleigh-driving and hockey have been the order of the day."

The British Columbian, a weekly paper begun only a month earlier, wrote: "A Day Upon The Ice—The Fraser River presented such a scene opposite this city on Friday last as we have rarely had the pleasure of looking upon—certainly such as the native red man never saw before. Upon Friday morning the ice bridge, which, 'Jack Frost,' had been busily engaged at was

---

[9] This reference was brought to my attention, and first researched, by Morey Holzman, author, (with Joseph Nieforth,) of "Deceptions and Doublecross, How the NHL Conquered Hockey," 2002, Dundurn Press, Toronto.

[10] Also brought to my attention by Morey Holzman.

thrown completely across the river, and pronounced safe for foot passengers. No sooner was this announcement made than scores of men might be seen running hither and thither in search of skates—an article which but few thought of bringing to this country—and in a wonderfully short space of time there was a busy throng upon the ice. All the available skates, both in camp and city, were brought into requisition, but still not one in ten was provided with the necessary article. But skates or no skates, all determined to enjoy themselves…but skating was by no means the only sport. Ladies, gentlemen and children might be seen in groups, engaged in sliding, running, playing at ball, etc., and every age and profession were represented. All seemed young again, entering into these boyish sports, just as they had done in other lands scores of years ago…"

New Westminster was only three years old, and had been cut out of the bush and the shore of the Fraser River, twenty miles from what would eventually become Vancouver, to be the new capital of British Columbia in 1859. There were many tradesmen and farmers who had traversed to the new colony, partly to take advantage of the two gold rushes in 1858 and 1862, but also to take advantage of the cheap land being offered by the government for colonization and the opportunities that meant for their future. There were many Upper Canadians, (Ontario), Nova Scotians, and apparently several Americans. It was most likely the Nova Scotians who avidly jumped at the chance to play hockey, since, as explained above, they had been developing a new hybrid game in places like Dartmouth, Halifax and Windsor for forty years, while it had been much slower to develop in Ontario. It might have been an Ontario man who described the scene in the British Columbian, since all he could think to call the shinny was, "playing at ball." Sheepshank, on the other hand, was born and raised in England, so he knew enough to call it hockey.

This kind of scene would most likely have been the same in new colonial outposts throughout Canada, where a window of opportunity provided a small group of men, with similar past experience, to relive their happiest days of sport.

But it could not be said that this was the beginning of the sport of ice hockey in British Columbia. In a way, it was similar to the game of hockey played by the explorer John Franklin on Great Bear Lake in 1825,[11] or the games of hockey played by the garrison soldiers of Kingston in 1843, as described in Freeling's diary. None of these games could be said to have started the general population on the way to emulating them on a regular basis, let alone developing an organized sport. It's not even certain, after all, that most of the games at New Westminster, or even those played by Franklin, were played with skates on.

Alas, it appears that the first hockey played in British Columbia was an ancestor that died out on the evolutionary trail.

But it was fun while it lasted.

---

[11] This reference was brought to light by Joseph Nieforth of Toronto in 2003. Franklin's diary said, "Till the snow fell, the game of hockey played on the ice was the morning's sport."

Plate 06. Map of South-Eastern British Columbia. Adapted from Water Powers in British Columbia, 1917. From author's collection.

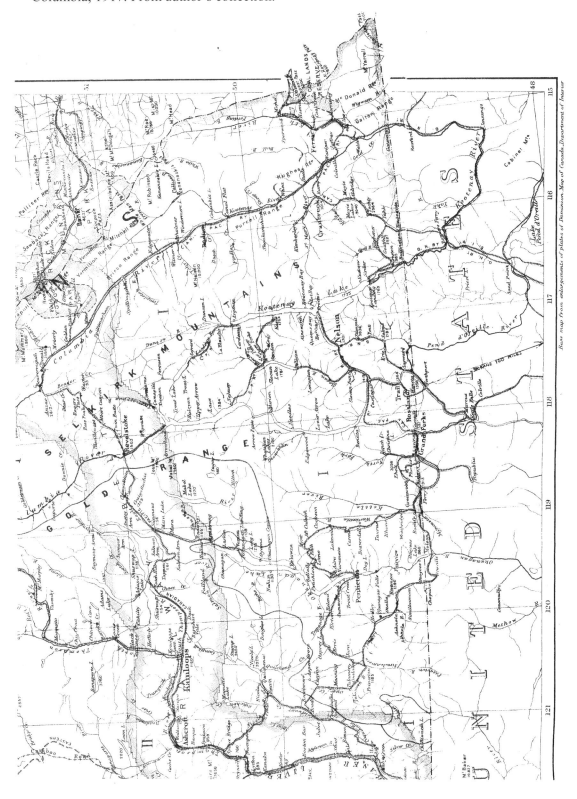

Plate 06a. Map of South-Eastern British Columbia. Adapted from Water Powers in British Columbia, 1917. From author's collection.

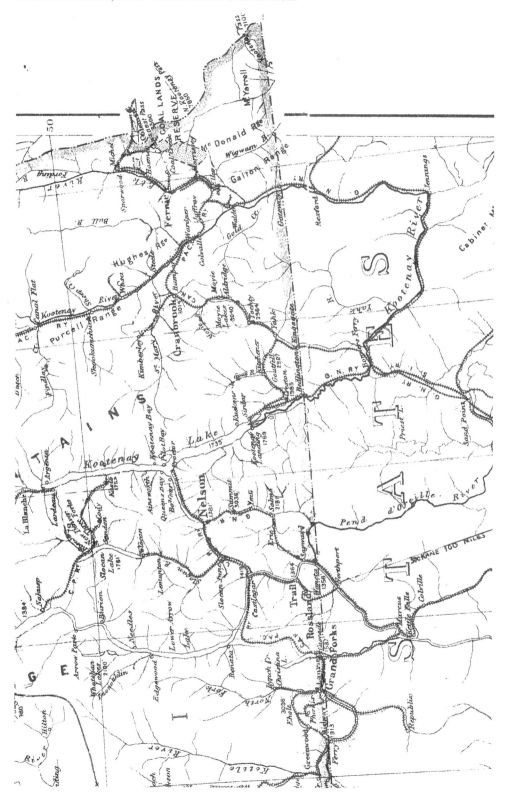

1895 SEASON

In the middle of January, 1895, a few leading citizens of the small town of Golden, B.C. including the town's Doctor, James Norman Taylor, and a business man named W.R. Hamilton, sat on the Columbia River bank and laced up a pair of their shoes, upon which they had attached thin metal, retractable skates. Then they stood up, picked up their new hockey sticks, and ventured out onto the bumpy ice where several other men were waiting to practise serious hockey for the first time in British Columbia.

This was not shinny; it was not a wild madcap game of boys thrashing at a makeshift puck in an ever-changing scramble, chasing each other in a perpetual keep-away. This was an adult attempt to play the new scientific sport, by passing, stickhandling, and shooting on a goal, but without any instruction, and little, if any, experience.

It would not have been pretty.

But it was probably exhilarating all the same.

The first notice of the new sport of ice hockey being played in B.C. came on January 12, 1895, in the Golden Era Newspaper, which said, "Steps are being taken to form a hockey club in town. Sticks and pucks were ordered and arrived this week and the boys are hard at work practising."

The Canadian Pacific Railway had blasted and carved its way through the Rocky Mountains into Golden in 1886. This was the direct route from Alberta, known then as the Northwest Territories, and Golden became a CPR construction town, set up to service the railroad, about sixty miles from the Alberta border. As it was also located in a valley, on the Columbia River, it became a kind of gateway to the rest of British Columbia.

Once hockey was introduced to Alberta, in 1893, or 1894, it was no accident that it would trickle across into British Columbia a year later.

By January 19, Bob Rusk had made a rink on the river, at "very little cost to skaters." It was not indicated whether this was a temporary structure on the ice itself, or a cleared space, beside the river, which could be flooded, as later became the custom. A curling rink had already been made in 1893, which could be used every winter. Similarly there was an ice rink constructed in Sandon, below Golden in the Slocan valley in 1893, and another rink, the Crystal Rink, constructed in Nelson, below Sandon, at the top of the West Kootenays, in 1893-94. But there is no indication that hockey was being played there yet.

An effort was being made to get an actual hockey game going in Golden, but it was not until January 23, 1895 that a hockey match was played, between two pick-up teams, captained respectively by W.R. Hamilton and Doc Taylor. "After a fast and exciting struggle," reported the Era, "the game resulted in a 4-4 tie. With a little practise a team could be selected which could hold its own with some of the neighboring hockey clubs."

Neighboring clubs?

In 1895 Golden was a small town of about 500 people, nestled, as it is now, at the junction of the Columbia and Kicking Horse rivers, in the middle of the Rocky Mountains. When they spoke of neighbors, they meant anybody along the Canadian Pacific Railway who had carved out a town, because if they weren't on the rail link somewhere, it was hard to get there.

The closest towns with organized hockey teams on the rail link were Banff and Calgary, in the Northwest Territories.

Revelstoke, about 100 kilometers away by crow, twice that by train, the other direction, might have had players at that time, but no record of them has shown up.

Nevertheless, the Golden Hockey Club was organized on February 7th 1895, electing the following officers: Honorary President, Mr. Foster; President, Mr. W. McNeish; Vice-President, J.Lake; Honorary Vice President, Captain Armstrong; Captain, Doctor Taylor; Sec-Treasurer, W.R. Hamilton. The membership fee was $1.00 and the next meeting was called for Saturday at the Queen's Hotel at 8:00.

It is not known what other hockey proceedings transpired that year in Golden. However, it was announced on February 23rd, that a team of curlers had left for Calgary. The curlers named, from the Golden Era, were: H.G. Parson, C.A. Warren, J. Rae, W. McNeish, J.N. Taylor, W.R. Hamilton, P.J. Russell and D.M. Rae. These men formed two "rinks," skipped by W.R. Hamilton and Dr. Taylor, and played several games against Calgary teams.

However, a day or two later, as reported in the Calgary Daily Herald, on February 25th, a Golden hockey team played the Calgary Fire Brigade hockey team. This was the first inter-provincial game between British Columbia and Alberta, which was still the North-West Territories until 1905.

Two of the curlers, W.R. Hamilton and Dr. Taylor played on the Golden team. The game was close in the first half, and the Golden team applied their new technique, which consisted of a battering ram formation running at the opponents, and then turning completely around, and ramming into the opposing players backwards. The score at the half was 4-3 for the Fire Brigade team, nonetheless. In the second half the referee informed Golden that he would not allow the new, wild charges, and Golden was left to play with their usual technique, which was very poor, in comparison to the seasoned Fire Brigade team, who proceeded to score 5 more goals and won the game, 9-3.

Golden Seniors		Calgary Fire Brigade (Tigers)
Marshall, C.	goal	Comer
Wheatley	point	Marshall, E.
Hamilton, W.R.	cover	Saunders
Mair	forward	Henderson
Taylor, Dr. J.N.	forward	Atkins
Vincent	forward	Watson
McColl	forward	Bruce

Goals: not known

(J. Rae, who traveled with the Golden players to curl against Calgary is possibly the same man as Jack Rae, who may have been a member of the Rossland Senior hockey team as early as 1897.)

Despite the enthusiasm of Dr. Taylor, and W.R. Hamilton, perhaps the most important of the officers of the Golden Hockey Club was Captain Frank P. Armstrong. Although he is only mentioned once, as a Vice President of the hockey club, Armstrong was a most remarkable man and a very consequential figure in B.C.'s pioneer days. Captain Armstrong constructed his first steamboat, the "Duchess," himself, and ordered a second hand engine from Winnipeg, which arrived on the first CPR train through to Golden. Armstrong then transported some of the first goods by steamboat up and down the Columbia River, and when the canal was finished, linking the Kootenay river system to the Columbia, Captain Armstrong was able to travel all through the Kootenays as well, down to the U.S. border, often reaching as far as Jennings Montana. The Duchess did not last long, grounding out, as many small steamboats did, but Armstrong piloted many subsequent vessels. He was known as the pioneer steamboat Captain of the Kootenays, and carried all manner of goods, mail and information to the towns littered over many hundreds of square miles.

In 1895 Captain Armstrong was one of only about fifteen people who were associated with, or who were playing, organized hockey in British Columbia. He was aware of how novel this was, and how interesting it would be to others. He probably spent more time traveling between towns in B.C. than anyone else and brought more news of B.C. activities to the towns of the Kootenays, than anyone else, and he could not have kept silent about playing hockey. He had seen it, he had possibly played it, and it would have made fascinating conversation. It is perhaps going too far to liken Captain Armstrong to the, "Johnny Appleseed," of B.C. hockey, but he must have been one of those who spread the word. [12]

It has often been supposed, however, that because people were skating in B.C. in the 1890's, that they must have been playing hockey. It was true that many small ice rinks had been erected in various small towns in B.C., such as the rudimentary arena built in Sandon in 1893, and the Crystal Ice Palace built in Nelson in 1894, etc., but one should not infer that hockey was involved at this time, simply from those facts. Those sticks and pucks, which arrived by train to Golden must have been enthralling to the new players. Skating activities were very much the rage, but hockey itself had a kind of supercharged excitement to it, and it appears to this writer that when it arrived, it was reported. Similarly, one could point to the many ice arenas in use in the Eastern provinces in Victorian times which never saw hockey for decades, until the 1880's. The same goes for the prairies. The erection of an ice arena did not equal ice hockey. The author has made exhaustive research into newspapers from the 1890's, and found no listings or mention of ice hockey until 1895. (Notwithstanding the one frolic on the ice in New Westminster). Curling, carnivals, speed races, and even brass bands were often found on the ice, but not hockey. So when it did show up, newspaper correspondents were often pleased to announce a town's first game of hockey, as something extraordinary. This author sees no reason to doubt them.

The word, then, was being slowly spread, but creating hockey teams was another matter. Victorians were certainly crazy about playing games, but ice hockey was not easy to develop. Sticks and skates had to be ordered, mostly by rail, from Winnipeg, and later Calgary. Players had to get time off from their mining (or other) activities, and if they were miners, they worked 10 or 12 hour days, cutting galena or silver out of the bare rock, although most hockey players were not miners, as will be seen below. In any case, games were most

---

[12] Captain Armstrong plied his trade for several decades in South-Eastern British Columbia. He was a major presence on business and sports committees and transportation boards etc. in Golden.

easily played in the evenings, after 8:00 p.m. but most towns didn't have electric lights until the late 1890's, which required large generators, and taxes to pay for the generators. Some towns had internal telephone systems, but few individuals had telephones in these small mining towns, and there might be just one central telephone office for the whole town, so rounding up a team was a major undertaking. Also, the ice had to hold for many weeks. There was usually six to eight weeks of freezing temperatures in the B.C. interior, but good ice, that was thick and not slushy, could be sporadic.

Furthermore, nobody as yet really knew how to play. There were no manuals on how to play the game.[13] There were the "Manitoba rules" formulated a few years earlier, and the "Montreal rules," but they weren't readily available in published form. As miners and lumbermen flooded into British Columbia from the East there gradually formed a group of men in each town who had some experience with this new game, but it could not happen quickly.

In fact it would take another two years before the players began to fully realize what the game would mean to them. As the true nature of competition on the ice began to infuse its way into their blood, they would become modern knights, jousting for the adoring crowds, who would revel in the speed, the action, and even the violence. Ostensibly the new sport, and science, of hockey, was highly civilized, but in practise it gave an outlet for aggression which was sanctioned and accepted by these frontier settlers. The players, both men and women, could experience bone crushing body checks, or even illegal smashes over the head, with few official consequences. So too was there both a written and unwritten code that said you played until you dropped, and even then there were usually no substitutions made.

The knights of old often fought for more than chivalry. There were honour and glory, but there were often wagers, and gold on the line, and on the battlefield there was ransom to be made from defeating one's opponent.

All of these aspects would be found anew on the jousting ground of the modern knight, who could now wield a hockey stick rather than a lance.

But all things considered, as enthralling as it was for those first few to play it, it could only be a modest beginning for hockey in 1895.

---

[13] The first ice hockey manual, by Arthur Farrell, was published in Montreal in 1899.

1896 SEASON

No hockey was reported in Golden. This must have been partly because the ice was poor that year, although hockey continued in Calgary and Edmonton, and a Calgary team traveled to Golden for a challenge curling match. However, the Golden newspaper was, as the Kaslo Claim remarked, the worst newspaper in the province, and the reportage of the paper, along with its technical execution was indeed somewhat lacking. The Calgary Herald also reported no hockey games with Golden.

There were, however, the seeds of hockey now being nurtured in Kaslo, ninety miles away from Golden, and in Sandon, close to Kaslo.

According to a phone conversation with New Denver resident and author Veronica Pellowski, Sandon had acquired about 5000 residents, in the late 1890's, although only about 2,000 had mailing addresses, and far less than that would show up in business directories. (Ms. Pellowski is an expert on Sandon, and the author of the book on Sandon: "Silver Lead and Hell.")

In actual physical size the town was smaller than Nelson or Rossland, compressed into the junction of a group of narrow mountain valleys at the top of the Kootenays. Its surrounding silver and galena mines had helped to spark a mining boom, and with it had come fast flowing money, and card sharps, who were as eager to mine the prospectors as those men were to dig the ore out of the ground. It soon became known as the gambling capital of Canada. Saloons, such as the Bucket of Blood, and gambling houses were often open twenty-four hours, with the poker tables constantly full, while the pianos played, or "shrieked" as one correspondent put it, adding that "it was one long carnival of cards, wine and women." (Kaslo Kootenian, Feb 24, 1910). As the Sandon Paystreak of Jan. 26, 1901 put it, "There is no brand of diversion that our professional entertainers cannot supply. All the games that have been invented since Pharo reigned will be on tap. Everything goes, from trifling with wild cats to bucking the tiger. Sandon is the only town this side of Monte Carlo that knows no limit: where the adventurous can stack 'em to the stars."

Kaslo was a growing mining town on the Northern top of Kootenay Lake, with a population of roughly 1200. Curling was becoming the rage in this city, and where curling sprouted, hockey often followed, as many curlers, especially the younger ones, were also hockey players, or would be lured by the other game to be played on the ice. Kaslo citizens were in the habit of sending away to Winnipeg Manitoba for all manner of equipment, (as was the rest of Canada), and had recently purchased 16 pairs of new curling stones from the Hington Smith Arms company. The stones cost $16.00 plus $2.00 to ship to Kaslo, through the CPR, the same route as that which travelled first through Golden.

As for curling, however, Kaslo and Golden were the only towns, according to the Kaslo Claim, with organized curling clubs, and it was difficult to get to Golden and vice versa, despite the railroad. Round trips would often take four days because the trains had to go slowly through the winding mountain passes; connections were often missed, and snow falls often blocked the tracks. Kaslo managed to send a curling team to Nelson, which was relatively easy, by steamboat, and defeated two Nelson rinks hurriedly put together.

Sandon also had some curling, but nothing was very organized. It's possible, however, that some hockey was also being played in Sandon in 1896.

A rudimentary rink had been constructed in 1893, which might have been used for skating. Ms. Pellowski says that the first true curling rink was built in late 1896, and the first annual general meeting of the Curling club was held on Dec. 11, 1896. But there are no known surviving newspaper records from Sandon until the fall of 1896, after the skating season was over, so the question of hockey remains open. Nevertheless, there are some indications of previous hockey activity in the 1897 reports.

Forinstance, the first mention of hockey in the Sandon Paystreak was on February 6th, 1897, when it said, "The Committee of the Hockey Club have arranged for a very interesting game of hockey to take place on Monday next, between the Fats and the Leans. The conditions are that none of the players shall have ever played hockey before…" When the above match itself was reported, the next week, it said, "The hockey match between the Fats and the Leans of Sandon on Monday last was one of the most exciting and laughable ever witnessed by the citizens of this town."

Sandon is the only town where the first notices of hockey in its paper refer to the game matter-of-factly, without announcing it as something new. This strongly implies that ad hoc hockey games had already been known to the residents the year previously, in 1896. In any case, the curling rink, which might have been used for skating, was torn down in the spring of 1897, according to Ms. Pellowski, to make room for new business premises on Reco ave. A much larger facility was then built to replace it, and this new facility, in late 1897, also served as a hockey rink.

As for the rest of B.C. a significant event took place in the town of Rossland, which was at the bottom of the Kootenays, nestled in the mountains, near the U.S. border. In January of 1896, Rossland implemented an electric light system for the first time, allowing its streets to glow in a few places after dark. Soon the other towns would begin their first attempts at general city illumination. This was enormously important for the development of hockey. So far, most sporting activities took place during the daytime, when events such as curling contests would be played on the natural river and lake surfaces on Saturday or Sunday afternoons. But in order to get two teams of hockey players together, i.e. fourteen men, for scheduled games, along with supporting crowds, the players had to get off work, which meant the late evening. Illumination was important for regular hockey games, and for paying spectators.

Veronica Pellowski indicated that Sandon achieved hydro-electric power in 1897, when several private power plants sprang up on Cottonwood Falls. There were at least eight, in fact, which were built in these early years, and J.M. Harris of the Sandon Power and Light company had a controlling interest. He was also the man who built the first arenas in Sandon, so it's clear that light was available for hockey games very early. However, most of these plants provided DC power, and only one, according to Ms. Pellowski, was AC, which means providing light for commercial buildings would have been difficult.

In any case it would take another year before large scale illumination was available in most major towns, and in the meantime the hockey infection began to gestate, with the word about the game being spread by men like Captain Armstrong.

In 1896 the stage was being set.

1897 SEASON

This was the year when hockey fever burst out in British Columbia.

Rossland, Nelson, Sandon, and Kaslo, had all sprouted competitive teams. Also, although there is only a slight mention to suggest it, hockey might have started, very rudimentaly, in Vernon and Kelowna.

Nelson and Rossland were major towns, near the top and bottom, respectively of the Kootenay pyramid. Rossland had a population of about 6,000, and was the fifth largest city in B.C. Nelson was about 5,000, and was the sixth. Official residents showed up fairly well in statistics for these towns, whereas a town like Sandon was often under-represented in official publications due to its transient population. Sandon's official population in the B.C. yearbook for 1898 was only 500, although in 1903 it was finally reported as 2000. All these towns were now booming from silver, gold, zinc, galena, and other mining operations. Rossland was a rail hub, about five miles from Trail, where a smelter was placed, close to the border with Washington State. It was high, amongst the mountains, and snow and ice were plentiful.

Sandon's city utility electric light system, with power possibly purchased from J.M. Harris, came on line with incandescent lights in March of 1897, allowing night games to take place at the end of the season, although they announced that they didn't have enough power yet for arc lights. Much of the problem with dim lighting in the rinks, according to Ms Pellowski, was probably caused more by the poor quality of the filaments in the bulbs, however, arc lights or not. Sandon was nevertheless hurriedly trying to catch up with itself in supplying infrastructure, and the town still didn't have an official Mayor. It was probably surprising then, even to the other more "mainstream" towns of the Slocan Valley, and Kootenay mountains, that out of this true "Wild West" town grew one of the top hockey teams in the province.

Golden, once again, did not register a mention of any games in 1897.

KASLO, SANDON, ROSSLAND and NELSON

The Kaslo rink company began construction of a new, enclosed skating rink on C. avenue, in December 1896, and completed it in January of 1897. The main building, under the roof, was 74 by 150 feet, while a centre space, reserved for skating, was 40 by 150 feet. On the sides were curling sheets of about 16 by 150 feet. For the first time, there were dressing rooms attached, and the whole structure was lighted by both arc and incandescent lights. As stated before, these lights were extremely important, since most official games were played in the evenings. It was also important to have separate sections for skaters and curlers because the curling rinks would not be appropriate for skaters, and would be hard to re-set every time the skaters finished. This way, both activities could take place simultaneously.

On January 16th, the Kaslo Kootenian, (formerly the Claim), mentioned hockey for the first time: "A hockey club is being organized in the city and will be ready to play as soon as the ice is ready in the rink. It will now be in order to arrange matches with Sandon and Nelson."

By January 30, the club had 30 members signed up, and the officers of the club were R.F. Green, Archie Fletcher, and O. Strathern. The members started practising three nights a week, very late at night, from 10:00 p.m. onwards at the new rink. The Kaslo rink management, according to the players, was very stingy with their practice times, as the 10:00 p.m. time slot implies, and they complained about this in later games. As well, their supply of sticks ran out and they had to order more by telegraph, presumably from Winnipeg. (In 1897 Kaslo finally had a working telephone system in the city, but it was very difficult to hook up telephone service to other towns in British Columbia, so most communication was still by telegraph.)

On Jan. 30 the Nelson Miner reported that in Kaslo, the first hockey match was played on Thursday at the skating rink. There were no other details and the Kaslo paper itself does not mention this game, which, if it existed, was probably just a scrimmage.

Nelson did not report its own town games until weeks later. However the first skating rink in Nelson had been built by the Turner brothers, in 1893-4, and stood in front of the Tremont Hotel on Baker St. In 1895 it was pulled down, and another was built in 1895 on Fort Street, which was where they began to practise hockey this year.

On Feb 13th the Nelson Miner reported that in Sandon, "skating was in full blast, curling and hockey being the chief features." In fact Sandon soon announced two inner-city games. The first was for fun, between the Fats and the Leans, and the Leans beat the Fats 2-1. The spectators had been charged a small admission fee to "defray hospital expenses." The game was considered both the "most exciting and the most laughable" the citizens of Sandon had ever seen, implying, as said above, that games might have taken place the year before.

The second game was between the Blacks and the Whites, and was more serious. This was the first mention of several famous Sandon players, including W.R. Hood, (or Hoods), and Andy Grierson. Robertson Hood's first name has only ever been given once, in a photograph. He is usually identified as either W, R, or W.R. Hood, or Hoods, but in each case it is the same man. Robertson Hood was a junior, with an attractive, fresh, but intense face, and a shock of dark hair parted down the middle, which probably flopped about when he dashed around the ice. He was a mainstay of the Sandon junior team, and often played for the seniors while he was still a junior. He became one of the top scorers in British Columbia, and played alongside most of the great players, including at one time, Lester Patrick. Andy Grierson and McVichie also became top snipers.

This Sandon game was also considered the most exciting game ever seen in the Kootenay. It was hotly contested, the Blacks beating the Whites 6-3.

Players named:

Blacks	Whites
Grierson, Andy	Walker
Hood	McVichie

Individual goals not known.

Kaslo then challenged the Sandon players to a match in Kaslo, and Sandon accepted. This was the first inter-city match between British Columbia teams, on Wednesday, February 24th, 1897. Many of these players, especially those from Sandon, went on to major hockey glory. Robert Hammond, Sandon's goalie, was an all-around player who also excelled as a forward. He worked in a livery stable, (probably Hammond Brothers), and had a strong sense of duty and love of adventure. He was one of the best goalies in B.C. during his short career. C.D. Blackwood was a strong defensive fixture for Sandon and later Nelson.

Sandon scored the first two goals, after some hard play. Then Kaslo scored on an exciting rush. In the second half there was much swift play on both sides, but Sandon pulled away, scoring 3 more goals. Near the end Kaslo scored once more, on a brilliant rush by Jackson. Sandon won 5-2.

Sandon		Kaslo
Hammond, R.	goal	Brown, A.
Blackwood, C.D.	point	Burchell, C.O. (or E.)
McVickie, D. (or J.A.)	coverpoint	Hunter, Sam
Grierson, A. W.(capt)	forward	Young, D.J. (capt)
Cameron, H. D.	forward	Donnelly, J.
Walker, J. (or F.A.)	forward	Jackson, W.
Kirvin, J. (or Kevin)	forward	Symonds, W. (or Simmonds)

Kirvin, or Kevin, as the Rossland Miner had it, was actually listed by Sandon as the second coverpoint, rather than having a rover. They seemed to be unaware that a rover was standard.

Goals: Grierson, (2), Young, D.J., (1); McVichie, (1); Blackwood, (1), Hunter, (1); Cameron, (1).

On January 20, the Rossland Newspaper reported that, "Secretary Watson, of the Rossland Hockey Club, will probably announce a hockey match tomorrow."

This match did indeed take place, on the 21st of January, and was reported the next day: "The Hockey Club and Bank Boys each scored twice—a hot contest. Those who attended the skating rink last night witnessed Rossland's first game of hockey. It was played between the Rossland H.C. and the Bank team. It was well contested, 2-2. There was a large attendance of fair size." The Bank team was probably an amalgamation of the Bank of Montreal, and one other bank.

Rossland Team (in Red)		Rossland Bank Team
Nash	goal	Egan
Campbell	point	Hobbs
Rae	coverpoint	McIntyre
McBride (capt)	forward	Chesterton
Prest	forward	Jeffs
Watson	forward	Ray

Goals: McBride (1); Watson, (1); Chesterton, (1); Jeffs, (1)

On Feb 27th, the Nelson Miner reported that "The Nelson Hockey Club will go to Kaslo this afternoon to play a match game with the Kaslo team this evening. A number of Nelson people will go along to witness the play."

On February 28th, the Nelson Hockey Club defeated the Kaslo club at the Kaslo rink. It was, "exciting and hotly contested," but Nelson won 5-1. "The first half was very tight on account of the Nelson team over-rating the ability of their adversaries, and standing wholly upon the defensive." There was one goal by Kaslo, in the first half, (of thirty minutes), then the Nelson team poured it on, scoring five goals. For an unknown reason, the Nelson goaltender left his net near the end of the second half, which allowed Kaslo to score. The Nelson Players were: McIntyre, Wm Duncan, Thos Duncan, Frank Smith, S. Seukler, (or Senkler), William Thurman, Charles Hipperson, Charles Donough and Jack McKanday, and H.T. Irvine, Manager. The Kaslo players named were: Jackson, Birchall and Gilman.

The Duncan brothers were especially effective.

Goals scored by: Duncan (Wm or Thos), (3); Hipperson, (1); Smith (1). The Kaslo scorer was not named.

(The Rossland Weekly Miner reported another game soon after this between Kaslo and Nelson, which was won by Nelson 4-1. However, even Kaslo and Nelson do not report this, and it appears that this was a mistaken account of the game on Feb. 28th)

On March fourth a mini-tournament, the first in British Columbia, took place in Sandon, between Sandon, Kaslo and Rossland. Nelson had refused to come for unknown reasons.

This marked the first moment that a true, organized hockey championship could determine the best hockey team in any part of B.C., and there were only four organized teams in B.C., not counting Golden, so when three of them showed up, it was highly significant.

The players would have been particularly excited. Just as the jousting grounds of the middle ages had pageantry, with banners, and clarions, these early carnivals and tournaments began to be accompanied by brass bands, with ladies and gents decked out in their finery. A fancy dress ball was the next day's accompaniment to the Sandon hockey tournament.

The men who were about to contest the ice would have begun to feel that they were celebrities, and even princes on the ice. But more than that, they were the best of a new breed of athletic pioneers and the ice was a kind of unknown territory. They had some agreed upon rules, but it would have been like flying the new-fangled aeroplanes which would also soon be invented; every moment with the equipment gave a new understanding. Each player would be watching the others closely to try to pick up new tricks. Each shot, each pass, would feel differently on their sticks and the experience would have been one of constant surprises and experimentation.

It was no wonder that the players couldn't get enough of the game, and during 1897 they challenged the other teams as much as they could, given the many constraints of time, work, geography and ice.

It was in Sandon that the players felt the thrill of the game the most, which was presumably why they had organized the first tournament. They also supplied the first silver cup to be played for, ostensibly for the championship of the Kootenays, which meant they felt rather confident about their abilities, and the chances of their winning. Indeed, any time in the next few years when the Sandon team did not win, they heard about it from their sarcastic news reporters.

Kaslo first played Rossland. The Rossland players had a strong edge in their combination play, but the Kaslo players were great individual artists, which was just as well, since they had been largely unable to practice with each other. At the first half, Kaslo was ahead 4-2. Rossland then, "got down to business," and came back, scoring three goals in succession, putting them ahead 5-4. Kaslo managed to tie the score, however, before time ran out. A sudden death overtime period was agreed upon and Dill from Kaslo scored on a brilliant rush from centre ice, giving Kaslo the game, 6-5. In contrast, the Rossland Weekly Miner reported that the Rossland team proved to be far superior to Kaslo in team work and playing, but the Kaslo team still won, finishing with a chance shot. Rossland also reported the final score as 7-6.

Kaslo was then forced to play their next game immediately after the first, against Sandon, and they did so very reluctantly because they were very tired. C. Kane had to replace Donnelly for Kaslo, who was hurt. The Sandon Paystreak was sympathetic to the effect of Kaslo's prior exertions on its team, suggesting that they would have put up a better fight, otherwise. It was a fast game, and Kaslo was plucky, but Sandon beat them, 10-2. According to the Rossland paper, it was "a very poor exhibition of hockey."

The next day, Friday morning at 10:00 a.m., Sandon played Rossland. It was an hour of "excitement and pleasure," and at the end of time, Sandon had won 5-2.

Sandon then became the first team to win a championship in British Columbia, and they were very proud of determining the resting place of the silver cup, which was nameless, and which gave them the right to consider themselves champions of the Kootenays. They could not quite call themselves the Champions of B.C. yet, since they had not played Nelson, and they were itching to do so. They immediately renewed their challenges to Nelson.

Goals scored by in the tournament: Dill, (1); the rest not known.

Sandon		Kaslo
Hammond, Robert	goal	Smith, A..
Merritt, J.	point	Jackson, W.
Blackwood, C.D	coverpoint	Kerr, C..
McVickie J. A.	2nd coverpoint	Donnelly, J.
Grierson, A.W.	forward	Dill, B.
Walker, F.A..	forward	Young, D.J.
Cameron, Howard	forward	Symonds, W. (or Simmons)
	spare	Kane, C.

Rossland

Watson, J, (or W.J. Wayson)	goal
Nash, George R.	point
Rea, T.H.	cover-point
Ray, Edmund E. (or Rae)	2nd cover-point
Prest, W.J.	forward
Turnbull, A.T.	forward
McBride, C.R.	forward
Cambell, Edwin	secretary

Nelson did finally heed the call, and travelled to Sandon. It would be the last game of the season, and would determine the unofficial ascendancy of hockey in the Province.

The Nelson team was similar to that which had played Kaslo above, except McIntyre was apparently absent, as well as Charles Donough and Jack McKanday, while W. Cooper was added. The Sandon team was the same as above, except Walker and Merritt were replaced by J. Henderson and W. Carnegie. H.G. Goodeve was referee.

The game was played on Saturday, March 19, at the Sandon rink, and Sandon demolished Nelson 14 to 3, upholding its claim to the name of Kootenay Champions, as well as, finally, their claim to being the Champions of B.C. "The individual playing on both sides was brilliant but the fine combination work of the Sandon team resulted in the defeat of the Nelson boys."

Unfortunately, no other stats were given.

Fittingly, the first season of hockey glory was over.[14]

---

[14] In 1909 the Nelson Daily News ran a retrospective article and reported 1896 as the first year of hockey in the Kootenays, but this was erroneous as they were clearly describing the events of 1897.

1898 SEASON

The Gold Rush was now a magnet, pulling in miners from all over North America, and they were pouring into all parts of British Columbia, not just the Yukon. The whole province was reaching its peak as a frontier. In February the mail coach in Rossland was robbed of $215 in registered letters. But as there were the usual vagaries of frontier living, there was also an overall constructive stability, as the North West Mounted Police kept order, and as the citizens strove to carve out their own outposts of the Empire. Every town was clamoring for a railroad extension. Local elections for every private and public organization were constant. Sandon incorporated in 1897, and finally elected their first Mayor. The Firehall was completed in December of 1897, and was fully paid for. Robert Hammond, the Sandon goalie, was a member of the Fire Brigade. In fact, most of the hockey players took part in numerous town activities, and just as the gold-seekers themselves had often been average city folk, who thirsted for adventure, many of the hockey players in these mining towns were not actually rough and ready miners, but rather clerks, or salesmen, who had come West looking for opportunity.

Cyril Archibald, who took the nickname, Barney, and who was soon to become the bruising terror of the ice for Nelson, was an accountant, or "tallyman." George Nunn, Nelson's goalie, was a bookkeeper. Arthur Brown, Kaslo's goalie, was a shoe salesman.

In any case, other town's hockey teams continued to grow, as Kamloops, Nicola Lake, Slocan City, Kelowna and Vernon all started practising seriously.

GOLDEN

In Golden, the only significant factor in their hockey history this winter season was the loss of one of their members, the afore-mentioned Captain Armstrong, who built another steamboat and headed for the Yukon with a group of miners. (He would soon be back). Apparently there were no games played, although they did mention that the Captain of the Calgary Fire Brigade Hockey Team, their old rivals, had his eye knocked out in a match. (Not with them.)

KASLO

(See also, the Kootenays, below)

Kaslo received an injection of new players to its practises, but these are not named. At the rink, the waiting room shed was torn down, and a new, larger one erected at one end. A gallery for spectators was also erected at that end.

The Kaslo hotel guests then challenged the Bankers team.

Kaslo Hotel	Kaslo Bankers
All positions unknown	
Byers, H.	Gerrard, G.B.
Sherwood, F.P.	Borradaile, A.L.T.
Boss, W.A.	Fletcher, H.R.
Arnold, C.M.	Allsion, W.
Montgomery, H.P.A.	Leslie, A.
Young, David Jackson	Irwin, F.L
Burchell, E.	Hill, F. Jim

This game supposedly took place on January 22, but there is no more record of it.

Many challenges and enquiries were sent back and forth about games. Initially Kaslo declined to play until they had practised more.

NELSON, ROSSLAND, SANDON and THE KOOTENAYS

Sandon started its season early, when on Saturday the 11th of December, 1897, a city challenge match took place between the "Recos" (a hotel, and a mine), and the "Ramblers," (a mine). The Ramblers won, but the score was not given. Several days later the official hockey club held a dance to raise funds. This was mainly because the small, make-shift rink which had been in use from 1896, had been torn down in 1897, and in the spring of that year a completely new arena had been built for curling and skating, by J.M. Harrris, but the upkeep was expensive. Hockey was such a major draw that the hockey team received 40 per cent of the gate receipts during its games. It was also one of the few arenas where hockey took precedence, having dedicated times two afternoons and evenings a week for practices. But the rink itself was always losing money.

On Christmas Day, Dec 25th, 1897 the Nelson team tried for revenge against the Sandon team.
This was the first hockey grudge match in B.C.
"The Game will last one hour, and promises to be an exceedingly interesting one as much care has been taken this year in the selection of the men and only the best players in the country will be on the ice. Provision for the accommodation of the spectators has been made and the outlook is that a large crowd will be present to witness the event. Hockey is wholly a scientific game and while it possesses some of the characteristics of the boyhood game of shinney, it is only played by the most skillful skaters. To persons unacquainted with ice skating the agility and dexterity of the players is wonderful and the novice, as he watches the rapid gyrations of the participants, at once becomes an earnest and enthusiastic advocate of the game. There is probably no game in which the movements of the players are more rapid. The ice is in good condition and the Nelson boys are going to fight hard for victory..."
The rink was badly lighted, as most rinks were then, until more arc lighting was available, or better filaments in the bulbs, and the ice was rough.

"All agreed that it was one of the best contests ever seen in Nelson. Many of the spectators saw their first hockey game that day and their enthusiasm knew no bounds. Both teams were in good condition and were very evenly matched. It was a fierce struggle from start to finish…" (Nelson Miner.)

This was the first mention of Joe Thompson, who became one of the greatest players in B.C. He was slightly over average height, strong, with a rugged face, and a mane of curly hair, which spread out in a triangular fashion. He had a mustache in his early years, but cut it off around 1902 or 1903. He had a sign painting business in Nelson for many years. Thompson could play forward or defense, and usually managed to score a goal from either position. He ended up with the second most number of known goals during the period of his long career with Nelson.

Sandon won the game 6-5.

The teams were:

Sandon		Nelson
Burceill, S	goal	Jeffs, A.
Blackwood, B.	point	Duncan, W.
Grierson, A. (Capt)	coverpoint	Nunn, George (capt)
McVichie, J	forward	Banning, W.
Cameron, J	forward	Smith, F.E.W.
Henderson, T	forward	Thompson, Joe
Hammond, R.R.	forward	Livingstone, W.M.
Martin, M.	spare	
McKinnon, Bob	spare	

Goals by: Not known

Nelson then practiced harder and challenged Kaslo and on Saturday, January 15th, the two teams met again, in Kaslo, after the the Nelson players had arrived on the steamer, Kokanee.

Nelson		Kaslo
Harrington, C.	goal	Kane, C.
Duncan, W.	point	Birchall, E.
Nunn, George	cover-point	Bordeille, L.
Thompson, J.	rover	Young, D.
Smith, F.	forward	Frost, S. (capt.)
Banning, W.	forward	Hunter, S.
Rutherford	forward	Dill, B.
Jeffs	spare	
Livingstone	spare	

H. Irvine, the Nelson manager, made the first goaltending change in B.C., dropping Jeffs, and substituting in C. Harrington. They also switched Livingstone for D. Rutherford.

Kaslo burst out with a three nothing lead in the first half, in a very fast game. The referee, Robert Carley of Nelson, was criticized by the spectators for not calling off-sides, which were more obvious in the early days of hockey, since the forward pass was not allowed. To be precise, one could pass the puck forward, but one would have to skate ahead of the intended recipient, to put him onside, before he could touch the puck. But the Nelson players had more stamina, and more weight, and the Kaslo players tired too soon. As a result, Nelson scored four of its own goals in succession in the second half. Just before time was called Kaslo managed to tie the game. Then they went into overtime, and Nelson quickly scored the game winner, finishing 5-4.

The individual goals are not known.

Nelson towns-people played some pickup games, including a match between the Go-Gos and the Wah-Wahs, who won 7-6.

Rossland travelled to Sandon, whose players were the defending champion of the Kootenays. After the ensuing game The Sandon Paystreak was disgusted with Sandon's play, relating that, "Shinny, offsides, flukes and fumbles followed each other in rapid succession…the Silver City Appolos, [sic], wrestled and floundered through till half time, when the flunkeys came forward and led the heroes to their corners to be rubbed down and prepared for the next spasm. But as to the next spasm—we will draw the veil of charity. Suffice it to say that Rossland made all the points they wanted and then waited calmly for the call of time. Score: Rossland 4; Sandon 0-0-0-0."

Rossland		Sandon
McBride	goal	Birchall
Becker	point	Hammond
Chester	cover	McVichie
Townsend	forward	Grierson
O'Brien	"	Henderson
McCreary	"	Gormely
Cleveland	"	Baxter

(Chester, named above, was probably Chesterton.)

Goals by: O'Brien, (1), the rest unknown.

It was reported by the Sandon Paystreak that Sandon then traveled to Rossland, and defeated Rossland on Feb. 18th, by a score of 3-0. No other paper, including Rossland's seems to report this game.

It was also reported by the Sandon Paystreak that Tom Bruce, from Calgary, has arrived in Sandon and "is a valuable acquisition to the hockey club." However it appears he never played.

Rossland travelled to Kaslo in January. The game was dominated from the beginning by Rossland so completely that the betting crowd could not get even 2-1 odds. The Rossland defence was almost invincible, while Kaslo's defense was like a sieve. The score was 6-0 at the end of the first half, and in the second, Rossland continued to dominate, scoring six to Kaslo's two, the game ending 12-2 for Rossland. Curiously, the Nelson Miner reported this game as 10-3. The Rossland Weekly Miner had it 10-2! But it is far more likely that the Kaslo records are more precise, since the game took place there.

After the game, the Rossland Weekly Miner's correspondent declared that the opinion was in Kaslo that the Rosslanders were invincible. This was the first year that Jack McCreary was mentioned as a goalie, and he became one of the best and most traveled goalies in the province.

Rossland		Kaslo
Rae and McCreary	goal	Burchell
Merritt (capt.)	point	Borradiale
McBride	cover	Strathern
Townsend	forward	Frost, C.E. (capt)
O'Brien	"	Hill
McCreary	"	Young
Chesterton	"	Hunter

(McCreary was named by the Rossland paper as goalie, while Beecher was named as a forward, and Rae was not named at all.)

The Kaslo Captain, C.E. Frost, fractured his knee cap and badly bruised the other, and was out for the season. (A carnival-like benefit game was played later for Frost.) Kaslo played no more games this season.

Rossland then travelled to Nelson to complete their tour.

This game was on Jan 29, and another rivalry was fuelled by heavy expectations. Large amounts of money were bet on the game, especially between the individual players, and the Arcade rink was standing room only.

At the end of the hour the game was tied, 4-4.

Then Rossland began another tradition, which they would carry on for many years—they cheated.

As the whistle blew, the Nelson team stopped playing and their goaltender moved from the goal. A Rossland player promptly shot in the puck. This was disallowed. But then Rossland refused to play any overtime, even though it had been agreed upon earlier. The reason was that the Rossland players were fading fast from their long trip, and it looked like they would lose not only the game, but also their money. So they left the ice. The Nelson players tried to claim the game as a forfeit, but the refs called it a tie.

The Rossland Weekly Miner had a slightly different view. Not only did they announce the result as 5-5, but their final remarks were somewhat cryptic: "Considerable money was wagered on the result, but the game was declared a tie, and bets were ruled to be off. The visitors leave for home tomorrow. Rossland refused to play off the tie."

ROSSLAND CARNIVAL

In January Rossland had made a significant announcement: they would hold a winter carnival, in February. It was suggested by the Carnival Committee that this event would determine the Championship of British Columbia, and there were no objections. As a result, with an official Championship finally scheduled, this event would soon galvanize hockey in the province, as the annual rush to be the best in B.C. prompted more teams to arise each year. The games took place in the new Palace skating rink, and the silver cup being offered was reported to be nineteen inches high, on a base of onyx. Years later, however, it was reported to be 27 inches high, on a base of ebony. What is known for certain is that it flared out at the top, and had a pair of miniature sticks and a puck at the bottom, with a "facing off" sketch on the cup itself. Two hockey players stood on either side of the final base as well.

Rossland first played Nelson. Rossland was ahead 2-1, after the first thirty minute half, and Rossland continued to pull ahead in the second half, defeating Nelson 6-1. According to the Rossland Weekly Miner, Nelson was simply, "outclassed."

Nelson Senior Team		Rossland Senior Team
Nunn, George (capt)	goal	McCreery, W.
Duncan	point	Merritt.
Livingstone.	cover	O'Brien, (capt)
Smith	forward	Becher
Thompson, Joe	"	Lahey
Rutherford	"	Harris
Jackson	"	Chesterton.

Goals: Becher, (2); Chesterton, (2); Lahey, (1); O'Brien, (1); Rutherford, (1)

Sandon then defeated Nelson 2-0.

Rossland then played Sandon. The game was intense but clean. Only Gormley from Sandon suffered a "scratch." Rossland went ahead 7-0 at the half, and finished off Sandon in the second, by the score of 11-1.

In this final game, the players named were:

Rossland		Sandon
?	goal	?
Lahey	?	Henderson
McBride	?	Gormley
Becher	?	
Chestertone	?	
O'Brien (capt)	?	

Goals scored by were: Becher, (4); Lahey, (4), Chestertone (1); McBride (2); Henderson (1).

Rossland then became the second Hockey Champions of B.C. One could say they were the first official hockey champions of B.C., but this is a matter of perspective. Sandon had asked all the towns the previous year who had teams to come to their championship, for the right to call themselves Kootenay Champions, and the only teams at the time were from the Kootenays. The Rossland Carnival committee likewise had asked that all teams interested in playing for the B.C. Hockey Championship come to their festival, and 3 teams from the Kootenays complied, agreeing that the winner among them would be named the B.C. Champion.

OKANAGAN

The first actual mention of hockey in the Vernon papers came on Feb 3, 1898: "An attempt is being made to arrange a hockey match at an early date between this city and the Kelowna boys."

Despite repeated attempts, this match never happened. It was specifically attempted to induce the Kelowna Dramatic Club, who apparently had a team, to arrange a match with a local Vernon team, but no one on the Dramatic Club felt competent enough to actually play a game against another team.

KAMLOOPS

Challenges were made as early as December 1897 between Kamloops and Nicola Lake, but no actual teams were formed, and no games were played that season.

LADIES

The ladies of Sandon were reported to be practicing, but it seems they could not form a team.

1899 SEASON

The telephone had made its way into the Sandon CPR depot in 1898, which was also connected to the Payne Mine Tram, up a large hill from Sandon, and there was a main telephone office in the town, operated by the Bell Telephone company.

Revelstoke and Enderby now joined the hockey battle. In Revelstoke, hockey equipment was offered for the first time in the town, and in January a team was formed, to go and compete in the Rossland Carnival. Revelstoke's team included Scott, McTavish, H. Pinkham, W. Sawyer, (Captain) and Estey.

This was the first mention of the great goalie, W. Sawyer, who had an amazing goals against average during his career but there is no record of any games he played as a goalie this year, and Revelstoke did not actually go to the Rossland Carnival. W. Sawyer's first name was never given in any published source related to hockey. However, he might have been the William Sawyer listed in the B.C. Directory for Revelstoke in 1902, 03 and 04, as owning a sash and door factory. But despite William being the only Sawyer listed in Revelstoke at that time, W. Sawyer actually played for Vernon from 1902-08. But there were no Sawyers listed in Vernon for that same period. Furthermore, it is apparent that W. Sawyer was not the only hockey player in the family. (See 1904 for a photographic mystery.)

GOLDEN

Golden finally started playing again, and they even constructed a new arena, 170 feet by 75 feet, receiving and accepting a challenge from Revelstoke. According to "Kinbasket Country," this rink was completed in 1898 at a cost of $2,500. A wire mesh was constructed around the centre ice area, which was used for skating and hockey, to stop the pucks from hitting the curlers, who had two rinks on the outer sides of the building.

A notice from the Revelstoke Herald in Dec. 1898, said, "Although there is no ice here as yet, nor have the Revelstoke boys ever played together, they intend to leave here on Christmas day and play Golden Monday morning, returning the same day." There is no record of whether this game took place. Later, on Feb 27, Golden traveled to Banff for a challenge match. The Golden Team was not used to the large ice surface and the keenness of the ice, and Banff won 8-0.

The teams were:

Golden	Banff
Positions not known	
Field	Black
Howden (capt)	Mather
Wilson	Frost
Grant	Douglas (capt)
Robertson	Hetherington
Knowlton	Brewster
Winn	Lindsay

KASLO

Kaslo organized its hockey club on Jan. 10th. Its Captain was Sam Hunter, who later became a mining property developer. There were 12 other members of the committee.

Kaslo had an inner-city match between the Hill residents and the Downtown boys, the Downtowners winning 3-1.

More Kaslo results are below, in the Kootenays.

NELSON, ROSSLAND, SANDON and the KOOTENAYS

Nelson was once again very serious. They also had built another new rink, on upper Stanley Street, (actually finished in late 1898). The location was one of the high points in the city, so the ice would last longer. According to Dr. D.M. Black, this rink was, "a very rough looking building, constructed of rough sawn boards which were left unpainted." But despite the roughness of the arena, the town did everything they could to promote the idea that, "a good hockey team is a valuable advertisement for a town."

A new rink was also opened in Rossland, at the corner of Spokane St. and 2nd ave. It accommodated 1500 people and had overhead arc lights.

A Rossland Junior team was formed, called the IXL, which was named after a mine. The President was Jack McQuarry, (or McCreary, whose name was often misspelled), and the secretary was Reynolds Turner. The players included Al Harris, captain, Reynolds Turner, Elgin Ferrier, John, (Jack) Donahue, John Laeler and Virgie Pownell. Jack Donahue eventually worked his way up from the juniors to the senior team and then became one of its stars, as well as its captain. He was a burly, strapping youth, with jutting swathes of curly hair, and although he was not known for scoring goals, he was an extremely effective defenseman.

Rossland had two Senior Teams which were great rivals. These were the Rosslands and the Victorias. They played a hard-fought challenge match in January. McCreary, the Rossland's goalie was outstanding. Chesterton had a two inch gash laid open in his head from the puck, but returned to the game after a few minutes. The Rosslands eventually prevailed 2-1.

The Victorias		Rosslands
Mackintosh, E.C.	goal	McCreery, J.
Merritt, J.N.	point	Lahey, Mike
O'Brien, Ed.	cover	Elwood, J.B.
Becher, A. Lorne	forward	Chesterton, C.W.
Warren, E.	"	McBride, C.R.
Harris, W.C. "Duke"	"	Rae, T.R.
Chalmers, F.W.	"	Davis, A.W.

Goals scored by: Davis, A.W. (2); Chalmers, F. W.(1)

Delaying games so players could recover from gashes in their heads, as above, or bruises or concussions, was becoming the custom. It was never explained clearly what rules were being followed in any of these contests. The rules for substitutions seemed to be a combination of the standard set by both the Canadian Amateur Hockey League, and the Ontario Hockey League, where no substitutions could be made except as a result of injury. However, as will be seen below there was often a determined desire not to replace anyone regardless of the injury, even if spares were available. Under mutual agreement, teams could both drop a man, but no one was under compulsion to follow this. The rules most often mentioned were the Manitoba rules, but I have never been able to find a copy of these.[15]

Another Rossland city league game took place between the Lions and the Tigers. The Lions were managed and possibly Captained by J.W. Spring, while the Tigers were managed, and possibly captained by Bert Hunter. The Lions wore red jerseys and yellow belts, while the Tigers wore white jerseys. The Lions won 2-1. Several articles were stolen from the players' dressing room including a pair of rubbers, a pair of gloves, and a hockey stick.

A Junior Championship cup for the city of Rossland was donated by Ross Thompson at a cost of $60.00. (This was a hefty sum. A miner might make approximately two dollars a day.) However, the only Rossland Junior game reported in the city was between the Rossland Junior Victorias and the Hunter Brothers Store, in March. The Juniors wiped the floor with the older team, 5-0, wherepon the seniors complained of being out of practise.

Hunter Brothers		Rossland Junior Victorias
Pollett	goal	Costello
McInnis	point	Robinson
Winters	cover	Wadds
Terneau (capt)	forward	Armstrong (capt)
Joiner	"	Kingsmill
Lawler	"	McIntyre
Martiu	"	De Voin

The Rossland Juniors (aka Victorias?) traveled to Sandon, where they played the Sandon Junior Team. According to the Sandon Paystreak it was the fastest hockey that had ever been seen in Sandon. "The combination work of the Sandon forwards was simply beautiful and showed an ability much beyond their years. Young Hood, who is the natural embodiment of greased lightning on skates, made some rapid transfers that were startling to the Rosslanders." While his team was generally excellent at passing, Jack Crawford of Sandon showed a very tough physical presence as well, to round out their overall abilities. The Rossland players also tended to bunch up in the scrimmages, reducing their own chances for creative combination plays. Sandon overpowered Rossland 8-4. (The Rossland Miner put the score at 10-4.)

---

[15] Unfortunately the Manitoba Hockey Association never returned my calls.

Rossland Juniors		Sandon juniors
Donahue, J.	goal	Crawford, Ernie
Farrier, Elgin	point	Crawford, William J. (Rusty)
Pownell, V.	cover	Crawford, Jack
Harris, Al	forward	Cliffe, William
Farrier, Roy	"	Hood, W.
Megans, F.	"	Carney, W.
Rae, Jack	"	Cliffe, W.

Goals by: Hood (3); Harris, Al, (1); the rest unknown.

According to Trail On Ice, the Sandon Juniors also defeated challenging junior teams from Kaslo, and for the first time, a team from Moyie. I did not find this information listed. (There is some evidence also that the Sandon Junior team then claimed the Ross Thompson Junior trophy for 1899.)

This Sandon junior team became the scourge of all other junior teams. They were so strong that they often played senior teams to a standstill, and when the juniors finally had to turn senior, their senior team was very strong, but there was a huge vacuum in their junior ranks. Once the Crawford brothers and Robertson Hood turned Senior, meaning they were approximately eighteen, as that was often the cutoff point, they were soon headhunted by other teams, and the Sandon juggernaut ran out of steam.

The Crawford brothers were a dynamic trio. Unfortunately, their place on various rosters has been confusing, since they were often referred to simply as Crawford. It's only from the photographic evidence that we know that William Crawford was also named William J. (Rusty) Crawford, and many times he might have been listed as W, J, or R. Crawford, confusing him automatically with his brother Jack.

The Kaslo Seniors then traveled to Sandon for another challenge match. It was a muddled game, which was sarcastically reported by the Sandon Paystreak: "After the educating influences of the junior match, this one was particularly grotesque." The game degenerated into, "an unregulated shinney match." Tripping was constant, and players were falling all over the ice. Combination play was forgotten. At the end of the game the score was 5-5. The Sandon reporter said afterwards, "A reward of $50,000 will be offered by the Humane Society, for the apprehension and conviction of the parties who told McVichie that he knew something about hockey."

Sandon Seniors		Kaslo Seniors
Birchall	goal	Conneley
Grierson, Andy	positions unknown	Frost, C.E.
Crawford, Jack	"	Dill, Bert
Hammond, Bob	"	Hunter, Sam
Hood - replaced Birchall in goal		
Blackwood, CD (possibly)	"	

Goals by: Hammond, Bob, (1)

The Rossland Senior Team arrived in Nelson on January first, for a challenge match, on January 2nd. They were the "Rosslands" as opposed to the "Victorias." It was a hard fought game, but Rossland was bigger, and better trained. Chesterton scored three for Rossland, McBride one, and Wetmore, the Nelson rookie scored their only goal, leaving the score 4-1 for Rossland. One lamp glass was smashed, but the new boards of the rink stood up well. Nelson lacked team play, and often one of their players would be stranded up ice, either because he wouldn't back-check or because he was goal-sucking. (My phraseology).

The Nelson Senior Team		The Rosslands
Bell, G.	goal	McCreery, W.
Blackwood, D. (or J.)	point	Lahey, M.
Duncan, W.	cover	Elwood, J.B.
Thompson, Joe	forward	Chesterton, C.
Duncan, T.	"	McBride, C.R.
Cowan, T. (or C.)	"	Rae, T.H.
Wetmore, M.	"	Davis, A.W.

Goals scored by: Chesterton, C. (3); McBride, C.R. (1); Wetmore, M. (1)

C. Archibald, D.W. Rutherford, George Nunn and A. Perrier tried out for the Nelson team, but didn't make it.

It was intended for the Nelson Fire Brigade hockey team to play the Nelson Seniors on the 13th of January but there is no record of the result.

At another Bonspiel in Kaslo, the hockey players waited until the warm-up curling was over, then the Kaslo and Sandon Seniors played to a 2-2 tie, with two 5 minute periods of overtime finally deciding the issue when Kaslo scored to make it 3-2. (The Sandon Paystreak said it was one 15 minute period of overtime.) The curlers then took over the ice for their official games.

Sandon		Kaslo
Hammond, R.	goal	Lovatt
Blackwood, D.	point	Moore
Gusty	cover	Dill
McVickie (capt)	forward	Young, D.J.
Cliffe	forward	Connelly
Grierson (capt)	forward	Frost
Crawford	forward	Hunter (capt)

Goals: Hunter (2); Blackwood (2); Connolly (1)

See also Slocan City's challenge of Nelson, in Other Games, below.

ROSSLAND CARNIVAL

The Rossland Carnival once again took place on Jan. 25th to Jan. 28th.

As stated, Ross Thompson, a politician, had put up a cup for a Junior contest, called the Ross Thompson trophy.

The format for determining a champion in the senior and junior events was rather ambiguous, and there were only a few teams competing. The Junior limit was initially 16 years of age. Then it was changed to 18, but it might have been changed back again.

Surprisingly, Revelstoke put up a good fight, although the powerhouse Rossland Senior Team defeated them 7-2.

Nelson Seniors were confident of getting through the first round easily, being matched with the Rossland's second team, the Victorias.

But they forgot they were playing on Rossland ice.

According to the Nelson paper the goal judges were slightly biased towards Rossland, as they refused to see two goals that went through the Rossland poles, and one goal awarded to Rossland actually did not go in. This, of course, is a matter of opinion, but even the Rossland sports reporters agreed. In any case, Nelson lost, 4-2. This was quite a blow to their pride, though they masked it well.

The Nelson Team was:

Nunn,	goal
Duncan, W.	point
Blackwood,	cover
Wetmore	forward
Henderson	forward
Thompson, Joe,	forward
Perrier, A	forward
Duncan, T.	spare
Archibald, B.	spare

Goals scored by: Wetmore, (2); the rest not known.

S. Neelands tried for the Goaler position and did not make the team.

This was the first game where Cyril, "Barney," Archibald was mentioned playing, as a spare, for Nelson. Soon he would become a stalwart defenseman for the Senior team. He was tall, strong, jug-eared, and mustachioed, with a mild, gentle face, and dimple in his chin, and he became the most hated man in hockey. An accountant by trade, working as a "tallyman" for J.A. Sayward, he was a bruising checker on the ice, and it appears he did not mind using his stick, or his elbows to foul his opponent. He was considered at one time an indispensable part of the Nelson squad.

The Rossland Victorias then surprised the Rossland Senior Team by beating them 2-0, and became the new Champions of British Columbia.

The Rossland Miner says the Rossland Senior Team also defeated the Sandon Junior Team 4-1. The Sandon Paystreak says the opposite, that the Sandon Juniors defeated the Rossland Seniors 4-1. The Paystreak also says that the Sandon Juniors defeated the Rossland Juniors, but there is no result available. However, the Sandon Juniors then defeated the Nelson Juniors 6-0 to win the first Junior Championship of B.C. (It was not stated that this was for the Ross Thompson trophy, but it probably was.) Rossland had a Kaslo junior playing for them named Hiram Carney. It was also said that Hood was a star for Rossland, although Hood was actually playing for Sandon.

Sandon Juniors

Cliffe, William (capt.)   (all positions unknown)
Hood, Robertson   (some first names taken from photographs)
Cliffe, Walter
Carney, C.
Crawford, W. Jack (Rusty)
Crawford, Ernie
McKinnon, Frank

When the Nelson team went home, they asked for a rematch with the Rossland Victorias, who obliged, and made plans to travel to Nelson. The Nelson Team practiced for two days straight, and the manager shuffled his lineup to get the best combinations.

Rossland couldn't make it. But the match was rescheduled for the next week. The Nelson Team played the Fire Brigade Team instead.

There is no record of whether Rossland ever showed up.

TRAIL

According to Trail On Ice there were regular matches taking place between Trail and Rossland in 1899, with a three car train called the "Hockey Special," shuttling players and fans back and forth, along the ten kilometers.

OKANAGAN

Vernon constructed a new rink, and began calling for a team to be formed amongst the casual players. By February a motley bunch had been formed and even accepted a challenge from Enderby, where they were playing their first hockey, but neither town could muster an actual team.

KAMLOOPS

Kamloops and Nicola Lake challenged each other, but again were all talk. In their defence, they did have to take a long stage coach ride, rather than a train or boat.

OTHER GAMES

Slocan City organized a Team and challenged Nelson. On March 11, the game took place at the Crystal rink, which still had reasonable ice, because it was on a high point, "up the hill" in the city. It appears that Slocan borrowed two players from Sandon, Grearson, (Grierson) and Jack Crawford.
Nelson finally won a game, 8-4.

The Teams were:

Slocan City		Nelson
Guest, H	goal	Nunn, G.
Henderson, T.	point	Archibald, B.
Nichols, Russell	cover Point	Jeffs, Alf
Berry, Robert	forward	Thompson, Joe
Crawford, Jack	"	Perrier, A
Grearson, Andy	"	Henderson, G.
Christie, H.R.	"	Wetmore, A.

This was the last game of the season for Nelson.

In the summer, the major cities in the Slocan Valley got together and decided to form an actual league—the first in B.C.

The British Columbia Hockey League was then announced, gestating until next winter.

On March 11th, the Kaslo Senior Team had their picture taken, commemorating their season.

VANCOUVER and VICTORIA

Finally, Vancouver and Victoria witnessed their first games of ice hockey.
All games previous to this in Vancouver and Victoria, reported in newspapers, are field hockey, and they did indeed compete in field hockey all year round in the mild climate of lotus land, especially in January, because the field was nice and hard. (Garth Vaughn, in his excellent book, The Puck Stops Here, states twice that records show that hockey started in Victoria in 1890. I

personally called Mr. Vaughn by telephone and asked him in which records I could find this reference. He indicated that he knew of none, and the information had come from a conversation with another man, whose name he had not recorded.)

This was a momentous event for Victorians because they were lucky if they received one week of ice a year. Vancouverites were lucky if they received two weeks. Thus, it required the conjunction of just the right cold weather, and a contingent of experts to show how the game should be played.

On Jan 7, 1899, this conjunction formed on Goodacre Lake, in the Victoria vicinity. The players were mostly from Eastern organizations, where they had all learned hockey, including Queen's university, Toronto U., Halifax Hockey Club, St. Francis Xavier College Hockey Club, North Sydney Hockey Club, Trinity College, McGill U., Winnipeg hockey Club, Osgood Hall, Hawthorne Hockey Club, Montreal, and the lone B.C.er, being Frank Smith from the Nelson Hockey Club.

"Victorians were treated to their first exhibition of ice hockey, the match between Capt. Langley's and P. Daniels' team being played on Goodacre Lake, Beacon Hill. Good play was next to impossible, but still there was enough fast play at times to keep the spectators interested, and even if British Columbians are not initiated into the mysteries of the game, they did not overlook one time when a player distinguished himself, natatorially, by swimming through one of the many slush puddles with another player on his back."

There was some reasonably good and interesting play, despite the slush, and the score ended 1-1. Len Campbell scored for Langley's team, and Doc Smith scored for Daniels'.

Langley		Daniels
Schultz, Sam,	goal	Blain, C.
Capt. Langley,	point	Daniels, F.J.
Greenflield, W.	coverpoint	Poff, G
Campbell, L	forward	Thompson, Crawford
Routh, Cliff,	"	Smith (Doc) F.
Moffatt, S	"	Gamble, C
Bullock, L.N.B.	"	Daniels, P.R.
McConnan, D.G.	spare	

As difficult as it may be to believe, that was the end of ice hockey in Victoria until 1911. It is possible that a bit of shinny was played from time to time when Victoria had its one week of frost, but it was impossible to form teams, practise, and then schedule games.

In Vancouver it was a bit different. With two weeks of ice (sometimes), one could practise and then challenge. And this is what they did, starting on January 7, 1899, when the first hockey matches in the lower mainland, (i.e. in the vicinity of Vancouver, which was a fairly small city then), took place. This was also the first year that hockey skates, as opposed to regular skates, were advertised in the Vancouver papers.

"The Shinney match between the Lacrosse Club and a picked team from the rest of the skaters, resulted in a victory for the club boys by two goals to one, after a very exciting match at Burnaby Lake."

Burnaby Lake was a preferred surface because it was very large, but it was also quite far from Vancouver proper, although it would end up being good for challenge matches with New Westminster.

Trout Lake was the easiest surface to get to, and there was a special cable car train that left half hourly from the Main St. Station, and traveled through the woods to a station very close to the small lake, about 3 or 4 blocks from the station in today's geography, but it was just bush then, with a cable car track laid through it. The ride probably took about twenty minutes. A game took place there the same day as the Burnaby Lake one:

"The hockey Team representing McLellan, McFeely and company, vanquished that of the B.C. Sugar Refinery at Trout Lake on Saturday afternoon by a score of three goals to one."

But thousands of skaters went out to Trout Lake daily, while the ice lasted. To Vancouverites it was absolutely magical, and was the most eagerly sought after event of the season.

New Westminster would also generate many hockey players, in years to come, but there were no records of New Westminster players or games this season.

1900 SEASON

The Boer War was now in full steam, and the papers were full of the results of the battles. Jack Rae, of the Rossland team, had enlisted, and was sent to South Africa. It's possible that Robert Hammond, the great Sandon goalie, also enlisted. There was an R.B.L. Hammond listed with Lord Strathcona's Horse, a B.C. regiment, in 1899, and this same private soldier was listed as killed in action on August 26, 1899, at a place called the Caucatiov Geluks. (At one point Hammond was listed in the Sandon Paystreak as R.R. Hammond, but many player's initials were erroneously listed). On the other hand, there is one more listing for R. Hammond on the Sandon team in February of 1900, so perhaps this is not him. In any case, Bob Hammond either disappeared from the Sandon scene before the 1900 season, or in the middle of the 1900 season, and never returned to the annals of hockey. He had never lost a game as a goalie.

There was also a smallpox epidemic in Southern B.C. and Washington, particularly in Spokane. Many towns implemented quarantines, whereby one would have to have a certificate showing that one had been innoculated, before one could enter the city. The quarantine was only partially enforced, but 1200 people in Rossland were innoculated.

Spokane, Washington, had started playing hockey, and the Spokane High School Hockey club applied to the Rossland Carnival, but according to the Rossland Miner, apparently were not allowed through the quarantine. Two people had died in Spokane, supposedly from the disease, but it was later considered a mild oubreak, with a hundred cases reported, and generally with symptoms more analagous to chicken pox.

Sandon was still collecting "one of the choicest aggregations of tin horn gamblers, sure-thing men, rounders, grafters, chair-warmers, chippies, pimps, etc., that has ever gathered within the city limits." (Paystreak, Mar. 24, 1900) They also collected William Howarth, a twenty-year old, from Slocan City, one of the top hockey players ever to play in B.C. He played no organized hockey this year, but quietly joined the typographical staff of the Paystreak, no doubt watching the final few games with a burning itch to play.

NELSON, ROSSLAND, SANDON and THE KOOTENAYS

The first match of the B.C. (Amateur) Hockey League was played in Rossland, Jan 6, 1900, between the Rosslanders and the Rossland Victorias. The Victorias won 3-1.

While waiting for better ice, these two teams played again in an exhibition match, where the Rosslands defeated the Victorias 5-3. At a late stage in the game, as the Victorias were losing, O'Brien was put in goal instead of Becher, but to no avail.

This was the first appearance of Eldon S.H. Winn in Rossland hockey circles. (He might have been the Winn who played for Golden in 1899.) Not only was Winn to become one of Rossland's best players, he was destined to be a major thorn in the side of Nelson when he became a referee, and a member of the Carnival committee, after 1905.

The Victorias		Rosslands (in Red)
Becher, A. Lorne	goal	Goninan
Adams.	point	Lahey, Mike
O'Brien, Ed. (capt)	cover	Elwood, J.B.
Winn	forward	Frost
Townshend	"	McBride, C.R. (capt.)
Harris, W.C. "Duke"	"	Rae
Howard	"	Perry

Goals scored by: Winn, (3); McBride, C.R.(1); Perry (2); two goals unknown.

Nelson also had two teams, and Greenwood, and Camp McKinney, each had formed a team, but in January they decided to combine their teams as one, calling it the Boundary Hockey Club, because they were near the U.S. border. However, it was also variously called the Greenwood Hockey Team.

Poor ice caused many scheduled games to be postponed. Eventually, Nelson Lacrosse-Hockey defeated the Nelsons in their first game, with the score being 8 to an unknown number. In their next game, Nelson L-H won again, 5-1. Tom Duncan scored the one goal attributed in the 5-1 game.

Nelson Lacrosse-Hockey		Nelsons (or Nelson City)	
Nunn, G.	goal	Neelands	
Archibald, B.	point	Duncan, W.	
Jeffs, A.	cover	Howden	
Wetmore, M.	forward	Duncan, Tom	
Greenley (or lees)	forward	Rutherford, Dave	
Perrier	forward	Hawkins	
Thompson, Joe	forward	Thompson, R.	
Blackwood	forward (at Rossland Carnival)		
		Zimmerman	forward (2nd game only)
		Pullen	forward (2nd & 3rd game)
		Cooke, R.F.	forward (3rd game)
		Martin	spare at Rossland Carn.

The Rosslanders then travelled to Greenwood for a league game. Greenwood was down 3-1 and tried to come back, getting one more goal, but even with a Rossland man off for two minutes they couldn't tie it up. Final score 3-2.

The Rossland Victorias traveled to Nelson, playing against Nelson City. In the first half, Rossland went up 5-0, largely due to the ineffective rushes of the Nelson players. In the second half, Nelson pulled themselves together a bit, scoring one goal, but the game ended 6-1. As the Nelson Daily Miner said: "The two most glaring faults of the Nelson team were the constant bunching of the forwards and their utter inability to shoot."

Rossland Victorias Team:		Nelson City Team:
McCreary, J.	goal	As above
Adams, E.	point	
O'Brien, E.M.	cover	
Winn, E.S.A.	forward	
Ross, Dr S.A.	forward	
Townsend, G.E.	forward	
Harris, W.S.	forward	

Other games results are not known, but the final standing in the league was as follows, before the Rossland Carnival:

Rossland Victorias	2 wins 1 loss
Nelson Lacrosse-Hockey Team	2 wins 1 loss
Rosslanders (or Rosslands)	2 wins 1 loss
Nelson City	1 win 3 losses
Boundary Hockey Club (Greenwood)	1 win 1 loss

Finally Rossland Victorias defeated Boundary (Greenwood) 2-1, one day after the Rossland Carnival games, as a league game, thereby winning the B.C. Hockey League trophy, with a record of 3-1. The Victorias seem to have got one more game out of the schedule, and Boundary one less.

Inner-city teams in Nelson provided the following game: The Hudson's Bay Stores defeated the Wholesalers 3-2.

The Rossland Junior Club the IXL's, began practising for a match with the Sandon juniors, but there is no record available of a game.

KASLO

There was an inner-city game in Kaslo between a team from the Hill, engineered by Alderman Hodder, and a team from the Flat, managed by alderman Archer. Archer's team won 3-2.

Archer's Flat Team		Hodder's Hill Team
Stewart	goal	Oliver
Carmichael	point	Morris
Grierson	coverpoint	Douglas
Hunter,	forward	Dill
Cody	forward	Palmer,S.
Stinson	forward	Miller, A.
Miller	forward	Beacher

After the Rossland Carnival, Sandon travelled to Kaslo for a challenge match, feeling confident with several members of their Junior winning team on the roster. Kaslo surprised the championship team, winning 6-3. They also surprised themselves, as they had not thought they were that good.

Sandon		Kaslo
Crawford, E.	goal	Stuart, J. (or Stewart)
Crawford, J.	point ?	Stenson G. (or Stinson)
Hammond, R	cover ?	Dill (Bert?)
McKinnon	f	Young, D.J.
Cliffe, W.	f	Cody
Hood	f	Grierson
Crawford	f	Hunter

Later Kaslo travelled to Sandon for a return challenge game, specifically against the Sandon Junior team which had won the B.C. Championships. (See the Rossland Carnival). It was a special event, bringing many of the Kaslo residents on a chartered train, including the Mayor. As the Kaslo Kootenian described the trip, "Given a special train, convivial company, a moonlight night, scenery weird in outline and awful in the semi-light, and you have a mixture of modernism and romanticism that not even the most matter of fact person can remain uninfluenced (by)."

The whole hockey club went over, which meant all the members who weren't even on the team. This included, A.W. Goodenough, N. Mackintosh, H. Fletcher, D. Carmichael, J.F. Maloney, J. Macpherson, E.L. Smith, O Strathern, P.H. Walsh, H.S. Whellams, T. Carrie, G. Hamilton, D. Kurtz, E. Shannon, J. Bjorn, H Sands, W.P. Evans, F.H. Hathaway, H.A. Blackburn, L. Palmer, J. Vivian, G. Hageman, C. Kettyle, W. Porter, J. Mackinnon, J. Miller, A.H. Esch, F.E. King, W. Walmsley and Master Alex McDonald, the "mascot."

They played that night, soon after they arrived, at 10:00 p.m. The Sandon team was basically the junior team this time, but they were just as good as the seniors. The game was a tough one one, but clean. The rink had a large boiler at one end, which caused a lot of interest, but the rink also had posts all though it, although it was not said exactly where, or how, the posts were situated. But not only did these posts impede the players, "the puck ricocheted about among the posts like a steer through a cornfield." Not only that, but the ice was warm, and, "the slush flew and the water splashed till the scene resembled Narraganset by moonlight or a naval display at Portsmouth." (Both quotes from the Sandon Paystreak, Mar. 10, 1900). Stewart, in the Kaslo goal, received essentially a "shower bath" from the opposing forwards. Gradually the Sandon team began to take control, and they finished with a 4-0 win. Then there was a banquet, and the Kaslo boys returned on their special train at 3:00 a.m.

Sandon (black)		Kaslo (red, white and green)
Hogan	goal	Stuart, J. (or stewart)
Crawford, J.	point	Grierson, Andy.
Crawford, W.	cover	Dill, J.
Crawford, E.	forward	Young, D.J.
Cliffe	forward	Cody, L.
Hood	forward	Stenson, G
Crawford	forward	Hunter, Sam

This game had marked the first appearance of George Hogan, or Hoggan, in goal for the Sandon Juniors. He later backstopped the Sandon Seniors as well, and quickly became one of the best goalies in the province. Hogan was small and thin, with a long, thin face. In 1902, when Hogan traveled to Brantford for the first part of the winter, the Galt Reformer newspaper sang his praises:

> There has appeared in the Brantford hockey firmament a star of considerable brightness. His certificate calls for Hoggan, Huggan, or some such name. Whether he's Huggin, Muggin, Mulligan, or what not, he's certainly a beautiful goal-tender. That fact was self-evident in the Galt-Brantford game here last week. He's scarcely the equal of the great "Dutchy' Morrison, but whoever christens Hoggan, Huggin, etc. a dub, is making the mistake of his life. Mister Hoggan, in his cage, is a bird and a high-flyer, one of the soarers whom the hockey bards sing about. Where did Brantford snare him? Well, that's the mystery. He loomed up on the horizon in the second game with Galt; but does not seem to have materialized when the season opened. At least neither Galt nor Paris remembers him in the first contests. A wireless dispatch says that this pearl of great price ambled along one day from British Columbia, a sort of gold nugget tourist. Brantford gathered him in, regretting that he had not arrived before, tho it is questionable if he could have turned the scale. Of course there may be nothing in the romantic legend of how Hoggan happened. Like Topsy, he may have 'jes' growed' in Brantford without anybody's knowledge. Strange things do happen in great cities. Anyway, he glistens like a genuine gem.

Kaslo was hoping for a third match to decide the series, but it does not seem to have taken place.

ROSSLAND CARNIVAL

The results were sparsely reported this year in all the papers.

Senior Men's championship:

Rossland Victorias defeated Nelson Lacrosse-Hockey 4-3.

Rossland Victorias defeated the Boundary-Greenwood Team 2-1.

Rossland Victorias thereby won the B.C. Championship. This team was the same as reported above in the Kootenays, except E.W. Monk replaced Dr. Ross.

Each member of the Senior Men's team received a golden locket. Each member of the Junior winning team received a silver match box, and each member of the Ladies winning team received broaches.

Junior championship:

The I.X.L's of Rossland defeated the Nelson Juniors 7-3.

The Sandon Juniors defeated the Rossland Juniors, and then the Spokane Juniors, with unknown scores, to win the Junior Championship.

Ladies Championship:

Rossland defeated Nelson 4-0. Nelson's cause was not helped by their Captain, Miss S. (or L.O.) Tamblyn, fainting on the ice.

Nelson Ladies Hockey Team:		Rossland Team
Harvey, Miss,	goal	Not reported
Tamblyn, Miss S,	point	
Lillywhite, Miss,	cover	
McDermott, Miss	forward	
Tamblyn, Miss L.O.	forward	
Hudson, Miss F.	forward	
Johnson, Miss,	forward	

The OKANAGAN

Vernon finally got a team together and tried a tour of the hockey towns in Southern B.C.

The team was:

Crowell, T.E., Captain,
Cochrane, A.O.
Jackson, Bert,
Jackson, R.
Taylor, K.
Edwards, J.
Shatford, S.A.
Crowell, T. Jr.

The only result reported was an 8-0 drubbing of Vernon by Revelstoke, which was North of Vernon. It was reported that Rossland had offered money for travel, and that Vernon was in Rossland on Feb 15th, but there is no other information available.

KAMLOOPS

Kamloops and Nicola appeared to have players, and they challenged each other, but nothing came of it.

LADIES HOCKEY

Ladies hockey started in 1900, with a championship event offered at the Rossland Carnival, where Nelson sent a Ladies team to compete against a Rossland team. (See Rossland Carnival, above).

Kaslo announced an effort to form a women's hockey club to compete at the Rossland Winter Carnival, but nothing came of it.

After the Carnival, the Rossland Ladies Hockey club formed two teams, for a challenge match in Rossland. These were the Stars, in black and gold, and the Crescents, in black and red. This was the middle of March, and the ice was poor, but the teams were evenly matched. Play was spirited at both ends, but only one goal was scored, giving the Stars a 1-0 victory.

Rossland Stars		Rossland Crescents
Burnet, Mrs.	goal	Haskins, Miss
Husband, Miss	point	Agnew, Miss
Fielding, Miss	coverpoint	Inches, Miss
Herchmer, Miss	forward	MacFarlane, Miss, (capt.)
Harris, Miss Mae, (capt)	forward	Northey, Miss
Inches, Miss B.	forward	Lockhart, Miss
Marshall. Miss	forward	Reagh, Miss J.

Goals by: Harris, Miss Mae, (1)

GOLDEN

There was no mention of local hockey in the Golden paper. However there appeared to be a growing disenchantment with the hockey players by the curlers, who were far more numerous, and who were apparently jealous of the time they could be spending, and space they could be using in the rink. According to Kinbasket Country, hockey was in fact dropped around this time from the rink, the curlers moved into the centre ice, and extra construction was added around the centre rink, so the skaters could skate all around it, using the previous area usually reserved for curling. The main hockey players did not put up much of a fuss, and these progenitors of the game now poured their efforts into curling. It was not until 1905 that another reference to local hockey was found in the Golden newspaper. However, the information from 1905 implied that hockey had been going on from time to time on a smaller scale.

VANCOUVER

In Vancouver the mild winter had prevented any hockey being played, although many players were chafing to get onto the ice. A large supply of sticks was ordered by McLennan and McFeely's hardware store, and a team formed under Mr. Spearman, but all they could do was issue challenges, one of which was to Armstrong and Morrison's Machine Shops. When the Stanley Cup was being played for by Winnipeg and Montreal, a large crowd gathered at the CPR telegraph office for regular bulletins. (Montreal won).

A cold spell peaked in middle February, but the ice just wasn't hard enough.

There is some photographic evidence of a team called "The Ramblers" being formed in Vancouver this year. (The new bicycle called "The Rambler" appeared in stores around this time.)

Plate 07. Rossland Ladies Team circa 1900, in the Rossland skating rink. Left to right are: Alice Cooper; E. Blackman; Nellie Inches, (also apparently known as Mrs. E. Morrison); Unknown; Effie Agnew; Alice Northy; Unknown. Some of these players were not named in the 1900 newspaper reports, and the roster of the official 1900 Ladies team remains unclear. Credit: Rossland Museum.

1901 SEASON

Queen Victoria died in January, with much ensuing lament and ceremony throughout the Empire. The Rossland Senior hockey team heard of the Queen's death when they disembarked from a train in Nelson. After a conference they decided to call the game off and go home, at Nelson's acceptance, even though the city of Nelson had paid for Rossland's expenses. (Rossland returned the next week.) A Kaslo curling team decided not to be represented in games for trophies, in deference to the Queen, although they still played exhibition games, without trophies.

In March, after the hockey season ended, moving pictures of the Queen's procession were shown at the Nelson Opera house for 50 cents admission. This was a major feat, considering the newness of moving pictures and the territory these prints had to travel, all over the globe, in just two months.

In May of 1900 a major fire had wiped out most of the city of Sandon. The townspeople were able to save the two ends of town, including the red light district, by blowing up part of the town with dynamite, but the rink was destroyed along with most of the other buildings. This was a huge blow to the city, which had already dealt with a decline in silver/lead prices, a miner's strike, and both a small exodus of miners searching for the new Eldorado in the Yukon, and then a glut of unemployed skilled miners clogging the streets aimlessly. But the town was quickly rebuilt, on a smaller scale, including the rink, and the intrepid hockey team managed to stay, and keep playing the following winter.

Jack Rae, of the Rossland Senior team, had seen a stint in South Africa, being present when the Canadians "rounded up" Cronje of Paardberg. (Army records show he actually enlisted with the Nelson Rifle company, and went with "A" company of the First Canadian contingent.) When he returned, Rae was quoted in the Sandon Paystreak of February 2nd 1901 as saying, "Being entrenched within eighty yards of Cronje's maxims was almost as exciting as playing hockey against Sandon." (This quote might have been a fabrication.)

The Sandon hockey club were presented with goal nets this year by N.J. Cavanaugh. Most teams had nets or acquired them around this time.

Scarlet Fever had broken out in many towns, but this was nothing new.

Silverton and Moyie began playing hockey seriously.

The afore-mentioned B.C. Hockey association fell apart, due to lack of anyone willing to provide the administration. Therefore, individual challenge matches continued, and it was generally assumed that the Rossland Carnival would decide the B.C. Championship.

The Sandon Paystreak announced that Vancouver would soon have artificial ice, but it was not to be.

NELSON, ROSSLAND, SANDON, KASLO and the KOOTENAYS

Sam Neelands became playing manager of the Nelson Senior Hockey Club, and the two clubs of the last year were combined for the best chance of winning against other cities. One rookie, however, cracked the lineup: O. Nace at forward. Two other newcomers almost made the team: C.E. Beasley and J. McLaughlin. Wetmore, who was said to be the fastest and smartest of all the Nelson players became Captain.

Nelson Seniors started off their season by defeating Sandon 7-2. This was the first league game in which Willie Howarth appeared. He would later go on to stardom for Sandon, and then Rossland. He was tall and strong, with a long face. He was reported to have a deceptive style, which seemed slow, but was actually fast.

Nelson Seniors		Sandon Seniors
		(All Sandon positions unknown)
Neelands, Sam,	goal	Crawford, E.
Archibald, B.	point	Crawford, J.
Jeffs, C.	cover	Grierson, A.
Wetmore, M. (or A)	forward	Howarth, William
Nace, O.	forward	Jackson
Perrier, A.	forward	McKinnon
Thompson, Joe.	forward	Cliffe
	forward	O'Neill

Nelson, Kaslo, Silverton and Rossland then traveled to Sandon, where another "Mid-Winter" carnival was taking place, to play for the "Championship of the Kootenays." The Nelson paper only reported its own team's final game. Sandon put up a set of mackinaw coats as prizes.

Nelson defeated the Rossland Victorias 5-4, reportedly coming back from a 3-1 deficit, and finally getting their revenge for several years of defeat. The Rossland paper agreed on the score, but stated that Nelson had a 4-1 lead, and it was Rossland that came back, but failed to win. The Sandon Paystreak agreed with Nelson's account. Joe Thompson was knocked out early on, with a stick to the head, which often happened to him, as he played low to the ice. Walker was sent off to even up the teams, playing six a side for the remainder of the game. Carmichael was severely shaken by a collision, and went off for six minutes while the game was delayed until his return. At the end, as the Paystreak put it, "it degenerated into a slugging match."

Nelson		Rossland Victorias
Neelands, Sam	goal	Leighton, A.G.
Archibald, C.	point	Rea, J. (or Rae)
Jeffs, C.	cover	O'Brien, Eddie
Perrier, A.	f	Winn, Eldon
Thompson, Joe	f	Carmichael
Wetmore (A. M. or R.)	f	Townshend, F. (or Townsend)
Nace, S.	f	Walker, J.

Goals: Thompson (1); Winn (1); Nace (1); O'Brien, (1); Townshend (1); 3 goals unknown for Nelson, 1 goal unknown for Rossland.

Nelson then left before they could play Sandon, for reasons unknown.

Rossland then played Sandon. At half time the score was 2-1 for Sandon, and they maintained control in the second half. Carmichael from Rossland was their star player, and he made several brilliant rushes, but he was not supported by his team. Sandon won 4-2.

Sandon		Rossland
Oliver	goal	Leighton, A.G.
Crawford, Jack	point	Rea, J. (or Rae)
Jackson	cover	O'Brien, Eddie
Grierson	f	Winn, Eldon
Howarth, Willie	f	Carmichael
Birchell	f	Townshend, F. (or Townsend)
Cliffe	f	Walker, J.

Goals: Carmichael, (1); Howarth and Grierson combined, (1); Crawford, Jack, (1); the rest unknown.

On the same day, Winnipeg Victorias defeated the Montreal Shamrocks for the first game of the Stanley cup, which they eventually won. Those towns which had accessible public telegraph systems would post the results on their boards as they came in, and the newspapers would print the scribbled play by play, by an overworked telegrapher, which appeared like this: "8:46 p.m. - Lining up. 8:50 p.m. – They are off. Game very even. Johnson has puck but loses. Woods shoots on goal. Grant lifts right on goal but misses. Brennan secures puck, going down to Victoria's goal. Brown makes a good stop. Bain shoots on goal, off side. It's very close. First game—Shamrocks in five minutes. [A game in this case meant a goal] Off again. Trihey secures, but loses to Bain. Bain is making a run, but is stopped. Play all in the Victorias' vicinity…", etc.

However, as exciting as this play-by-play was, it was not generally used for provincial games, possibly because no one wanted to be the runner, carrying news to the telegraph office, and have to miss the game. Occasionally the results would be projected on a screen at the local theatre. Twenty years later, when radio was common, this fast and exciting description would be heard across thousand of miles of households.

Kaslo then played Silverton. The Silverton players were not very experienced, and, "collisions and catastrophes followed in such rapid succession as to be bewildering." (Sandon Paystreak Feb. 2, 1901) Silverton scored first, but then it was mostly Kaslo, finishing with a 6-2 win.

Kaslo		Silverton
Brown	goal	Not Named
McIntosh, G.	point	
Dill,	cover	
Carney,	forward	
Moore, C.	forward	
McIntosh, A.	forward	
Bloomfield	forward	

The Rossland and Sandon Juniors also played at this carnival – see Juniors, below.

The winner of the Carnival was not formally announced, but the Sandon players claimed the Mackinaw coats.

Later, Nelson traveled to Revelstoke for a tune-up game prior to the Rossland Carnival, but lost, by an unknown score.

Nelson Seniors played one more exhibition game against Rossland after the Rossland Carnival. There were 350 spectators, who paid 25 cents each. Both teams played with only six men, as Rossland had to drop a player before arriving. Nelson then dropped a rookie who was going to be given a chance—Crough. Nelson's team was otherwise the same as the rest of the season. In this game, several goals were scored by Rossland from the cover point position, with long shots, presumably high "lofting," ones, which had become a favorite tactic for clearing the puck. (In the late nineteenth century, "Lofting," was performed backhand. But there is no indication whether these lofts were backhand or forehand. "Lifting" was becoming popular, and was the equivalent of today's forehand wrist shot.) A goal post broke and delayed the game for 15 minutes. McCreary, the Rossland goalie, reportedly became disheartened, and played poorly in the second half. Nelson won 12-6.

Rossland

McCreary, J.	goal
Warren, E.J.	point
Carmichael, G.	cover
McLennan	f
Walker, C.C.	f
Townshend, J.	f

Goals: Wetmore, (4); Carmichael, (3); Thompson, (3); Mclennan, (3); Perrier, (3); Nace (1); Archibald (1).

Sandon seniors traveled to Revelstoke and encountered one of the top goalies in B.C. history, W. Sawyer, as well as Revelstoke's coverpoint, W. MacDonald, who had been purportedly the Captain of the Winnipeg team. Sawyer was sturdy, if a bit fleshy, sardonic faced, and surprisingly adept.

MacDonald had an "imported Winnipeg lift," and could easily throw the puck into the net from a hundred feet. Furthermore the Revelstoke rink was poorly lighted, and shots could come from dark corners, without warning. Revelstoke was too strong for Sandon, and won 6-2.

Sandon		Revelstoke
Hogan?	goal	Sawyer, W.
?	point	?
?	cover	McDonald, W.
?	f	?
Grierson	f	?
Birchell	f	?
?	f	?

Goals: MacDonald, W. (3); Birchell, (1); Grierson, (1); rest unknown.

Sandon later played another game in Kaslo, in March, against the Kaslo Seniors. It was after ten at night when the game commenced, because the train was late, and midnight when it ended. The ice was very heavy, and the game unremarkable, according to reports. Sandon won 5-1, according to Kaslo, and 6-1, according to Sandon.

Kaslo	Sandon
(Positions not known, except Hogan would be goal)	
Brown, A.H.	Hoggan, G
McIntosh, G.	Crawford, J.
Young, D.J..	Crawford, W.J.
Bloomfield, E.V.	Howarth, William
Hunter, S.	Jackson, H.
Carney, H.	Hood, R.
McIntosh, R.M..	Grierson, A.

<u>Inner-City Play</u>

Kaslo

In Kaslo, two town games took place:

The Business Men defeated the Clerks, 5-3.
The St Pancras Inn team defeated the Town team 7-5. There was a big supper at the Pancras Inn after the game, and a party that lasted till 2:00 a.m.

Rossland

The Rossland Victorias played the Rosslands to a 4-4 tie.

Victorias		Rosslands
McCreary	goal	Leighton
Winn	point	Ferrier
O'Brien	cover	Donahue
Bonter	forward	Harris, Al
Rea	forward	McLellan
Harris	forward	Townsend
Ferrier	forward	Carmichael
Walker	spare	

The Bankers of Rossland formed two teams, combining the Bank of Montreal and the Canadian Bank of Commerce, against the Bank of Toronto and the Royal Bank of Canada. J.H. Watson had played hockey in Eastern Canada, but it was G. Carmichael who was the best player, scoring two goals in the Toronto/Royal Bank's 2-0 win.

Bank of Montreal/Can Bank of Com.		Bank of Toronto/Royal Bank
Foster	goal	Leighton, A.
Brown, C.M.	point	McNaughton, W.
Lamont, N.	cover	Carmichael, G.
Phipps, (or Fipps) W.H.G.	forward	Morkill, A.B.
Walker, C.C.	forward	Watson, J.H.
Fisher, H. G.	forward	Hughes, W.G.
Dewdney, E.L.	forward	Leighton, G.A.

Nelson

The Nelson Hardware men beat the Grocery men 7-2.

Teams:

Hardware		Grocery
R.Shields	goal	Bride, Roy
Beer, G.S.	point	Proudfoot, D.
Hipperson, B.	cover	McDonald, D.
Downey, M	forward	Nunn, G. (captain)
McLean, W.	forward	Wilson, D.
McHardy, C.	forward	Benedict, C. e.
Hunter, J. (Capt)	forward	Longhurst, A.

The Grocers then played the CPR staff, winning 3-1

Grocers		CPR
Nunn, G	goal	McMillan, W.
Phillps, G.	point	Newport, J.
Wislon, D.	cover	Hurley, J.
Longhurst, A.	f.	Holmes, J.
McDonald, J.	f.	Whittet, E.
Wright, P.	f	Moe, R.S.
Benedict, C.	f	McAstocker, C.

The Nelson Electric Tramway Company defeated the Nelson Tennis Club 6-4.

The Tramway Co. then defeated the Militia Company 4-3 in overtime.

Nelson Tramway		Nelson Militia
Champion, W.	goal	Wadds, Seargeant J.
Ford, J.	point	Beer, Lieut G.S.
Mason, A.V.	cover	Wilson, Pte G.
Dunne, C.	f	McHardy, pte.
Hawkins, J.	f	Downey, pte
Ault, Z.	f	Coxhead, pte
Pullen, F.	f	Hunter, pte

The CPR team played the Wholesalers, but the result is not known.

Sandon

Sandon had five inner city games. The first was between two hotel teams, the combined Miner's and Kootenay; and the combined Palace and Filbert. Most of these players were newcomers to the sport and the game was rather farcical. The Miners and Kootenay Hotel won 6-2.

Miner's and Kootenay Hotels		Palace and Filbert Hotels
McLeod, Ed.	goal	Newell, Wm
Walmsley, Chas.	point	Burns, Ernie P.
Hanson, Chas.	cover	Angus, Johnny
Hulten, Fred	2nd cover	MacDonald
McLeod, Wm.	f	Peck, Bill
Slinger, Steve	f	Carmichael, Duncan J.
Milne, Jack	f	Murat, Jack C.

Goals: Peck, (2); the rest unknown.

The second game was between the Merchants and the Saloons. Only one man, Charles Carmichael, had experience at the game, and there were many crashes and falls. The Merchants won 9-2.

Merchants		Saloons
Ritchie	goal	Gagnon, Louis
Winters	point	Walmsley
Cameron, Jack	cover	Carmichael, D.J.
Weir, Jimmy	f	Gardner, Martin
Cliffe, B.	f	Hanson, Charlie
Carmichael, Charles	f	Murphy, Paddy
Ross, Albert	f	Richards, Billy

The Seniors and Juniors played three games over the season. All of them ended in ties, 3-3; 4-4; and 3-3. (Lineups were as above in previous games).

ROSSLAND CARNIVAL

The Sandon Seniors dropped out due to business commitments, but the Sandon Juniors were chomping at the bit to defend their title. This was the last year that most of them could be juniors and they had already proven they were a tough match for any senior teams. They were normally the toast of the town in Sandon, and as the Paystreak said, "With the hockey boys and their followers out of town the camp [i.e. Sandon] assumes the calm quietness of a Bruce cemetery."

Sandon Juniors defeated a combination Rossland Senior team in what the Rossland papers described as an exhibition match, but which Sandon described as a match against the Victoria Juniors of Rossland. The score was 5-0, according to Rossland.

Rossland Seniors		Sandon Juniors
McCreary, J.	goal	Hogan, G.
Leighton, A	point	Crawford, J.
Leighton, G.	cover	Crawford, Ernie
Morkill, D.B.	forward	Hood, Robertson
Pownell, R.	forward	Crawford, Wilaim
Bonter, C.	forward	Cliff(e),W.(probably William)
Phipps, W.H.G.	forward	McKinnon, John

Rossland Juniors, also called the Columbias, then defeated Nelson Juniors 6-5.

Rossland Juniors		Nelson Juniors
Ferrier	goal	Brown
Ferrier	point	Rutherford
Donahue	cover	Crow
Clothier	forward	Greenless
Harris	forward	McFarland
O'Hearn	forward	Pullen
McEvoy, C.	forward	Beasley

Goals: Clothier (1); Cliffe (3); McKinnon (1); Hood, (3); Carmichael (1); one goal unaccounted for.

It appears that the Sandon Juniors were considered such favorites that they were given a bye into the final game, waiting for Rossland and Nelson to fight it out. Sandon Juniors then played the Rossland Juniors in the final junior game. Ewing of the Phoenix Seniors was inexplicably allowed to play for Rossland, but only after a protest. Carmichael was also playing as a ringer, from the Rossland Senior team. Donahue had to retire after an injury, and it's not clear whether Sandon sent off one of their own men to even up, or whether Rossland played a man short, or used a spare. The teams were basically the same as above, except for Ewing and Carmichael replacing O'Hearn and Harris. Sandon slowly overpowered Rossland and won 8-2, to take the Junior Championship. One report had it the other way around, but it was clearly Sandon which won. Sandon also won the right to keep the cup permanently, as they had won it three years in a row.

When the Juniors returned to Sandon they received a large reception and a dance in their honour.

Rossland Seniors seemed to be a combination of the two Rossland teams. They first played Revelstoke Seniors, whose best player was W. McDonald, formerly the captain of the Winnipeg senior team, and the betting on the game was fairly even as a result. Wynn, (actually Winn), of Rossland had his hand broken by a stick and was out for the season, being replaced by McLellan. There were many lifts, back and forth, but no goals were scored this way. O'Brien, of Rossland went off for a five minute major penalty for tripping, but it didn't seem to help Revelstoke very much, and it was Rossland which scored a power play. In the last minute four Revelstoke men piled up in the Rossland goal, on top of the goalkeeper, McCreary, but the puck managed to stay out. Rossland prevailed 6-1, mostly because the Revelstoke men wore themselves out too quickly.

Revelstoke		Rossland
Sawyer, W. (capt)	goal	McCreary, J.
Edwards, E.	point	Warren, E.G.
McDonald, W.	cover	O'Brien, E.M. (capt)
Graham, J.	forward	Wynn, E.S.H. (or Winn)
Johnson, J.D.	forward	Harris, W.S.
Hault, W.	forward	Neelands, P.N.
Brewster, W.	forward	Carmichael, G.A.
	spare	McLellan (or McLennan)

Goals: Johnson J.D. (1); Carmichael, G.A. (1); O'Brien (1); Harris, W.S. (1); McLellan (1); Neelands, P.N. (2);

The Nelson Seniors played the Phoenix Seniors. McArthur and Monk, playing for Phoenix, were old hands from Rossland, having been on the 1899 and 1900 team. One goal was scored by Nelson when a clearing lift, behind the Phoenix goal, struck the Phoenix goaltender and dropped in front of the goal. Joe Thompson swatted it into the goal. There was a long delay when a skate broke, and they had to find another one. Nelson finally won, 4-2. (Another report says 3-2, and the Rossland paper says 4-1, although it lists 6 goals).

Nelson		Phoenix
Neelands, Sam,	goal	Mitchell
Archibald, B.	point	McPherson
Crough	cover	Lyons
Wetmore, M. (or A), (capt)	f	Monk
Nace, O.	forward	Niles
Perrier, A.	forward	McArthur, P.C.
Thompson, Joe.	forward	Ewing

Goals: Nace, O. (1); Thompson, Joe (1); Niles, (1); Wetmore, (1); Monk (1); Perrier, A. (1)

The Nelson Seniors then played the Rossland Seniors. The Nelson team was the same as above, while the Rossland team had another Thompson in place of P.N. Neelands, (or Newlands). Nelson played a much better game of combination play, and pulled away quickly from Rossland, despite Rossland getting the first goal. 3 goals were scored by lifts from the defense. Nelson finally won 8-1, for the biggest win of their history, finally securing the Rossland Carnival Cup, and consequently the Championship of B.C.

Goals: O'Brien (1); Archibald, B. (2); Thompson, Joe (1); Perrier, A. (2); Nace, O. (2); one goal unknown.

OKANAGAN

Vernon lost a challenge match to Enderby 2-0 at home.

Vernon	Enderby
Jackson, E.R.	Oliver, E.
Crowell, Thomas E.	Lawes, T.
Cochrane, A.O.	Nelson, A.
Taylor, K.	Siwash, Alec
Little, C.	Bailey, W.
Smith, George	McCleod, D.
Christian, C.	Johnston, A.

Positions are not known.

GOLDEN

No local hockey was reported

JUNIORS

The Junior Rossland teams, the Cyclones and the Invincibles, made up of boys under 14 years of age, played a game won by the Cyclones 3-2.

Cyclones		Invincibles
Stanaway, E.	goal	Simpson, V.
Harris, Edgar	point	Lockhart, H.
Cross, Floyd	cover	Berger, Charles
Dickson, J.	forward	Erickson, Al
Inches, R.	forward	Smiley, Oliver.
Hickinbottom, E.	forward	Funk, Ed
Rawlings, Beecher	forward	Lewis, R.

The Invincibles then changed their name to the Hurricanes, and played several games against the cyclones. One further result is known, a 2-1 win for the Cyclones. The teams were basically the same, except H. Coleman replaced V. Simpson in goal for the Hurricanes, and F. Burns replaced E. Stanaway in goal for the Cyclones. Beecher Rawlings scored both Cyclones goals and Al Erickson scored for the Hurricanes.

The Cyclones beat the Hurricanes again, 4-1. F. Biglen replaced Hickinbottom for the Cyclones and A. Braden and O. Lemrise replaced Erickson and Smiley for the Hurricanes. J. Dickson scored all the goals for the Cyclones, and Lemrise scored the Hurricanes' goal.

Once again the Cyclones beat the Hurricanes 4-1. J. Dixon (or Dickson) was in goal this time for the Cyclones, and Hickinbottom was back in as a forward. R. Inches scored two goals, Hickinbottom one, E. Harris one, and the lone goal for the Hurricanes was by R. Lewis.

The Cyclones then met the Nelson Juniors in Nelson, and tied two-two. Rossland declined to continue, to play off the tie. They also protested at the replacement earlier of a Nelson player who became sick, wanting Nelson to play with only six men.

Teams:

Nelson Juniors		Rossland Juniors
Johns, Steve	goal	Higinbotham, F. (or Hickinbottom)
McBeath, Les	point	Inches, Bob
McDougal, J.	cover	Harris, E.
McLean, Homer	f	Dickson, J.
Wallace, Bert	f.	Keating, A.
Gichrist, L.	f	Rowlings, B.
Gilchrist, P.	f	Lockhart, H.

Harris, the Rossland Captain, tended to swear a lot, and received a cut over his eye. Keating scored two goals and Wallace and McLean scored for Nelson.

Goals: Keating, (2); Wallace, Bert (1); McLean, Homer, (1)

Later in the season, the Hurricanes finally beat the Cyclones 2-0.
Goals: Lewis, R. (1); Funk, E. (1)

At the Sandon festival, the Rossland Columbias, a junior team, defeated the Sandon Juniors, 8-5. (The Sandon paper says 7-6.) Two goals were scored by long lifts. Apparently the Columbias and Sandon juniors had met three other times in the last three years, with Sandon winning all three games.

Columbias		Sandon Juniors
Ferrier, R.	goal	Hogan (or L. Gagnon)
Ferrier, E.	point	Crawford, J.
Carmichael, G.	cover	Crawford, E. (or W.)
Harris, A.	forward	Hood(s), R.
McAvoy, C. (or McCreary)	f	McKinnon, J.
O'Hearn, E..	forward	Crawford, R. (or E.)
Donahue, J	forward	Cliff, Billy (William)

Goals: Harris, A. (2); Crawford, E. (1); McAvoy, C. (2); Carmichael, G. (2); Cliffe, Billy (1); Hoods, (1); McKinnon, J. (1); Donahue, J. (1)

Two junior Kaslo teams played each other in the town. They called themselves the "Hill" and the "Town". They only played five a side, and after sixty minutes the game was tied 1-1. In a ten minute overtime, Tom Carney scored twice, making the score 3-1, winning for the Hill team.

Hill (Kaslo Junior)		Town (Kaslo Junior)
Bruce, Douglas	goal	Lindsay, J.
Carney, Tom	forward	McKinney, R.
McKenzie, Erl	forward	Grotie, R.
Bishop, Harry	forward	Stephensen, J.
Carney, Augustus	forward	Lindsay, B.

Goals scored by: Grothe, (1); Bishop, Harry, (1); Carney, Tom, (2)

On the way home from the Rossland Carnival, the Sandon Junior team defeated a Silverton team in Silverton, but the score is not available.

LADIES

Rossland once again had two ladies teams, the Crescents and the Stars, which were both members of the Rossland Ladies Hockey Club. There were reports of teams at Revelstoke and Nelson, but there were no reports of games.

Rossland Crescents		Rossland Stars
Bogart, Miss	goal	All names unknown
Hewing, Miss Eva	point	
Agnew, Effie, Miss	cover	
Barton, Ona, Miss	rw	
Reagh, Jeannie, Miss	lw	
Inches, Bella, Miss	f	
Spellman, Mrs.	f (capt)	

Despite the names of the Stars being unknown, the other women involved in the club were: Lalonde, C.O., Mrs, President of the Crescents; Inches, Nellie, Miss, Secretary of the Crescents; Mae Harris, Miss, overall club Vice President; Palmer, R.E., Mrs, overall club President; Roff, Miss, Secretary, and Smith, John, overall Treasurer.

OTHER GAMES

Revelstoke had an inner-city game, between "...a team from the Wigwam, [reference unknown] and a team from the City." The Wigwams won 5-2. An invitation was made to the CPR team from Calgary.

Ashcroft began playing hockey, and formed a hockey club, receiving an invitation from Revelstoke. Ashcroft's players were:

McQuarrie, W.G.,	goal
Bremner, J.A.	point
Leslie, H.E.	cover
Reynolds, F.L.	f
Haddock, A.	f
Beattle, G.A.	f
Cameron, W.	f

The author found no record of any games. However, a week after this notice it was reported that F.H. Springs, a member of the hockey team, had injured his hand by a fall on the ice, and that the players are practicing a lot.

Moyie finally organized a team, with P.J. McMahon as manager, but it appears they played no games.

Phoenix was now playing hockey, as seen above at the Rossland Carnival.

VANCOUVER

In Vancouver a match was attempted several times between Vancouver teams, and New Westminster, but the ice was poor. However, on February 5, the first match between a Vancouver and New Westminster team took place at Trout Lake, with a thousand people watching or skating around. New Westminster beat the CPR seven from Vancouver 2-1. The Vancouver team included K.A. Campbell, Dunn, and their star player, Sandy Cowan.

The ice lasted for a few more days and thousands fled from the city to Trout Lake, buying up all the skates in town. As the Vancouver Province related: "skating has become the ruling sport, and skates a something everyone must have…out at the lake….men, women and children invaded the frozen sheet of water in hundreds—even thousands; the tram-way people found even the extra cars inadequate at times, and secured at least partial compensation for the losses sustained by the tie-up of snow storm week: hockey claimed the attention of all its devotees; the squeal of the learner was heard in the land. By evening the bonfires blazed brightly in all their mystic charm; peregrinating peddlers of coffee, sandwiches and cigars did a thriving business; the last objection to the impost of an admission fee was removed when the tramway people hastily wired the trail to the lake, and had it brilliantly illuminated by electricity ere the coming of evening. The skating fever has seized young and old in earnest, banishing the grippe to the back shelves of oblivion. The only question now is, 'how long will the ice last?'"

Before the trail was illuminated, many people had got lost, wandering in the woods. Several young men had actually missed the lake and walked all the way to New Westminster.

Another practise game took place at Trout Lake. A return game with New Westminster was anticipated, and this time A.E. McNaughton was to be asked to play, although he didn't, but the weather turned mild, melting the ice. Many of the players came from the Lacrosse club, and it might be said that the Lacrosse Club had a hockey team.

The ice was better at Burnaby Lake and the players took the tram there, playing on February 9. Fifteen hundred people ended up on the lake, which was a mile wide and three miles long, dwarfing Trout Lake. The trams ran all day, and often were so crowded they were suffocating. The ice was perfect, smooth and thick, and many scratch games of hockey were played. But everybody stopped to watch the main event—the game between the picked teams of New West and Vancouver. Vancouver was called by some the Terminals. The papers called this the best hockey match ever played in British Columbia, but they obviously had not traveled to the Kootenays.

New Westminster won 2-1, again.

Cheyne, the New West goalie was prone to making body checks, as he normally did in lacrosse. Parr broke his skate, so could only play goal, and Dunn had to move out to play forward, which was unfortunate, because Parr was a poor goalie.

The Teams were:

Vancouver		New Westminster
Dunn, N	goal	Cheyne
Elwood	point	Malcomson,
Bailey	cover	Ryall, H.
Cowan, Sandy	f	Southon, H.
Merritt	f	Burden, F
Gilmour	f	Turnbull, A.
Mearn	f	Lynch, F.
Parr	spare	

A.E. McNaughton ended up as referee, replacing an absent Mr. Bogardus.

Then the ice turned soft for the final time.

Plate 08. Sandon Senior Hockey Team 1901. The players are unnamed, but four can be determined from other sources. These are: William Cliffe, bottom, far left; Jack Crawford, to William Cliffe's left, with his arms on two player's knees; William Howarth, at far right, bottom corner; and William MacAdams, top row, far right, in his suit. the other players are possibly A. Grierson; H. Jackson; O'Neill; Oliver, or Birchell. Photo from author's collection.

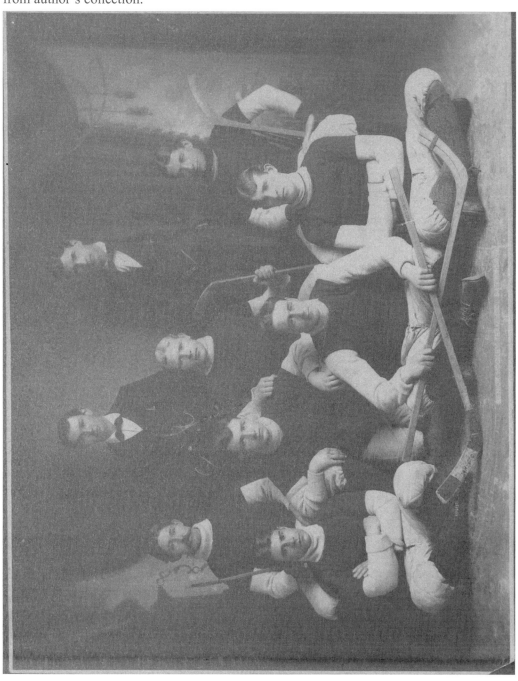

Plate 09. Sandon Junior Hockey Team 1901 (Names as shown) Photo from author's collection.

Plate 10. Nelson Hockey Team 1901. Back row, left to right, George Bell, Manager, C.I. Archibald, Point, Joe Thompson, forward, R.Carley, Coach. Middle row: C.Jeffs, cover point, O. Nase, forward, J.A. Wetmore, forward and Captain, S. Neelands, Goal. Front row: J.E. Crough, cover point, A.A. Perrier, forward. (Note the use of two cover points, which were sometimes used instead of a rover.) Credit: Nelson Museum.

1902 SEASON

The town of Fernie was completely under quarantine in Jan-Feb, due to smallpox. No one could enter or leave.

Spokane apparently had a junior team, as they sent a request to the Rossland Carnival committee for entry, but were turned down, due to the events already being full. A senior team from Lethbridge Alberta, and other junior teams from Sandon, Slocan City, and Nelson were also turned down.

The B.C. Hockey League was again dormant. Challenge matches continued as before, constituting unofficial rivalries. This was the first year that newspapers began reporting the positions of center, rover, left wing, and right wing, as a matter of course.

NELSON, ROSSLAND, SANDON and THE KOOTENAYS

Nelson had new uniforms! For the first time they wore their distinctive, new colours of green and white. It was reported in the Rossland Miner that the green sweaters of the Nelson team had been donated by Alf Jeffs. Photographic evidence shows that it was probably the chest and back which were green, and the sleeves and turtleneck which were white, with a white trim at the waist.

Sam Neelands, the great goalie and manager of the Nelson team had gone off to the Boer War. The Sandon Paystreak had announced he had left in January of 1901, but he was still playing games for Nelson into February, so he must have deferred his leaving somehow. In any case, fortunately for Sam, the war was basically ending, although there is no record available of Sam's return. He was replaced as Manager by W.J. Astley. Also leaving was J.W. Nunn, the Secretary of the Nelson Team, for a job in Winnipeg.

Nelson played its first game of the year against Sandon, at home, with a rookie in the lineup—T.Collins, at Point. He beat out J. Nunn, who then promptly left for Winnipeg as stated. This was the first organized hockey game which featured William Howarth for Sandon, who would later crack the Senior team as one of its stars. The Nelson goalie, Nunn, was considered to be the determining factor by Sandon. Nelson won 7-4.

Sandon		Nelson
Bloomfield, E.	goal	Nunn, G.
Crawford, J	point	Collins, T.
Crawford, W. (capt)	cover	Jeffs, C.
McKinnon	f	Nase (Nace)
Hood, R.	f	Wetmore, A.
Howarth, W.	f	Thompson, Joe
Grierson	f	Pullen

Goals by: Wetmore, (2); Nace, (2); Howarth (2); Pullen, (1); Hood, (1); Grierson, (1); Thompson, (1). (One goal unknown. Wetmore probably scored 3, but it's not clear which of the Nelson team scored the extra goal.)

One more challenge match was played in Sandon against Nelson, in March. The Nelson team was missing Wetmore, their ace forward, and Nunn, their best goalie, as well as the rookie, Collins. Paul Greyerbiehl once more stepped into goal, with D. Rutherford, at point, and A. Perrier as centre.

There was some disagreement over who actually accompanied the Nelson team. The Sandon account is probably more accurate, as there was no Nelson reporter on the scene. According to the Sandon Paystreak Nelson only brought six men and Sandon dropped one of their own to even up. The Nelson team was not a weak one, but according to the Paystreak they admitted before the game that they expected to lose. Nevertheless Sandon was itching for the win, and gave no quarter. Sandon started piling up the goals, and the game became rough, as Nelson became frustrated. As the sarcastic Sandon reporter remarked, "Jack Crawford did a Japanese wrestling turn with Nace over in the corner...Joe Thompson did the Sandow act[16]...Grierson broke his shinney over Bullen just merely to make things interesting." The referee did not keep a tight control on these transgressions, and Arthur Perrier was heard to shout several times, in his thick French Canadian accent, and somewhat broken English, the equivalent of, "Jesus Christ, play hockey!"

During half time, with the score 6-3 for Sandon, a supporter of the Sandon team offered Robertson (W.R.) Hood one dollar for every goal he scored in the second half. This was possibly offered by Paddy Murphy, who was the manager of the Clifton Saloon, and who would soon hire Hood to clerk at the Filbert saloon and café, when Murphy purchased it. Murphy later played briefly for Sandon in 1903. In any case, Hood roared out of the block when the game started, and immediately scored an unassisted goal with a "grand-stand rush," from end to end. He scored two more before the game was ended. But for all that, it was still a disappointing game for the spectators because the flow of the game had been slow, with heavy, slushy ice and a generally torpid and sullen group of opponents in the Nelson team. Sandon won 11-4.

Goals: Thompson, (2); Hood and Grierson combined, (1); Hood and Howarth combined, (10; Crawford, William (Rusty); (1); Hood, W.R. (5); Perrier, (1); one goal unknown.

A combined Rossland seniors team also traveled to Sandon after the Rossland Carnival, in late March. They were without their stars, Winn and Carmichael, and it showed, as "the Sandon boys put in goals whenever they had a mind to." According to the Paystreak, McCreary, the Rossland goalie, played a strong game, but, "The playing of the balance of the Rossland team is hardly fit for publication." Sandon massacred Rossland, 14-3.
Goals, and full roster, not known.

Sandon played a match in Slocan City, but the result is not known.

Trail finally began playing hockey seriously this season, and organized a senior team to challenge the Rossland Victorias. The Trail fans had composed

---

[16] A famous German strongman, operating mostly in England.

a song, sung to a popular melody, and carried many tin horns. The Trail team was much heavier, but the Rossland players were better skaters, although their former Captain, Eddie O'Brien, had moved to Seattle, and declared himself out of hockey. Rossland scored first with a long lift, which was misjudged by Conklin. The score then alternated, until the last half, when Rossland pulled away, scoring 3 unanswered goals, to win 6-3.

Victorias		Trail
Leighton	goal	Conklin
Ferrier	point	Blaylok (capt)
Carmichael	cover	Viets
O'Hearn	rover	Barrough
Walker	centre	Clark
Phipps	lw	Brew
Rae	rw	Buggins
Donohoe	spare	

Goals: Carmichael (1); eight goals not known.

Rossland Victorias and the Trail team played a rematch in Trail, during the afternoon, since the lighting at the Trail arena was poor. Rossland had Winn back at centre, while a spare man, Lawe, was also part of the team. The teams were otherwise basically the same. This time Rossland won 4-0.

A third match was played between these two teams, and was won by Rossland 10-5. The teams had already changed somewhat from the first game, but Trail then announced it would start beefing up its team, and began its long tradition of bringing in ringers, which it would practice often over the years. A Trail spokesman indicated they would be bringing in Jack Gibson, "who played point for the Berlin Ontario team during the season when Berlin was disqualified for professionalism....he was rated as the best man in Ontario at point, and doubtless retains much of his old skill." Another, tougher Buggins brother was to play for Trail as well.

Rossland Victorias		Trail
Leighton	goal	Brock
Ferrier	point	Blaylock (capt)
Carmichael	cover	Darragh
Meegan	rover	Bingay
Winn	centre	Ayres
Rae	lw	Shoemaker
Harris	rw	Buggins

Inner City play:

Nelson

Rocky Mountain Rangers (in Nelson) defeated Nelson CPR 4-3.
Retail Clerks (Nelson) defeated the Rocky Mountain Rangers 10-5.

Sandon

Sandon started a City League in December of 1901. The Printers played the City, and the game was evenly fought, with the score ending 6-6. Three Cliffe brothers were with the Printers, while three Crawford brothers were with the city team. This was the only game in the city League to be reported. William Howarth was finally getting into the game.

Printers of Sandon		City (Sandon)
Potter	goal	McKinnon, F.
Cliffe, R.	point	Crawford, J.
MacAdams, W.	cover	Crawford, W.
Howarth, W.	f	Gusty, J.
Cliffe, Wm.	f	Crawford, E.
Hood, R.	f	Grierson, A.
Cliffe, W. (probably Walter)	f	Clothier, Roy

ROSSLAND CARNIVAL

The hockey winners received the following prizes:

Seniors: One pair of military brushes in silver.
          One desk clock.
          One pair of opera glasses.
          Two pairs of gold links.
          Two diamond studs

Juniors: Seven gold scarf pins.

Rossland Seniors, (who were the Victorias), first played the Trail seniors, who were without the vaunted player from the East, Jack Gibson, and still had only one Buggins. There was a scheduling mixup, to the consternation of the Trail team, and they started off badly in the match, trying to catch up in the second half, but to no avail, as Rossland won 9-3.

Trail		Rossland Seniors
Borck	goal	Leighton, (A. or G.)
Blaylock	point	Ferrier
Darragh	cover	Carmichael
Ayres	rover	Winn, Eldon S.H.
Lynch	centre	Harris, Al.
Brew	lw	Clothier, Roy
Buggins	rw	Rea

Nelson Seniors then played the Rossland Seniors, (or Victorias). Considerable attention was paid to who would referee and as the first choice was injured, and the third was not acceptable to Rossland, William Howarth, the Sandon Captain, was pressed, reluctantly, into service. The Nelson men were heavier, and had played more as a team. Rossland's Captain, Winn, was not playing. But Rossland scored first. However, this was all they could muster, as the superior team work of Nelson overpowered Rossland, 7-1. (In this Carnival, the puck was referred to several times as the "gypsum." One wonders if the puck was actually made from this mineral, or whether it simply resembled a gypsum crystal, which can be roughly disc shaped).

Nelson (green and white)		Rossland Victorias (white)
Greyerbiehl, Paul	goal	Leighton, (A. or G.)
Archibald, C. (Barney)	point	Ferrier
Jeffs, C.	cover	Carmichael
Perrier, Arthur	rover	Davis
Wetmore, (A. or M.)	centre	Harris, Al.
Nase, or Nace, O.	rw	Higgins
Thompson, Joe	lw	Clothier, Roy

Goals: Harris, (1); other goals not known.

Sandon Seniors played Phoenix in the other semi-final. Two goals by Sandon were disallowed for being offside. McArthur tripped Hood and was given a stern warning from the referee. The first half ended with the score 3-1 for Sandon. In the second half McArthur was sent off for five minutes for "fouling." Hood also indulged in "fouling," and was sent off for five minutes. He redeemed himself by scoring 3 goals, and was also injured for several minutes while the game was delayed until he could continue. Sandon eventually prevailed 8-4. (Sandon put the score 9-4). Hogan had played his usual sterling game. It was said by the Sandon Paystreak that, "Phoenix could not keep pace with the lightning changes of the Sandon boys," i.e. passing successively in combination.

Sandon Seniors		Phoenix Seniors
Hogan,	goal	Mitchell
Crawford, J.	point	Warren
Crawford, W.	cover	Stutzel
Crawford, E.	rover	McCarthur
Hood, R.	centre	Monk (capt)
Howarth, W.	rw	Ewing
Grierson, A.	lw	Chesterton
Cliffe	spare	

Goals: Grierson (1); McArthur, (2); Howarth, (3); Hood, (3); Monk (2); one goal unknown.

Nelson then played Sandon for the Senior Championship. The Nelson team appeared to be the same as its previous challenge matches. The ice was soft, and slow, but the men were fast. There were only two penalties, both to Nelson. Jeffs and Archibald were a battle-worn defensive duo who had played well together before. They were constantly clearing their zone with long, accurate lifts. Sandon's defense, although also used to playing together, was not as strong. Sandon had a more experienced goalie in Hogan, however. Sandon scored first, but Nelson roared back, and after the first half it was 2-2. In the second half, the Nelson team seems to have employed a new strategy which might have consisted in counter-attacking swiftly, once the Sandon forwards had been stripped of the puck by Nelson's crack defence. Nelson scored three unanswered goals, and won the game 5-2, gaining once again the Championship of B.C., (and presumably a lot of money).

Goals: Howarth, (1); other goals not known.

The Junior Championship for the Thompson Cup was played between Rossland and Nelson, and Rossland completely overpowered Nelson 11-1.

Rossland Junior Victorias		Nelson Juniors
McQuarrie	goal	Moe
Ferrier	point	Rutherford
Carmichael	cover	Sprye
Donohue	rover	Ross
Harris	centre	McFarland
Miggins	rw	Pullen
Clothier	lw	Wright

(According to the Nelson paper, the Nelson hockey team wanted a tune-up before their final game with Sandon, and so, after beating Rossland 7-1, they played another exhibition game with Rossland, which then beat Nelson 11-1. The Nelson paper tried to justify this crazy score by saying that the

Sandon team was evidently betting heavily on their game with Nelson, which would decide the championship. When Nelson lost 11-1, the Sandon team sent back home for more money. Then the Nelson contingent obliged with renewed betting. However, what appears to have happened is that the Nelson paper got the whole game mixed up with the Junior Championship. The Junior Rossland team was also called the Victorias, and several of the players played for both Junior and Senior teams. The Rossland Miner does not mention this supposed senior game, but does report the junior championship, while the Nelson paper does not report the junior championship at all. It would have been bizarre for the Nelson Seniors to expend their energy like that before an important game.)

THE OKANAGAN

This was the first year that W. Sawyer, the great goalie, switched from the Revelstoke team to Vernon. But at first he did not play goal, finding a place on defense. There is no available record showing whether he played goal this year for Vernon.

The Vernon Team travelled to Revelstoke and won a game, 5-3. The Vernon Team was:

McLaughlin, J.	goal
Sawyer, W.	point
Jackson, R.	cover
Elworthy, E capt	rover?
Jackson, B.	f
Shatford, S.A.	f
Crowell, T.E.	f

A week later they played Revelstoke again. My records do not show what the score was, but with 2 ½ minutes to play, Vernon players refused to continue due to the roughness of the game. Three of their players had already been knocked out. Although the crowd cheered the Vernon players, the refs awarded the game to Revelstoke, which was important to give a definite result for the side bets.

THE BOUNDARY REGION

Phoenix played a game against Greenwood. They appeared to play with six men a side, instead of seven. Chesterton scored a goal with one of his "Cyclonic dashes," reminiscent of the way another Cyclone got his nickname. But Phoenix put the game away in the second half, winning 5-2

Greenwood		Phoenix
Stowe	goal	Mitchell
McPherson	point	Lyon(s)
Warren	cover	McArthur
Chesterton,	centre	Monk
Steer	rw	Coulton
Dill	lw	Ewing
McKinnon	spare	Coles

Goals: Steer, (1); McArthur, (2); Coulton, (1); Monk, (2); Chesterton (1);

Grand Forks formed a hockey club, and played their first game ever, against Phoenix, at Grand Forks, on January 18. It was described as a "donnybrook," in the first half, due to the rough play. Phoenix was ahead 1-0 at the half. In the second half, the Grand Forks spectators became so excited that they often crowded into the ice, preventing the players from performing properly. Grand Forks pulled ahead by one, but then Phoenix tied it up, and with 45 seconds to go, Monk scored the winning goal for Phoenix, making it 3-2. Phoenix colours were white, while Grand Forks was red and white.

Grand Forks		Phoenix
Cochrane,	goal	Mitchell
Jackson,	point	Lyons
Grant	cover	Stretzel
Brown,	rover	McArthur
McQueen	forward (rw)	Ewing
Baker	forward (lw)	Monk
Vahey	spare	Fulton
Farrell	spare	

Goals: McArthur, (1); McQueen, (1); Baker (1); Monk (1)

Another game was played between these two teams in Phoenix, with Phoenix winning 10-5. Grand Forks had the same team, except Niles was the rover, and Farrell and Vahey didn't play.

Phoenix:
(positions not known)
Stow
Lyons
Stretzel
McArthur
Ewing
Monk
Wood

KAMLOOPS and NICOLA

The Kamloops Team traveled to Nicola Lake, to play their first game. The result is not known, but the Kamloops players were: J.C. Holmes, Angus Nelson, K. Bayntun, E. Unwin, W. Jarvis, and B. Prior (capt.). (Who was the seventh man?) The Nicola Team is not known. But a week later a rematch took place in Kamloops. The teams were:

Kamloops		Nicola Lake (positions not known)
Dennings, T.	goal	Cropp, Rev.
Adams, H.A.	point	Godlich, E.
Cornwall, H.A.	cover	Riley
Nelson, Angus (capt)	f	Murray, W.
Bayntun, K.	rover	Murray, J.
Holmes, J.C.	f	Carlington, A.R.
Prior, B.G.	f	Duncan, J.H.

Kamloops won 8-1. Despite huge enthusiasm, no other matches took place that season.

GOLDEN

No local hockey was reported.

JUNIORS

The Nelson Juniors played the Rossland Juniors, swearing to wipe the floor with them. (Rossland was called the Mountaineers in one report). But Nelson lost, 4-2.

Nelson		Rossland
Davidson, W.	goal	Johns, D.
Steele, L.	point	Preston, Jack
Curran, Joe W	cover	Harris, Edgar
McLean, H.	rw	Keating, Al
Gilchrist, Lance.	center	Funk, Ed.
Wallace, A.N.	rover	Dixon, James
Steed, W.B.	lw	Goninan, D

The Nelson Juniors then swore they would not lose again, strengthened their team with new players and challenged again. But they lost again, 6-3.

Nelson		Rossland
Davidson,	goal	Johns, B.
Greyerbiehl,	point	Inches, R.
Stewart, N.	cover	Harris, E.
Sharpe, Roy,	center	Funk
Moe, Roy	rover	Dixon, E.
Wallace, A.H.	lw	Preston, J.
McLean H.	rw	Goninau, D.

The Slocan Juniors traveled to Sandon and played the Senior team, losing 11 to 6. (Sandon no longer had a junior team, as the former juniors were now too old, and there were not sufficient numbers to take up their positions.)

LADIES:

The Rossland Girls Hockey Club was organized and began practicing regularly at the rink. Eldon S.H. Winn, Captain of the Victorias, had the plum job of coach. There are no results reported of games, however.

VANCOUVER

In late January New Westminster and Vancouver challenged each other, but conditions conspired against them. A lot of snow fell, on various days, causing great mounds to build up, eventually turning into great mounds of slush. Everyone at Trout Lake was charged ten cents to go on the ice by the men who cleaned off the snow, and took care of coats and boots. Nevertheless, two hockey managers in Vancouver rounded up some of the best men and had a practise on the ice. These players were: Sandy Cowan, Billy Flood (the fastest), Bailey, Charlie Herman, Nelson Dunn, who had learned hockey at Upper Canada College, Clarence Marpole, E. Birchall, who had played hockey in Nova Scotia, Charlie Grassie, and Dick Worth. The managers were Quigley and Frank Burde. The New West Manager was Herb Ryall.

But sadly, no game ever took place.

1903 SEASON

NELSON, ROSSLAND and THE KOOTENAYS

A city ordinance ordered that gaming come to a complete close in Rossland, in January. No more card games or roulette wheels were allowed in any of the saloons, which made wagering on hockey games all the more urgent.

Nelson's uniforms had changed, so that the sleeves were also green, while the only white was around the neck, and cuffs of the sleeves.

In December of 1902, Kaslo announced, to the surprise of everyone, that they would have no hockey team this season. This was a major blow to Sandon, since the two cities played each other the most, and Sandon's other competitors were much farther away. There were only a few clues regarding Kaslo's hockey hibernation. The Kaslo Kootenian mentioned that, "Basketball is attracting more attention than any other sport in Kaslo at the present time. Three games a week are played in the drill hall…"

The Sandon Paystreak of December 20, 1902 said, "The [Kaslo] sports are too busy playing ping pong and parlour croquet. Later on ante-over, blindman's buff, pussy wants a corner, and other new fangled games will be indulged in. Kaslo is bound not to be before (sic) the times."

Apparently the new sport of basketball had reached across the country faster than hockey and grabbed the attention of the young men of Kaslo.[17] This was anathema to the Sandonites, as evidenced by the reporter's sarcasm. It is nevertheless surprising that the young men could not break themselves away from what was more a summer sport, to play hockey for at least two months, but such was apparently the case. It was two years before they gradually began to play hockey again.

A proposal was advanced by several representatives to set up a Kootenay Hockey Association, but nothing official came of it.

The Kootenay teams played a series of challenge matches, preparing for the Rossland Carnival. Nelson first played Sandon. They played six a side because McIntyre was delayed and Nelson then dropped Rutherford.

This was the first senior game which saw the inclusion into the Nelson team of the great goaltender, Harry Bishop. At first glance his inclusion would have seemed bizarre. Bishop was very small, and cherubic, and he looked like he was in the wrong league. He appeared to be between twelve to fourteen, but in fact he was already twenty-one. His previous experience in B.C. had been playing for the junior team in Kaslo even though he actually would have been overage. But with Kaslo no longer playing hockey, Harry had moved to Nelson.

Harry had been playing ever since he was very young in Niagara, and then for a senior team in London Ontario, so he was actually very experienced. He was a late bloomer, physically, but not in the fast reaction category. Frank Patrick was to say of him, many years later, that, "Bishop was a fine athlete, and a grand hockey player. As a goal-keeper he was good enough to have made professional company had he cared to make the jump."[18] His debut for Nelson was very strong, as Nelson defeated Sandon 3-1.

---

[17] Invented by James Naismith in December 1891.
[18] Nelson Daily News, October 31, 1924.

Nelson		Sandon
Bishop, Harry	goal	Hoggan, G.
Archibald, C. (Barney)	point	McIntyre, R.J.
Jeffs, Charlie	cover point	Crawford, W
Perrier	forward	Grierson
Blackwood	forward	Hood
Thompson, Joe	forward	Cliffe
Rutherford	forward	Crawford, E.

Goals were by Thompson, (2), Hood, (1) and Perrier, (1). Nelson was the heavier team, and although play was generally clean, Archibald and Jeffs threw their weight around constantly, wearing out the smaller Sandon team.

Sandon then moved on to a tour of games with Grand Forks, Phoenix, Rossland.

Rossland and Grand Forks met for a "league game," in Rossland. The game almost didn't take place because the train carrying the Grand Forks team was blocked by snow somewhere near Silica. Somehow word was received of the exact location of the train, and the Rossland team sent out sleighs to pick up the Grand Forks players. (Presumably the other passengers, not being hockey players, were out of luck). The game started one hour late as a result. It was hard fought, but Rossland Victorias won easily, 6-1.

Grand Forks		Rossland Victorias
Cochrane, A.O.	goal	McCreary
Jackson, Harry	point	Winn
Mitchell, W.	cover	Carmichael
Niles, C.H.	rover	Felion
Perrier	center	McPherson
Ewing, George	left wing	Clothier
McQueen, A.	right wing	Harris, Al
	Manager	Davis, Al

Goals were scored by: McPherson, (1); Felion (3) Clothier, (1); Harris, (1); and the Grand Forks goal by an unknown player.

Sandon and Rossland met for a senior challenge match. It was hotly contested, with rapid dashes from both sides. Howarth fell and was gashed under the eye by someone's skate. The game was delayed for fifteen minutes while a doctor bandaged him up, and play then resumed with Howarth again on the ice for Sandon. Harris outran the Sandon defense to get under a long lift, and grabbed the puck ahead of them, to score for Rossland. In the end, Rossland was just a bit too strong, winning 5-3.

Sandon		Rossland Victorias
Hogan, G.	goal	McCreary
McIntyre, R.J.	point	Winn, Eldon
Crawford, J.	cover	Carmichael
Crawford, W.	rover	Felion
Hood	center	McPherson
Crawford, E.	left wing	Clothier
Howarth	right wing	Harris

Goals: Felion, (3); Carmichael, (1); Hood, (2); Harris, (1); 1 goal unknown.

Cyril, (Barney), Archibald, gave up the post of captain of the Nelson hockey team, and C.D. (Dudley) Blackwood was elected to that post.

Nelson intermediates defeated Rossland intermediates 8-2 in Nelson. Nelson wore green jerseys and white trousers. Johns had been acquired by Rossland from Nelson. Preston scored both Rossland goals, and the Nelson goals were by: Wallace, (2); Sharpe; (3); Baker, (1); and Steele (2).

Nelson		Rossland
Greyerbiehl	goal	Johns
Stewart	point	Inches
Curran	cover	Harris
Wallace	forward	Preston
Sharpe	forward	Keatings
Steele	forward	Gininan
Baker	forward	Dixon

Barney Archibald was going to have to be away in the territories for the carnival, but so great was the need for him to be on the team, that his employers made new arrangements, allowing him to play.

Due to the recent movement of players, there was great concern that all players be amateurs and actually live in the cities they played for.

<u>Inner-City Matches</u>

Rossland

The Rossland Victorias played the Citizens Team in early January, to determine who would play against outside teams. The Victorias won 9-3, although there is some confusion about the score.

Rossland Citizens		Rossland Victorias
Leighton	goal	McCreary
Donohoe	point	Winn
Rea	cover	Carmichael
Sangster (forward)	rover	Felion
?	center	McPherson
?	left wing	Clothier
?	right wing	Harris

Goals: Felion, (5 ?); Clothier, (1); Sangster, (1); 5 goals unknown.

The Rossland Bank of Montreal played the Associated Banks of Rossland. G. Carmichael of the Associated Banks was the big star, getting two goals, and smashing one of the overhead lights with a high lift. The Associated Banks won 3-1.

Bank of Montreal		Associated Banks
Fraser, J.S.C.	goal	Leighton, A.G.
Stricland,, A.	point	Lewer, C.E.
Lamont, Robert	cover	Carmichael, G.
Phipps, W.H.G.	rover	McKenzie, J.K.
Clark, W.	center	Carpenter, W.
Gibbs, M.	left wing	Anderson, J.
Falding, H.	right wing	Gillard, J.

Goals: Carmichael, G. (2); McKenzie, (1); Phipps, (1)

The West Kootenay Power and Light Company of Rossland challenged the Hunter Brothers Stores, and played to a 2-2 tie.

Hunter Bros.		West Kootenay Power and Light Company
Hunter, Robert	goal	Campbell, Lorne A.
Morrison, E.	point	Logan, Gordon
Ternan, W.G.	cover	Grant, G.P.
Joiner, P. (forward)	rover	Somers, C.
Andrews, R.	center	McKibbin, R.S.
Lawler, G.	left wing	McDonald, D.
McLaughlin, J.	right wing	Waide, James

Nelson

In Nelson the Wholesalers beat the Bankers 5-2. Two hundred spectators witnessed the match. The first goal was scored by Wallace, with a lofting shot that went end to end. There was some controversy about Barney Archibald's roughness, and the Bankers then refused to play any more scheduled games against the Wholesalers unless Archibald was not playing, which meant that no further games were played.

Wholesalers		Bankers
Nunn	goal	Bamfield
Archibald, Barney	point	Wallace
Benedict	cover point	Dumoulin
Fraser	forward	Hedley
Sharpe	forward	McFarland
Wright, Perry	forward	Eden
Hipperson	forward	Pinkham

The CPR and the Rockey Mountain Rangers, (of Nelson), played a game against each other, but there is no other info.

ROSSLAND CARNIVAL

Much boasting preceded this contest. The Sandon paper, forinstance, was replete with criticism of the Nelson team, such as: "Nelson can play nothing but a butcher's game, and a good referee will change all that." And, "Nelson will now have to play hockey, not shinney." Sandon also felt that their team was so good, "it will be like taking candy from a baby…"

Barney Archibald, the accountant, was once again singled out as being Nelson's equivalent of today's "goons."

Just prior to the Carnival, at a hockey banquet in Rossland, Arthur Perrier of the Nelson Team, (who had been playing as a ringer for Grand Forks), stood up and announced that in order to secure the Rossland Carnival Cup this year, Nelson was going to bring in three players from Winnipeg. Large amounts of alcohol were consumed at these banquets, so one can assume that this might have been what prompted Perrier, who was also the secretary-treasurer of the Nelson team, to let the cat out of the bag. A deeper possible motive might have been that since Perrier was one of the weaker members of the Nelson team, he was likely to be one of those who would be supplanted before the Carnival, and he purposely leaked the information to guarantee his place in the contest, after the impending protests.

Immediately this announcement sparked indignation and debate, especially since it was obvious "professionalism." However, the fact remained that there was no rule against it. But the loophole was swiftly closed by the Rossland committee, who decreed that players had to be residing in their cities for at least thirty days. Perrier then found himself back in the Nelson lineup.

Many teams were announced as entering the festival but the ones who actually took part were: Nelson, the Rossland Victorias, Rossland City, Sandon,

(Rawhiders), Slocan City, Grand Forks, and Medicine Hat and Pincher Creek, both from Alberta, who combined into one Crow's Nest Team, although it was also called the Pincher Creek Team. Initially, it was proposed that it wouldn't be fair for Pincher Creek to be eliminated from the whole contest if they lost their first game, so it was decided that the B.C. team who had defeated all the others would then play Pincher Creek for the final game. One might consider this bizarre, but the result of this drawing ended up being even more distorted, as will be seen below.

Also, despite the fact that the Rossland Victorias had defeated the Rossland Citizens team, to decide which team would play against outsiders, another Rossland team was formed for the Carnival out of the defeated Citizens team, and they were called the Rosslands, or the Rossland City Team.

Nelson played Grand Forks. Nelson jumped out to a 3 goal lead in the first half, but Grand Forks, who were very fast, started to come back, narrowing the score to 3-2. Then the game see-sawed and Nelson ended up winning 5-4. According to the Nelson reports, despite the close score, they apparently did not use much energy. Grand Forks felt otherwise, calling it a great game, with a much improved Grand Forks team, which appears to be true.

Nelson		Grand Forks
Bishop	goal	Cochrane, A.O.
Archibald	point	Jackson, Harry
Jeffs, Charlie	cover point	Mitchell, W.
Perrier	forward	Niles, C.H.
Blackwood	forward	Coulson, or Colton
Thompson, Joe	forward	Ewing, George
Hacker, A.	forward	McQueen, A.

Goals: Thompson, Joe, (2); Hacker, (2); Niles, (2); Colton, (1); McQueen, (1); one goal unknown for Nelson.

The Rossland Victorias then played the Rossland City Team. (The Victorias had the same team as usual.) The Rossland paper considered it a dull affair, with the Victorias only playing hard when they needed to, and eventually winning 9-5.

Rosslands (City)

Leighton	goal
Donohoe	point
Ray, J.	cover
Preston	rover
Keating, Al.	center
McLaughlin	lw
Clark, X	rw

The Rossland Victorias played Slocan City. The York boys, a feature of the Slocan Team, were sons of the mayor of Slocan City. The goalie, L. York, was pummeled by shots from the Victorias, who won either 4-2, or 4-0. (The newspaper is damaged here.)

Slocan City Seniors

York, L.	goal
Barber	point
McMillan	cover
York, J.	rover
McKinnon,	centre
Smith	rw
Bull	lw

Nelson played Sandon in a very close game. According to the Rossland Miner, the Sandon team was the stronger, as a result of their great combination work. Nelson had a very strong defense, however. Sandon scored first to great pandemonium. Baker for Nelson then tied it up, although it was an offside play, according to the Rossland Miner. (Baker had been promoted from the junior team to the senior team.) Hood put Sandon ahead again just before the half. In the second half Cliffe put Sandon ahead 3-1. But soon Nelson came roaring back, as Sandon became too concerned with their offense, and neglected their defense. Nelson scored 3 unanswered goals to put them ahead 4-3. Archibald, Sandon's nemesis, scored one of the goals through lofting the puck end to end. Jeffs was hit on the head by the puck, and knocked out, but returned to the game later. It's not known whether a spare filled in for him or not. Just as the whistle was blown to end the game, Sandon scored, but it was disallowed, and Nelson was declared the winner, 4-3. Sandon was very disappointed. It was said in the Nelson Daily News that Nelson won a thousand dollars through betting as a result. (The Daily News also put the score at 5-3).

Nelson		Sandon (red and white)
Bishop, H.	goal	Hoggan, Geo.
Archibald, C. J.	point	Crawford, J
Blackwood, C.D. (Dudley)	cover	Crawford, W.
Baker, C	forward	Hood, W. R.
Jeffs, C.	forward	Howarth, Wm.
Perrier, Arthur A.	forward	Cliffe, Wm.
Thompson, Joe	forward	Crawford, E.
Hacker, A.	spare	Murphy, P.H. (Manager)

(P.H. Murphy was probably Patrick or Paddy Murphy, who had become the owner-manager of the Filbert Saloon and Café.)

Goals: Hood, (2); Cliffe, (1); Baker, (1); Thompson, Joe, (1); Blackwood, (1); Archibald, (1)

Nelson then played the Rossland Victorias in what was billed as the final game for the Championship of British Columbia, and therefore, the final game for the Carnival Cup. However, Pincher Creek was still waiting to play their final game, but somewhere in the last two days, it had been quietly decided that Pincher Creek would not play for the cup, and that their game would be essentially meaningless. There does not seem to be a protest reported on the part of Pincher Creek for this downgrading.

In any case, the "final" match between Nelson and Rossland Victorias was a bitterly contested one, and the enthusiasm of the crowd of 1500 was unparalleled, according to the papers, in the history of local amateur sports. It was reported that four hundred people traveled by train from Nelson just for the final game.

McPherson of Rossland was knocked out, and Blackwood and Thompson of Nelson were both injured, and several penalties were called, putting men "on the fence." It appears that the Rossland players tired in the second half, possibly due to the physical play of the burly Nelson players, but the Rossland Miner disagreed with the Nelson paper, making it seem as if the Nelson players were falling all over the place after being checked by the Rossland players. The Nelson defense was very strong, and according to the Rossland Miner, all the players would bunch up around the Nelson goal whenever it was threatened. Pandemonium reigned as supporters shouted themselves hoarse. Green and white flags and pennants were waving everywhere, along with the Rossland colours. (Red?)

Clothier scored the first goal for Rossland, but then Thompson, (2) and Archibald scored in the second half for Nelson. One of Joe Thompson's goals bounced off Felion's foot, hit the goal post and went in. Incredibly, Archibald had scored again on one of his patented lifts, probably backhanded, from one end of the ice to the other. The Rossland reporter said of this shot that it, "looked easy to the majority of spectators, [but] was a most difficult shot to handle." The final score remained 3-1 for Nelson.

Goals: Thompson, (2); Archibald, (1); Clothier, (1)

Huge amounts of money were reportedly won and lost on this game.

Boasting of the money won was prevalent and very vocal, with men marching through the streets, waving the bills in the air. (Although side bets were often made in gold dust, since cash was not always available, and as many of the spectators were miners, or worked in related fields.)

It was reported that the Crow's Nest team had actually raised ten thousand dollars as a betting pool, and hired an auctioneer, to "raise pools." They traveled to Rossland and put this money up for betting, but "no pools were sold."

As the Nelson Daily News said, "The Game was for blood and was won more through the great work of the Nelson defence than through any brilliant work of the forward line." There was great jubilation over this in Nelson, as that meant they could permanently keep the Cup, having won it three times in a row. (Ironically Rossland had also won the cup in its first three years, but the first year was by the Rossland City team and the next two years by the Rossland Victorias.)

The same day Nelson then played Pincher Creek, aka the Crow's Nest Team, who had yet to play a game, and the Nelson players were exhausted and disheveled. Several were now wearing bandages. The Pincher Creek team didn't even bother to body check any of the Nelson team, because it was not much of a challenge to beat them. The Nelson, "Champions," lost 9-3.

Pincher Creek (or the Crow's Nest Team) (Red and White)

Sharp	goal
Turnbull	point
Gunn, A.	cover
Moore, J.	rover
Turnbull, C.	centre
Kastner, M.	rw
Fair, Wm	lw
Schofield, J.H.	Manager (?)

A grand testimonial dinner was then arranged in Nelson for the victorious players, and tickets were proposed for the general public, as well as presentations, but the organizers and team officials were anxious that this would not affect the men's amateur standing. Incredibly, at the same time, they were fielding challenges from teams such as Sandon, to play a match for $500 a side. Apparently Vice-President of the Nelson Team, J.S. Carter replied, (by cable), "Amount too small—one thousand dollars a side least Nelson can consider. Nelson now only does business with people who have a reputation or money."

This was from the man whose description in the papers often made him seem the the most vocally ardent defender of amateurism.

There was never an attempt to explain this dichotomy of ethics, either by the men themselves, or by the rules. It was simply accepted that men had to gamble on games, and that they had to receive appearance money, or money for "expenses," and that had nothing to do with being a professional, even though the men received the money they won. But they weren't paid a salary, (most of the time), and that, apparently, made all the difference to them.

The Cup was displayed in the window of Patenaude Brothers, Engravers. Just as is done now with the Stanley Cup, the Carnival Cup was filled with alcohol and the players drank from it.

A running newspaper battle then ensued over where another game would be played against Sandon, and for how much. Sandon insisted, ultimately, on playing in Rossland and Nelson insisted on playing in Nelson. As G.E. McGlaughlin, the Nelson manager stated, "The Nelson team will not play at Rossland, nor will the Montreal Victorias play Sandon for the Stanley Cup at Los Angeles or New Orleans." Although the one thousand dollars seems to have been put up by both sides, they could not agree, and this game was never held. Sandon maintained that it insisted on playing in Rossland for "its own reasons." They couldn't come right out and say it, but the fact was that playing in Rossland would have provided a substantially larger Gate receipt, which both clubs would have shared. If Sandon had lost the huge side bet, they would have made it up with the Gate receipts. As for Nelson, pride seems to have been more the deciding factor, and since they had already won a huge amount of money they were satisfied.

(Robertson Hood of Sandon, then traveled to Calgary to play for that city against Edmonton in a series for the Stephen trophy.)

THE SLOCAN

Slocan City defeated Silverton 6-5 on March 6.

Silverton		Slocan
Bowes	goal	Hamberger
Byrons	point	Barber
Bains	cover	Hicks
Elliott	forward	Milne
Pinchbeck	forward	Brown
Yorke	forward	Tier
Bull	forward	McRae

After the Rossland Carnival, Sandon played Slocan City in Slocan, but the result is not known.

THE CROW'S NEST

Both Medicine Hat, who won the Crow's Nest League, and Pincher Creek, the two Alberta teams, announced they would enter the Rossland Carnival, but only Pincher Creek showed up.

Medicine Hat traveled to Fernie and defeated Pincher Creek there 7-3, thereby winning both the Liphardt and Henderson trophies.

THE BOUNDARY

Grand Forks played Sandon, on Sandon's tour. The game ended 1-0 for Grand Forks when, "The puck was lost in the course of the game and could not be replaced." Grand Forks thereby was awarded the game, since it appears there were no more pucks in Grand Forks.

Greenwood and Phoenix played a match which was won 5-0 by Greenwood, who had acquired Phoenix's best player, although it's not clear who this was.

Grand Forks announced they had acquired Sandon's star player, "Weary Willie" Howarth. However, there are no games with any results for Howarth, playing for Grand Forks.

Phoenix traveled to Grand Forks and defeated Grand Forks 3-1. (Only 6 men a side were played, due to an unnamed accident.)

Phoenix		Grand Forks
Cole	goal	Cochrane
Cook	point	Grant
Church	cover	Ewing (capt)
Strutzel	forward	McQueen
Colton	forward	Mitchell
Mead	forward	McDougall

Grand Forks then traveled to Phoenix. Both teams made changes: Grand Forks had replaced Grant with Jackson, H., and added Niles; Phoenix had replaced Church with Lyons, and added Clark. Phoenix defeated Grand Forks again, 8-2.

Phoenix then returned to Grand Forks, whose team had been practicing diligently in anticipation, and juggling their players again. As a result they reversed the previous decisions and Grand Forks won 8-1. Grand Forks then claimed the "Championship of the Boundary." (This seems odd, since Phoenix had beaten Grand Forks twice, and both had 2-2 records, but perhaps there was another game, unreported.)

Phoenix		Grand Forks
Lyons	goal	Cochrane
Cook, W.	point	Jackson, H.
Cook, P.	cover	Mitchell
Clarke	rover	Niles
Strutzel	forward	McQueen
Colton	forward	Ewing
Mead	forward	McDougall

In Grand Forks an inner-city game took place between the Heroes and the Hoboes, which was won by the Hoboes 2-1.

Heroes		Hoboes
Miller	goal	Donaldson, John
Jackson	point	McIntyre
Petrie	cover	Savage
Woodland	forward	Spier
Hankinson	forward	White
Miller, Alex	forward	Bower
Campbell	forward	Stewart

VERNON

Vernon now had a new rink, and the first match against an outside team ever played in Vernon took place January 19, against Kamloops. Vernon won 7-0.

Vernon		Kamloops
Sawyer, W.	goal	Blair, Clifford
Robertson, R.W. (or H.)	point	Dean, D.W. (or S.W.)
Elworthy, E. (capt)	cover	Winters, A
Crowell, T.E.	rover	Nelson, Angus (capt.)
Jackson, E.S.	center	Baynton, K.
Shatford, S.A	r. wing	Adams, H
Mabee, C.	l. Wing	Cornwall, H.A.

Goals were scored by Shatford (2), Crowell (2), Mabee (2) and Jackson. The Vernon goalie only had 2 shots on him the entire game.

A month later the return match was played in Kamloops, and Vernon won 3-2. Vernon goals were scored by Crowell, Elworthy and Jackson. Kamloops had A. Greatrix and G.R. Mason instead of Winters and Adams. Angus Nelson had formerly been with Vernon, but was now Kamloop's star.

Vernon defeated Revelstoke 2-0 in Vernon. Robertson scored in a long lift from point. Elworthy also scored.

Revelstoke		Vernon
Allum, E. M.	goal	full team as before
Hyatt, A.	point	
Moir, J.	cover	
Douglas, R. (capt)	rover	
Boyd, J-P	centre	
Bews, W.	r. wing	
Chambers, W.	l. wing	

Goals: Robertson, (1); Elworthy, (1)

A return match in Revelstoke resulted in Vernon defeating Revelstoke, again, 2-0. Crowell and Jackson scored for Vernon. Revelstoke had changed two players, but it's not known which two.

Goals: Crowell, (1); Jackson,(1)

Vernon Seniors then challenged Nelson, which declined, and Sandon, which accepted. (Vernon was prepared to pick up Nelson's expenses of $235). The confident Sandon Seniors traveled to Vernon for the game.

Sandon appeared to be superior right from the start with much better combination play, and indeed they scored the first goal in two minutes. They scored again, and made it 2-0 in the first half. (Both goals by Howarth.) In the second half Vernon adjusted to Sandon's style of play and stormed the Sandon end, scoring two goals. (Elworthy and Robertson). Howarth scored another goal, but it was offside. Tier then scored for Sandon, but in the last two minutes, Elworthy scored again for Vernon, against the visibly sagging Sandon players, preserving a tie, 3-3.

Vernon was very proud of its achievements this year, not losing a game, and standing up to one of the province's powerhouses. It was a harbinger of things to come.

Vernon		Sandon
Saywer, W.	goal	Hoggan, I.G.
(same as above)	point	McIntyre, R.J.
	cover	Crawford, E.
	rover	Crawford, W.
	center	Guerson, A.(Grierson)
	l. wing	Howarth, W.
	r. wing	Tier, J.

Goals: Howarth, (2); Elworthy, (2); Robertson, (1); Tier, (1)

(An Edward Elworthy was listed in the 1904 B.C. Directory as a clerk at W.R. Megaw, General Merchant. R.J. McIntyre, of the Sandon team was formerly minister of the Methodist church at Enderby and was also a pitcher for the base-ball team of that district.)

KAMLOOPS

(See also Vernon)

Town games were played in Kamloops between the CPR, Kamloops College, and the Town Team. According to Wind and Ice, players involved included the Munn Brothers, Parsons, Fred Irwin and Angus Nelson.

An inner-city match took place between the original seven Kamloops Seniors who had played the first game that season against Vernon, and a picked town team. The Senior Kamloops team defeated the picked team 5-0.

Kamloops Picked Town Team	Kamloops Senior Team
Mason, G.R.	As above, (see Vernon)
Greatrix, Alf	
Bayntun, E.	
Willing, Ed	
Unwin, J.M.	
MacCormick, Alf.	
Stroeger, A.	
Edmonds, W.H.	Manager/coach

JUNIORS

Rossland Juniors beat Trail Juniors 6-2.

Phoenix Juniors defeated the Grand Forks juniors 4-1.

Grand Forks		Phoenix
Taylor	all positions	Biner, G.
Traunweiser	unknown	McAuliffe
Sloper		Biner, A.
Michner		McKelvey
Birbeck		Pierce
Hay		Trainer
Feeney.		Hudson

Vernon Juniors (blue jerseys) and Vernon High School played to a five-five tie.

Vernon high school		Vernon Juniors
Christien, H.	goal	McCluskey, J.
McCoy, O.	point	Scott, W.
Birnie, H.	cover	Mohr. W.
Robbins, F.	rover	Thomas, J.
Graham, D.	center	Carey, J.
French, P.	r wing	Meyer, R. (capt.)
French, G. (capt)	l wing	McQueen, T.

A second game between these two teams resulted in another 5-5 tie.

A third game resulted in a 3-2 win for the high school boys.

LADIES

The Rossland Ladies started a club, and had a practice match. Miss Shrapnel showed up well in goal.

VANCOUVER

In mid February the ice finally firmed up and New Westminster and Vancouver challenged each other once more. However, when the hockey players ventured onto the ice at Trout Lake and Burnaby Lake, it was not strong enough, and many youngsters fell through the ice for a dunking, before they finally gave up.

Plate 11. Nelson Hockey Team 1903. Back row: left to right, J. Fred Hume, (Hon. President), J.F. Thompson, forward, I. Archibald, point, G.E. McLaughlin (Manager). Middle row: H.J. Hacker, forward, C. Jeffs, forward, W.A. Macdonald, K.C. (sic), President, A.A. Perrier, forward, C.D. Blackwood, cover point and captain. Front row: H. Bishop, goal, C. Baker, forward. Credit: Nelson Museum.

1904 SEASON

The world watched as Japan and Russia began a war, keeping the headlines full of the generally constant Russian defeats, well into 1905.

More importantly for the Kootenays, Trail upgraded its telephone system this year, so that forty new poles, and 1500 insulators were added.

Nothing seems to have come from another attempt to set up a Kootenay Hockey Association. However, Rossland implemented a new, Industrial City Hockey League, which could not be made up of any players already playing for a current senior team.

Hockey skates were on sale in Nelson from 35 cents to $4.00 a pair.

NELSON, ROSSLAND and THE KOOTENAYS

Eldon Winn was now retired from active competition. But this retirement was ironically one of the most important developments in inter-city rivalry in the Kootenays, because he became a referee.

Eldon S.H. Winn had been an articling student during the first years of his playing career, with MacNeill and Deacon, in Rossland. By 1905 he was a partner in his own law office, McDonald and Winn.

He was a self-assured, smug, smooth-featured man, who had become the Rossland team's Captain, as much for his leadership qualities as well as his scoring ability. But Winn was also a lawyer, and evidentally gave the Rossland team an aura of learned authority. He began refereeing seriously in 1905, and appeared to be acceptably impartial, and very stringent regarding the rules and infractions. (He was the only referee to give a man a penalty for grabbing the puck and throwing it away from his goal.)

In 1906 that began to change. This was the first time Winn was made a member of the Rossland Carnival Committee, and he was simultaneously the President of the Rossland Hockey Club. From then on, for the next three years, he became the referee of choice for all of Rossland's important games, and no protest on the part of Rossland's rivals could dislodge him.

Winn was still, it seems, a competent referee, but from 1906 onward he chose his moments to apply a little hometown help to his team, causing much consternation to Rossland's arch-rivals, Nelson. This situation continued even when Lester Patrick arrived on the scene in 1908. In a way, Winn became the obdurate yin to Lester Patrick's haughty yang.

In Sandon the team had lost at least six of its main Senior players. This was a blow from which Sandon never really recovered. William Howarth, their star forward, who had acquired the nickname, "Weary Willie," was head-hunted by Rossland. Howarth's nickname was given him because he had, "…an easy method of skating, with a long swing, and seemed slow, but in reality was very fast."[19] Grand Forks had also first announced that they had acquired Willie Howarth from Sandon at the end of the last season. They might have done so, but there are no records showing any games he played for them. In any case,

---

[19] Rossland Miner, Feb 6th, 1913.

Howarth was not with Grand Forks long, because Rossland definitely acquired him at the beginning of the 1904 season.

Rossland had also acquired two other top players from Sandon: Andy Grierson, and Robertson Hood. It's not known what inducements were made.

The Crawfords appear to have left, to towns nearby, such as Lardeau, Arrowhead, or Ferguson, and their great goalie, Hogan, is unaccounted for during the rest of his career. Eventually some of the Crawfords moved to Saskatchewan.

In Nelson, Roy Sharpe was promoted from the intermediates as cover-point, and there were several other changes. According to the new Manager, Musselman, it was agreed by the previous regulars to open up the field and try out every good hockey player in Nelson for the team. Gone was their feisty defenceman, Barney Archibald, as well as some of the other stalwarts who won the cup the previous year, Charlie Jeffs, Blackwood, Perrier and Rutherford, at least temporarily. (Perrier was back intermittently).

This is a remarkable event in the history of sportsmanship, but may also reflect the aging of the team, and their satisfaction in winning the Rossland Carnival trophy for all time. Many players in subsequent decades felt the same way, including the 1980 United States team after they won gold at the Olympics from the Russians. It may seem silly to equate these two events, but to the Nelson team, they had achieved the highest level available to them. It was not really feasible to challenge for the Stanley cup at this time, but an advertisement for the next year's Rossland Carnival indicated that the winners would be eligible to play for the Stanley Cup. This was only technically true, and would, of course, still be up to the trustees.

Nelson intermediates voted to merge with the Nelson Senior Team's management, and although it was never stated in that way, it was essentially to provide a farm team for the Seniors.

D. McNichol resigned as manager of the Nelson Seniors and Frank Musselman was elected in his stead.

Brandon Manitoba challenged the Nelson Seniors to a series of games, but nothing came of the challenge.

Hockey Sticks were on sale for between 20 to 50 cents, along with other hockey equipment at Nelson Hardware.

Rossland Seniors went on a tour and defeated Revelstoke 11-3, tied Vernon, 5-5, and lost to Silverton 5-2. It was implied by some in Nelson that the heavily favored Rossland team lost to Silverton on purpose in order to cash in on bets against themselves. However, the Rossland paper related that the Silverton team was made up of a conglomeration of "all the fast men" of the Slocan district.

Rossland		Vernon
Leighton	goal	Cochrane
Donahue	point	Robertson
Powers	cover	Elworthy
Hoods	center	Jackson
Clothier	rover	Smith
Grierson	r. wing	McQueen
Howarth	l wing	Mabee
Dickenson, H.P.	manager	

Nelson played Rossland, with the biggest crowd watching ever assembled in Nelson. It was specifically stated that all the Nelson men were residents of Nelson and played the game for the love if it, alluding, probably, to the mass defection of Sandon players to Rossland.

The Rossland players averaged 165 pounds, as they added muscle to contend with the toughness of the Nelson team. The game was accordingly very roughly played. Four players were penalized, for two minutes, i.e. "put on the fence." Joe Thompson was injured. "Weary Willie" Howarth played a strong game for Rossland. Bishop's goaltending was magnificent, and Joe Thompson was the best Nelson forward. However, after the first quarter, Rossland was ahead 2-1, and "the Rossland contingent shouted loud and long and offered their money freely."

In the second half Nelson began to pull away, scoring their fifth goal with a contingent of players following the puck into the net and ripping it off its moorings. Finally Nelson won 6-3.

Nelson:		Rossland (blue jerseys)
Bishop	goal	Leighton
Deacon	point	Donahue
Guay	cover	Powers
Baker	center	Hood
Robertson	right wing	Grierson
Thompson, J	left wing	Howarth
Sharpe, Roy	rover	Clothier
Kern	spare	

Goals were scored by: Sharpe, (1); Clothier, (1); Howarth, (1) Robertson, (1) Thompson, (3). The 2 other goals were unaccredited.

Rossland then traveled to Phoenix for a challenge game. Phoenix went ahead 3-1 at the half, and then they traded goals, with Phoenix ending the game as the winner, 4-3. One of the Rossland men was injured, and both teams played a man short to compensate. However, once the Rossland players came home from their tour, they protested that they had not lost this game, but rather, for reasons unexplained, they had actually been the winners. One report described the Phoenix team as a, "…composite Boundary team," with it being reported that one player at least, G.M. Carmichael, had been borrowed from Grand Forks.

Phoenix		Rossland
Haverty, John	goal	Layton
Collins, T.E.	point	Donohue, Jack
Carmichael, G.M.	cover	Powers
Steel, L.	forward	Howarth
Trainner	forward	Clothier
Coulton	forward	Hood
Carmichael, R.	forward	Grierson

In a return match in Rossland, the Phoenix team was weaker, dropping G.M. Carmichael, Coulton and Trainner, and playing A. Clarke and George Franier. Phoenix was still a man short, so the teams played six a side. The game was all Rossland, scoring the first three goals, and then scoring at will, but the final score is not given. This was lauded, however, as proof of who should be considered the winner of the previous game.

The Rossland Carnival then took place. (See the results below.)

Immediately after the Carnival, Nelson invited Revelstoke and Fernie to play further games in Nelson.

Nelson Seniors then defeated Revelstoke Seniors, 7-4, Thompson scoring 5 goals. (Although one account shows him scoring 4 goals and Baker 2.)

Revelstoke		Nelson
Woods	goal	Bishop
Sawyer	point	Deacon
McAnn	cover	Robertson
Graham	rover	Guay
Barber	center	Baker
Allan	left wing	Thompson
Bews	right wing	Perrier

Goals were scored by: Baker, (1) Allan, (2) Thompson, (5) Graham, (2), Perrier(1)

Nelson then played Fernie and won 2-1.

Fernie

Rutherford	goal
Miller	point
Kastner	cover
Turnbull	forward
McLachlan	forward
La Fortune	forward
Brown	forward

Goals by: Thompson,(1); McLachlan (1) and Guay.(1)

Nelson played one more challenge match with Rossland, in Rossland, after the Carnival, with Nelson only getting 40% of the gate receipts, as a result of their newly diminished status, after their Carnival showing.

All the goals were scored in the first half, and Nelson won 2-1. Thompson scored three goals, but two were disallowed, one for being offside, and one because the goal judges didn't see it. Thompson was also playing with a severe cold. Guay also scored for Nelson, and Hoods scored for Rossland. Nelson newspapers called this the Championship of the Kootenays, since they had now won 2 out of 3 contests with Rossland. Although the arena was packed, betting was somewhat slow, and the Nelson team only made about 300-400 dollars on side bets.

Nelson		Rossland
Bishop	goal	Leighton
Deacon	point	Powers
Robertson	cover	Grierson
Steele	forward	Hoods
Thompson	forward	Howarth
Perrier	forward	Donahue
Guay	forward	Clothier

Goals: Thompson, (1); Guay, (1); Hoods, (1).

Rossland was not satisfied with this result, and demanded a rematch, as usual. It looked like one would take place, but then the weather turned warm, and that was the end of the series for the year.

Nelson tried to arrange further games with Cranbrook and Fernie, but minimum guarantees of money were not forthcoming, so they cancelled.

The Nelson Intermediates played the Rossland Intermediates.
Rossland won 4-3. Steele was now playing for Phoenix and Baker with the Nelson Seniors.

Nelson int.		Rossland int.
Inches, R.	goal	Johns, D.
Harris, E.	point	Stewart, J.
Crosse, D.	cover	Curran, J.
Funk, Eddie	forward	Sharp, R.
Dixon, J.	forward	Wallace, Bert
Preston, J.	forward	Gallon
Keating, A. (capt.)	forward	Greyerbiehl, P.
McCabe, A.E.	spare	McDougall, N.

<u>Inner-city play</u>

Industrial League

In Rossland the new Industrial League was a big success. The teams were the Le Roi Mine, The War Eagle Mine, Hunter Brothers Stores, The Bank of Montreal, and The Kootenay Power and Light Company. The players all had to be from the clerical or engineering force of the firms involved, although it was simple enough to put a miner on the clerical payroll. More importantly they had to play exclusively for those teams.

Hunter Brothers

Hunter, Robert	goal
Hicks, W. G.	point
Ternan, W. G.	cover
Hattrup, E. H.	rover
Costello	centre
Lavasseur, T.	lw
Lee, J.	rw
Brown, G.	f
Burke, W.G.	tried out for team

West Kootenay Power and Light Co.

Barrett, Charles E.	goal
Parker, J. W.	point
Fortin, F. D.	cover
Summers, Charles E.	rover
Grant, Garnet, P.	centre
McDonald, John D.	lw
McKibbin, Robert S.	rw
Campbell, L.A.	tried out for team
Schulfer, J.	tried out for team
Rich, A.J.	tried out for team

Le Roi Mine

Bowers, A.E.	goal
Fraser, George	point
Clothier, George	cover
Keating, Al	forward
Anderson, John	forward
Tonkin, G.	f
Morkill, D.B.	f
Robbins, J.	tried out for team
Anderson, Robert H.	tried out for team
Simpson, C.E.	tried out for team

Bank of Montreal

Winter, C.B.	goal
Falding, Homer	point
Lamont, R.	cover
Phipps, W.G.H.	f
Dewdney, E.E.	f
Sutherland, E.G.	f
Padden, A.E.	f
Duthie, E.	tried out for team
Fraser, J.S.C.	tried out for team

War Eagle Mine

Cosgro, John, P.	goal
Davis, Carl R.	point
Emery, A.B.	cover
Cram, James, K.	f
Dunne, W.	f
McBride, C.	f
Tuttle, Jay	f
Oliver, H.G.	tried out for team
Cole, Arthur A.	tried out for team
Jenkins, Charles V.	tried out for team
Kirby, E.B.	tried out for team
Cruikshank, G.	tried out for team

Hunter Brothers first defeated West Kootenay Power in overtime 4-2. Ternan for Hunter Brothers was the only named scorer, on a long lift.

Le Roi defeated the Bank of Montreal 5-3.

Le Roi defeated War Eagle 4-0.

It was then decided that Hunter Brothers and Le Roi would play a final game for the Championship, because they were the only two teams with wins so far. This seems a rather unfair system, but no one is on record as complaining.

Hunter Brothers controlled most of the early game, and Ternan's lift was the tactic, "...that the mine boys feared more than aught else in the game," but, "Ternan's deadly lifter only got into full working order once, [and] that secured Hunter's sole tally." The sore was tied 1-1 after regulation time. It took four overtime periods of five minutes each for Le Roi to score the winning goal, giving them the game 2-1, and the Industrial League Championship.

Goals: Ternan, (1); 2 not known.

Nelson

In Nelson the Reilly Hockey Team lost to the Wholesalers 8-4. Grierbiehl and Deacon scored goals, but the rest were not reported. Unfortunately for the Reilly club, their goaltender, Paxton, was "rotten."

Reilly Club		Wholesalers
Paxton, A.	goal	Nunn, George
Colpitts	point	Holmes, Joe
Deacon	cover	Greyerbiehl, P.
McLachlin	forward	Benedict, C.
Wright	forward	Dill, A.
Gallon, T.	forward	Sharpe, Roy
Kydd, N.	forward	Hipperson, W.
Hiams	forward/spare	Ferguson
Kydd D.M.	spare	
Misses Reilly, mascots		

A game was announced by the Canadian Foresters team and the Retail Clerks of Nelson. The result is not known.

ROSSLAND CARNIVAL

Harry Dickenson of The Giant Powder Company now donated the next cup for the B.C. Championships, replacing the, "Citizen's Trophy," which had been retained by Nelson permanently for 3 straight victories. This new Cup was called the Giant Powder Cup. It was closed at the top, with one hockey player standing on it, with his stick down and one foot in the air. The cup had two handles, and in the middle were two hockey sticks crossed, with the base underneath.

The betting on the games went as follows, according to the Rossland Miner: "Last night wagers were offered on Rossland at ten dollars even against each of the clubs entered, ten dollars to forty that Rossland would capture the trophy, even money that Vernon or Fernie would defeat Nelson, even money that Boundary would defeat Revelstoke. Such are the features of this aspect of the sports."

It was ordered that an end be put to whistles, bells and horns at the events. Special "officers" would be distributed throughout the spectators to crack down on these nuisances.

The hockey opened with an exhibition match between the Rossland Ladies teams. The team rosters were all mixed up from the previous games. The Whites won 3-1. Miss Kit Hamilton, captain of the Whites, had instilled a fine sense of combination play into her team, while for the Blues, Miss Goninan played a strong game at point, lifting admirably. Lilly Demuth made, "a series of fine rushes in a futile effort to capture the game for the Blues."

Whites (white sweater)		Blues (blue sweaters)
Milne, Mary	goal	Aconitt, Johanna
Bogart, Eva	point	Blackman, Evelyn
Demuth, Reba	cover	Goninan, Minnie
Donahue, Flossie	forward	Stanaway, Olive
Hamilton, Kit	forward	Demuth, Lilly
Honey, Edna	forward	Demuth, Selma
Honey, Francis	forward	Adams, Dot

A major controversy erupted between Vernon and Fernie. The star player for Fernie, Turnbull, had not quite achieved the thirty day residency status necessary to satisfy the rules. However, they assured the Rossland Carnival that Turnbull was there to stay, as a permanent resident. The Carnival committee acquiesced and allowed Turnbull to come. But when Vernon heard of this, prior to their game with Fernie, they absolutley refused to play, causing their scheduled game to be cancelled. Fernie insisted that Turnbull be able to play, so all day, until midnight, the committee conferred. Finally they offered a solution: Turnbull could not play against Vernon, but if Fernie progressed after that, then Turnbull could play in any of the other games. Fernie grudgingly agreed, and the next day the game was played.

Despite losing their best player, the result was a surprise to Fernie, and everyone else, when Vernon crushed them 7-4. Vernon had displayed, "…unexpected skill and staying ability." There was a large crowd in attendance, cheering for both sides. The goal judge at Fernie's end, (Nelson's manager, Mussleman), was removed after he, "didn't, or wouldn't," see one of Vernon's goals, which would have made the score 8-4.

This knocked Fernie out of the competition, and they were very disappointed.

Fernie		Vernon (blue and white)
Rutherford, C.	goal	Sawyer, W.
Miller, R.	point	Robertson, R.H.
Kastner, M.	cover	Ellworthy, E.
Stevens, J.	rover	Smith, A.
McLaughlin, J.	center	Jackson, E.S.
Brown, C.	l. wing	Mabee, C.
Lafortune, (or Lafontane), D.	r. wing	McQueen, A.
	spare/or manager	Crowell, Thomas Edward
Turnbull, C.	spare	

Rossland played Nelson. It's not stated whether this was the Rossland Victorias, or a picked Rossland team. It seems more likely that it is a picked team. The Nelson team had lost several of its members from the previous championship years, including Archibald, Jeffs and Blackwood, and this weakened their defense considerably. There were many end to end rushes by both sides which did not score. All the goals came in the second half, when Rossland finally scored first. Then Nelson's new defenseman, Roberts, lifted the puck toward the Rossland goal, and when it came down, Donahue swiped at it and missed, Leighton moved out of the crease to play it, and it slipped past him into the goal. But Rossland scored one more with ten minutes remaining, and it stood up as the winner, making the final score 2-1 for Rossland. This was the first time in four years that Rossland had beaten Nelson.

Rossland (blue and white)		Nelson (green and white)
Leighton	goal	Bishop, H.
Donahue	point	Roberts
Powers	cover	Deacon
Clothier	rover	Guay
Hood	centre	Baker
Howarth	l wing	Thompson, Joe
Grierson	r wing	Perrier

Rossland then played Revelstoke. Two thousand spectators, by that time, reportedly, were watching the games. Revelstoke stunned Rossland by a, "…rush line that would organize near the flags and come down the ice with a speed and cleverness that made the outlook ominous." Revelstoke went ahead 2-0 with this tactic, and Rossland was slow to counter it. But soon they organized their own teamwork in a similar fashion and, "worked the puck down the sides in terrific charges," and soon tied the score. Then they took a four-two lead by the end of the half, and never looked back. The Revelstoke Captain, Barber, was a, "veritable cyclone," and led many attacks down the ice, but he was actually too fast for the rest of his team, and they often couldn't catch up with him. Barber was left to make single dashes many times as a result. He scored on one of these, but it wasn't enough, as Rossland defeated Revelstoke 10-4.

Revelstoke (green sweaters)

Wood, (or Woods), W.	goal
Sawyer	point
Edwards, E.	cover
Barber, W.J. (capt)	rover
Graham, C.	centre
Allen, (or Allan), J.	lw
Bows, (or Bews), H.	rw
McCann, Barney	spare, or manager
Granger, H.	spare, or manager
Johnston, C.E.	spare, or manager

Goals: Barber, (1); all other goals unknown.

Rossland and Vernon then played for the B.C. Championship. Rossland seems to have been forced to play one more game than Vernon, as a result of there being five teams, which is certainly not fair, but there is no record of dispute. Vernon was wearing blue and white, and Rossland switched as a result to red, usually playing this year with blue sweaters. The referee was Turnbull, of Fernie, who had reason to hate Vernon, but he seems to have judged fairly all the same. Vernon had a great rush, which they employed immediately and quickly rammed in one goal. They scored a second goal the same way, and Rossland was hard pressed to pick up their game, seeming a bit, "stiff," from the previous day. But they battled back and scored a goal. In the second half both sides assailed the goalies who were playing the game of their lives, stopping many hard shots. In the end neither side could score again, and Vernon won 2-1.

Vernon had won the B.C. Championships.

The Vernon players were ecstatic and they were well feted by their town when they returned home, drinking champagne from the cup, as was becoming the custom. This report might be apocryphal, however, since the new cup had a closed top, with a hockey player on top of it, but it could possibly be detached.

There remains, however, a small mystery. As explained above in 1899, William Sawyer was the only Sawyer listed in Revelstoke between 1902 to 1904 in the B.C. directories. But there were no Sawyers listed in Vernon in 1902-04. Yet there was at least one other Sawyer playing for Revelstoke in 1904: an H. Sawyer, as evidenced by the 1904 Revelstoke team picture. But these two players look exactly alike! Both were playing at the same Rossland Carnival, but on two different teams. H. Sawyer has his hair a bit shorter than W. Sawyer, but the picture could have been taken earlier in the season. One is left with the probability that these two hockey playing Sawyers were twins. In the 1910 B.C. directory for Revelstoke, the Sawyer Brothers, Richard H. and Henry, are listed as sash and door factory workers, just like William before them, who is no longer there, while there is still no Sawyer listed in Vernon. (In 1918 an H. Sawyer was listed in Revelstoke as a mixed farmer. In 1922 a Harry Sawyer was listed as a shingles manufacturer in Revelstoke.)

At the very least, these two Sawyers had to be brothers, and it appears that Revelstoke was probably more of a home to W. Sawyer than Vernon.

As for the Nelson players, they returned home as quickly as possible and the result was not spoken of in the press. The Rossland Miner praised Vernon, where "hockey is played for the sport it affords, and where hockey is not a 'business proposition,' as it is in at least one town that sent a team to the carnival." This probably meant Nelson, although the sentiment is clearly hypocritical.

The Rossland Junior team defeated the Trail juniors 3-0.

Trail Juniors
    Positions not known
Coleman
Isley
Tyson
Glover
Cunningham
Callaghan
Tyson
Chapman

After the Carnival, The Nelson Daily News implied that there was much razzing of Joe Thompson in the Rossland press, who were claiming that he should retire and that he was now a "back number." Joe Thompson apparently became very irate and reportedly was, "devoting several hours daily to telling his friends in Nelson what an awful roast the Rossland Miner handed him and what big stunts he is going to do when Nelson and Rossland next meet, just to show that he isn't a dead-un." But the Nelson Daily News had misrepresented what the Miner had said, which was: "Much was expected of Joe Thompson on Nelson's forward line, but for some reason he did not deliver the goods. It would be rank heresy to hint that Thompson's days as a star are over, but this may be the explanation of his lack of effectiveness last night."

When the Rossland Miner heard that Thompson was upset they pointed out that they had not meant anything personal, and in fact they admired Thompson as being, "the fairest, cleanest, player in the Nelson team, and one of the best athletes in the whole Kootenays."

Presumably, Joe Thompson was mollified.

The BOUNDARY
(See also the Kootenays, above)

Phoenix intermediates defeated Greenwood intermediates, 6-5 in Phoenix.

CROW'S NEST

Fernie had defeated Medicine Hat in two games.

Fernie became the champion of the Crow's Nest League.

Cranbrook now formed a hockey club.

TRAIL

It was announced that the Bank of Montreal team would play the Trail Team, but there is no record available.

In March it was announced that the Trail Smelter team had won the Championship of Trail. This team challenged the Banks of Rossland to a game, where "Gold bars, silver-lead and slag will be bet against dollars, dimes, and worthless checques." However, there was no record of this game available.

OKANAGAN

Some Vernon teams actually placed challenges in the local paper. The Commonage Intermediate Team, whose president was James McQuarrie, challenged whoever was the poorest Vernon team. The guests of the Coldstream Hotel, whose Captain was H.G. Muller, and guests of the Victoria Hotel, also posted challenges. The Commonage appears to have been a residence of some kind, and they formed a club, with officers, including James McQuarrie, Albert Campbell, William Johnston, George Dayton, (Captain,) and Horace Dayton.

In Vernon, the Coldstream and Victoria hotels played initially to a three three tie, whereupon they agreed to a five minute overtime, and Coldstream scored the winner.

The Vernon High School beat the Mic-Macs, a city junior squad, 4-0. A rematch resulted in Vernon high school winning 4-3.

The Vernon Commonage Hockey Team played the Enderby intermediates, who won 5-3. Enderby then traveled to Vernon for a rematch and won 9-1.

Commonage		Enderby
Dayton, H.	goal	Johnson, H.
Kennedy, G.	point	Hale, A.E.
Dayton, G.	cover	McCormick, W.H.
Johnson, C.	rover	Woods, W.
Woods, G.	center	Lawes, F.R.
Carey, J.	r. wing	Johnson, A.
Riddle, R.	l wing	Hancock, C.

The Vernon Rink Company declared it would offer a trophy for an intermediate city championship.

Vernon Intermediates beat the Revelstoke intermediates in Vernon, 12-1. The Vernon paper was extremely condescending to the Revelstoke team, suggesting they not bother playing, and that they wasted Vernon's time.

KAMLOOPS

Kamloops did not challenge outside the city and there were contests between the CPR, Kamloops College, and the Town team. Players involved were: Parsons, the Munn brothers, and Angus Nelson.

LADIES HOCKEY

The Rossland Ladies were practicising in full form this year, and they split into two teams, the Whites and the Blues, for some inner-city matches. The first result is not available, but the second game was won by the Whites 2-1 over the Blues. Miss Helen Falding fell and broke her wrist. This was possibly the first time the ladies wore abbreviated skirts, but it's not known exactly what these looked like, although they might have been partial bloomers.

Whites (white sweater)		Blues (blue sweaters)
Milne, Mary	goal	Preston, Ella
Blackman, Miss, E.	point	Aconite, Joanna
Goninan, M.	cover	Falding, Miss Helen
Hamilton, Kit	rover	Honey, Francis
Adams, Dot (capt)	center	Donahue, Flossie (capt)
Demuth, Lily	r. wing	Demuth, Selma
Stanaway, Olive	l wing	Bogart, Eva
Hook, Ruby	spare	Honey, Edna
	spare	Cosgriffe, Ella

The Rossland Ladies Hockey Club then tied the Bank Clerks 2-2.

The Silverton Ladies team then played the Slocan Ladies in Silverton. (One report says it was Silverton which traveled to Slocan, but I favour the other account, since it is much more detailed.) A special steamship was chartered to bring both the Slocan Men's and Ladies team.

The Silverton paper described the game this way: "This was the greatest game ever played with hockey sticks. The audience roared with laughter and the rooters tumbled over each other in their excitement. Three goals were scored, and all of them by the Silverton lassies. It is said that the Slocan girls shut their eyes every time they threw the puck, and when the Silverton girls could not shoot the goals they sat on it. Billy Hicks refereed the game. He hasn't done much of anything since."

The score was 3-0, all of the goals scored by Miss Coburn, for Silverton. There was a dinner and dance afterwards.

Silverton		Slocan
Miss Vetterhaus, Lena	goal	Miss Few
Miss Lawson	point	Miss Webb
Miss Findlay	cover	Miss Cavan
Miss Barclay	rover	Miss Tipping
Miss Coburn	forward	Ball, N. (or Bull)
Miss Horton	forward	Christie, P.
Miss Lawson	forward	Mrs. Hicks

Goals by: Miss Coburn, (3)

The Revelstoke Ladies Hockey Club traveled to Rossland and played the Rossland Ladies at the end of February. It was stated twice in the Rossland Miner that the Revelstoke team had unusually good looks. The costumes were a big hit as well, and apparently the Rossland Ladies' skirts hampered them less than the visitors, but it's not stated why. They played two games. In the first game the Rossland team worked together very well, while the Revelstoke team did not work together at all. This was partly because Rossland had good ice for a much longer time, and was able to practice. Rossland won easily, 6-1.

Rossland Ladies (In dark skirts, white sweaters and white tocques.)		Revelstoke Ladies (In dark skirts, green sweaters and tweed caps.)
Milne, Mary	goal	Dunne, M.N.
Blackman, Miss, E.	point	Pettipiece, E.
Goninan, Minnie	cover	Coleman, M.V.
Hamilton, Kittie	forward	Corley, M.
Honey, Edna	forward	Buck, A.
Demuth, E.	forward	Buck, M.
Honey, F.	forward	Sawyer, B.

In the second game, the Revelstoke ladies had learned a few things, and put up a much better fight. But the Rossland Ladies had substituted their B team, and so were weaker. The score ended 4-4.

Rossland Ladies, 2nd team

Aconite, Johanna	goal
Harris, Kittie	point
Demuth, Reva	cover
Bogart, Evat	rover
Demuth, Lily	centre
Demuth, Selma	l wing
Adams, Dot	r wing

OTHER

The Slocan City men's hockey team traveled to Silverton to play in the same contest listed above in the Ladies section. The rink at Silverton was packed with supporters of both teams who were tremendously noisy. There are two accounts of this game which do not agree in the result. The first, from the Silverton paper was very confused, and didn't give a final score, but from the goals reported, appeared to show the result 5-3 in Silverton's favour. The other report from another paper showed Slocan City winning 9-4. (The first newspaper report is not dated, or attributed, and was taken from "Old Silverton," by John Norris.)

Silverton		Slocan
Thorbun	goal	Tams
Linton	point	Pinchbeck
Bain	cover	Gormley
Bowes	rover	Hicks
McKinnon	forward	McMillan
Mills, Billy	forward	Milne
Blomfield	forward	Terry

Goals by: Mills, (2); Blomfield, (1); Bain, (1); McKinnon, (1); McMillan, (2); Milne, (1).

Soon after, Billy Mills from the Silverton team married Lena Vetterhaus, the goaltender of the Silverton Ladies team..

JUNIORS

Two Nelson junior teams played to a draw. They were the Nelson Champions, captained by W. Riley and the Nelson Amateurs, captained by L. McCandlish.

Rossland and Trail Juniors played a game on January 12th, with Rossland winning, but the score is not known.

Rossland Juniors		Trail Juniors
Darling, F.	goal	Coleman, H.
Hering, W.	point	Moran, J.
Griffith, C.	cover	Isley, C.
Demuth, O.	rover	Callahan
Braden, A.	center	Chapman
Forteath, D.	r. wing	Cunningham
Stanaway, E.	l wing	Malsley

Rossland then traveled to Trail, which was strengthened by a forward named C. Zithen. The score was 0-0 after regulation play, and after a few minutes of sudden death overtime, Trail scored to win 1-0. The Rossland Team was the same, while Zithen replaced Malsley and Moran was replaced by G. Glover.

VANCOUVER

Capt. Logan, manager of the Vancouver Ice and Cold Storage Company offered to erect an artificial ice rink with some assistance from the city, but this did not happen.

Otherwise, there was no hockey this year in Vancouver, due to lack of ice.

Plate 12. Nelson Hockey Team 1904. Back row, left to right, J.H. Fox, Sec-Treasurer, L. Steel, forward, I.G. Robertson, cover point, F. Thompson, [actually Joe F. Thompson], forward, J.F. Musselman, Manager. Middle Row, A. Guay, forward, W.H. Deacon, point, W.A. McDonald, K.C. (sic), President, H. Bishop, goal, and captain, A.A. Perrier, forward. Front row: C. Baker, forward, Roy Sharp, forward. Credit: Nelson Museum

Plate 13. Revelstoke Hockey Team 1904. Top row (l-r): E.M. Allum (executive); A.J. McDonell (vice-president); D.G. Mackenzie (secretary-treas.); Middle row (l-r): W.D. McCann (rover); W.J. Barber (centre, captain); E. Edwards (cover point); H. Bews (right wing); Bottom row (l-r): H. Sawyer (point), R.H. Wood (goal), J.S. Allen (left wing). Credit: B.C. Sports Hall of Fame and Museum.

Plate 14. Vernon Hockey Team, 1904. Back Row, left to right: A.O. Cochrane, Secretary-Treasurer; L. Norris, Vice-President; T.E. Crowell, Manager; S.C. Smith, President; O. J. Vail, second Vice-president. Middle row: A. McQueen, r.wing; R.H. Robertson, point; E. Elworthy, cover-point and Captain; W. Sawyer, goal; O. Q St. Clair Mabee, l.wing Bottom row: E.S. Jackson, centre; E. smith, rover. From author's collection.

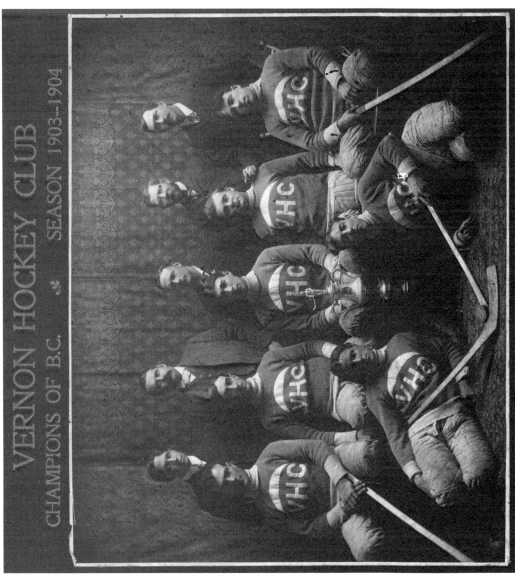

H. Sawyer

W. Sawyer

Plate 15. Silverton Men's Team, 1904. The only positively identified player is William, "Billy" Mills, forward, top row, centre. The other players are probably Linton, point; Bain, cover; Bowes, rover; McKinnon, forward; Blomfield, forward. Photo from author's collection.

Plate 15 (a). Silverton Ladies Team, 1904. The only positively identified player is Lena Wetterhaus, goal, bottom row, far right. She became Mrs. William Mills. The other players are probably Miss Lawson, point; Miss Findlay, cover; Miss Barclay, rover; Miss Coburn forward; Miss Horton, forward; Miss Lawson, forward. Photo from author's collection.

1905 SEASON

Telephone lines were finally extended from Kelowna to Vernon. Telephone service rates were 25 cents for the first five minutes, and ten cents for the next five minutes.

Goal Nets began to be introduced, between the posts, and the goal was now described occasionally as the net, as opposed to the flags, or the posts, which were generally two posts with flags.

Rossland entered serious negotiations with the famous Dawson hockey club to play in Rossland on their tour to the Stanley cup, but Dawson was unable to come.

Dawson did manage to play for the Stanley Cup against Ottawa, and that series is well chronicled in the Trail of The Stanley Cup.

It was reported that the Rossland Hockey Club was having difficulty placing its members in jobs at the local rink, and they called for the resignation of the rink manager as a result, suggesting that his place be taken by Andy Grierson, who had experience in Sandon as an ice maker. It was also announced that the hockey boys were in need of funds, and that the whole town should attend the games, so the team could be remunerated. This was clear evidence of professionalism, but no one seemed to notice or care.

NELSON, ROSSLAND and THE KOOTENAYS

Rossland started their season by playing Grand Forks in Rossland. Grand Forks had not had much time to practice, and it showed, as Rossland won 12-2.

Grand Forks		Rossland
Wilson	goal	McCreary
Grant	point	Donahue, J.
Manly	cover	Jameison
Moe	rover	Wilson
Ross	centre	Hood
McCallum	lw	Grierson, Andy
McMillan	rw	Howarth, W.

Nelson and Rossland played their first challenge match of the season, on January 2nd, in Nelson.

Harry Bishop, Nelson's crack goalie, was away back east. Barney Archibald had returned, and Arthur Perrier, and C D Blackwood were apparently still playing, but none of these three could crack the lineup.

The game was quite rough. But there was exciting play. Nelson was ahead 4-2 at the end of the first half. Then Rossland tied it up in the second half, but Nelson went ahead by two goals again. Robertson of Nelson, "stopped the flying rubber with his hand and facing about, in infinitely less time than it takes to tell it, sent the puck like a rifle ball over the heads of all the players, straight into the net." Howarth, for Rossland, seized the puck at center and cleverly dodged around his opponents to score unassisted. Jamieson scored on a long lift. Rossland had to score two goals in the final couple of minutes to attain a tie- 7-7.

Nelson Seniors		Rossland Seniors
Greyerbeihl	goal	McCreary
Deacon, W.H.	point	Donohue
Robertson, I.G.	cover	Jameson
Thompson, H.V.	rover	Wilson
Baker	center	Hood
Armitage	r.w.	Grierson
Thompson, Joe, F.	l.w.	Howarth

Goals were scored by Howarth, (3); Hood, (2); Wilson, (2); Armitage, (1); Thompson, Joe, (1); Robertson, (2); Baker, (2). (One goal by Rossland was unaccredited to any player.)

An excellent article on how to play the game appeared in the Nelson Daily news. Some of the best points, especially as they relate to modern hockey are as follows: "In fact, all the forwards are now supposed to take part in the defence work by what is called, checking back...with a line that is good at checking back a team should have very few goals scored against them...some forwards depend on the following in [i.e. rebounds] to score than they do on the shooting...the point is usually a big husky fellow [playing closest to the goal], though the custom is dying out [an oblique reference to Barney Archibald and C.D. Blackwood losing their places on the team] ...the rover is generally the fastest skater on the team. He is able to play defence or forward...and will always step into a vacant position when any of the other men are ruled off...the forwards ...must be able to shoot well and do it while skating at full speed. Each forward is expected to check his own man, get away from him when one of his own team has the puck and cover him when the other team has it, to prevent his getting it...theoretically, hockey perfectly played, will result in no scores...The players often try to settle old scores, and the spectators too frequently in the excitement cheer for any piece of rough work. To keep the game clean, one who should be most severely dealt with is the player who is known to be attempting to settle some old score on the ice."

Harry Bishop returned from back East and brought his brother, Archie, "a very fast forward, who may be given a place on Nelson's line." This was to be a major understatement. Archie Bishop was to prove one of the greatest players in the history of B.C. hockey. He was also short, with innocuous features, but he was a whirlwind as a forward. He started right away on the Senior team and never left it until 1912. Although he was not the scoring leader in 1905, he eventually scored more goals than anyone by far in B.C. during these early years, and according to the unofficial statistics compiled by this author, led the province in goals scored five times.

A return challenge match took place between Rossland and Nelson, with Nelson changing its lineup: (Joe Thompson, and Deacon were unavailable.) Rossland jumped out to a 3-goal lead. Robertson of Nelson had to leave the game due to injury. It's not known if the teams then played six a side, or whether only Nelson played with six men. In the second half, Nelson began to assert itself, with Archie Bishop getting his first goal for Nelson. Then Baker scored for Nelson, but Grierson of Rossland scored to end the Game 4-2 for Rossland.

Nelson		Rossland (same as above)
Bishop, Harry	goal	
Robertson, I.G.	point	
Thompson, H.V.	cover	
Bishop, Archie	centre	
Cody, E.	rw	
Armytage	lw	
Baker	rover	

Goals: Hood, (2); Wilson, (1); Grierson, (1); Bishop, Archie, (1); Baker, (1).

A third game took place in Nelson. Joe Thompson and Deacon returned to Nelson. But Rossland had head-hunted A. (or C.) Baker, one of Nelson's stalwarts. It was said that Baker would play in place of Wilson, who apparently resigned. However, Wilson continued to play. It was Howarth who was unable to play in this game, and the loss of their star player showed. Joe Thompson scored the first goal in twenty seconds, and the rout was on. The score stood at 7-0 at half time for Nelson. Harry Bishop only had 3 shots on goal to contend with in that half. In the second half Rossland picked up their pace a bit and managed a couple of goals, but the score ended 10-2, despite renewed vigour by both teams. Rossland also complained of bad ice.

Nelson		Rossland
Bishop, Harry	goal	McCuaig
Deacon, W.H.	point	Donahue
Robertson, I.G.	cover	Jamieson, H.
Bishop, Archie	r. wing	Jameison, A.
Thompson, Joe	l. wing	Baker
Armytage	rover	Wilson
Thompson, H.V.	center	Hood

Goals were scored by: Thompson, Joe, (3), Thompson, H.V. (4), Armytage, (1), Bishop, Archie, (2), Hood (2).

Rossland then moved on to Fernie, where they played to a 4-4 tie, and then played a second game, winning 4-3. The exact teams are not known, but

McQuaig was probably the goalie. It seems that the Rossland team was essentially the same as above, however, as it was the same tour.

A fourth challenge match between Nelson and Rossland took place at the end of January. The lineups were exactly the same as the last game, above, and this game was, "stubbornly contested." Hood, for Rossland was missing, as he had a severe cold. In his place was Conroy. The first half was scoreless, as the Rossland defence had improved. Donahue and Jameison were constantly breaking up Nelson's attacks with long lifts down the ice, but the Nelson defence were expert at getting the puck back up to their forwards. In the second half Wilson and Armytage got into a scuffle, Armytage hitting Wilson in the nose. Both players went off, Wilson for two minutes, and Armytage for ten. Robertson of Nelson was struck in the eye with the puck, and there was an intermission while they waited for him to recover. Finally the fast, and heavy Nelson forward line wore down their opponents in the second half. H.V. Thompson drove the puck into the net from between the legs of a scrum of players. Deacon scored on a long lift, and Joe Thompson slammed in the puck from another scrimmage, leaving Nelson the victors, 3-0.

Goals were scored by: Thompson, H.V. (1), Thompson, Joe, (1), Deacon, (1).

Rossland then traveled to Revelstoke and defeated Revelstoke 11-7. (Exact teams not known).

Rossland then traveled to Vernon and defeated Vernon 5-4.

Vernon		Rossland
Sawyer	goal	McCreary
Robertson	point	Grierson
Taylor	cover	Jameison
McQueen	r. wing	Baker
Jackson	center	Hood
Mabee	l. wing	Howarth
Oliver	rover	Wilson

Goals: Howarth might have scored 3 goals. The others are unaccredited.

Nelson then split up its Senior Team, to play two games at once, one in Vernon and one in Nelson. A round trip took 4 days, and not everyone could get away. This split seemed like a good idea, since the "bench strength" of available players was very strong, but the competition was ultimately too strong for the bench. Vernon defeated this team, 8-2. The Vernon players were generally older and heavier, and the Nelson team had several juniors.

Nelson (B team)		Vernon
Bishop, Harry	goal	(same as above)
Greyerbiel	point	
Sharp	cover	
Bishop, Archie	rover	
Armytage	r. wing	
McIntosh	center	
Cody	l. wing	

In Nelson the second team, (which I call Team A, just to distinguish it from the one which played in Vernon), played Rossland.

Nelson started the scoring when Guay was accredited with a goal, but this was quickly disqualified when it was found that it was a piece of Guay's broken stick that had ended up in the net, while the puck was in the other end of the rink. Nelson then scored for real with a goal by Joe Thompson. Then the game see-sawed, and after the first half it was tied 3-3. Guay, of Nelson had three penalties. In the second half Rossland scored three quick goals, and then hung in, finally winning 8-6. Nelson complained of not having their full team, but this was not justified, since their team was strong as it was, and they were the ones who had split up their own team, causing the city to lose its first game in Nelson in six years.

Nelson (Team A)		Rossland
Nunn, George	goal	McCreary
Deacon	point	Grierson
Robertson	cover	Jameison
Thompson, Joe	right wing	Howarth
Perrier	left wing	Baker
Guay	center	Hood
Thompson, H.V.	rover	Wilson

Goals were scored by: Thompson, Joe, (1), Howarth, (2), Guay, (4), Hood (1), Baker, (1), Wilson (1). (3 goals by Rossland, and one goal for Nelson, were unaccredited.)

The two Nelson teams that both lost to Vernon and Rossland respectively then might have played in Vernon as a warm-up for the Carnival. The result is not known.

After the Rossland Carnival it appears that Nelson and Fernie played a match, which was won 4-2 by Nelson, but no other info is available.

Inner-city play

Industrial League

The Rossland Industrial League, now called the Kootenay Industrial League, expanded to include the Trial Smelter team, and they invited the Northport, Washington team to join. Northport was just across the border, South of Rossland, by a half hour train ride, but they chose not to be part of the league, for reasons unknown.

Much of the Industrial League's results this season are unclear. The War Eagle Mine was supposed to be part of it, but I can find no record of its results. The Trail paper reported that The Centre Star Mine played a game against the Trail Smelter, but the Centre Star Mine was not supposed to be part of the League.

Hunter Brothers

Gill	goal
Hicks, W. G.	point
Ternan, W. G.	cover
Carmichael	rover
Brown, G.	centre
Cross	lw
Hatrup	rw

West Kootenay Power and Light Co.
Not known this year.

Le Roi Mine

Bowers, A.E.	goal
Townsend, A.F.	point
Peters, F.S.	cover
Keating, Al	rover
Dixon, J.A.	centre
Tonkin, S.G.	lw
Scott, O.N.	rw

Bank of Montreal

Winter, (or Winters), C.B.	goal
MCosh	point
Leighton	cover
Lamont	rover
Lee	centre
Dewdney	lw
Phipps, W.H.G.	rw

War Eagle Mine
Not known this year.

Trail Smelter Team

Buchanan, J.	goal
Blaylock, S.G.	point
McNabb, A.J.	cover
Turnbull, J.M.	center
Bingay, T.W.	rover
Sullivan, M.H.	l wing
Grosvenor, F.E.	r wing
Morgan, J.	coach

Centre Star Mine
Not known this year.

It was announced that Hunter Brothers and the War Eagle Mine would play the first game, but there's no record of it available.

Le Roi defeated the West Kootenay Power and Light Company 8-2.

The Trail paper reported that the Trail Smelter Staff defeated the Rossland Bank officials, 3-0. Was this the Bank of Montreal? Blaylock, of Trail scored one goal with a high lift from near his own goal. Grosvenor was injured, and was "...now a qualified authority on astronomy." The Trail coach was "Capt" Morgan.
(The Trail Smelter Staff appears to be the same as the Trail Smelter Team.)

Goals: Blaylock, (1); 2 goals unknown.

Hunter Brothers played the Bank of Montreal. Once again, Ternan's lifts were the scourge of his opponents as he scored twice with this tactic. However, the score was tied 3-3, late in the second half, when Lee of the Bank of Montreal rushed in for a rebound, swatted in the puck and smashed into the goalie, who was injured. A short intermission lasted while Gill made himself ready to play, and when the game resumed it was only a few minutes before time was called and the Bank emerged the winner 4-3.

Goals: Ternan, (2); Dewdney, (2); Leighton, (1); Brown, (1); Lee, (1).

The Le Roi Mine played the Trail smelter, and won 4-3 after being down 3-1.

Goals scored by: Sullivan (1); Keating (1); Turnbull (1); Grosvenor (1); Dixon (2); Scott (1)

The Centre Star Miners of Rossland defeated the Trail Smelter Team 2-1.

Le Roi and Hunter Brothers were supposed to play a final game which would determine the winner of the League, but many of the players came down with the flu, and the game was postponed. Then the wheather turned mild, and soon the season was over, without a final game being played, leaving the championship undecided.

W.H.G. Phipps, of the Bank of Montreal team, was then transferred to Victoria.

The Rossland Upper Town team defeated the Rossland Lower Town team 11-2.

ROSSLAND CARNIVAL

One of the events decided upon was a championship between the best B.C. team, and the best Northwest Territories team. (i.e. Alberta). However, this arrangement did not come to fruition.

Nelson Seniors had their full, top team in this event and it showed, as they first encountered Vernon. About one thousand people were at the rink to watch the game. Vernon was confident, as they were the defending champions, and they had also defeated Nelson at Vernon already this season. However the team they defeated was only half of the top Nelson team, and Vernon was now without their star forward, Ellworthy, who had departed for places unknown. Vernon started out with a fast game, but began to sag as the score went against them. On both sides the players began to give up team work for the tactic of repeated one man rushes.

H.V. Thompson was struck by the puck and there was an intermission of a couple of minutes while he recovered. He was also checked so hard into the "side of the rink," that he needed another intermission. The seasoned Vernon goalie, Sawyer, allowed in 4 goals from long shots, as far away as centre ice.

In the end, the Nelson team was heavier, and also in better shape. They beat Vernon easily, 6-1. Vernon was crushed, and they slunk away from the tournament. This was the most devastating loss to any team in British Columbia, as evidenced by the fact that the Vernon Seniors *never returned*. They never played another game the whole next season, (1906). They never played in the Rossland Carnival again, and they never played any team outside of the Okanagan again, for twenty years, until 1925, when the Vernon Seniors played an Intermediate series against Vancouver and Trail Intermediate teams in Vernon, which they lost.

Vernon Seniors did content themselves with defeating many Okanagan teams, but there was never any satisfactory explanation given for their total reticence to try their mettle again in the mainstream hockey world.

Nelson		Vernon
Bishop, Harry	goal	Sawyer, W.
Deacon, F., (or W.H.)	point	Robertson, R.H.
Robertson, J. (or I.G.)	cover	Taylor, S.S. (or F.G.S.)
Thompson, H.V. (or F.V.)	rover	Oliver, Bert
Bishop, Archie	centre	Jackson, E.A. (or E.S.)
Armytage, A. (or R.)	rw	McQueen, A.
Thompson, Joe	lw	Mabee, O. St. C.
Cody, E. D.	spare	
McIntosh, J. (or G.)	spare/manager	
Musselman, J.F. (?)	manager	Shatford, S.A.

Goals: Thompson, H.V. (1); Thompson, Joe, (2); Armytage, (1); Robertson, J. (or I.G.), (1); Deacon, (1); McQueen, (1)

Fernie then played Rossland. Fernie's combination work was excellent, while the Rossland men, although not lacking in this area, had difficulty shooting. Twice Hood hit the post, with two lifts. Fernie jumped out to a four one lead, and in the second period Rossland tried to come back. Someone hacked Kastner, Fernie's star player, so hard in the leg, that he had to retire to the dressing room, and the surgeon attending him thought the leg was fractured. Kastner returned in ten minutes, however, and continued to play, although someone else whacked him in the leg again later, causing another delay in the game while he recovered. Hood for Rossland ran into the fence and had to be carried off the ice. He later returned. Rossland brought the score up to 4-3, but near the end Fernie scored another goal, and that became the final score: 5-3 for Fernie. This was a major upset, although Fernie was known to be an excellent team.

Fernie		Rossland
Miller, J.	goal	McCreary
Dalmage, F.	point	Donahue
Kastner	cover	Jameison (or Jameson)
Smith, Y.	rover	Wilson
Fraser, J.	center	Hood
Martin, W.	l. wing	Grierson
Steele, L.	r wing	Howarth

Goals: Smith, (2); Martin, (3); Wilson, (1); Fraser, (1): Jameison, (1); Howarth, (1).

Nelson then played Fernie in the final Senior B.C. Championship game. The teams were the same as above. Almost 2,000 people watched the game. The ice was soft and slow. The Fernie contingent had many injuries from the previous game, but at least this game was clean and sportsmanlike. Kastner, however, was cut on the nose and was allowed 3 minutes to recover. Fernie jumped out to a 2-1 lead, but Nelson was solid in every area, and gradually began taking control, despite the fact that F.V. Thompson accidentally scored on his own goal. Fernie just couldn't keep up with the punishing pace, having to slog through the wet, slow ice, and Nelson ended up winning the B.C. Championships once again, 7-4.

Goals: Thompson, F.V. (2); Armytage,(3); Bishop, Archie, (2); Kastner, (1); Dalmage, (1); Fraser, (1); F.V. Thompson scored a goal for Fernie, accidentally.

A. Armytage caught pneaumonia and had to go to the hospital. (He recovered.)

A Junior Championship game was played between Rossland and Trail, the perennial combatants. Rossland dominated, winning 6-3. The winners received solid silver medals.

Rossland		Trail
Bradshaw	goal	Prescott
Harris	point	Isley, C.
Griffith	cover	Isley, M.
Trezonna (or Trezona)	rover	Tyson
Stanaway	center	McFarlane
Ferteath	rw	McLane
Demuth	lw	Callahan

Goals: Stanaway, (2); Trezona, (2); Demuth, (1); McLane, (1); McFarland, (1); Isley, (1); Forteath, (1).

In the Juvenile Championship Rossland defeated Nelson 4-1.

Rossland		Nelson
Keefe	goal	Ellis, E.
Trezona	point	Howell, P.
Fox	cover	Gore, G.
Inches	rover	McDonald, A.
Demuth	center	Riley, W.
Braden	rw	McCandlish, M.
Griffith	l. wing	Davidson, (or Davison)

Goals: Braden, (3); Demuth, (1); Riley, (1).

A Ladies Championship was played between the Rossland Reds and Blues, since none of the other ladies teams had been able to come. The Ladies' ensembles were, "most pleasing." The Reds wore, "pretty red blouses, with sailor collars, trimmed in white, with blue short skirts, beneath which was displayed a considerable expanse of black hose. Each wore dark little shoes, and nickel-plated hockey skates. On their heads they wore togoggan caps, which gave a fetching finish to the costume. The Blues wore blue blouses with sailor collars trimmed with white braid, blue skirts, dark hose, black shoes, shining hockey skates, and white tobbogan caps or lark caps."

The teams played six a side. Once again, the lineups were changed drastically from previous practices. The game was a very spirited one. Frances Honey was sent to the bench once for body checking one of the Miss Demuths to the ice. But there were many altercations, and, "the players in the excitement of the game frequently fell, and this was often the case in the mix-ups, and the gallant referee, Mr. Bonter, had a busy time of it, assisting the fallen ladies to their feet."

Slowly the Reds began to pull away from the Blues, and the score ended 4-0 for the Reds.

Reds (red blouses and blue skirts)   Blues (blue blouses and blue skirts)

Reds		Blues
Hattrup, Edna, Miss	goal	Aconite, Miss
Agnew, Effie	point	Agnew, Miss W.
Milne, Mary	cover	Bogart, Mis
Honey, Frances (capt)	center	Smith, Mary (or May)
Blackman, Ethel	r. wing	Demuth, Reba
Blackman, Hazel	l. wing	Demuth, Lilly

Goals: Honey, Frances, (2); Blackman, Ethel, (1); Blackman, Hazel, (1).

An exhibition game was played between the Rossland Intermediates and the Lardeau Seniors, who appeared to have gained several of the Sandon players, the Crawford brothers. However, the Lardeau team was not quite up to the previous Sandon standard. After exchanging goals, Rossland began to pull away. Inches received a two minute penalty from Eldon Winn for picking up the puck and throwing it from his goal. But Rossland overpowered Lardeau 9-2.

Lardeau		Rossland Intermediates
Schultz, W.G.	goal	Inches
Crawford, Jack	point	Conroy
Crawford, Wm.	cover	Carmichael
Crawford, E.	rover	Keating
Cliffe, Wm.	centre	Funk
Richards, Bert	rw	Baker
Boyd, J.P.	lw	Dixon

Goals: Keating, (3); Crawford (?), (2); Funk, (3); Conroy, (1); Baker, (2);

OKANAGAN

Summerland opened a hockey rink and played a game against Prairie Valley. (Result not known).

Vernon Intermediates formed a team, with McQueen, A. as Captain. They intended games with Kamloops, Revelstoke and Kelowna Seniors. Against Kamloops Intermediates they won 7-0.

The Coldstream Valley team (ranch) challenged the Bankers of Vernon. (Result not known).

Vernon played a game against Kamloops, and won 7-6, but it's not ckear if this was an intermediate match or not. The Kamloops players included Angus Nelson, Lapoiinte, J., the Munn brothers, and Barber, G.

Vernon Seniors lost a challenge match to Rossland, 5-4. (See the Kootenays.)

See Vernon in the Rossland Carnival and the Kootenays above.

TRAIL

The rink was upgraded, including renovations to its foundation and the addition of six arc lights. A new, apparently cantankerous manager, G.F. Weir, made for new, stringent rules, and the hours for practising hockey became difficult. Everyone wanted to skate on the rink as much as possible and hockey was restricted only to late night hours, from 9:30 to 10:30 p.m. on 3 days, and from 7:00 to 8:00 p.m. on three days (Tuesday, Thursday, Saturday.) Sunday was right out: no one could skate on the sabbath. This made practising difficult for any teams. Also, "Any person refusing to leave the ice after hours or in any way annoying the caretaker will be barred from the rink."

According to Trail On Ice, The Arlington Hotel Shin-Peelers played the Meakin Never Sweats. W. Rob from the Shin-Peelers scored 2 goals.

In the Rossland Carnival, the Rossland Juniors defeated the Trail Juniors 6-3.

See also the Industrial League above in the Kootenays, and the Rossland Carnival.

The CROW'S NEST

Grand Forks had hockey going, and amongst those playing steadily were: Moe, C.E.; Grant, F.; Manly, W.J; Birnie, H.; Ross, N.; Lawson, A.; Woodland, H.E.; Haverty, G.; Hay; Baker, W; and McDonald, C.D.

Phoenix lost to Grand Forks in a game after the Rossland Carnival, 2-0.

Grand Forks		Phoenix
Woodland	goal	Hilliard
Rea	point	Thompson
Birnie	cover	Collins
Moe	forward	McMillan
Ross	forward	McKelvy
Baker	forward	McCallum
Hay	forward	Buchanan

Goals scored by: Moe (1); Birnie, (1).

A return match was scheduled, but any result is not available.

(See also the Kootenays, where Grand Forks played Rossland.)

GOLDEN

At the end of December 1904, The Kootenay House defeated the Columbia Hotel 7-0. At the rink it was announced that season ticket holders would be able to see any hockey games free, but that games with outside teams would cost extra. It was also announced that the Hockey Club had exclusive use of the rink on Thursday evenings and on Tuesdays and Saturdays after 10:00 p.m.

In January the Lumber Company and the Town played a game with a large crowd watching, and the Town team won 3-1. No names were given.

It was announced that Rossland would challenge Golden during Rossland's tour of the Kootenays. But there is no record of a game, and the Rossland Miner never mentioned Golden as a possibility.

In February Dr. Taylor, the same man who had helped to start hockey in Golden ten years earlier, dislocated his shoulder in a local hockey game, and had to stay in his own hospital.

Later, the paper bragged about the ability of its players and announced a game against Wilmer, whose team travelled 80 miles to play against Golden. The Golden team won 5-1.

OTHER GAMES

The Lardeau Hockey Club of "Trout Lake" issued some challenges, and apparently played a team from Arrowhead, but no result is available. The Lardeau Manager was J.J. Atherton. Lardeau did play a game against the Rossland Intermediates at the Rossland Carnival. (See above.) Lardeau was actually not very close to Trout Lake, but was rather at the top of Kootenay Lake.

LADIES HOCKEY

Rossland Ladies had two teams, and the Nelson ladies also had a team. The Rossland combined Team was to travel to Nelson in February, but it appears the match was postponed, even though tickets had been sold . (The ice was becoming poor). The Nelson team was composed of: Miss Evans, Kate; Baldwin, Wilhelmina; MacDonald, Greta; Graves, Greta; Gore, Hazel; Nagorssen, Mabel; Blakemore, Barbara.

The Rossland Ladies' two teams were the Reds and the Blues. William Howarth, the great Rossland men's player, was the coach.

Reds (red sweater)		Blues (blue sweaters)
Milne, Mary	goal	Raymer, Mrs. Frank
Blackman, Miss, E.	point	Demuth, Selma, Miss
Agnew, Effie	cover	Blackman, Ethel, Miss
Hattrup, Mrs. E.H.	rover	Cosgriff, Ella
Honey, Frances (capt)	center	Smith, Mary
Demuth, Reba	r. wing	Donahue, Flossie
Demuth, Lilly	l. wing	Blackman, Hazel, Miss

(Eva Bogart tried out but didn't make the team.)

Vernon formed a Ladies Team with Miss Byers as Captain.

Revelstoke had a Ladies Hockey Club. Their secretary was Miss C. Adelaide Buck.

(See also the Rossland Carnival.)

JUNIORS

Rossland Juniors defeated Trail Juniors 7-2.

Trail Juniors		Rossland
Prescott	goal	Bradshaw, Reggie
Isley, Claude	point	Harris, Edgar
Isley, Matt	cover	Griffith, Charles
Chapman, Arthur	right wing	Braden, Alf
Callahan, John	left wing	Forteath, D.
McFarlane, F.	rover	Stanaway, Edgar
Tyson	center	Trezona, J.

Goals: Callahan,(1); Tyson, (1); Forteath, (1); Trezona, (1); Stanaway, (1); Harris; (1), 3 goals for Rossland shared by the previous 4 players.

A junior match between the Nelson Invincibles and the Rossland Invincibles took place in February. The players ranged in age from 10-14. The Rossland team took the lead and held it, winning 5-3.

Nelson		Rossland
Ellis	goal	Keefe
Finerty	point	Trezona
Grant, James, (capt)	cover	Fox
Howell	right wing	Demuth, B.
Gore	left wing	Jones, Stanley
McDonald	rover	Inches, Jack, (Jimmy) (capt.)
Bell	center	Demuth, J.
	Forward	Griffith, George

Goals scored were by: Inches, (2), Griffith, (1), Jones, (1), Gore, (1), Bell (1), Demuth, (1), McDonald (1).

A return match yielded a tie between these teams, 2-2.

Nelson Juniors defeated Trail Juniors 6-2.

VANCOUVER

Finally the ice was good!

A match between the employees of McLennan, McFeely and Co. and the Hudson's Bay Company, at Trout Lake, was announced in February, but was cancelled because all the players couldn't make it. Alex Turnbull, the Lacrosse star, announced he had a New Westminster team ready to play a Vancouver team. Fred Lynch was also a member of that New Westminster team. R.E. Broadhead, a former Ottawa hockey "expert" put together a team called Broadhead's Boarders, and issued challenges which were never fulfilled.

Trout Lake was full of skaters nonetheless and the BC Electric Railway ran cars packed with skaters, on a half-hourly basis, to the lake. Throughout February the BCER would mark bad patches of ice with red markers, have skiffs ready to rescue people who fell through, and constructed lanterns all along the pathways.

Scrub games did take place, but it was hard to get genuine matches going. Challenges and counter challenges were announced, but the organization proved difficult. It was announced that a team from Vancouver would be finally formed, from the following players: K. Campbell, Ted Brown, J. Hawman, Soucie, Nelison, [sic] Fraser, Williams, Haller, Thompson, Clarence, O'Malley, and Anderson. Unfortunately the rains came and ended the game before it could start.

1906 SEASON

On January 2nd Rossland, which was built on the crater of an old volcano, experienced an earthquake, which seemed, from the rumblings, like a series of explosions to the towns around it. Many enquiries came flooding in by telegraph and telephone to help with the wounded. However, there was no major damage, and, fortunately for the hockey players, the arena was still sound.

In late January, the steamer Valencia, of the Pacific Coast Steamship Co. sank off Vancouver Island, losing 145, (almost all), of its passengers. Several Kootenay citizens went down with the ship, which was as ill prepared as the Titanic. The sailing master had never passed through the dangerous strait they were trying to cross, and the weather was bad. When they went aground, they saw other ships leaving the area, apparently abandoning them to their fate. It turned out the life preservers were stuffed with "rushes" instead of cork, or other floatable substances, and they tended to sink. It was one of the worst disasters on the Pacific Coast.

NELSON, ROSSLAND, SANDON and the KOOTENAYS

The first artificial ice rink played in by a British Columbia team was not one of the arenas built in 1911 by the Patrick Brothers in the Pacific Coast League. It was in Spokane, Washington in 1906.

Spokane was a much larger city than Rossland or Nelson, but it shared a constant flow of mining personnel, and other technical workers with the Kootenay towns. It was, in a sense, one of the Kootenay towns itself. There were essentially no restrictions on cross border employment. Many Spokane residents competed in the various Rossland Carnival events and it was natural for them to eventually start up a senior hockey team.

The Star Shingle Company surprised the hockey world by developing an artificial ice rink at their plant on the corner of Canon street and Sinto avenue. On February 6th, 1906, they opened it unnofficially to the public as soon as it provided an ice surface, and they were surprised when three hundred people showed up. The rink had a surface of 200 by 88 feet, which made it larger than Nelson or Rossland's ice surface, and could accommodate a standing crowd of spectators of 700-800. There were separate men's and ladies dressing rooms, and a café which served hot coffee and sandwiches.

The Schaeffer brothers, Jacob and E.M., (or E.W.), were the leading proponents of the company, who managed the rink, and they immediately announced their intention of having serious hockey games there, including matches with the top B.C. teams. As will be seen below, their calls were answered. (See Spokane, after the Rossland Carnival).

Rossland and Nelson played many regularly scheduled games this year in a kind of informal Kootenay league.

In the first game the Rossland Victoria hockey team played Nelson. There were over 400 paid admissions and the crowd, "went crazy with excitement." The first goal was scored by Robertson for Nelson in four seconds, which appears to be a record for B.C., at that time. Nelson went ahead 3-1 in the first period, but Rossland battled back, and the score ended 6-6.

Nelson Team		Rossland Victorias
Bishop, H.	goal	Leighton
McIntosh, J.	point	Robertson (with Fernie in 1905)
Robertson, J.	cover	Donahue
Bishop, Archie	center	Hood
Guay, A.	rover	amieson
Steel, L.	r wing	Crawford
Thompson, Joe	l wing	Howarth

Goals scored by: Robertson (N) (1); Bishop (2); Thompson (1); Jamieson (1); Crawford (2); Howarth (3); Guay (2).

Nelson then traveled to Rossland, but without Harry Bishop, and they put in a newcomer, N. Stewart. Rossland jumped out to a 4-0 lead. Joe Thompson broke his stick trying to jam the puck in the net. Nelson battled in the second half, getting two fast goals, but Rossland pulled away and won 7-3.

Nelson		Rossland
Stewart, N.	goal	Leighton
McIntosh, R.	point	Robertson
Robertson, I.G.	cover	Lafferty
Guay, A.	right wing	Crawford
Thompson, Joe	left wing	Howarth
Steel, L.	rover	Jamieson
Bishop, Archie	center	Hood

Goals scored by: Hood (3); Crawford (2) ; Howarth (1) ; Bishop (2); Robertson (Nelson) (2).

Rossland then tied Nelson 4-4. (Nelson scored the final goal by piling into the goalie when the puck was caught in his jersey.)

Nelson		Rossland
Bishop, H.	goal	Leighton
Mcintosh,	point	Donahue
Guay, A.	cover	Lafferty
Thomson, F.V.	rover	Jameison,
Bishop, A.	center	Hood
Thompson, Joe	left wing	Howarth
Steel, L.	right wing	Crawford

Goals scored by: Crawford (1); Howarth (1); Bishop (2); Jameison (1); Thompson, Joe (2); Hood (1)

Nelson then played Rossland again. The Rossland defencemen Donahue and Lafferty, kept sending the puck into the rafters with their lifts, causing great uncertainty about where it would fall back down. Leighton, the Rossland goalie, was warned several times for kneeling, which was illegal for goalies. But Nelson defeated Rossland 5-2.

Nelson		Rossland
Bishop, H.	goal	Leighton
Stewart,	point	Donahue
Guay, A.	cover	Lafferty
Thomson, Frank, V. (cap)	rover	Jamieson
Bishop, A.	center	Hood (s)
Thompson, Joe	left wing	Howarth
Steel, L.	ight wing	Crawford

Goals by: Bishop (2); Thompson, Joe (2); Steel (1); Hood (2)

Nelson then played Rossland to determine the winner of the Kootenays. Lafferty was knocked out, "struck over the heart," according to the Rossland Miner, while checking Joe Thompson. There was a five minute intermission while they waited for Lafferty to recover, which he did, and then continued to play. However, Dr. Kenning convinced him to retire a few minutes later, and he was replaced by Jameison. Hood was cut on the temple by a skate, and there was a short intermission while the wound was bound up. Crawford for Rossland, scored the first goal, but Archie Bishop scored two to put Nelson ahead at the half. In the second half, Rossland scored two, and Nelson one, leaving the final score 3-3. For some strange reason, neither side pressed for an overtime period, which would have determined the ultimate status of the inter-city challenge series. As it was, there were no more games between these two teams, outside of the Carnival, so that meant there was no winner of the informal Kootenay League.

Nelson		Rossland
Stewart	goal	Leighton
McIntosh,	point	Robinson
Sharp	cover	Donahue
Guay, A.	rover	Lafferty
Bishop, A.	center	Hood
Thompson, Joe	left wing	Howarth
Steel, L.	right wing	Crawford
	Spare	Jameison

Goals were scored by: Crawford (2); Bishop (2); Howarth (1) Steel (1).

Nelson intended to play Fernie, but the result is not known.
Rossland Seniors traveled to Grand Forks and defeated them 6-3.

Rossland Intermediates defeated Trail Intermediates 2-0.

Trail Intermediates

Chapman	goal
Isley	point
McFarlane	cover
Tyson	rover
Callahan	centre
Cunningham	rw
Friez	lw

Goals: Dixon, (1); Keating, (1)

The Rossland Intermediates again defeated the Trail Intermediates, 6-2.

Rossland Intermediates		Trail Intermediates
Inches	goal	Chapman
Braden	point	Isley
Griffith	coverpoint	McFarland
Trezona	rover	Frieze
Keating	centre	Tyson
Dixon	rw	Callahan
Stanaway	lw	Cunningham

Goals by: Keating, (3); Trezona, (2); Stanaway, (1); Frieze, (1); McFarland (1)

<u>Inner city games</u>

Industrial League

The Rossland (or Kootenay) Industrial League expanded its mandate to include teams from Northport Washington, but once again, no team from that city ultimately played any games. The Centre Star Team and War Eagle Team amalgamated because their two mines had formed a merger.

A warm-up exhibition game was first played by the Trail smelter's office staff, against the combined Banks team, the Trail Smelter winning 4-1.

Rossland Bankers		Trail Smelter
Winter	goal	McGregor
Lamont	point	Blaylock
Allen	coverpoint	McNabb
Falding	rover	Grosvenor
Lee	centre	Bingay
Goodeve	rw	Noble
Dewdney	lw	Sullivan

Goals scored by: Allen (1); Sullivan, (3); Blaylock (1)

The first official game of the Industrial league was played soon after by these two teams, and the Trail Smelter Team then defeated the Rossland Bankers 5-0. "Mr. Watson, of the Bank of Toronto, the fourth forward on the Bank's team, was struck early in the evening on the nose, and the continued flow of blood greatly handicapped him in manipulating his hockey stick. His best playing was done after half time." There were about 150 spectators, but so ardently were the general skaters wanting to get on the ice, that they forced the game to last only two periods of 20 minutes each, rather than 30 minutes.

Rossland Bankers		Trail Smelter
Winter	goal	Moore
Lamont	point	Blaylock
Allen	coverpoint	McNabb
Watson	forward	Grosvenor
Lee	"	Bingay
Goodeve	"	Noble
Dewdney	"	Sullivan

The combined Centre-Star/War Eagle Team then played the Le Roi Mine Team, and defeated Le Roi 7-0.

Le Roi		Centre Star/War Eagle
Brown	goal	Walters
Stevens	point	Reed
Jones	cover	Smith
Marshall	rover	Buchanan
Neill	centre	Neill, H.
Acorn	lw	Rodgers
Cooper	rw	Lewis

Goals: Neill, H. (4); Buchanan,(2); Rodgers, (1)

The Rocky Mountain Rangers played the Grocery Clerks and beat them 6-1.

Rockey Mountain Rangers		Grocery Clerks
Griffith	goal	Gill
Kelly	point	Jones
Brown	cover	Driscoll
Inches	rover	Glencross
Goodeve	centre	Stanaway
Linquist	lw	Braden
Forteath	rw	Penrose

Goals not known.

Centre Star played the Trail Smelter in one semi-final game. There was huge betting, especially by the Centre Star supporters, who, "had coin to back up their faith in the team." The cheering for both sides was more raucous than usual as a result. Centre Star went ahead 2-0. Then Trail scored, leaving the score 2-1 at the half. Neither side could muster a goal in the second half, as the Centre Star team played extremely defensively, preferring to win by a slim margin.

Centre Star		Trail Smelter
Ried	goal	Buchanan
Harris	point	Blaylock
McQuade	cover	McNabb
Buchanan	rover	Grosvenor
Neil	centre	Bingay
Lewis	rw	Noble
King	lw	Sullivan

Goals: Buchanan, (1); Neil, (1); Blaylock, (1)

The Rockey Mountain Rangers then played West Kootenay Power and Light in the other semi-final game. They played six a side. The Rangers had a much modified lineup, with Stanaway and Trezona essentially as ringers, playing forward, and a new goalie, Futcher. (There is no record of West Kootenay Power playing any other games to get to this semi-final.) Trezona scored 4 goals, and Stanaway 3 goals, in a 9-2 romp over the Power company, who had protested before the game began that the Rangers had men who had played for other teams prior to this game, which was clearly against the rules. In fact, while Trezona and Futcher had replaced some original men from the Ranger's lineup, it was actually Stanaway, Rinquist and Goodeve, who were the principal part of the protest, as they had played for other teams. Ironically, Trezona, a hired gun for many teams over the years, appears to have been technically acceptable.

Rockey Mountain Rangers		West Kootenay Power and Light Co.
Futcher	goal	Pemberton
Griffith	point	Cameron
Trezona	cover	Patton
Stanaway	centre	Raymer
Ringquist	lw	Graham
Goodeve	rw	Connell

Goals: Trezona, (4); Stanaway, (3); Ringquist, (2); Cameron, (2).

The League committee quickly conferred and decided the next day that the West Kootenay Power company had indeed won the game because the Rangers were clearly in contravention.

Centre Star then played West Kootenay Power and Light for the Championship. The Centre Star Mine had 300 men to choose from, while the Power company had only a small number of electricians, meaning they couldn't be choosy. But the Power company put up a good fight, only losing 3-0. Centre Star was then acclaimed the champions of the Industrial League.

Centre Star		West Kootenay Power and Light
Walters	goal	Young
Harris	point	Patton
McQuade	cover	McKibbon
Buchanan	rover	Cameron
Neil	centre	Raymer
Reid	rw	Pemberton
Lewis	lw	Graham

Goals: McQuade (1); Neill, (1); Lewis, (1).

The Nelson Diamond A-Ashdown Hockey Club (Hardware) played the Bell Trading co. (Grocers).

Diamond A-Ashdown		Bell Trading (Grocers)
Bennett, C.	goal	Nunn, George
Dill, A.J.	point	Manhart, C.
Holmes, J.W.	cover	McDonald
Hipperson, W.J.	rover	Laughlin, M
Blackwell, A.E.	center	Partington, C.T.
Ball, R.	rw	Lavasser
Wilson, G.	lw	McLeod
	spare	Starkey, F.
	spare	Irving, A.
	spare	Scanlan, T.J.
	spare	Joy, R.G.
	spare	Fleming, G.

The Nelson East Ward team defeated the West Ward Team, 6-5

East Ward		West Ward
Greybiehl, F.		Steel, L.
Davison, W.	(positions not known)	McIntosh, R.
Guay, A.		Deacon, W.H.
Thompson, Joe		Stewart, N.C.
Bishop, Archie		Bell, Ole
Sharp, R.		Perrier, A.
Davison, W.	spare	Belrose
Thompson, F.	spare	Smyth, Plum

Club Colours: black and white   red and yellow

THE ROSSLAND - ALBERTA TOUR

The Rossland Victorias left on January 26th for a tour against Alberta teams. The Victorias were without either of their star goalies, Leighton, or McCreary, and Jack Donahue, one of the up and coming juniors, was listed as spare.

The replacement of Leighton in goal, with a new man named MacDonald, was a big gamble.

Rossland Victorias Alberta Challenge Team

Team colours were: red and white sweaters, white pants, and red stockings.

McDonald	goal
Robertson, "Mary"	point
Lafferty	cover
Jamieson	rover
Hood (s)	centre
Howarth	lw
Crawford	rw
Donahue	spare
Thomas, Dan	manager

Rossland first played the Edmonton Thistles. The ice was very soft, quite contrary to what Rossland expected, and they had sharpened their skates to a fine edge, which caused them to sink into the slush. Their biggest advantage had been their fast combination play, and this was also hindered by the puck sticking to the ice, preventing fast passing. But their biggest disadvantage was the goalie, McDonald, who, as the Edmonton Journal said, "is not qualified for the company he is in." Rossland couldn't score a goal, and lost 5-0.

    Goals: Dobson, (2); Deeton, (1); Johnston, (1); Powers, (1).

That evening Rossland then played the Strathcona Team, which was just on the other side of the river. The Headline in the Edmonton Journal ran, "Rossland Colours Trailed in Slush." The first paragraph ran, "The gang from the Kootenay, who came over here on the understanding that they knew something of the general principles of the hockey game, were so badly beaten by the Strathcona bunch last night that the score got lost in the shuffle, and it would have taken an actuary to keep track of the goals as fast as they were made. The Rossland bunch not only did not play, but they did not try, and if the authorities of the sister town, [Strathcona], had followed the law of the land literally they would have raided the house and pulled the door keeper for taking money under false pretenses. The intimation that the four bits was admission to a hockey game made it little better than petty larceny."

MacDonald was playing worse than the previous night, and seemed to let in everything shot his way. He even put one goal in on himself. The Edmonton Journal sarcastically called him the, "child wonder...from the mines." The Rossland team stopped trying, in a very unsportsmanlike way. Howarth was very tired anyway, and couldn't keep up the necessary pace. Hood was just disgusted and "loafed" around, as did most of the team, inneffectually. At the end of the first half the score was 5-1, and in the second half, the floodgates poured open and the Edmonton Journal stopped counting who had scored for Strathcona. The game ended officially at 14-1. (Another account put it at 18-1).

    Goals: Hampton, (2); McArthur, (2); Ritchie, (2): Crawford, or Hood, (1), the rest apportioned between the first three mentioned Strathcona players.

After this second loss, the Rossland Miner reported that, "It has been definitely decided not to bring in a team from Alberta to play the champion hockey team at the conclusion of the championship series. [Rossland Carnival] The medals for the competition would run up to between $425.00 and $450.00. It was felt that the gate receipts would not be equal to meeting this sum, and the idea of bringing the team was, therefore, abandoned."

But the Rossland Team shouldered on, despite the lack of support. They begged their hosts for another goalie, and were given the more experienced C. A. Wilson from Edmonton for their next game, the next day, against Strathcona. This did make a difference, and gave Rossland the confidence to pick up their game. Howarth was still worn out, and his place was taken by Donahue. The game was very rough, with lots of penalties being called. Wilson was a better goalie, but he had his faults, as he broke a skate, and made his way to the sidelines, while, "wildly gesticulating to the referee to delay the game until he got his feet into some new shoes." The referee either did not see him or did not care, as Hampton of Strathcona shot the puck into the empty net. Another goal was scored on Rossland when both Hood and Crawford were playing with broken sticks. Despite all this, however, the score was still only 4-1 at half time for Strathcona. In the second half, Rossland got lucky when the Strathcona goalie reached out and tipped a wide shot into his own goal. Rossland got one more goal, but Strathcona pumped in 5 more, and ended up winning, 9-3.

Goals: Ritchie, (3); Richards, (1); Kent, (2); Crawford, (1); Jameison, (2); Hampton, (3).

That evening Rossland played a second game against the Edmonton Thistles. This time they had been given the star, "stonewall," of the Strathconas, as goalie, Sam Humeson, (or Humeston). The Edmonton Journal reported, "The men from the mines evidently were of the opinion that they simply had to win a game, or all that was left for them was to go back to their homes in the mountains and die a natural death as a hockey team." Howarth was back in for Rossland, and he was back to his old self. But Edmonton went up 2-1 at the end of the first half. At times the game was like, "chain lightning," and in the second half Rossland picked up the pace, and scored 4 goals to Edmonton's 1, winning the game 5-3.

Goals: Johnston, Arnold, (1); Howarth, (1); Powers, (1); Chester, (1); 4 goals unknown.

So Rossland had got their win, (and they made a lot of money from bets on that game), but they still had two games scheduled against Calgary, on their way back home.

In the first game against Calgary, Rossland would not allow McDonald to play in goal despite the fact they would not be given a goalie by the Calgary team. As a result, Hood and Lafferty shared the goaltending chores. The ice was very slushy and soft, which as usual hampered the Rosslander's style. But the Calgary Team tended to outwork the Rosslanders, all the same. At half time Calgary was ahead 2-1, and they kept up their superiority in the second half, winning 6-3.

Goals: McLeod, (1); Lafferty, (1); Bates, (2); Jameison, (2); King, (2); Rouleau, (1)

The next day these two teams played again, and Rossland appeared very tired. Even so, it was only 1-0 at the end of the first half. But in the second half Hood slashed the Calgary Captain, Rylance, and was sent off for the rest of the game, leaving the team to play shorthanded for a long time. Normally this didn't cause a huge problem, as six men was sometimes better than seven, but in this case, being as tired as they were, the Rossland team couldn't keep up the pace, and faded. Calgary poured in 5 more goals and won the game 6-0.

Goals: McLeod, (3); Rylance, (1); Flummerfelt, (1); Rouleau, (1)

Thus the tour ended, and Rossland limped home in time for the Rossland Carnival. The Calgary results were not reported in the Rossland Miner, except to say that they lost twice.

ROSSLAND CARNIVAL

The return train fare, on a special CPR train from Nelson to Rossland, and back, to watch the Hockey Finals, cost $2.50.

Eldon Winn was put in charge of most of the important games, including those between Rossland and Nelson.

In the Senior Championship, Nelson first played the Boundary Team, also called the Greenwood Team. In the first half, "It was hockey of the slap-bang order that the crowd was treated to, and at times it was almost thrilling in its intensity. The players soon had the audience going, giving them glad-hand applause and cheers. Once in a while, in their eagerness to check, a player or two would fall with an audible thud, and then the tension would be relieved by little shrieks from the feminine portion of the audience." (Rossland Miner). Only one goal was scored in the first half, by Archie Bishop of Nelson. But in the second half, the Boundary team seemed to, "go to pieces." Nelson started racking up the score, and the Boundary team seemed powerless to stop them. Finally the game ended, 7-1 for Nelson.

Boundary		Nelson
Wade, M.P. (or W.C.)	goal	Bishop, H.
Dill, E.B. (or E.P.)	point	Deacon, W.H.
Jost, J.M. (or J.S.)	cover	Guay, A.
McKinnon, F.	rover	Thomson, Frank V.
Baker, B.	center	Bishop, A.
McQueen, A.	right wing	Steel, L.
McMillan, W.	left wing	Thompson, Joe
	spare	Stewart, L.

Goals: Bishop, A, (3); Thompson, Frank, (3); Thompson, Joe, (1); McQueen, A. (1)

The Rossland Seniors then played the Fernie Seniors. Before playing, one of the Fernie squad, Edward Sherman, was barred from the game because he had not fulfilled the thirty day residency requirement. But instead of playing their spare man, who is not named, they decided to play with only six men. Rossland had the option of dropping a player from their team to make it fair, but they declined, citing the importance of the game. (It is not explained why the Fernie team made their poor spare man, who had travelled all the way to Rossland, sit on the bench for the entire game. However, this was not unheard of, and happened several times over the course of the period covered by this book. It has never been satisfactorily explained, and must be left for conjecture.)

Kastner of Fernie got a severe smash over the left eye, and the game was suspended for two minutes while the doctor patched it up. Hood was struck on the leg, and the game was delayed for thirty seconds while he recovered. Rossland scored first, however, and began to pull away. It was 4-2 at halftime, and in the second half Rosssland continued to pour it on. Near the end of the game, the Fernie goalkeeper, Miller, fell down, and four of the Fernie players fell on top of him, with two other Rossland players on top of the bunch. No goal was scored on the play, but Rossland overpowered Fernie, winning 9-2. The Nelson Daily news had the score 2-1, but the Rossland Miner's account is clearly more accurate.

Fernie		Rossland
Miller	goal	Leighton
Dalmage	point	Robertson
Kastner	cover	Lafferty
Chalk, "Chic"	rover	Jamieson
Sherman, Edward	center	Hood (s)
White	left wing	Howarth
Armitage	right wing	Crawford

Goals: Hood, (5); Howarth, (1); Chalk, (2); Lafferty, (1); Jameison, (2)

The Senior Championship Game, for the B.C. and Kootenay Championship Cup, was then played by Rossland and Nelson.

Eldon Winn, a member of the Rossland Carnival Committee, and the President of the Rossland Senior Hockey club, was referee.

The reporter for the Rossland Miner complained that two goals for Rossland had not been allowed by the goal judge for Nelson, Charles Longhurst. But Lafferty of Rossland scored the first goal on a high lift from cover point. Bishop then scored for Nelson. The Miner reported that the puck was in the Nelson end three quarters of the game. Lafferty was struck over the head by a stick and an intermission of nine minutes was taken while the doctor sewed up the gash. But after a scrimmage the bandage was struck off of Lafferty's head, and the stitches broke, so they had to wait for another intermission while they were sewn up again. The first half ended tied, 1-1.

In the second half, Hood scored for Rossland, and then Crawford was struck in the head and had to be bandaged. Hood was then struck in the hip by a stick, and it was so bad that a serious discussion arose over whether this warranted substituting Keating for Hood. But Hood decided to stick it out. Eldon Winn seems to have allowed most of these assaults to take place without much in the way of penalties. The Rossland Miner dismissed these assaults, by both sides, as merely, "a too eager desire on the part of the players to win." Guay of Nelson had sprained his ankle so badly that he couldn't return and Bellrose took his place. (A rare substitution!)

F.V. Thompson then scored to tie up the game, and it ended 2-2. There is some disagreement over who wanted to continue and who didn't, but in any case the teams agreed to a sudden death overtime. This then resulted in one of the most grotesque spectacles of cheating on the ice so far, by the Rossland Team, at least according to the Nelson Daily News, and the Spokane Spokesmen Review. With the overtime period becoming prolonged, every time the Rossland goal was in danger a Rossland player would collapse to the ice and stop the game while he was carried off. This sham was allegedly performed by the goalie, Leighton, and by Lafferty and Hood, many times. At one point the Nelson manager, Bunyan, eventually went to the Rossland dressing room, where Eldon Winn was allowing the men to recuperate, and found no one there. When Bunyan complained to Eldon Winn, he was told, with a wink, there was nothing to be done. The Rossland players continued feigning injuries, pretending to go to the dressing room, and then coming back on later, after "recovering" until, after an hour, Eldon Winn declared the game could no longer continue. He declared all bets off, and that the contest would have to be played off at a later date. It was later intimated by a Nelson reporter that the tactic had something to do with a gate receipt dispute with the management of the rink, but this seems unlikely. There were always disputes with the rink management over gate receipts. The Nelson team was furious, but there was little they could do.

Rossland		Nelson
Leighton	goal	Bishop, H.
Robertson	point	Deacon, W.H.
Lafferty	cover	Guay, A.
Jameison	rover	Thomson, Frank, V.
Hood	center	Bishop, A.
Crawford	right wing	Steel, L.
Howarth	left wing	Thompson, Joe
	spare	Bellrose

Goals: Lafferty, (1); Bishop, A. (1); Thompson, F.V. (1); Hood, (1).

The next bizarre chapter in this saga depends on who you believe, the editor of the Rossland Miner, and the Rossland manager, or the editor of the Nelson Daily News, and the Nelson Manager. Rossland claimed that Nelson was being obstructionist in setting up another game, and Nelson claimed the same about Rossland. Finally Rossland set a date for the big game between the two teams in Rossland and advertised it in their paper, as the Great Hockey Match, Nelson Vs. Rossland, for the Championship of British Columbia. The day before the contest, a long article, entitled, "Hockey For Blood," ran in the Rossland Miner, announcing one of the most exciting matchups ever in the history of B.C. The Rossland team practiced for two days beforehand. The management sold tickets to a large crowd, and when the time arrived for the big game, everyone showed up, except the Nelson Team. The referee started the game, a Rossland player shot the puck in the "Nelson" net and the Championship Game was given by Eldon Winn to Rossland. The Carnival Committee made a big show of presenting the cup to the Rossland team, and even impugned the character of the Nelson players as part of the ceremony.

The players, along with their President, Eldon Winn, soon after had their pictures taken with the cup.

There was much ensuing vilification of the Nelson Team. Eldon Winn related at a Carnival committee meeting that Nelson had been given more than the required 3 days notice, (in this case, six days notice), and that meant that Nelson had clearly defaulted. The Nelson manager, Bunyan, related that the major bone of contention had actually been the replacement of Eldon Winn as referee. Nelson had agreed to play, as long as someone else was appointed referee. Bunyan had been promised a definite answer before game day—Wednesday, but when Tuesday midnight arrived, he was still not given an answer, and was forced to cancel the travel plans of the team, sending a wire to that effect, as he, "could not be responsible for inviting hundreds of Nelson people to travel to Rossland to see a hockey game that might not be played."

The Rossland authorities countered in the press that Nelson had no right to dictate who would be the referee. However, this is not the point. Rossland knew that Nelson would not play with Winn as referee, but Rossland refused to say whether Winn would be the referee or not, evidently preferring to see Nelson show up and have to accept a fait accompli. It was a win-Winn situation for Rossland, for either way they got what they wanted—the B.C. Championship—whether they actually had to play for it or not.

However, in defense of the Rossland team, it was evident that several members were not satisfied with this, and a game was tentatively scheduled unofficially in Spokane. In fact, several Rossland players apparently left for Spokane, believing they were going to play Nelson there, but it appears that the game was called off. The Rossland players instead played a Spokane team. (See SPOKANE.)

The Rossland Carnival Committee wrote its own history, and the Rossland team therefore became the official B.C. Champions.

The Intermediate Championships:

Rossland Intermediates played the Phoenix Intermediates. Kelly, of Phoenix was knocked partially out by a fall and took ten minutes to recover. But in the second half he couldn't play at all. Phoenix had not brought a spare, so Rossland graciously dropped one man. Rossland won, 6-0.

Rossland Intermediates		Phoenix Intermediates
Inches	goal	Bluer
McCreary	point	Thompson
Brown	coverpoint	Kelly
Preston	rover	Pierce
Keating	centre	McMillan
Dixon	lw	Clark
Bloomfield	rw	McKelvie

Goals: Dixon,(2); Keating, (3); Preston, (1)

Nelson Intermediates played the Trail Intermediates. The score was 0-0 at the end of the first half. Then the more aggressive Nelson forwards went to work and scored 3 goals. Trail scored one goal near the end, but Nelson won 3-1.

Nelson Intermediates		Trail Intermediates
Greyerbiehl, F.	goal	Buchanan
Stewart	point	Blaylock
Bellrose	coverpoint	McNab
Perrier, (or Ferrier)	rover	Isley
Bell	centre	McFarland
Gigot	rw	Tyson
Clunis, M.	lw	Isley

Goals: Bell, (2); Clunis, (1); McFarland, (1).

Rossland Intermediates then met the Nelson Intermediates for the B.C. Intermediate Championship. The game see-sawed for awhile, then Rossland went up by two goals, and Nelson tried to battle back, scoring one, but time ran out and Rossland won the championship 5-4. Goals: Keating, (3); Brown, (1); Dixon, (1); Clunis, (2); Bellrose, (1); Weir, (1)

A Juvenile game was played between the Rossland Stars and the Nickel Plate teams, with the Rossland Stars winning 2-0 on two goals by Phil Donahue.

Rossland Ladies met the Nelson Ladies for a challenge game. The Rossland Ladies wore red sailor waists, trimmed with white, red skirts trimmed with white and white touques. The Nelson Ladies wore green jerseys trimmed with white, and dark skirts, and no head coverings. Their combination work was excellent. The referee, Eldon Winn, who apparently had helped the ladies up when they fell the year before, declined to do so this time. The Rossland Ladies won 2-0 on goals by Hazel Blackman and Reba Demuth. Mrs. Wragge was touted as the best player for Nelson. All the Rossland ladies received gold lockets from the carnival committee.

Nelson Ladies		Rossland Ladies
Gigot, Rose	goal	Blackman, Eva
MacDonald, Miss Helen	point	Aconite, Johanna
Cummins, Miss Dorothy	cover	Milne, Mary
Wragge, Mrs.	rover	Blackman, Ethel
MacDonald, Greta	centre	Honey, Francis
Blakemore, Miss Teenie	lw	Demuth, Reba
Blakemore, Gladys	rw	Blackman, Hazel
Gigot, Miss D.		
Robertson, Miss		

(Also possibly, for Nelson, Miss Poppie MacDonald, Miss M. Blakemore. And Mrs. W.A. MacDonald)

Goals: Blackman, Hazel, (1); Demuth, Reba, (1).

Rossland Juniors defeated the Nelson Juniors 3-1. This was not indicated as a junior championship game.

Nelson Juniors		Rossland Juniors
Howell, P.	goal	Griffith, G.
Lindsay, I	point	Trezona, B.
Bell, J.	cover	Wilson, J.
MacDonald, N.	rover	Keefe, Ed.
Cummings, C.	center	Inches, Jas.
Gore, G.	right wing	Linquist, A.
Cummings, J.	left wing	Penrose, William

Goals: Linquist, (1); Cummings, (?), (1); Inches, (1); Penrose, (1)

SPOKANE

The call went out for local hockey players to christen the new artificial ice, and on February 7, 1906, the seniors had their first practise at the Star Shingle arena.

The Spokane Amateur Athletic Club had taken the lead in trying to form a team, and they received about ten hopefuls. They were given three hours a week to practise. C.C. Walker was the coach and trainer. The best candidate was Hunter Wurtele, (or Wurtell), who had played with the "Montreal club." [sic]. He was now employed at the Washington Water Power company as an assistant superintendant. Wurtele was clearly in a class above the rest and quickly became the team's Captain. Other players who practiced were: McBurney, Walker, Channer, and Tatro.

Several other possible teams were announced, including the High School, Gonzaga college, and Blair Business College. None of these teams answered the call, however.

Another team, called the Independents, was formed, from former Canadian players living in Spokane. Roy Ferrier, Virgil Pawnell, M.R. Turner, George Schroeder, and Al Harris had all played for Rossland, while the Brandon brothers had played in eastern Canada. The Brandon brothers, however, never actually made the team.

The Independents then changed their name to the Eagles. They scored a major coup in getting Jack McCreary, formally of the Rossland Seniors to play goal for them, and they then challenged the SAAC. On February 27th they played their first game. McCreary was immediately under siege. He turned aside many sharp shots from constant rushes. The star of the game was Wurtele of the SAAC. "The dashing rushes of Captain Wurtele of the club called forth many bursts of applause. Wurtele showed superior speed on the skates and was especially skillful in dodging through the players with the rubber puck under his stick, and he proved exceptionally accurate in locating the goal."

Unfortunately for McCreary this meant one of the worst defeats of his career as he and his team lost 7-0. One of his own defensemen, Ferrier, even scored on him accidentally. The Eagles had played with little teamwork, but they had had little time to practise.

Eagles		SAAC
McCreary, Jack	goal	Rae, (or Rea), J.E.
Turner, M.R.	point	Schaeffer, W.
Ferrier, Roy (Cap	cover	Smith, H.
Kelly, E.	centre	Tatro, O.U.
Trezona, Jim	rover	Walker, C.C.
Pawnell, V.	wing	Wurtele, Hunter (capt)
Munroe, A.	wing	Sanderson, C.B.

Goals by: Wurtele, (3); Walker, (2); Sanderson, (1); one goal scored on the Eagles by their own player, Ferrier.

Immediately after this game, the members of the "B.C. Champion" Rossland team arrived in Spokane for a challenge series of two games against the SAAC. The Rossland players were under contract to the Spokane management and all received an undisclosed amount of "expense" money. Jack McCreary promptly switched back to play goal for Rossland.

Artificial ice tended to be a bit softer than the hard winter ice Rossland was used to, but after their debacle in Alberta, the Rossland players quickly became accustomed to the artificial ice in the first game. There were about 500 spectators. Spokane started out by rushing repeatedly and kept the Rossland team on the defensive. But most of their rushes became individual efforts by Wurtele, Walker or Tatro, and they didn't have enough combination teamwork to break through the tough Rossland defense. "There were frequent outbursts of commiseration when a luckless player tripped and crashed upon the ice or against the walls of the rink, from the feminine spectators....Captain Wurtele had two or three hard falls that dazed him for several moments and he was hardly in condition to play his best game. Had he another forward or two who could work combinations with him, there might have been a different story to tell, for he was the fastest man on the ice, individually."

The Rossland team hit the goal post several times, and Rae, the Spokane goalie was considered a hero by the Spokane reporter, stopping many hard shots. But Rossland controlled the game, passing the puck across the ice in combination, and eventually won 2-0.

Rossland		SAAC
McCreary, Jack	goal	Rae, (or Rea), J.E
Robertson	point	Smith, H.
Lafferty, H.	cover	Schaeffer, W.
Jamieson, H.	rover	Walker, C.C.
Hood, W.R.	f	Tatro, Oliver U.
Trezona, J.	f	Wurtele, Hunter (capt)
Crawford, (?)	centre	Sanderson, C.B.
Howarth, W.	spare	Ferrier, Roy
Donahue, Jack	spare	

Goals by: Hood, (1); Jamieson, (1)

In the second game Hunter Wurtele was unable to play, and Rossland took complete control. The Spokane players never gave up, but Rossland overpowered them easily 10-1. W. Schaeffer scored the lone goal for Spokane on a pretty passing play from Oliver Tatro and Tom Neil. (Neil was from Montreal.)

The teams were basically the same as the first game, except Neil had replaced Wurtele for Spokane.

Goals by: Hood(s), (3); Jamieson, (2); Crawford, (2); Trezona, (1); Robertson, (1); Lafferty, (1); Schaeffer, (1)

Spokane tried to interest other B.C. teams in playing this season in the artificial rink. The Rossland team's manager, A.D. Davis, was hoping that some of these B.C. towns would come down and play them in Spokane, but although there were discussions, no other games took place.

Spokane's season ended, along with the rest of B.C.

TRAIL

The Rossland Intermediates defeated the Trail Intermediates 6-2.

Rossland Intermediates		Trail Intermediates
Inches	goal	Chapman
Braden	point	Isley
Griffith	cover	McFarland
Trezona	rover	Fries
Keating	centre	Tyson
Dixon	rw	Callahan
Stanaway	lw	Cunningham

Goals by: Fries, (1); McFarland (1); others not known.

(See also the Rossland Industrial League, above, and Juniors, below

The BOUNDARY

Greenwood Seniors traveled to Phoenix and defeated their seniors 5-2.

After the Rossland Carnival, Rossland Seniors traveled to Greenwood and defeated Greenwood 7-5.

OTHER GAMES

New Denver defeated Sandon 8-4, and also defeated them in another game, but the score is not known.

OKANAGAN

It was a mild winter in the Okanagan and the papers did not even mention the Winter Carnival.

The Vernon bank employees formed a hockey club, with the Captain being Wright, H.K. They expected to play with Coldstream Valley and Enderby.

The Bankers of Enderby formed a team. A.E. Taylor, manager of the Bank of Montreal at Enderby, broke his collar bone in a practise game.

It was hoped that the Okanagan would have a ladies team this year. Nelson and Rossland both had Ladies Teams, but no results are known.

In Vernon the Single and Married men challenged each other to a game. The Married men included Jackson, Mabee, Hilliard and Cochrane. However, the result is not known.

The Armstrong Hockey Club was formed, with George Wilson as Captain and Manager.

KAMLOOPS

Kamloops did not play much this year. There were no challenge matches with Vernon. The Kamloops Lumber Company formed a team.

GOLDEN

An odd notice was given in the Golden Star: "Fernie is to be in the Crow Hockey League. Now all Fernie needs is a hockey club." Since there was only the most minor mention of hockey players practising in Golden this year, it seems hypocritical to ridicule Fernie's hockey status. It was mentioned that the Rossland Hockey Team had passed through Golden enroute to Edmonton to try and capture the "capital." Rossland apparently disdained to play against the Golden Team, or perhaps the Golden Team was not up to the challenge.

LADIES HOCKEY
See the Rossland Carnival

JUNIORS

The Rossland Stars and the Nickel Plate Flat, both juveniles, played a match in January. The Rossland Stars won 3-0. In February they played another game, which was won by the Stars, 2-0.

Rossland Stars		Nickel Plate Flat
Townsend	goal	Braden, (Putnam 2nd game)
Goodeve	point	McLean, Milton
Luff	cover	O'Brien
Donahue, Phil	rover	Senoith
Keefe, Willie	centre	McCullouch, Luther
Boultbee	lw	Stevens
O'Brien, R.	rw	Mitchell
Rutherford	point in 2nd game	
Johnson	rw in 2nd game	
	rover	Owens (2nd game)
	rw	McLean, A. (2nd game)
	lw	Tees, R. (2nd game)

Goals in first game: Donahue, Phil (1); Keefe, W. (1); Luff, (1)
Goals in second game: Keefe, (1); Donahue, (1).

Trail Juniors defeated the Rossland Junior Invincibles, 1-0, in overtime.

Trail Juniors		Rossland Invincibles
Robinson	goal	Griffith
Brown	point	Trezona
Truswell	coverpoint	Fox
Swartz	rover	Inches
Morgan	centre	Demuth
Morrow	rw	Lindquist
Weir	lw	Owen

(Chapman is reported in goal for Trail by Rossland)

Trail Juniors lost to the Rossland Juniors 2-0.

The Trail Juvenile Team played the Rossland Juveniles, but the result was not reported.

VANCOUVER

No ice! The mild winter killed any chance of a hockey game in either Vancouver or Victoria.

Plate 16. Centre Star, Industrial League Team, Rossland, 1906. (shows Industrial League Trophy) From left to right, J. Murphy, H.A. Harris, J.P. Gamble, A.K. Keating; B.W. McQuade; R.C. Buchanan; R.J. Walters, (goal); At this point one player's name seems to be missing, and it's not certain which it is; W.N. Reid; Togo, mascot. Credit Rossland Museum.

Hunter Wurtele, captain of the first hockey team of the Spokane Amateur Athletic club. Mr. Wurtele is assistant superintendent of light and power of the Washington Water Power company. He is an old Montreal star, and en coming to this city his remarkable ability on the ice and in handling the puck quickly won him the leadership of the club team, which is practically new at the game.

Plate 18. Hunter Wurtele, Spokane's Star. From the Spokane Spokesman-Review, March 4, 1906.

Plate 17. Rossland Ladies Team 1906. From top row, left to right: Mary Milne, Eva Blackman; Ethel Blackman; Frances Honey. Bottom row: Reba Demuth; Hazel Blackman; Johanna Aconite. Credit Rossland Museum.

1907 SEASON

NELSON, ROSSLAND and THE KOOTENAYS

Yet another attempt to set up a hockey league in the Kootenays failed, and challenge matches were once again the result.

William Howarth, the great star of the Rossland team, married Reba Demuth, one of the Ladies on the Rossland team which Howarth coached. They moved to Anaconda Montana, where Howarth worked at the Anaconda Standard, in the printing room. Reba Demuth's father was Fred Demuth, the superintendent of the Kettle Valley Railway. Howarth continued to play for the Rossland team for some of its games in 1907, but this was the last he played for teams in B.C.

Frank Thomson of the Nelson Team was transferred this year to Revelstoke.

NELSON, ROSSLAND and the KOOTENAYS.

Rossland Seniors played the Phoenix Seniors, who were made up almost entirely of professional players who had composed the Rossland team the previous year. Much was made of the contrast between the supposed "amateurs" of the new team, and the professionals, but nothing was mentioned about the ethics of paying players for supposedly amateur games. This was the first time, in fact, it was stated categorically in print, and in a most blasé fashion that professionals existed in B.C. hockey. Most of the controversy over this kind of issue had usually centred on the fact that players were not from the town they were supposed to be playing for, not the fact they were paid. It took several years yet before this issue would become truly controversial. (See the 1911 season).

The Rossland players seemed to have more stamina. Jack Collins of Phoenix was hit between the eyes with the puck and required a surgeon. Thomas Lafferty of Phoenix had a bad fall, and was out for the last 18 minutes. Neill went off to even things up. Rossland finally won 7-4.

Phoenix		Rossland
Wade	goal	McCreary, John (Jack)
Collins, Jack	point	Donahue, John
Lafferty, Thomas	cover	Deacon
Hood, W.R.	centre	Keating
Jamieson, Harry	rover	Howarth, William
Robertson, R.H.	lw	Neill
McQueen	rw	Dixon

Goals: Lafferty, (1); Jamieson, (1); Dixon, (1); Keating (3); Howarth, (2); Robertson, (1); Deacon, (1); McQueen, (1)

Nelson then played Phoenix in a challenge match in Nelson. At the beginning of the game Ferguson broke his leg in a hard check with Hood, and was replaced by Clunis. Otherwise the Nelson team seemed to score at will, winning 14-3.

Phoenix		Nelson
Wade	goal	Bishop, Harry
Robinson	point	Sharpe
Lafferty	cover	Ferguson, w.
McBeth	rw	Steele
McQueen	lw	Thompson, Joe
Hood	center	Bishop, Archie
Jameison	rover	Bishop, Eddie
Frazer	spare	Perrier, A.
	spare	Clunis

Goals: Bishop, A (7); Bishop, E. (2); Thompson, Joe (3); Clunis, (2); Robertson (Phoenix) (1); Lafferty (1); McQueen (1).

Nelson played Rossland in their first challenge match of the season. Archie Bishop scored the first goal in 8 seconds with a "lift" which caught McCreary off guard and rolled into the goal on its edge. In the second half three Nelson forwards rushed the Rossland net and smashed it over, and while a heap of players were on the ice, the goal judge signaled that the puck had crossed the line. The Rossland players were generally heavier, but the faster Nelson players eventually won 8-3 through their combination play. Rossland reported the score as 6-2.

Nelson		Rossland
Bishop, H.	goal	McCreary, John
Sharp, Roy	point	Deacon, W.H.
Steel, L.	cover	Howarth, William
Bishop, E.	rover	Keating, Al
Bishop, A.	centre	Brown, C.C.
Clunis, J.(?)	lw	Neil, Herb
Thompson, Joe	rw	Dixon, James

Goals: Bishop, A. (2); Thompson, Joe (1); Clunis (3); Bishop, E. (1); Neil (1); Keating, Al (1); Dixon (1); Uncredited goal (1)

Nelson played a second, return challenge match in Rossland, with basically the same Rossland team, but Nelson was without two of their stars, Harry Bishop and Roy Sharp, and they were replaced by Greyerbiehl and A. Perrier. The result shows just how important a top goaltender can be to a team, as Nelson lost 8-0, although that doesn't explain their total lack of scoring. In the second half, Archie Bishop was severely hurt, and was off for seven minutes, while the game was delayed. The Nelson papers were so ashamed they did not even mention the result. The Rossland paper considered it a great victory.

    Goals: Dixon (3); Keating, (4); Howarth, (1)

Nelson then traveled to Phoenix for a challenge match. Archie Bishop was again the star of the game, especially when he broke his stick, but managed to use one of the pieces to poke the puck through the opposing goal posts. Harry Bishop was back in goal and Roy Sharp was back at point for Nelson, which won handily 9-3.

Phoenix		Nelson
Kelly,	goal	Bishop, H.
Collings	point	Sharp, Roy
Lafferty	cover	Steel, L.
Hood	rover	Bell, R.
Fraser	centre	Bishop, A.
Robertson	rw	Clunis, M.
McQueen	lw	Thompson, Joe

    Goals: Bishop, A.(5); Fraser (1); Hood, (1); Sharp, Roy, (1); Lafferty (1); Thompson, Joe (1); Clunis, M. (1); Bell, R. (1)

After the Rossland Carnival Spokane traveled to Nelson for a challenge match, and benefit for Ferguson, the Nelson player who broke his leg. Spokane was without their best goaltender, Charles Robertson, as well as their best forward, Wurtele. Nelson won 8-5.

Nelson		Spokane
Bishop, H.	goal	Ferrier, Roy
Jeffs, C.	point	Russell
Steel, L.	cover	McCaugherty, Ernest
Bellerose	rw	Schaefer
Thompson , Joe	lw	Sims (or Simms)
Bishop, A.	center	Niblett
Bell, R.	rover	Trezona, (J ?)

    Goals: Bishop, A. (2); Thompson, Joe, (2); Jeffs, C. (1); Bellerose, (1); Steel, L. (1); Bell, R. (1); Niblett, (2), McCaugherty, (2); Trezona, (1).

The Nelson team was to travel to Spokane on February 24th for a return match, but they did not attend. See SPOKANE below.

Inner-City matches

Nelson

A Nelson inner-city Hardware match was played between the Ashdowns and Wood-Vallance. Wood-Vallance won 7-3.

Ashdowns		Wood-Vallance
Brown	goal	McBride (R?)
Holmes	point	McIntosh
Hipperson, C.	cover	Bell
Ball	center	Sharp
Parry	lw	Middleton
Hipperson, W	rw	Jackson
Blackwell	rover	Riley

Goals: Sharp (3); Jackson (2); Hipperson, W. (2) Bell (1); Ball (1); Riley (1)

The Nelson Ashdowns then met the Retail Grocers, but the result is not known. The Ashdowns had the same men as above. The Grocers were:

Grocers

Teague	goal
Knott	point
Manhart	cover
Bell	forward
Mcalman	forward
McLaughlin	forward
Nagle	forward

The Nelson West Ward (the "Hand-Warmers") played the Nelson East Ward (the "Stick-Arounds") The West Ward won 6-4 primarily because Fotheringham, the East Ward goalie, tried to play forward at the same time.

West Ward (colour white)		East Ward (colour green)
Smythe, Plum	goal	Fotheringham, Billy (?)
Hipperson, W.	point	Manhart
Davison, W.	cover	Bell, F.
McLaughlin	rover	Fife, F.
Hannah, H.	forward	Petersen, R.
Douglas, K.	forward	McCandlish, S.
Perry, Fred	forward	Larson, C.
Harris	spare	

Goals: Perry, F. (3); Hannah, H. (1); McCandlish, S. (1); Bell, F. (1); Harris (1); Unknown (3).

The West Ward "Handwarmers" then played the Nelson Band Team.

Hand Warmers		Band
Smyth, Plum	goal	Fleming
Davison	point	McCandlish
Bell	cover	O'Connor
Riley	rover	McAlman
Hannah	forward	Perrier
Ball	forward	McLaughlan
Perry, Fred	forward	Oliver

The Handwarmers won 5-2, despite the various marches, fugues, etc. played by the other bandsmen during the game.

Goals: Perrier, a. (1); Bell, (1); Riley, (1); Ball (1); Hannah (1); McAlman (1)

Another game between the West Ward and the East Ward (Handwarmers and Stick Arounds) took place with the score ending 3-2 for the Handwarmers. Blackwell replaced Bell for the Handwarmers and Keefe replaced Larsen for the Stick Arounds. The referee, Ed Bishop, sent Perry and Hannah to the penalty box for one minute and 3 minutes respectively, showing that the referee determined how long a player was to be off.

<u>Inner-City Matches</u>

Rossland

In Rossland, the Le Roi Team (mining) played the Bankers, and beat them 10-0.

Bankers		Le Roi (Mine)
Machin	goal	Reid (capt.
Mills	point	Graham
Chubb	cover	Waring
Lee (capt)	centre	Rinquist
Dewdney	lw	Inches
Owens	rw	Penrose
	spare	Allen

Goals: Penrose, (1); Rinquist, (4); Waring, (1); Inches, (3); Allen, (1)

Le Roi then defeated the Rocky Mountain Rangers of Rossland 2-1.

Rocky Mountain Rangers		Le Roi (Mine)
Gill, B.	goal	Reid (capt.
Brown	point	Penrose, B.
McDonald, A.S.	cover	Werring, F.
Stanaway, E.	centre	Inches, B.
Forteath, D.	rover	Allen, P.
Goodeve, H.	rw	McDougall, G.
Braden, A.	lw	Rinquist, A.

Goals: Allen, (1); Forteath,(1); Inches, B.

Le Roi was now on a roll, having defeated the Bankers 10-0, the Centre Star 3-0, and now the Rocky Mountain Rangers 2-1. The Rangers had been winning, (results not known), and they took this loss hard. They were scheduled to play the Bankers, but their players couldn't get away.

In any case, Le Roi became the winner of the Industrial League Cup for 1907.

THE CROW'S NEST

Fernie beat Coleman Alberta, in Fernie, 6-5.

ROSSLAND CARNIVAL

A new event was added this year; the International, or Open Challenge. The Cup was presented by J.S.C. Fraser. It had no hockey players on it, but rather silver roses all along the top. (It resides today in the Rossland Museum, without its base). As well, there was the Senior B.C. Championship, the Intermediate B.C. Championship, the Ladies event, and a challenge match between the best two Industrial League teams from the Trail area. Coleman Alberta was disqualified from the event when they asked the committee to drop the 30 day residency rule, so they could bring in outside players.

Eldon Winn, President of the Rossland Hockey Team, was the chief referee.

Nelson Seniors met Revelstoke for a preliminary game and handily beat Revelstoke 11-4.

Nelson		Revelstoke
Bishop, Harry	goal	Bush, W.
Jeffs, C.	point	Sawyer, J.
Steel, Les	cover	Sissons, C.B.
Bishop, Archi	rover	Barber, W.J. (Allen)
Bell, Ole	centre	Dunn, P.
Thompson, Jo	lw	Allen, J.
Bellrose	rw	Knight, G.
Grosvenor, F.	spare	
Clunis, M.	spare	

Goals: Bishop, A. (5); Allen, J. (1); Thompson, Joe (4); Steel, (1); Barber, Allen, (2); Bell, O. (1); Dunn, P. (1)

Rossland then played Phoenix. Phoenix scored the first goal, but Rossland came roaring back. It was argued that one of Rossland's goals had not crossed the line, and a Phoenix player was angered so much he smashed the goal judge over the head with his stick. Such a transgression would mean instant and indefinite dismissal from any league today, as well as criminal charges and lawsuits. But the player appears to have received no punishment for this infraction from Eldon Winn. In contrast, in 1955, when the great Maurice Richard smashed Hal Laycoe over the head and back several times with three different sticks, and then punched a referee twice in the face, all in the same incident, he was only given a suspension of three days, plus the playoffs, which caused a major riot, so perhaps the idea of punishment for assaulting referees has been a gradual development. Nevertheless Rossland overpowered Phoenix 9-1.

Rossland		Phoenix
McCreary	goal	Kelly, C.
Donohue, J.	point	Robertson, R.H.
Deacon, W.H.	cover	Lafferty, T.
Keating, A,	center	Hood, W.R.
Howarth, W.	rover	Fraser, J.
Dixon, S.	rw	McQueen, A.
Neil, H.	lw	McBeath, H.

Goals: Hood, (1); Howarth, (2); Keating, (2); Dixon (4); Neil (1)

Rossland then played Nelson in the final game for the B.C. Championship. It was a furious game right from the start, but clean. The score was tied at the half. In the second half, Rossland went ahead by one, when Deacon from Rossland, made a cross-ice pass to Neil, who sped up the side, and around five men, closed in on the goal, and scored. The fans were jubilant, throwing their hats and causing pandemonium. But Nelson tied it up, and no one scored until late in the final minute, when Dixon scored for Rossland. The rink then became a "seething mass of yelling humanity in a flash. Players on both teams were caught in a frantic jam and enthusiasts pounded and slapped the victors and their hands were almost shaken off." (Spokane Spokesman-Review Feb. 15, 1907).

There was just one problem: time had not run out. From the accounts it appears there might have been as much as ten seconds left. This certainly would have been enough to mount a charge and get several shots on goal by Nelson. In contrast, the Rossland Miner related that, "as it was close to the end of the last half, it was almost certain that it would be impossible for either side to make another tally before the end of the match." The Nelson players immediately tried to protest but the referee was Eldon Winn, and as Winn was also the President of the Rossland club, and as the Rossland townspeople were already celebrating, he would not listen to the protest. Rossland was ahead 3-2, the game was declared over, and Rossland had thereby won the B.C. Championship once more, with a little help from Eldon Winn.

Goals: Howarth, (1); Bell, (1); Neil (1); Bishop, A. (1); Dixon (1)

Spokane then played Revelstoke for the first game of the Open, or International cup. It was a close game, but Spokane fought like "Trojans," working very aggressively. According to Spokane, the Revelstoke players excelled at roughing and tripping, and the Spokane men had many bruises. One of Spokane's goals was scored when a Revelstoke defenceman fanned on a rolling puck, and watched as it rolled over the foot of the goalie, into the net. Spokane won the game 4-2.

Spokane		Revelstoke
Robertson, Charles E.	goal	Bush, W. (or Buck)
McCarthy, Ernest (actually McCaugherty)	point	Sissons, C.B
Ferrier, Roy	cover	Barber, W.J.
Trezona, Jim	rover	Dunn(e) P.
Niblitt, J.	centre	Hope, T.
Trainer, George	lw	Allen, J.
Schafer, W. (or Schaefer)	rw	Knight, G.

GOALS: Trainer, (3); Dunn, (2); Niblitt, (1)

Rossland then played Spokane. It appears they might have played six a side. Niblitt dropped out for Spokane. One of the Spokane players got caught in the fence and only extricated himself with great difficulty. Except for McGaugherty, the Spokane players could not shoot that well, although McGaugherty tended to score on long shots, as did many of the Rossland men. The first half ended 3-2 for Rossland, but in the second half, Rossland overpowered Spokane, and won 6-3.

Goals: Keating (3); Howarth, (1); McGaugherty, (3); Donahue (1); Dixon, (1)

Nelson Seniors then met the Phoenix Seniors in the next International, or Open Championship game. Nelson pulled ahead 3-0, but Phoenix began to get stronger as the game went on, and Nelson became weaker. However, Nelson held on to win 4-3.

Goals: Bell, (1); Bishop, (2); Thompson (1); Hood(s), (2); Mcqueen (1)

Nelson then met Rossland for the final game for the International Cup. Before the puck was dropped, the fans were silent in anticipation of this great contest. But when the action started, they began to cheer themselves hoarse. Bellrose scored first for Nelson with a long high lift that disappeared into the rafters, and surprised the Rossland goalie, by landing in the net. The Rossland Miner's reporter excused the goalie, McCreary, by saying that it was a shot that the best of goaltenders could have missed. This sounds fantastic to a modern player or fan. But the fact remains that a large proportion of goals were scored by long lifts, over the entire period covered by this book. One has to wonder how the goaltenders could not have countered this better, but one has to remember that the goalies couldn't kneel, and the lighting was sometimes dim. It is also true that some goals have been scored in the modern NHL this way. Also, the original lofting and lifting, which was done mostly backhand, had been slowly developing into a type of forehand wrist shot, whether used to flip the puck high, or to drill it directly at the goal. In both cases it was now being called lifting, and the term wrist shot, was still a long time coming.[20]

Nelson pulled out to a three nothing lead, and then began playing more defensively, playing for time. The Rossland reporter says that the evidence of this was the many offsides that the Nelson team now made. One has to wonder what he meant by that. Since it was very easy to make an offside play, simply by passing the puck forward, it might be that Nelson purposely stalled the game by doing this, since there was no penalty, usually, for delay of game, and considering what Rossland had done the year previous, with their feigned injuries, it seems a small example of "gamesmanship." (Cyclone Taylor himself related that whenever he felt tired, he just flipped the puck out of the rink.)

Rossland started to come back, but it was too little, too late, as Nelson won 4-2, and took the International Cup home.

Goals: Bishop, (2); Bellrose, (1) (the Nelson paper credited Jeffs with this goal); Thompson, (1); Donahue, (1); Deacon,(1)

Rossland Intermediates played the Phoenix intermediates, and beat them 3-0.

---

[20] J. MacDonald Oxley, who played hockey around 1895, described the experience this way: "A lift at the goals is very hard to stop, if sent in low and swift, as I know by personal experience; for once, when tending goal, the point of my opponents charged down the length of the rink, and without slackening speed, "lifted," the puck, and sent it past me like a bullet, while I was making ready to receive it on the ice, not imagining that he could lift successfully while at full speed." My Strange Rescue, and Other Stories of Sport and Adventure in Canada, by Oxley, 1895.

Rossland Intermediates		Phoenix Intermediates
Goninan, Dick	goal	Besner
Harris, E.	point	Percell
Warren, A.	cover	Clark
Allen	rover	Russell
Inches	centre	Fraser, J.
McDonald, A.	lw	Gigot
Brown, C.C.	rw	McMillan

Trail Intermediates then played Rossland, and gave them their toughest fight so far, but Rossland won 3-2. This meant that Rossland won the Intermediate championship. (The Nelson papers indicated that this final game was against them, but I can find no record of it.)

Trail Intermediates	
Chapman, A.	goal
Robb, E.	point
McNabb, A.J.	cover
Stanaway, A.	centre
Ritchie, B.	rover
Sullivan, M.	lw
Buchanan, J.	rw

The Nelson Juveniles beat the Rossland Juveniles, 1-0. T. Cummings scored the only goal.

Rossland beat Nelson for the Junior B.C. Championship, 3-0

Rossland		Nelson
Keefe	goal	Cummings
Griffith	point	Jackson
Stanton	cover	Bell
Inches	centre	McDonald
Demuth	rover	Bergman
Cosgriffe	lw	Miller
Owen	rw	Gore

SPOKANE

Once again Spokane formed two city teams. The Spokane Athletic Association Club started off the season as before, but the Eagles changed their name back to the Independents, although because they were now managed by a fellow named John W. Wood, he had them call themselves Wood's Independents. They were still mostly former British Columbia players.

Jake Schaeffer was now the manager of the rink, and the management quietly suggested that the future of the sport in Spokane depended on large crowds showing up.

In the first match between the SAAC and the Independents, Hunter Wurtele was again the star: "Wurtele's brilliant dashes through the flying field of skaters fairly electrified the crowd, and a wild cheer was sure to arise the moment this young man shook himself loose from the bunch and started on a sprint for the goal. He scored all five of the club's goals on excellently placed shots, but two of the successful tries were not allowed."

It was a fast and exciting game, but the Spokane Amateur Athletic Club prevailed as it had the year previously, this time 3-1.

Wood's Independents		SAAC
Leighton, Jack	goal	Rae, (or Rea), J.E.
Simms	point	Neil
Ross	cover	McGaugherty, (E or T) (called McCarthy)
Trainer	centre	Munroe, A.
Trezona, Jim	rover	Wurtele, Hunter, (capt)
Kelly, E. (capt)	rw	Tatro, O.U.
Nicholls	lw	Eede

Goals by: Wurtele, (1); Trezona, (1)

In the second game between these two teams, it was evident that the Independents, after practicing together more diligently, had finally become the equal of the SAAC. However, as the game became more equal, the players became rougher. The Independents were more schooled in the use of the body check and the trip, and used them often. The SAAC complained that two of their best men were missing, Rae and E. McGaugherty, who they kept calling McCarthy half the time, but the Independents had a change in lineup too, missing their former captain, Kelly, and their top goalie, Art Leighton. Wurtele was his usual electrifying self, but couldn't put the puck in the net this time. Schaeffer had mastered the art of bouncing the puck off the boards to the consternation of his opponents. In the end, the Independents prevailed for the first time, 6-4.

Wood's Independents		SAAC
Robertson, Charles E.	goal	England
Trezona (?)	point	Simms
Ferrier, Roy	cover	Feill (probably Neill)
Trainer, G.	centre	Eede
Trezona, Jim	rover	Wurtele, Hunter, (capt)
Niblett	rw	Tatro, O.U.
Carmichael	lw	Schaefer

Goals: Niblett, (3); Trezona, (2); Eede, (2); Schaefer, (2); Trainor, (1); Tatro, (1)

In the third and final game these two teams fought even more roughly. The complete lineups are unknown, but were probably very similar to the previous game. Four of the Independent's goals were protested by the SAAC, but were allowed to stand. The Independents won the game 6-2. About 150 people watched the game, a disappointing number for the rink management.

The Independents therefore could call themselves the victors of the city challenge series, although there was apparently no formal cup.

Immediately after this game, Roy Ferrier was asked to select a team to travel to the Rossland Carnival, which he did, but Hunter Wurtele, their best player, was unable to attend.

See the ROSSLAND CARNIVAL, above.

After the Rossland Carnival Spokane traveled to Nelson and fought a hard contest, eventually losing 8-5. Wurtele was still unable to play with the team. (See NELSON, above). Spokane then returned home, but they challenged several B.C. teams to come down and play. Nelson and Rossland were anxious to do so, and Nelson even announced that they were on the way, with the support of $300 from the community for the trip. The Spokane business men raised a fund to provide the Spokane team with new uniforms. This was the biggest moment of the Spokane hockey scene, where they would have finally proven the worth of an artificial rink to the hockey world, and reaped its benefits. But it all came to naught from an unexpected source.

The Electrical Workers union announced that the Star Shingle company was on the "unfair list." This meant that several other hockey players from British Columbia, who were union members, would not be allowed to play. But the biggest blow to Spokane was that Ernest McGaugherty, who was a member of the Electrical Workers Union would be punished if he played, and he was considered the best player for Spokane, outside of Hunter Wurtele.

Other local unions took up the "threatening cudgel," in sympathy with the EWU. The rink management couldn't guarantee Nelson's, or any team's expenses, as a result. The whole series of games, which would have brought in a much needed profit for the Star Shingle company, were dropped. The season ended, and so did the arena's existence. The rink itself had never been profitable, and as the labour situation remained unresolved, the Schaeffer brothers sold the entire artificial ice section of their business to an ice making company.

The meteoric rise of top level hockey teams in Spokane would have one last gasp of glory the next year, as a team was assembled, despite the lack of ice, to compete in the B.C. championships, but with the death of the arena, professional level hockey would not rise again in Spokane until Lester Patrick started the Spokane Canaries of the Pacific Coast League in 1917. (They folded the same year.)

The OKANAGAN

W. Sawyer was elected Captain of the Vernon senior team. Politician, (MPP) Price Ellison offered a silver cup to be played for by the Okanagan area teams. A league was suggested with Vernon, Armstrong, Enderby, Revelstoke and Kamloops. However, the League did not take place on an organized basis this year.

The Vernon Town team beat The Vernon Bankers, 6-2.

Vernon Bankers		Vernon Town
May	goal	Sawyer, W.
Smith	point	Hilliard, W.B.
Bennett,	cover	Elliott, P
Mabee,	forward	Mohr
Myers, B	forward	Smith
Lang	forward	Morrison, R.
Myers, R.	rover	Burnette, C.

The Vernon Bank Team defeated the Coldstream Team 5-1.

A return match saw the Vernon Bankers defeating Coldsteam 8-4.

Vernon Seniors beat Armstrong Seniors 6-2.

Armstrong		Vernon
Burnyeat, D.	goal	Sawyer, W.
Breedon, F.W.	point	Hilliard, W.B.
Reid, J.	cover	Elliott, P.
Daykin, J.	rover	Burnette, C.
Stewart, J.	center	Morrison, R.
Stewart, C	lw	Mabee, O St. C.
Graham, D.	rw	Lang, J.

The Vernon Senior team played the Enderby Senior Team in Enderby, defeating them 6-3. The Vernon Lineup was the same as above, except Mohr, W. replaced Morrison.

TRAIL

(The games listed below were not reported as Industrial League games, so it's unclear if they were single challenges or not.)

The Trail Smelter Team tied the Rossland Rocky Mountain Rangers, who were a militia unit, 1-1.

Rossland Rocky M. R.		Trail Smelter
Gill, H.B.	goal	Chapman, A.
Brown, C.C. (or T.D.)	point	Robb, W.
Griffith, Charles	cover	McNabb, A.J.
McDonald, A. S.	rover	Bingay, T.W.
Stanaway, Edgar	centre	Richie, A.B.
Braden, E. (or A.)	rw	Buchanan, J.
Goodeve, H.	lw	Sullivan, M.
	spare	Babington, A.R.

Goals by: Mcdonald, A. (1); Sullivan, M. (1).

Trail Smelter played the Rossland Centre Star Mine, At half time the score was 0-0, and the referree, Donahue, had not kept the players in check, resulting in a "donnybrook" of rough play. In the second half, McQuade scored on a lift from his own end. Then Bruce Ritchie evened the score, and the game ended in a tie, 1-1. Five minute periods were then played to break the tie, and the Centre Star scored a controversial goal in the second five minute period, winning the game 2-1. At the final whistle, the Trail player, Buchanan, was knocked out, and the Trail goaltender and defencemen skated out of the goal, "when the Rossland forwards finding it not convenient to hear the referee's whistle, passed the puck through the undefended Trail goal. An argument ensued, but the goal was allowed."

Rossland had cheated again.

A further note was illustrative of the contest: "A number of the Trail boys look as if they have been through a Custer massacre."

Rossland Centre Star		Trail Smelter
Goninan, D.	goal	Chapman, A.
McQuade, E.M.	point	Robb, W.
Byram, H.	coverpoint	McNabb, A.J.
Harris, E.	rover	Bingay, T.W.
Herr, E..	centre	Ricthie, A.B.(Bruce)
Griffith, F.E.	rw	Buchanan, J.
McDougall, C.	lw	Sullivan, M.H.
	spare	Babington, A.R.

Goals by: McQuade, E.M. (1); Ritchie, Bruce (1). Last goal unknown.

Ed Stanaway, the best player on the Rossland Rockey Mountain Rangers, was head-hunted by the Trail smelter team, given a position at the smelter, and added to the Trail Team from February onward.

The Arlington Hotel, "Shin-Peelers," defeated the Meakin hotel, "Never-Sweats," 3-2.

Arlington		Meakin
Williamson, Jim.	goal	Moore, "Maggie"
Rob, W.	point	Cunningham, Jimmy
Robb, Herb.	coverpoint	McPherson, W. (Happy)
Simm	rover	Young, Jack
Williamson, Cliff.	centre	Driscoll
Tyson, C.	lw	Cunningham, P.
Chambers	rw	Morgan, R.

Two of the players from Trail, Happy McPherson, and Jack Young, then announced that they had received "flattering" offers to play with the Kenora Thistles. This offer seems to be apocryphal, since the Kenora Thistles were one of the top teams in the country and were after only the very best, which these two players were not. Kenora went on to win the Stanley Cup that year, without McPherson and Young, who inexplicably turned them down.

Not to be outdone, two other Trail players, Maggie Moore and Jim Williamson, announced that they would not go East to play in the Stanley Cup matches.

KASLO

No hockey reported.

KAMLOOPS

Kamloops challenged no outside teams this year.

GOLDEN

No local games were reported this year. Harry G. Parson, one of the founding father's of hockey in the area was elected the conservative member of the British Columbia Legislature for the Columbia region.

JUNIORS

The Nelson Juniors played the Trail Juniors in Nelson. The score is not known.

Nelson		Trail
Cummins	goal	Melligan
Jackson	point	Truswell
Bell	cover	Brown
Bergman	forward	Swartz
McDonald	forward	Morrow
Gore	forward	Morgan
Miller	forward	Driscoll

The Trail Junior Hockey team defeated the Nelson Juniors 4-2.

Trail Juniors		Nelson Juniors
MilliganWinter	goal	Cummins
BrownLamont	point	Jackson
Russel, R.	coverpoint	Miller, F.
Swartz	rover	Bell
Cunnigham, P.	centre	Yelmer
Driscoll	lw	Gore
Morgan, R.	rw	Miller, J.

The Trail Juniors then left for Nelson to play the Juniors there. The result is not available.

The Enderby Juniors defeated the Armstrong Juniors in Enderby 5-1.

Armstrong Juniors defeated Vernon Juniors 4-3.

The Vernon Juniors beat the Armstrong Juniors in a return match, 5-0.

Armstrong Juniors		Vernon Juniors
Francis, A.	goal	Baker, R.
Barnes, .F.	point	Reinhard, F.
Fisher, S.	cover	McClusky, F.
Christian, L.	rover	Reinhard, F.
Murray, F.	rw	Maxwell, G.
Maundrell, .F.	lw	French, S.
Symmington, F.	center	Polson, W.

LADIES

The Rossland Ladies Hockey Club was practicing this year, in anticipation of the Rossland Carnival. It was announced at one point that the

Rossland Ladies would play the Phoenix Ladies at the Carnival, but no record of this game is available.

Rossland Ladies

Blackman, Eva	goal
Harding, Mrs. Fred	point
Goninan, Minnie, Miss	cover
Fox, Ethel	rover
Blackman, Hazel	centre
Demuth, Lily, Miss	rw
Lee, Sarah	lw

The Vernon Ladies played the Armstrong Ladies in Armstrong. Armstrong won, 2-1. It was a hard fought match, with the puck in the Armstrong end the majority of the time, but the Vernon Ladies couldn't shoot very well.

Vernon Ladies		Armstrong Ladies
Miss Smith, K	goal	Miss Hill, L.
Mrs. Kenny,	point	Miss Francis
Miss Elizabeth Ellison	cover	Miss Hamill
Miss Polson, O.	rover	Miss Murray
Mrs Welton, J.R.	lw	Miss Batho
Mrs. McIntyre	rw	Miss Daykin
Miss Smith, A.	center	Miss Periard
Miss McAllister	spare	

Goals: Murray (1); Periard (1) (Protested); Welton (1)

A return match in Vernon resulted in Armstrong winning again, 2-1. The Vernon Ladies were faster, but the Armstrong women were heavier, and, according to the Vernon News, therefore had the advantage most of the game. The crowd numbered about 500 and the gate receipts were $114.85. The teams were similar to those above, except for Vernon Miss Joyce Morkill replaced Miss Kenny, and for Armstrong, Miss Harding replaced Miss Francis.

The Vernon Ladies played the Vernon Junior Ladies, with a 6 person team, and beat the Juniors 6-4.

Vernon Seniors:		Vernon Juniors
Miss Smith, A.	goal	Miss Smith, K.
Miss Bell, Dora	point	Miss Gibbs, Ethel
Miss Polson, O.	cover	Miss Ellison, E.
Miss McAllister	center	Miss Morkill, Joyce
Miss Welton, J.R.	rw	Miss Kennedy, Jessie
Mrs. McIntyre, A.	lw	Miss Jacques, Hazel

VANCOUVER

Finally there was ice!

The populace thronged to any surface that would carry them on skates. At Trout Lake the B.C. Electric Railway ran cars continuously, from Main Street, every fifteen minutes, during the cold snap and there were 2000 people on or around the lake during peak times. The Lake was technically owned by a man named Mr. W.M. Reeves, and the city had to rent it from him, in order to have people skate on it.

A long anticipated match between a Vancouver Team, and a New Westminster team for the lower mainland championship was negotiated, but as usual, the teams dithered while the cold snap progressed. New West wanted more time to prepare a team, but there was no telling how long the ice would last. Meanwhile a Vancouver team calling itself the new Ramblers, announced a challenge to anyone who would take it up, but there is no record of any game. Answers to the challenge were to contact Mr. O. Hemphill, 727 Hornby st. in Vancouver.

However, the Fraser River froze over solidly, a rare event, which meant that the ice was staying for at least a week. The New West Team announced that a game would be played, in fact, on the North Arm of the Fraser, forty-five years after the first shinny games there!

Finally a Vancouver Team took the train to New Westminster and played on the river close by. Vancouver wore white and New West wore Crimson.

Vancouver (The Terminals)		New Westminster (Royals) (positions not known)
McQueen	goal	Gifford, T. (probably goal)
Pindle,	point	Turnbull, Alex
Beyley	cover	Turner, Alf
Wheeler,	rover	Ryall, H.
Herman, Charlie	rw	Cheyne, R.H.
Tait, W.	lw	Malcomson, Sid
Sangster	center	Lynch, Fred
Neilson, Oscar,	spare (and manager)	
Pringle	tried out	
Bailey (same as Beyley?)	tried out	
Schwartz	tried out	

This was the first time in known history that an organized hockey match was played on the Fraser River. Nearly a thousand spectators saw the teams play to a three three draw. Vancouver scored a 4th goal just as time ran out, but it was disallowed, by the referee, A.P. Garvey of Vancouver. However, it appears that the goal was in fact in time, based on the testimony of the time keeper, who had a stop watch, and was on his way to the referee to show him the time, during the game, when Vancouver scored, and there was still 3 seconds on the watch when he reached the Referee. The New West spectators complained, apparently for the sport of it, and the Ref wanted to be fair, so he cancelled the goal, but ordered two minutes of overtime, which did not result in a score.

It looked like the ice would then melt, but it rallied, making a return match the next week possible at Trout Lake, for the inter-city championship.

New Westminster was missing a few players, so they were replaced by some Vancouver players, including Charlie Egan who played goal. Alex Turnbull, the great Lacrosse veteran of New Westminster was injured when a collision caused his own stick to slash across his face and cut his forehead over his left eye. Tait of Vancouver was also injured. But the loss of Turnbull opened the floodgates for Vancouver, and they scored five goals, with New West not scoring any. A sixth goal for Vancouver was scored, but was called offside.

Vancouver		New Westminster
McQueen	goal	Egan, Charlie
Neilson, O.	point	Chene, L.
Herman, Charlie (Captain)	cover	Carley
Pringle,	rover	McLean
Tait, W.	centre	Turnbull, Alex
Sangster	rw	Sutherland
Laidlaw	lw	Galbraith

Vancouver then declared itself Champions of the Pacific Coast. They were promptly challenged by the Bankers team, and another game took place on Trout Lake. Vancouver was also called Herman's Champions.

Vancouver		Vancouver Bankers
McQueen	goal	Townley
Neilson, Oscar	point	Smithe
Herman, Charlie	cover	Frazer, E.W.
Pringle,	rover	Orr, J.
Smith	center	Campbell, W.J.
Sangster	rw	Rhodes
Laidlaw	lw	Mitchell
	spare	Swartz

Oscar Neilson collided violently with an opposing player and was cut over an eye. This bled profusely and he had to go back into Vancouver for medical attention. The Bankers could generally pass well, but they couldn't skate as well as the regular Vancouver players, and as a result the score ended 7-0 for Herman's Champions. The score was erroneously announced as 8-1 by the morning papers, but the goal judges cleared this up. The Bankers did score one goal but it had been disallowed as offside.

After this there was a general thaw and no other challenge matches were reported, leaving Herman's players as Champions.

Plate 19. Nelson Senior Men's Hockey Team, 1907. (Showing the International or Open cup, and the previous B.C. Championship Cup, which they did not win this year.) Top row, left to right: H. Bishop, goal; L. Steel, cover; J. Thompson, l wing; R. Bell, r. wing; C. Jeffs, point; R. Sharp, spare. Middle row: A. Perrier, Secretary; M.R. McQuarrie, Manager; A Bishop, centre. Bottom row: W. Davidson, spare; M. Clunis, spare; J. Bellrose, rover; F. Bishop, spare. (This is actually E. Bishop.) Credit Rossland Museum.

Plate 20. Rossland Senior Men's Hockey Team, 1907. Back Row, standing, left to right: Burken, Manager; Neil, wing; Winn, President; Howarth, rover; MacKenzie, secretary, (A.B. ?); Keating, centre. Bottom row, sitting: Dixon, wing; Donahue, point; Deacon, cover; McCreary, goal.
Credit Rossland Museum.

Plate 21. Le Roi Industrial League Team, Rossland, 1907. (Showing the Industrial Hockey league trophy). J. M. Donahue, trainer; K.C. Allen; P.S. Peters, Manager; A.L. Acorn; W.F. Townsend; J.A. Waring; W.H. Read; R. Inches; W. Penrose; A. Rinquist. Credit Rossland Museum.

Plate 22. Spokane Senior Hockey Team, 1907. Back row, left to right: George Schroeder, Trainer; Schaeffer, rw; Niblett, lw; Trezona, rover; Simms, spare; F.A. Tamblyn, Manager. Seated: Roy Ferrier, cover point; Robertson, goal; E. McCaugherty, point. Not shown: Trainor, centre. this is the only known image at this time. From the Spokane Spokesman-Review, Mar. 3 1907.

Plate 23. Vancouver Team, Herman's Champions, 1907. (Shows the cup they had made for the Championship of the lower mainland, which they considered the Pacific Northwest.) Top row (l-r): W. Laidlaw (right wing); J. Sangster (cover point); Middle row (l-r): F. Tait (centre), T. Wheeler (rover), W. Bailey (manager); Bottom row (l-r): C. McQueen (goal); C. Herman (left wing, captain); O. Neilsen (point). Credit B.C. Sports Hall of Fame and Museum.

1908 SEASON

NELSON, ROSSLAND, and the KOOTENAYS

A momentous event took place in the spring and fall of 1907; the Patrick Family moved from Montreal to Nelson. Father Joe Patrick had already moved part of his lumber business to the area in 1906, and in the next few years his two eldest sons, Frank and Lester, were enlisted, at various times, to act as camp bosses and administrators. Both Frank, 23, and Lester, 25, had been major hockey stars with Eastern Teams, as indicated in their biography written by Eric Whitehead in 1980. Lester had assumed now that his hockey career was effectively over, but he could not have been more wrong. Frank was still playing with the Ottawa Vics, in his last year of college. He even refereed a Stanley Cup match in 1908.

Lester's inclusion into the Nelson hockey scene in 1908 was not as meteoric however, as Whitehead has implied. First, Lester began playing in a few local scrimmages, and as the players began practising for the season, Lester Patrick became part of a team of newcomers who challenged the regular members of the team. In this, Lester was very shrewd, as he was bound to shine on the 2nd string team, and he could probably control the proceedings better, as he was wont to do. It's not certain whether the full import of Lester's past was known to the majority of players. Certainly, there was no announcement in the paper that a major star was in town, as it normally would be for any other sport or activity. However, there was a lot of anticipation and betting on this challenge match. The older team was called the "Fossils," and the newcomers were called the "Tenderfeet."

Lester had already played directly for the Stanley Cup 5 times. After playing for the Westmount Club in Montreal, he travelled to Brandon Manitoba, becoming a member of that team when they challenged Ottawa for the cup. He lost that time, but then the next year he was back in Montreal, on the Wanderers, and played a challenge series again against Ottawa, losing again. Finally, the Wanderers, with Lester, wrested the cup from Ottawa the next year, 1906. That series was one of the most amazing in history, as the Wanderer's won the first game of the total goals 2-game series, 11-2, in Montreal. There seemed no possibility they could lose, but in the next game, in Ottawa, the Silver Seven scored nine unanswered goals and tied up the series. Although Lester had played defense all through the game, he then skated through the entire Ottawa team twice, in the last two minutes of the game, and scored two goals, giving the Wanderers the slim margin of victory they needed.

Later the Wanderers, with Lester, lost the Cup in a challenge by Kenora Thistles, but then won the Cup back again later in the same season.

The very first newspaper notice of Lester Patrick's hockey career in Western Canada, excluding Manitoba, was not auspicious, however, and read as follows: "Patrick lost the puck to Bishop and presently the latter scored on a neat pass from Bellrose." The score was not favorable to Lester either as the oldtimers won 10-4. It's not known if Patrick scored any goals.

Fossils		Tenderfeet
Bishop, H.	goal	Harding, H.
Deacon, W.H.	point	Wilson, W.
Steel, Les	cover	Patrick, L.
Bell, R.	rover	Jamieson, H.
Thompson, Joe	rw	Kent, B.
Belrose, J.	lw	Newton, C.R.B.
Bishop, A.	center	Hood

Goals by: Bishop, Archie, (1); the rest unknown.

Nevertheless, Lester was seen for what he was: the best hockey player at his position in Nelson, and he won a spot on the senior team just in time for the first regular game of the season, in Nelson, which was against Rossland. Kemp, also from the East, was in the lineup, and Nelson was quick to point out that these were not ringers, but genuine Nelsonians, i.e they lived in Nelson. Joe Thompson was moved to defence, as he seemed to work well with Lester.

This 1908 team, although it changed a few of its personnel here and there, was something of a strange sight. Most of the players were small, even undersized for the low average height of the times, while they had only two tall men, Joe Thompson, and Lester Patrick, who was about six foot one, towering over everyone else.

It was in this game that Lester Patrick introduced his distinctive, "Loop the loop," style to a large audience in British Columbia. He tended to employ this as he made rushes up the ice, but he was unable to score in this game, generally because he was tripped and smashed into the ice by the Rossland players. In fact, at one time he was tripped and then jumped on, bruising his ribs; and in another altercation was bashed over the head with a stick. The players were sometimes warned for this, and not given penalties, although several penalties were dished out, including one to Lester. The referee, Deacon, who was from Nelson, announced in the second half that the first player who was caught using rough tactics would go off for ten minutes, and this type of play then subsided somewhat, while Nelson succeeded in winning 7-3.

Lester Patrick's reputation had not quite made it to Rossland. The Rossland papers referred to him usually as Patrick, not Lester Patrick, and did not mention his illustrious past.

Nelson		Rossland
Bishop, H.	goal	McCreary
Patrick, L.	point	McCaugherty
Thompson, Joe	cover	Donahue
Kemp	lw	Dickson, (or Dixon)
Bishop, A	center	Keating
Bellrose	rover	Riliance (or Rillance)
Steel	rw	Neal
	spare	McCarthy (?)

Goals: Steele (1); Keating (1); Bishop, A. (2); Bellrose (1); Neal (1); Kemp (2); Thompson, Joe (1); Dickson (1)

The "Loop the Loop" style became all the rage of the Nelson players from junior to senior as many attempted to emulate Lester. Horswill, another player from the East, Kenora Ontario, often attempted this style. It's not clear exactly what this was, however. One correspondent, while assessing his commercial league opponents said they did not have the weight or length, or vocal abilities necessary in loop the loop hockey.

Lester was very fond of another action, the "Loft," which relieved pressure on his own goal, by flipping the puck backhanded far into the air and down to the other side. In fact many goals were scored this way because the goalie often lost sight of the puck. Modern rules would normally penalize this action, unless the puck was shot on net, because of icing. However this tactic, which was a staple of Eastern hockey at least as far back as 1895, was already being employed, and was not new.

After this game a photo was taken of the Nelson team by the Ping Pong Photo Gallery, in the Alan Block, and prints were made available to the public the next day.

Nelson then head-hunted Robertson Hood from the Rossland team. This gave them an extremely strong offense, and with Lester Patrick and Joe Thompson often scoring from defense it was a formidable combination. However, some time before the Rossland Carnival, Hood appears to have left Nelson and was playing for Armstrong, in the Okanagan. It's doubtful he was actually headhunted there because Armstrong was not an important team, and would have had only a few games. Hood probably had gone where he could get the best employment.

A return match at Rossland had the following lineup:

Nelson		Rossland
Bishop, Harry	goal	McCreary, Jack
Patrick, L.	point	Allen
Thompson, Joe	cover	Donahue
Bishop, Archie	rover	Rillance
Hood,	center	Keating, C.
Dunn,	rw	Neal
Kent,	lw	Dickson
Bellrose,	spare	
Bell, R.	spare	
Steel, L.	spare	

Approximately 1000 people saw this game, which was a lot for the Kootenays. Rossland scored the only goal in the first half, by Rillance, apparently when Harry Bishop was not looking. According to the Rossland paper, "Patrick," the Captain of the Nelson team, had evidently been lecturing his team during the break, in the dressing room. When they came back on the ice, the correspondent continued, "In order to encourage the boys of his team, he took the puck from near the Nelson goal and brilliantly zigzagged his way through the Rossland's forwards and through their defense, and scored himself. It was a beautiful piece of work, the best perhaps of the evening. Patrick is very fast, most elusive, and is very cool and uses his head to advantage, as well as his feet. During the remainder of the game he was not allowed to repeat the performance, and he was checked with so much vigor, and particularly by Neil, that he experienced 3 or 4 falls." i.e., he was tripped or hooked, very often after that, but there does not seem to be too much of a penalty to the Rossland players for that. They were playing in Rossland, but the referee was Father McCullough, not Eldon Winn. He did give out some five minute penalties for roughness. The minor penalties were two for Rossland and two for Nelson. However, Lester Patrick had finally scored his first goal in league play, and with his famous loop the loop rushing, which had, apparently, a zig-zag component.

Nelson began to pull away now, with Hood scoring two goals, and then Bishop on a nice combination play. However, Rillance and Dixon both scored for Rossland. The game was rough all around. Dunn, from Nelson got a stick in the mouth and the game was delayed for several minutes while he recovered. Archie Bishop and Neil had a fight, which gave them both five minutes for fighting. The game ended 4-3, for Nelson. The Rossland Miner's reporter does not seem too concerned about the roughness, but the Nelson paper was not particularly happy with it.

Goals: Patrick, L. (1); Rillance, (2); Hood (2), Bishop (1); Dixon, (1).

Nelson and Rossland Intermediates challenged each other to a game, and the Nelson Team was chosen from the following players: Bell, R; Gore, G.; Bishop, E.; Moodie, J.; Greyerbiehl, F.; Manhart, H.; Fife, F.; Bell, J.; and Millar, E.

The Nelson Intermediates then played two challenge matches against Rossland, defeating and tieing Rossland in a two game series. (Goals not available)

Then Nelson Intermediates played Kaslo, winning 5-3.

Nelson Int.		Kaslo Int.
Cummins, C.	goal	Weir, A. (or Ware)
Riley (or Reilly)	point	Blackwell, Bert
Miller, S.	cover	Weir, B. or L. (or Ware)
Bishop, E.	rover	McDonald
McDonald, A.	center	Anderson, A.
Forteith, D.	rw	Carney, A.(or G.)
Miller, J.	lw	Carney T.
	spare	Jenkins, H.

Goals: Miller, J. (1); Ware, L. (1); Carney, T. (1); Forteith, (1); Reilly (1); Bishop (1); Jenkins (1)

(Also named in the Kaslo paper as possible players, O. Tapinalla, R. McKinney).

Inner-City Games

Nelson

(see also Lester Patrick's first game, above)

The Combined Banks met the Imperial Bank and the Imperial Bank won 13-3.

Imperial Bank		Combined Banks
Seatle, W. R.	goal	Not known
Ferguson	?	Nickerson Brothers
Swan	?	Starr
Hartin	?	Machin
Swannell	?	Rhinehardt
Lawrence	?	Nixon

The Wholesalers beat the Retailers 10-3.

Wholesalers		Retailers
Nunn	goal	Teague
Page	point	Horswill
O'Connor	cover	Pool
Rason	rover	Stevens,
Lavasser	center	Partington
Longhurst	rw	McLaughlin
Miller	lw	Jackson
		Party, C.D. (defence)
Starkey, Fred	spare	
McDonald, J.A.	spare	
Brown, George	spare	

Goals by: Party, C.D. (2); rest unknown.

The Real Estate men beat the Retailers (Grocers) 5-2.

The Real Estate team then made a big push to form a major competing team, and announced that their patrons would be the Prime Minister, Wilfred Laurier, and the B.C. Premier, Richard McBride. These two men were actually visting Nelson at the time, and did indeed agree to be patrons. Their Manager would be the same as the Senior team, M.R. McQuarrie; their Captain would be the old stalwart player, C.D. Blackwood, etc. They would be willing to take up challenges just as soon as they formed a suitable lineup. Dr. Wolverton, their President and Banker, agreed to put up any expenses involved in administering the challenges.

Another game against the Retailers was arranged, but at the last minute it was called off, as there was to be a large amount of money bet on the game, and the Retailers got cold feet. After their bombastic announcements, this was the only result of the Real Estate team's aspirations this year, leaving the Premier and the Prime Minister without any games to officially patronize.

A City Team Cup was offered this season for Nelson Teams by the Nelson Daily News. The Daily News Cup was to be played for, according to whatever league or challenge series the main hockey fraternity thought best. The Senior team's management was put in charge, and they decided to use the Daily News cup for an inner-city Senior challenge series. One such unofficial city game had already taken place, which was Lester Patrick's first game, but it was decided to start from scratch with three teams, the Mountains, the Lakes and the Rivers, who had previously called themselves the Bloods, or Sanguinaries. The first game was between the Mountains and the Lakes, and included Ferguson, who had broken his leg the previous year. Harry Bishop was not allowed to play goal, because that would have practically guaranteed victory for whatever team he played on.

The Mountains won the first game, 11-8.

Mountains		Lakes
Greyerbiehl	goal	Cummins, N.
Riley	point	Horswill
Deacon	cover	Ferguson
Bell, J	rover	Bishop, Harry
Bishop, Archie	center	Swan
Bellrose,	rw	Gore
Steel,	lw	McDonald
Newton	spare	Bishop, Ernie

Goals: Bishop, Archie, (5); Bishop, Harry (5); Steel, (2); Swan, (1); Bellrose (3); Ferguson, (1); Riley (1) Bishop, Ernie, (1)

The Mountains and Rivers played next, and although Lester Patrick was on the Rivers, they lost 18-6. The Mountains had decided to use more and better combination play, as opposed to individual rushes and badly outplayed the Rivers.

Mountains		Rivers
Greyerbeihl	goal	McLaughlin
Deacon	point	Patrick, L.
Steel	cover	Wilson
Chave, (E.J. ?)	rover	Thompson
Bishop, A.	center	Hoods
Bellrose	rw	Perrier
Bishop, H.	lw	Bell, R.

Goals: Bishop, Archie, (5); Chave, (5); Bishop, Harry, (4); Bellrose, (4); Patrick, Lester, (4); Hood, (1); Bell, R, (1)

After the Rossland Carnival this city championship was resumed.

A benefit game was first played between the Lakes and Mountains, to raise money for Frank Nott, a fringe player, but fine athlete, who lost an eye while practicing.

Rivers	Lakes	Mountains	
Greyerbiehl	Fotheringham, W.	Bishop	goal
Rielly	Horswill	Deacon	point
Bell, J	Miller	Steel	cover
Hood	Bishop, E.	Bishop, A.	centre
Swan	Chave	Bell, R.	rover
Clunis	Gore	Belrose	rw
Moody	Mcdonald	Patrick (?)	lw
Wilson	Miller, J.		spare
Newton	McLaughlin		spare

The Teams were re-arranged somewhat as the manager of the Nelson senior team was preparing for a big match against Grand Forks.

The Mountains defeated the Lakes 11-5

Mountains		Lakes
Greyerbiehl	goal	Bishop, Ernie
Hood	point	Deacon
Horswill	cover	Patrick, L.
Bishop, H.	rover	Chave
Bishop, Archie	center	Gore
Perrier,	rw	Miller, Jack.
Belrose	lw	Steel

Goals: Patrick, Lester (4), Bishop, H. (3) Bishop, A.(3) , Bellrose, H. (3) Horswill (1) Perrier, (2), Miller, Jack (1)

Another game was played between the Mountains and the Rivers, with the Mountains winning, but no other details could be found.

The Mountains played the Lakes again, and several players either switched teams, or didn't play. Lester Patrick sat out the game.. The result was the Mountains 8 and the Lakes 5, with the Mountains then winning the Daily News Cup. (The actual roster of the teams was not given.)

Goals scored: Bishop, A. (2); Bishop H. (2); Miller, J. (1); Miller S. (3); Perrier, (2); Moody, (1); Thompson, Joe (2)

A Nelson hockey "minstrel show" was organized for the first time this season. Presumably the hockey players put on black face and performed a grotesque pantomime, as was the custom. Since Lester Patrick was known to be the most gregarious and entertaining member of most parties he attended, it is likely he participated. One is left with a disturbing image of a great hockey player, but he was, after all, a product of his times.

Archie Bishop was by now the manager of the Stanley St. rink.

Rossland Industrial League

Between the Rossland and Trail papers, only three games were reported from the Industrial League.

Trail Smelter defeated the Rocky Mountain Rangers of Rossland 4-0.

Trail smelter tied the Centre Star Mine 7-7.

Trail Smelter		Centre Star Mine
Chapman, A.	goal	Goninan, B.
Robb, W.	point	Griffith, F.
McNabb, J.	cover	Rollins, A.
Shorey, M.	centre	Stanaway, E.
Sullivan, M.	rover	Trezona, J.
Buchanan J.	lw	Cole, H.
Schwartz, R.	rw	Hamilton, B.

The final game was then announced, to decide the championship, between Le Roi, and Centre Star.

Le Roi won 4-1. All four of the Le Roi goals were scored by Rinquist.

Le Roi		Centre Star Mine
Inches	goal	Goninan, B.
Penrose	point	Griffith, F.
Waring	cover	Rollins, A.
Griffith, C.	centre	Stanaway, E.
Harris	rover	Trezona, J.
Wilson	lw	Cole, H.
Rinquist	rw	Hamilton, B.

Goals: Rinquist, (4); Trezona, (1).

ROSSLAND CARNIVAL and B.C. CHAMPIONSHIP

As indicated in the previous year, Spokane had been forced to drop out of regularly organized hockey this year because their rink was taken over by an ice-making company. However, most of their best players were still in the city, and they were itching to play, despite there being no ice. Most importantly, the McGaugherty brothers, Ernest, and Tom, who had been playing for Rossland this year, were both available, but Wurtele, once again, was not.

This time the team traveled early to Rossland to acclimatize themselves to the ice, and to get in some practise before the big games.

In the preliminary International event, Spokane faced Coleman Alberta, a very strong team, who had been Alberta provincial champions a few years earlier.

At the start Coleman pulled away with a 2-0 lead, and at the end of the first half, was still ahead 3-2. In the second half Coleman pulled away again, scoring two goals to make it 5-2. But Spokane furiously fought back, and scored 4 unanswered goals, pulling out an amazing 6-5 victory over the disappointed Coleman team.

Spokane		Coleman
Robertson, Charles E.	goal	Higgins
Ferrier, Roy	point	White
McGaugherty, Tom	cover	Simms
Trezona, Jim	rover	Jamieson
Turner	centre	Baker
McGaugherty, Ernest	rw	Gresack, f.
Cardiff (or Cradiff), L.	lw	Lewis
Mohr	spare	

Goals: Baker, (1); Lewis, (2); McGaugherty, T. (4); Gresack, F. (1); Jamieson, (1); Trezona, (1); Cardiff, (1). (It's possible that one of Tom McGaugherty's goals was actually scored by his brother.)

Eldon Winn then presided over a bizzare series of events involving Nelson and Rossland. This might have been the first time that Eldon Winn had refereed a match with Lester Patrick, who had been warned about Winn's previous decisions. Therefore, Nelson had requested, a month before the carnival, that a judge of play be added to the officiating staff, i.e. a second referee, and not someone from Rossland.

This request, by the Nelson manager, McQuarrie, can be traced to the probable influence of Lester Patrick, who was possibly the only one on the Nelson team who had played under the two referee system being employed for a couple of years in Eastern Canada.

According to McQuarrie, after sending two letters with his requests, he received one phone call from the head of the Carnival Committee, Mr. McKenzie, who told McQuarrie that, in McQuarrie's words, "everything would be arranged to our entire satisfaction." McQuarrie made another phone call himself to Mr. McKenzie two days before the team left for Rossland, iterating that because of the difficulties they had had previously in Rossland, there would be no use going to Rossland if there would not be a judge of play added from a neutral city. Mr. McKenzie repeated his words that everything would be arranged to Nelson's entire satisfaction.

When the Nelson team arrived for their first game, they found that Eldon Winn was once again the only referee the Rossland committeee would consider. Winn himself made it clear at that point that he would not referee the game with anyone under him, and if there were any changes, he would leave the ice. Winn apparently knew his men, because they backed him up. Winn himself was not on the hockey committee this year, although he was on the skating committee, but two other important people were: John (Jack) Donahue, the Rossland team's Captain, and K.C. Allen, one of the Rossland team's defencemen. Winn then made assurances to Nelson that he would give the Nelson team "the squarest of square deals."

Very reluctantly, the Nelson team decided to play anyway, with Eldon Winn as the sole referee. This match against Rossland was their preliminary international, or open match, although it was also a knockout match, the loser being eliminated. The Rossland paper indicated that the Nelson team was not aware of how diligently the Rossland team had been practicing, especially in designing and executing combination plays. The Nelson correspondents indicate that the game was unnecessarily rough. In any case, Rossland was ahead 4-0 at half time. When the next half started, Joe Thompson of Nelson had to retire because of a cut over one eye. For some reason, which has never been explained, Nelson did not insert a spare player to take Joe's place, but rather played on with six men. No spare was named on their roster, so it's possible no spare was brought. Sometimes a team played with spares, and sometimes not, but it seems short-sighted of their Captain, Lester Patrick, not to bring a spare to the championships, as they had done in the past, even though there were plenty of good players to choose from. Was it because the Rossland organizing committee would not let them use a spare? It's true that Rossland basically made up its own rules at the Carnival, but the unfairness of this would have been immense. The Rossland paper merely reported that Joe Thompson was struck in the eye and had to retire. In any case, from previous game results it does appear that there was nothing extraordinary about one team continuing a man down, for the remainder of a game, and indeed, many games had been reported in this way.

However, the ramifications of this, in terms of the evolution of the game were considerable, and what happened next should have had major significance to someone like Lester Patrick. In the second half, despite being one man down the entire time, Nelson finally figured Rossland out and scored three goals, while Rossland was unable to score even one. Lester Patrick scored two of the goals, and Archie Bishop the third. Rossland managed to squeeze out a victory 4-3, but the Nelson team was soundly beating the Rossland team while they were short handed for about half an hour! What had happened here? The empirical evidence shows that six man hockey was superior to seven man hockey. Suddenly the ice surface, which was the largest rink in B.C., had opened up to allow more freedom of movement to one particular side. One of the two defensemen, Lester Patrick, then scored two of his team's three goals, where he was unable to get through before.

Of course there might have been other factors. The Rossland players might have become overconfident. The Nelson players might have started playing better than before. The game was apparently very rough, especially from the Rossland players, and they might have stopped playing so roughly, allowing the Nelson players to use their abilities better.

But something should have been considered here, for future reference, by one of hockey's best players, Lester Patrick. Although the impetus for changing and improving rules came more from his brother Frank than himself, the two brothers began revolutionizing hockey a few years later. But the one rule that Lester would never change, until he had to, in the NHL, was the team size of seven men. He always maintained that the change by the NHA, and later the NHL, to six man hockey was a cynical attempt to save money and cheat the fans.

Nelson		Rossland
Bishop, Harry	goal	McCreary, Jack
Patrick, L.	point	Donahue, Jack
Steel, Les	cover	Allen
Dunn	rover	Rillance
Bishop, Archie	center	Keating, C. (?)
Thompson, Joe	lw	Neal
Bellrose	rw	Dixon, Scotty

Goals: Keating, (2); Patrick, L. (2); Dixon, (1); Neal, (1); Bishop, A, (1)

After the game, the Nelson team decided that "Mr. Winn's methods were…unsatisfactory from every standpoint," and they unanimously decided to insist on the appointment of a judge of play for their next game. It was not clear exactly why Eldon Winn was considered unsatisfactory, but in any case, they informed Mr. McKenzie, in the presence of witnesses, on the day before their next game, of their decision not to continue without a judge of play.

Once again, the committee appeared to acquiesce, and asked for a list of possible judges from Nelson. It's not known whether this was the overall Carnival Committee, or the Hockey Committee, or a combination, or just A.B. McKenzie.

Several names were given, and Nelson also indicated that they would still play with Winn as referee as long as a neutral man was judge of play.

Everyone waited while the hockey pot was being stirred.

In the meantime, the Carnival then continued with Rossland playing Spokane in the final of the Open, or International Cup.

According to the Rossland paper, Rossland started with a lead and Spokane never caught up. But according to the Spokane paper, the Spokane team actually led briefly in the first half, 2-1. But before the first half had ended, Rossland had gone ahead 5-2, and Spokane had a tough time trying to come back. In the second half they poured it on, as they had with Coleman, but they couldn't quite make the comeback, as Rossland won the Open Championship 7-5.

Rossland		Spokane
McCreary, Jack	goal	Robertson, Charles E.
Donahue, Jack	point	Ferrier, Roy
Allan	cover	McCaugherty, Tom
Rillance	rover	Treazona
Keating, Al	center	Trainer,
Dixon, Scotty	rw	McCaugherty, Ernest
Neil	lw	Cardiff

Goals: Neil, (3); Dixon, (2); Keating, (2); McCaugherty, T. (3); Trezona, (2)

Then Nelson was to play Rossland for the B.C. Championships. (Oddly, they were the only two Senior teams to have attended from B.C.)

In the afternoon, before the game, according to M.R. McQuarrie, he again approached Mr. McKenzie and he was assured that everything would be arranged for the evening's match to Nelson's satisfaction. Soon after McQuarrie then asked Mr. McKenzie who it was they had arranged as a judge of play and Mr. McKenzie instructed him that McQuarrie himself would have to, "fix it up with Winn when he came." This alarmed McQuarrie, and he immediately sought out Eldon Winn. He found Winn and asked him about the judge of play. Winn indignantly replied that he would not go on the ice with any judge of play. McQuarrie hurried back to the rink, where the Nelson team was on the ice, warming up for the game. When they heard what Winn had said they felt they had had enough and left the ice, awaiting events.

McQuarrie sought out Mr McKenzie again, who was now obdurate: he could do nothing about it, but McQuarrie could appeal directly to the Rossland players. McQuarrie then did this, but they "collectively stated that they would not go on the ice with any judge of play, or any referee but Winn."

Lester Patrick, the Captain of the Nelson team, then sought out the committee and made an appeal, explaining the professional nature of a judge of play, and requesting a "square deal." He was refused any compromise point blank, and according to Patrick, the committee told him, "they would not be dictated to by Nelson people." It's not clear if this is the executive committee or the hockey committee.

Patrick then said, in the Nelson Daily News, "Having failed in my effort, I then took my men off the rink and we all went down to the hotel. While we were down there, Winn, the referee, awarded the cup to the Rossland team."

The Rossland paper had a quite different view of the whole affair. Apparently the eager fans, reported to be around 1300 by the Rossland paper, and 1800 by the Nelson paper, were made to wait three hours in the nighttime cold while an argument they couldn't see went on between the two teams. Simply put, the Nelson team had again demanded a judge of play, as well as a referee. The Rossland organizing committee had refused and Nelson then refused to play. Then Nelson pulled its team and went home, leaving the B.C. championships once again to Rossland.

Accusations then flew back and forth.

What had actually happened?

The Rossland committee agreed that the request for a judge of play had come weeks earlier, but they swore that no agreement had been given, except to consider it. They also denied that any verbal agreement had been given by telephone. In fact, all the games so far in the tournament had been played without a second referee, and Nelson had not apparently disputed any of them. (i.e. the one game they had played).

In fact, according to the Rossland committee, they did try to effect a compromise at the eleventh hour. The Rossland officials had, in fact, offered A.B. McKenzie, the head of the Carnival committee, as judge of play, but Nelson had rejected him. Then Rossland offered Judge Wilson, another Rossland man, but this fellow had no skates, and said he would have to officiate from the time-keeper's bench. Nelson also rejected Judge Wilson. The Rossland Miner also pointed out that right after the game was given to Rossland, Nelson offered to play an exhibition game in its place. This was part proof of a favorite conspiracy theory of the correspondents: that the Nelson team was aware they would lose, due to being physically unfit, after the last game, from a combination of bruises and drinking. They then searched for a way out, as enormous amounts of money had been bet on the game, by gambling elements which controlled the team. Offering to play an exhibition game right after showed that they actually had no objections to the refereeing situation.

It was true that a large amount of money had been bet, and those Nelson supporters who had lost huge amounts on the previous game were not happy about the prospect of losing the next one. But the Nelson account of this exhibition game was entirely different from the story promulgated by Rossland. According to M.R. McQuarrie, while the players had gone back to their hotel, a telephone call had come for him from the organizing committee. They had asked Spokane and Coleman to play an exhibition game in the place of the cancelled game, but had been turned down. If Nelson would consent to an exhibition game, "We will give you anything you want." The Nelson players then dressed back into their uniforms, trudged back to the rink, and took the ice. This time there was indeed a judge of play, Blake Wilson, (not Judge Wilson), from the the P. Burns Company, and he did have skates. In fact P. Burns and Company had offered $200.00 for Nelson's expenses if they played. Nelson assented to this, but then the Rossland players announced once again that they would not consent to a judge of play, and would not consent to play with anyone except Winn alone. With that, the Nelson team once again left the ice, and went back to the hotel, leaving the spectators to freeze by themselves.

In any case, Winn, and his co-horts Jack Donahue, and K.C. Allen, had won, and they had made sure that Rossland would be the cup holders of the B.C. championships.

So who does one believe? The Nelson account of events is much more detailed than the Rossland one, which tends to gloss over the account, and stress over and over that Nelson had no right to ask for a judge of play.

The whole affair is in fact reminiscent of the old "bait and switch" method employed by Rossland in the 1906 delayed playoff for the B.C. Championship, when Nelson didn't actually take the bait, but wound up losing the trophy all the same. This time the bait had been taken, and the switch made, regardless of whether Manager McQuarrie had been given a definite answer or not. It's clear that he was led to believe his request would be granted. The situation is also reminiscent of the 1972 Canada-Russia summit series when the

Canadians were denied their choice of referee for the final game, as had been promised, and were saddled with the referees they considered the most incompetent instead.

Furthermore the idea that Lester Patrick would be controlled by gambling interests would not have been consistent with his character. It is probable that he, along with many others of the team, would not have cared about the betting, since he had a stern religious background to which gambling was anathema. Furthermore, the whole issue of asking that a judge of play be added to the game, had certainly been introduced much earlier than the final game, when it looked, before the Carnival, like Nelson had the stronger team.

But another possibility exists along these lines: without money being an issue, Lester Patrick thought he was doing the right thing, to save his team from ignominious defeat because he had seen the debauched state of his men, and knew they were too weak. They hadn't brought a spare, and the referee was known to be partial to Rossland. Did Lester Patrick then decide that their original request be made into a rigid, face-saving device?

This is highly doubtful.

It's far more probable that the Nelson team had finally reached the point where the straw had broken their camel's back. It's possible that Rossland had underestimated the resolve of the Nelson team, because after all, the situation had always worked in years past.

There was another element to the affair, which would not have escaped manager McQuarrie's, or Lester Patrick's notice, however. There was one way that Nelson could hurt Rossland, and that was by depriving them of a large amount of gate receipts, which had to be given back, and a large amount of money bet on the game. This would be the conspiracy theory in reverse, and although it might not have been a major factor in the team's immediate decision, it was certainly felt by the Rossland committee, who ultimately paid dearly for the championship cup, which could now be retained forever by the Rossland team, after "winning" it three years in a row.

(Speaking of money, Nelson attended the Carnival under a contract for $150.00 expense money, and they were technically breaching their contract.)

Oddly, the root cause of the issue can be traced directly to two very strong-willed men, Eldon Winn and Lester Patrick. On the one hand, Eldon Winn had previously guided the Committee in its carefull manipulation of fairness, and his control of the hearts and minds of the players was reminiscent of Svengali. His refusal to step down, or agree to any compromise shows that he had reached a peak of hubris hitherto unequalled in B.C. sports.

On the other hand, the introduction of Lester Patrick had provided the first possible legitimate solution to the influence of Winn. No one had known what to do about changing the appalling referee situation, and it was probably Lester Patrick, who had played league matches in Eastern Canada for three years with the new judge of play and referee system, who had first suggested this plan.

However, Lester Patrick was also a stubborn man, and this insistence on a judge of play did cost the Nelson team the right to play for the B.C. Cup.

But Nelson's withdrawl had its sting. The Rossland players began to feel cheated themselves of a chance for glory and money, and appeared belatedly to come out of their stubborn trances, some of them agitating, days later, for a proper finish to the game. The Rossland management also felt the loss of money keenly and began to make overtures to Nelson. But Nelson refused to play another game in Rossland, despite the fact that Rossland offered a challenge match for a lot of money and finally relented to adding a judge of play, with Manitoba rules to be followed. At this point Lester Patrick's indignation should have turned to acceptance. He had got what he wanted, and it would have been simple for written guarantees to be exchanged. But Lester Patrick had spoken, and he chose to remain aloof, and savour his pyrrhic victory. This attitude was to cost him and his team dearly three years later.

Grand Forks and Fernie both offered their rinks for a neutral game site to finish the tournament in later weeks, but although Nelson seemed to consider it, Rossland refused this. (Rossland's rink, and population, was much bigger and would have afforded a much bigger gate receipt, while the others would have been small.)

The Rossland Ladies Hockey Club announced a derisive challenge to the Nelson Seniors, promising not to rough them up, while the Rossland reporters also called into question Nelson's fortitude.

However, even with this taunting, no further championship game was played.

Other results at the Carnival:

Phoenix Intermediates defeated Trail Intermediates 10-8. (The Nelson paper says 9-8.)

Phoenix then played Rossland Intermediates for the Intermediate Championship, and defeated Rossland 6-5.

Phoenix Intermediates		Rossland Intermediates
Biner	goal	Inches, B.
Clark, H.	point	Penrose
Jost	cover	Brown
McKelvie	centre	Griffith
McDonald	rover	Stanaway
Longhurst	lw	Cole
Clark, R.	rw	Harris

Goals: Cole, (3); Stanaway, (2); Longhurst, (2); McKelvie, (2); Clark, R. (2).

Rossland Juniors defeated the Trail juniors 8-1.

Rossland Juniors		Trail Juniors
Keefe, E.	goal	Robinson
Griffith	point	Brown
Stanton	cover	Milligan
Demuth,	rover	Morgan
Inches, J.	centre	Cunningham
Braden	rw	Swartz
Cosgriff, F.	lw	Morgan

There is no indication of who ultimately won the Junior Championship, although it's possible that Rossland was declared the winner from this one game.

Rossland Juveniles and Trail Juveniles played to a 1-1 tie.

TRAIL

Arlington Hotel defeated Crown Point Hotel 6-2.

The Meakin Hotel challenged Arlingto, but the result is not available.

The CROW'S NEST

The Phoenix Intermediates defeated the Greenwood Intermediates 6-0.

Fernie defeated Coleman Alberta in the new Fernie rink, 7-2. The two teams played two more times, Fernie winning each of them, and consequently they became Champions of the Crow's Nest Pass, and the Whelan Cup. (Coleman was the previous year's winner). Cowly also defeated Coleman, 1-0, and Coleman had defeated Macleod Alberta 10-4.

Fernie challenged the Nelson Senior Team in March, (after the Rossland Carnival), and Nelson traveled to Fernie for this prestigious contest.

Nelson		Fernie
Bishop, Harry	goal	Morrison
Deacon	point	Kent
Steel	cover	Wright
Patrick, L.	rover	Pever
Bishop, A.	center	Kemp
Thompson, J.	rw	Rilance
Bellrose,	lw	Therin

Fernie won a very close match, 6-5.

The OKANAGAN

Vernon and Armstrong played a best three out of five series through the season to decide who would win the silver cup donated by Price Ellison, MP. The teams were as follows, for the three games:

Vernon		Armstrong
Sawyer, W.	goal	Maundrell, S.
Jackson, E.S.	point	Bodden, S.G. (or Bawden)
Elliott, P.	cover	Willis, J.B.
Myer(s), B. (or H.F.)	rover	Burnyeat, D.
Morrison, R.S.	center	Daykin, J.
Speers, S.J. (or S.H.)	rw	Johnson, C.
St. Clair Mabee, O.	lw	Towl, J.
		Pelly, R. (rover, 3rd game)
McKinnon, A	center (3rd game)	

Vernon won the first game 4-2.
Vernon won the second game 7-1.
Vernon won the third game 2-1.

Vernon therefore won the Ellison Cup, which was put on display in F.B. Jacques' jewelry store. Vernon declared itself Champion of the Okanagan Valley as a result.

A later challenge match between the Vernon Senior team and Armstrong yielded a 6-2 win for Vernon. The Teams were mixed up with several players changing sides, and new players added, as follows: (although the reporter might have got things mixed up himself).

Vernon		Armstrong
Spencer, H..	goal	Maundrell, S.
Birnie, H..	point	Maundrell, A
McKinnon, A.	cover	Mills, W
French, P.	rover	?
Middleton, W.	center	Hood, W.
Cary, J.	rw	Morrison, P
Speer, S.	lw	Daykin J.

Armstrong finally got its revenge in another challenge match with Vernon, when they trounced Vernon 7-1. The lineups and stats are unknown.

Boarders at the Royal and Coldstream hotels in Vernon, challenged each other to a match. Coldstream won 6-3.

Coldstream		Royal
Adams	goal	Armitage
George	point	Kennedy
Kearns	cover	Elliott
Spencer	rover	Fred
Forrester	center	Power
Speers	lw	Bustin
Duncan	rw	Turnbull, H.

Summerland defeated Peachland 2-0, playing their match in the reservoir in the hills behind Summerland, which took many hours of hiking to get to, presumably with skates and sticks on their backs.

Penticton players drove to Prairie Valley where they met the Summerland Team and lost 2-0. Richard Powers is the only player named for Penticton.

Kelowna defeated Summerland 2-0 in a challenge match, which was apparently a return match, but I cannot find the first match mentioned.

KAMLOOPS

In Kamloops an official team was finally organized again, run by the Kamloops Athletic Association and challenged Nicola at the Nicola Rink for the "Haddad" Trophy, of which little is known. Nicola won this game, 2-1.

The players known were:

Kamloops		Nicola
Brennan, William	goal	?
Nelson, Angus	forward (?)	Curtis, C.
Lapointe	?	Neal
Somes, T. (Captain)	?	Murray
Irwin, Fred	?	Charlton

Thomas Munn was a player but which side isn't known.

Nicola later traveled to Kamloops for a rematch and won again by a 2-1 score.

KASLO

Kaslo enthusiasts finally began to take hockey seriously again, and put great pride in their intermediate team. They organized a game against Sandon, in Kaslo. One of their players, Thomas Carney, had been so anxious to play again, after several years absence, that he began playing for Sandon, when he was stationed there for a week, and when the Intermediate game was announced, he still played for Sandon when he returned to his home town.

The first goal was scored in 23 seconds by Langille of Sandon, but North, of Kaslo quickly tied it up. After a hard fought game it ended 3-3.

Kaslo		Sandon
Walter, R.	goal	Tattrie, W.
Blackwell, B.	point	Langelle, S.
Hunter, Sam	rover	McDougall, F.
Cliffe, W.	cover	McDonell, F.
Anderson, Allen	rw	Hope, G.
North, C.	centre	Charbonneau, F.
McDonald, H.	lw	Carney, Thomas

Goals: Langille (2); North (1), Anderson (2); McDougall (1)

Kaslo Intermediates then played a game against Nelson Intermediates, who beat them 5-3 (See Nelson above for details). There was to be another game against Sandon, but I have not found a record of it.

GOLDEN

No local games were mentioned.

OTHER GAMES

Coeur D'Alene Idaho announced a team, with E.J. Blanchard as Captain, but no games are known.

Camborne (near Sandon B.C.) defeated Ferguson, 3-1 to take the "Silver Cup" for 1908.

Camborne		Ferguson
Dunn (scored)	forward (?)	Garrett, "Rusty"
Smith, "Dutch"	forward (?)	Barber
Marten	?	Blackie
Orr	?	

JUNIORS

The Rossland and Nelson Junior teams challenged each other to a match, and Nelson won 8-0.

Nelson Juniors		Rossland Juniors
Hartin, D.	goal	All unknown
Hardie, (or Hardy), D.	point	
Cumming (or Cummins), T.	cover	
Smith, F.	rover	
Patterson, W.	center	
Boyce, G.	rw	
Brown, R.	lw	

Goals: Boyce, G. (4); Cummins, T. (3); Brown, R. (1)

Another game took place between the juniors of Nelson and Rossland, Nelson winning 7-4.

Nelson Juniors		Rossland Juniors
Cummins, T.	goal	Keefe
Riley,	point	Stanton
Bell, J.	cover	Braden
Miller, S.	rover	Demuth
McDonald	center	Inches
Gore,	rw	Cosgriff
Miller, J.	l w	Griffith, G.

Goals: Gore, (2); Miller, J. (2); Demuth, (2); Inches (1); Griffith (1); Bell, S. (1); Miller, J. (1); McDonald (1).

Another game between these two junior teams was announced later in the season, but the result is unknown. The teams were as follows, however:

Nelson Juniors		Rossland Juniors
Hartin, D.	goal	Team not known
Hardy, D.	point	
Cummins, T.	cover	
Grant, J.	rover	
Paterson, W.	centre	
Boyce, J.	rw	
Brown, R.	lw	
Stewart, J.	spare	

Rossland Juniors defeated Trail Juniors 3-2.

Rossland Juniors		Trail Juniors
Keefe, E.	goal	Robinson, C.
Stanaway, H.	point	Brown, D.
Griffith, G.	cover	Truswell, D.
Demuth,	rover	Milligan, F.
Inches, J.	centre	Morgan, D.
Owen, H.	rw	Morrow, C.
Cosgriff, F.	lw	Schwartz, B.

Armstrong juniors defeated the Enderby juniors by two points. (Score unknown).

Vernon Juniors defeated the Armstrong Juniors 6-3.

Vernon Juniors defeated the Kelowna juniors 3-1.

In Kelowna the High school and the Public School challenged each other to a match, and the Public School won. In a later match, the High School defeated the Public school 6-1.

VANCOUVER

There was some ice this year. The Bank clerks of the city organized a team for challenges, and Alex Turnbull, the Lacrosse player, began organizing a team. Unfortunately the ice did not last, and there were no organized games. This was a great pity, especially because one of the greatest players in the game, Tom Phillips, was now residing in Vancouver, and he must have been itching to play.

A roller polo game was played against Victoria at the Imperial roller skating rink, Vancouver winning 3-0. Some of these players, who are named below, would undoubtedly also have played hockey:

Vancouver: Wagner, Howell, Sidsworth, Charbonneau, Burns; Victoria: Burnett, Thrall, Burnett, Regan, Medrich.

Nelson's Speedy Hockey Team

Plate 24. Nelson Senior Men's Team, 1908. Left to right: Bellrose, cover; a. Bishop, rover; H. bishop, goal; J. Thompson, wing; L. Patrick, cover; Steub, point; Steel, centre. This is the only known image at this time.
>From the Spokane Spokesman-Review, Feb. 9, 1908.

Plate 25. Rossland Senior Men's Team, 1908. Top row, left to right,: C. Griffiths (?); S.J. Martin; W.C. Allan (?); Jack Donahue. Middle row: J,W. Dixon; A.J. McCreary; Herb Neil. Bottom row, J. Rilance; Al Keating. Credit Rossland Museum.

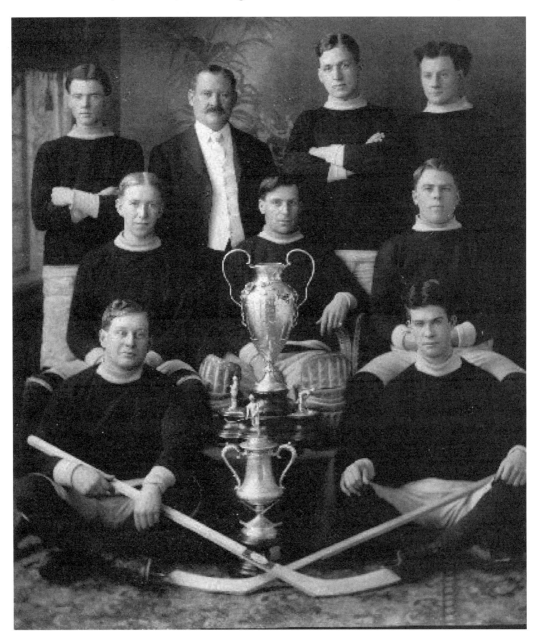

Plate 26. Rossland Senior Men's Team, 2nd photo 1908. (Showing the Giant Powder B.C. championship Cup, provided first in 1904, and the Fraser International or Open Cup) This photo has been catalogued in the Rossland Museum as being from 1905. However, in fact, this is another team photo from 1908, taken with more of the principals present. (Or perhaps the other way around, with less principals, but the first seems more logical.) There was much controversy this year, and the result was not confirmed by the committee until months after the carnival. As for determining the date, the International cup was not provided until 1907, and Rossland won both the B.C. Championship Cup and the International cup in 1908. The photo therefore can't be 1905, or 1906, or 1907, since Nelson won the International cup in 1907, and it can't be 1909, 1910 or 1911, as Nelson won both the B.C. and International cup in 1909, as well as the B.C. championships in 1910, and Greenwood won the International in 1910, and Phoenix won both cups in 1911. The players named also indicate a date of 1908. Top row, left to right, J. Rilance; J. McArthur, (Manager); S.J. Martin, (Sec-Treasurer); E.S.H. Winn, (President ?); Herb Neil. Centre Row, J.W. Dixon; Al Keating; W. C. Allan; Joe Deschamps; J. Donahue; A.J. McCreary, goal. Seated, Phil Donahue; C.Griffiths. Credit Rossland Museum.

Plate 27. Vernon Senior team 1908. (Showing Cornwall cup) Back row, left to right: E.S. Jackson, point; T.E. Crowell, Manager; W. Sawyer, goal. Middle row: R.S. Morrison, centre; A. McKinnon, spare; P. Elliott, cover point and Captain; O.S. Mabee, l.wing. Bottom row: S.H. Speers, l.wing; H.F. Meyer, rover. From author's collection.

1909 SEASON

This was the last year, (up until April 1st), that cocaine, morphine and opium were publicly legal in Canada. No longer could the Coca-Cola company put cocaine in their Canadian bottles, and all druggists had to register their ingredients with the federal government.

After this season, hockey enthusiasts had to content themselves only with alcohol.

NELSON, ROSSLAND and the KOOTENAYS

Frank Patrick had returned from his studies in the East to take over one of his father's logging camps, but he was itching to play hockey with Lester. He finally convinced his father, Joe, to allow him to take time out from administering the logging camp, and play. At the same time, the finishing touches were being put on a brand new, enclosed rink, on Hall Mines Road, which was said to have all of the best features of the best rinks in Canada,

It has often been said that this was the rink built by the Patricks, but this is misleading. A subscription was taken round by the Patrick brothers, as well as others, and many large contributions were made by leading citizens, of about one thousand dollars each. That is to say, promises were made and shares issued, with money to be paid in installments over a year. The leading contributors were Joseph Patrick; George P. Wells; Toye, Taylor and McQuarrie; Harry Wright; A.G. Lamber (?) company; William Waldie; J.Fred Hume; P.Burns and co.; J. Laing Stocks; and William Gillette. The total cost of the rink was $16,176.00. It was W.G. Gillette, former mayor of the city, who actually built the rink, and they started construction as soon as they could, in 1908. The finishing touches were still being added in February of 1909. G.W. McBride was the first President, W.J. Wilson was V.P.; and William Waldie Secretary.

According to Dr. D.M. Black, "The roof was curved and was carried on trusses which rose from the outside walls so there were no posts to interfere with the view of the spectators seated along the sides. Of course, [there was] no refridgeration, and [they] had to depend on natural ice with the result that some of the games were played under rather sloppy conditions."

Tungsten bulbs had come in around 1908, so the lighting in the rink was better now, whereas earlier it had been very yellow, and somewhat dim.

Before the regular season started in Nelson, however, Lester was asked to join a team of ringers, in December of 1908, being put together by Fred Whitcroft in Edmonton to challenge the Montreal Wanderers for the Stanley cup. Lester joined the team, along with Tom Phillips, the great Kenora left winger, who was then living in Vancouver.

The Wanderers won the first game, 7-3, during which Tom Phillips broke his foot, or ankle. Edmonton won the second game 7-6, but lost on the total aggregate score.[21]

---

[21] Eric Whitehead, in "The Patricks," has unfortunately mixed up the chronology of events for Lester's first years in Nelson. He has the Edmonton Stanley cup challenge take place in Lester's first season, early in 1908. Whitehead also reports the Wanderers winning both games.

Back in the Kootenays, another attempt to formalize a B.C. league was given firm ground when the B.C. Hockey League was announced, having two distinct parts: East Kootenay League, comprising Coleman Alberta, Fernie and Moyie; and the West Kootenay League, or division, comprising Rossland, Nelson and Grand Forks. Both divisions were under the jurisdiction of the B.C. League, and Manitoba rules were to apply, including two referees. Grand Forks dropped out, and became part of the Boundary League, while Moyie moved to the West division. The East division then fell apart. The Crow's Nest Pass teams then played several unofficial games with each other, including Moyie.

The Boundary Hockey League was announced, which included Greenwood, Phoenix and Grand Forks. They considered themselves Intermediate, but they had no other Senior teams, so these teams were their best.

Other leagues were announced, including one between Revelstoke, Vernon, Enderby and Armstrong; and between Ashcroft, Kamloops and Nicola. However none of these leagues materialized, and throughout the province there were many challenge matches instead.

Trail was not a factor in these league announcements, but a newspaper account refers to "frantic bidding" for the services of Trail players. But although this appeared to be happening in Trail, there is very little indication that anyone outside of Trail was actually frantic to pick up any Trail players for their teams. There is a great deal of boasting and hyperbole among proud hockey communities, however, and one or two incidents of requests for players could easily have been blown out of proportion to make good newspaper copy.

The principal B.C. League was between Nelson, Rossland and Moyie. However, for the usual reasons of distance and time, it was difficult to play all the games desired. In any case the addition of Frank Patrick served to put the final piece of the puzzle into a great Nelson team.

An unusual element had also been inserted into all the senior games this year—two referees. Every game had a referee and a judge of play, even in Rossland. Furthermore, Eldon Winn was not refereeing. This was so for "league" games with Nelson, as well as the Rossland Carnival. Did this mean that Lester Patrick's stand had paid off? Possibly. Everyone seemed tired of controversy, and anxious not to lose their money. However, the ghost of Eldon Winn would rise again, two years later.

In the meantime, however, the Nelson team, with the Patrick Brothers, enjoyed an unfettered playing field.

Rossland Seniors warmed up for the coming battles with Nelson by playing the Trail Seniors in a non "league" game. Rossland had spent a lot of time practicing and put everything they had into this contest, and they crushed Trail 13-0.

Nelson and Rossland then played their first Senior league match in Nelson. However, Rossland had lost two of their best players. Donahue was playing for Moyie this year, and their top goalie, McCreary, was unavailable for the time being. A new man, Carruthers, was put in McCreary's place for this first "league" game.

The Nelson team was heavier, with perhaps an average of 150 pounds to 120 pounds for Rossland, so their checking gave them an advantage, apart from their fine play. Frank Patrick was particularly effective. He was rock solid on defense, and added his weight to the offense many times, often rushing through the Rossland defense. He scored the first and last goals, with one more in the middle for a hat trick, in a 14-1 romp over Rossland.

Sheelah Castle, Frank and Lester's niece, who is one of the last people still living who saw the two men play, in exhibition games in the late 1920's, says that Frank's body was more like a hockey player's than Lester's, as it was lower to the ground and a little stockier. As a result, Sheelah has the impression that Frank might have been the better skater of the two.

Archie Bishop had six goals. Approximately 1000 people watched the game.

Nelson		Rossland
Bishop, H.	goal	Carruthers
Patrick, F.	point	Griffis, C. (or Griffith)
Dunne, T.	cover	Allen, K.C.
Patrick, L.	rover	Neil, H.
Bishop, A	center	Keating, A.K.
Thompson	lw	Stenaway
Steel	rw	Dixon
Bell, R.	spare	
Gore, George	spare	

Goals: Bishop, A, (6); Patrick, Frank, (3); Thompson, Joe, (3); Patrick, Lester, (1); Dunne, T. (1); Dixon, (Rossland) (1).

Rossland went home and practised harder. Then came the return match in Rossland, where Frank Patrick was unable to play, as he was kept in the logging camps by his father, and his place was taken by Al Horswill. For Rossland, McQueen replaced Stenaway, (or Stanaway), and McCreary was in goal instead of Carruthers.

Lester Patrick took up the slack, and seemed to score at will, according to the Rossland Miner's reporter. However, Frank Patrick's departure was reflected in the score being reduced for Nelson by exactly the number of goals he had scored in the previous game, and 3 goals more scored against, 11-4, for Nelson. But the main story was still Lester Patrick's performance, as he scored seven goals.

The Rossland Miner had the score 8-4, denying three of Lester Patrick's goals and giving two of the Rossland team's goals to Neill, instead of K.C. Allen, as reported by Nelson. I favor the 11-4 score as the Nelson reporting seems more accurate, but I've split up the individual goal results, according to Nelson's reporting of its goals, and Rossland's reporting of its goals, below.

Goals: Patrick, Lester, (7); Allen, K.C. (Rossland), (1); Neill, (2); Bishop, A, (2); Steel, (1), Dixon (Rossland) (1); Dunne, (1).

Frank Patrick was back for the final game of Nelson's B.C. League contests against Moyie, in Nelson.

According to the newspaper evidence the Moyie team tended to cheat a lot, by tripping, and general rough play. Clothier, forinstance, was considered a cheap shot artist. At one point, he tripped Frank Patrick, and while the referee wasn't looking, kicked him a couple of times with his skates. Patrick got up and retaliated, jabbing Clothier in the face, which was seen by the referee and cost Frank a penalty. In fact, most of the Nelson team's penalties were for retaliation.

Nelson certainly didn't need to cheat to win, as they smothered Moyie 16-3.

Nelson		Moyie
Bishop, H.	goal	Grady
Patrick, F.	point	Donahoe
Dunne, Tim	cover	Kelly
Patrick, L.	rover	Sherman
Bishop, A	center	Bawlf
Thompson, Joe	lw	Demock
Steel	rw	Clothier

(Others who had tried out for the Moyie team were: Langille, Kamm, Foote, Flemming and Simms.)

Goals: Bishop, A. (7); Patrick, L. (5), Patrick, F. (2); Bawlf (Moyie), (2); Thompson, Joe, (1); Steele, (1); Clothier, (Moyie), (1).

Although it was not celebrated yet, because they were not sure of more league games, this meant that Nelson had won the League Championship.

Rossland made a tour with its intermediate team. (See also KASLO)

Rossland Intermediates		Nelson Intermediates
Cosgriffe	goal	Greyerbiehl
Stanton	point	Riley
Braden	cover	Bell
Davidson & Stanaway	rover	Gore
Griffith (s), G.	center	MacDonald
Demuth, O. (or Demouth)	lw	Miller
Hamilton, B.	rw	Belrose

Rossland defeated New Denver 4-2.
Rossland lost to Kaslo 5-2
Rossland tied Kaslo 4-4
Rossland had 2 other victories.

	Victory	Loss	Tie
Rossland	3	1	1
Nelson		1	
Kaslo	1		1
Sandon		1	
New Denver		1	

Known goals were scored by : Griffith(s), G. (2); Demuth (or Demouth), O., (1); Bell, (1); Gore (1)

(Kaslo's roster may be seen below, in KASLO. Sandon's and New Denver's rosters were probably similar to the ones noted below, in SLOCAN VALLEY.)

Inner-city games

Rossland

The Industrial League seems to have been rendered unofficial or discontinued this year, despite the fact that some of the teams still existed. (See Trail).

Nelson

Nelson City League (Daily News cup)

Only two games were reported, each side winning one, which leaves the question open over who won the trophy.

Victorias (blue & white)		Thistles (red & white)
Bishop, H.	goal	Greyerbiehl
Horswill	point	Patrick, F.
Thompson, Joe	cover	Dunn(e) tim
Gore, George	centre	Bishop, A.
Patrick, L.	rover	Bell, Bob
Steel(e) Les	rw	Belrose, T.
Belrose, G.	lw	Perrier, Arthur (Alf)
Clunis	spare	Sharpe
Palmer (or Balmer)	spare	Miller, Jack

The score of the first game, won by the Victorias, is unknown, the second was 3-2 for the Thistles. The goals in the second game were: Patrick, L., (1); Patrick, F. (1); Perrier, (1); Bishop, A. (1); Balmer (or Palmer) (1).

Lester scored his goal by deking out his Brother Frank and going around him. Frank scored his by going through the whole Victorias team, and also assisted on Perrier's goal. Greyerbiehl stopped a breakaway by Lester by charging out and swiping the goal away from him.

Arthur Perrier was back playing hockey after a few year's absence.

ROSSLAND CARNIVAL

The Giant Powder Cup was now kept by the Rossland team, for having won it three times in a row, albeit by dispute. The Giant Powder company put up another trophy, this time a shield, also called the Hamilton Shield.

A new arrangement was made between the Rink management and the Carnival committee, to ensure that the rink would share in the profits.

Pincher Creek dropped out because there was some question of whether several of their players were professionals.

Spokane enthusiasts agitated for a Spokane hockey team, but even if they had wanted to practise without their old artificial rink, the winter had been too mild to give them even natural ice, and the players of their glory years of 1906-08 had largely dispersed. Hunter Wurtele was still in Spokane, but Ernest McCaugherty was now at Cleveland Ohio, while Tom McCaugherty was in Vancouver. B.C.

The teams entering the Senior championship then were Nelson, Rossland, and Moyie. The Intermediate Teams were Nelson, Rossland and Trail. There were also two Junior Teams from Rossland and Nelson, and two Juvenile teams from Rossland and Nelson.

All games were now played under the "Manitoba Rules," not the rules arbitrarily set down by the Rossland committee, and the two referee system was in place.

However, Eldon Winn was actually still on the hockey committee, along with K.C. Allen, who was both the chairman, and one of the Rossland players. But just before the Carnival started, Eldon Winn caught "la grippe" and was confined to his bed. This boded well for Nelson.

Rossland played Moyie in the first game of the Senior Championship. Both teams were evenly matched. Rossland scored first, when a long shot skipped between the legs of the Moyie goalie, who had been caught napping. But Moyie tied it up when McCreary, the Rossland goaltender, left his crease to clear the puck, but lost it to a Moyie player, who quickly passed to Sherman, who did not miss the open net. In the second half, the afore-mentioned Sherman, was bashed in a scramble and was carried off. The game was delayed for several minutes until he could return. Later, the crush of the spectators was so great a portion of the boundary fence caved in and the game was delayed for 8 minutes, putting it back up. Rossland scored again by swarming the Moyie net, and that was the game winner, makng it 2-1 for Rossland.

Rossland		Moyie
McCreary	goal	Grady
Jost	point	Donahoe (orDonahue)
Allen	cover	Kelly
Dixon	lw	Dimmock
McQueen	rw	Langille
Keating	center	Clothier
Neil	rover	Sherman (possibly W.H.)

Goals: Dixon, (2); Sherman, (1)

Nelson then played Rossland for the International Cup, despite there being no team from outside B.C. in attendance.

The Rossland team had improved and their play showed it as they pressed Nelson from the outset, nearly scoring when the puck hit the post. But Lester Patrick skated through the Rossland team and scored the first goal. After several close calls around the Nelson net, Lester again broke away and scored the second goal. Keating kept Rossland close, however, scoring on a "brilliant," long shot, and the half ended 2-1. In the second half the teams traded goals. Rossland hit the goal post again, while later, their goaltender knocked the puck into his own goal during a scramble. Rossland scored the final goal, but the score ended 5-3 for Nelson. This result gave Nelson the Open, or International Championship.

Nelson		Rossland
Bishop, H.	goal	McCreary
Dunne, T.	point	Jost
Thompson J.	cover	Allen, K.C.
Patrick, L.	rover	Neil, H.
Bishop, A	center	Keating, A.K.
Patrick, Frank	lw	Dixon
Steel	rw	McQueen

Goals: Patrick, Lester, (2); Bishop, A. (2); Allen, (Rossland) (2); Keating, Rossland (1); Unknown credited player for Nelson in a scramble, (1).[22]

Nelson then played Rossland the next day for their first game of the British Columbia Senior Championship. The Rossland lineup was the same, while for Nelson, Frank Patrick was moved back to point, and Joe Thompson took left wing. With Frank back on defense and the Nelson boys utilizing their superior speed, the tired Rossland players were overwhelmed, 10-1. Lester Patrick scored 5 goals, and then left his brother Frank to score the last two goals for Nelson.

---

[22] The Rossland Miner gave one more goal to Lester Patrick, and one less for Archie Bishop, but I have gone with Nelson's report.

Goals: Patrick, Lester, (5); Patrick, Frank, (2); Thompson, (2); Bishop, A, (1); Neil, (1).

As Eldon Wynn was reportedly confined to his bed, one can imagine him gnashing his teeth as the results came in.

The next day Nelson played Moyie for their second match for the B.C. championship. The lineups were the same except that Bawlf had replaced Clothier for Moyie. Frank Patrick played forward again, at left wing, Dunne moving to point. Nelson went ahead 4-0 at the end of the first half. Moyie became somewhat disheartened in the second half, and couldn't stop the relentless Nelson onslaught, finally losing 15-0.

Goals: Bishop, A, (6); Thompson, Joe (4); Patrick, Lester, (2); Patrick, Frank, (2); Steele, (1).

Nelson therefore won the B.C. Senior Championship, with the biggest aggregate margin of goals the province had ever seen. The players received seven individual medals for the Championship, and seven individual lockets for the International Cup. The International trophy was put on display in the window of Toye, Taylor and McQuarrie's office in Nelson.

Much hyperbole was expounded about the new class of hockey being displayed by the Nelson Team, and how it was unlikely anyone could beat them. It was conveniently forgotten that "lowly" Fernie, winners of the Crows Nest Pass League had defeated this Nelson senior team 6-5 the year earlier, the only substantial difference this year being the new presence of Frank Patrick. Furthermore, with Frank Patrick, Nelson had played one close match against Rossland, only winning 5-3. It was also important to note that the Senior Nelson team had only actually played two other teams the whole season, being Rossland and Moyie.

However, having outscored their opponents 71-12, in 6 games, this Nelson team, with two of the greatest Hockey Hall of Famers on it, was undoubtedly the toughest force in the province.

The Rossland paper philosophically explained this defeat by saying, "It is certain that it would be injurious to the Carnival for Rossland to win the hockey championship all the time, as in time, outside teams would not compete."

When the Nelson team had their picture taken, they ensured they would appear in the best light possible by including not only the Giant Powder Shield, and Fraser trophy, but also the Daily News Cup, which they did not win, and the original B.C. Championship Cup, which they also technically did not win. The Daily News Cup was supposed to be awarded to the Thistles or the Victorias, both Nelson city teams, but the result was left open, as the teams had tied. However, the 1904 and 1907 Nelson teams had also included the former B.C. Championship Cup in their team photo, which they also did not win, so it appears it was a tradition. (The city had won the cup three years in a row, 1901-03, and had been awarded the actual cup permanently).

In the Intermediate Championship Rossland defeated Trail 8-2

Rossland Intermediates		Trail Intermediates
Cosgriffe.	goal	Chapman
Stanton	point	Sullivan
Braden	cover	Milligan
Owen	rover	Shorey
Griffith	center	Swartz
Demuth (or Demouth)	lw	Dawson
Hamilton	rw	Weir

Goals scored: Griffith, (4); Hamilton, (2); Braden, (1); Demuth (1); Weir (1); Shorey (1).

Rossland Intermediates then defeated the Nelson Intermediates 4-0.

Nelson Intermediates

Greyerbiehl	goal
Hardy	point
Riley	cover
Gore	rover
MacDonald	centre
Miller	lw
Bellrose	rw

Goals: Hamilton, (1); Owen, (1); Braden (1); Demuth (1);

This meant that Rossland won the Intermediate Championship.

(E. Stanaway, who sometimes played for the Rossland Intermediates, won the skating race championship of B.C.)

Nelson Juniors and Rossland Juniors played to a 4-4 tie, then played 35 minutes of overtime without result. Players mentioned in this game were: Rossland: McDonald, Donahue, Davison, and Nelson: Mathews, Boyes, Hardy. The Juniors then played another game a day later, Nelson finally winning the Junior Championship, 3-2.

Rossland Juniors		Nelson Juniors
Evans	goal	McLeod
Ehlers	point	Mathews
McLane	cover	Hardy
Keating	rover	Miller
Donahue	centre	Grant
Davisdon	rw	Boyes

McDonald   lw   Hardy

In the final game, Hardy scored 2 goals and Grant 1, for Nelson. For Rossland it was Keating and Davidson.

The Nelson paper called these contests the Juvenile championships, but it seems clear that these were actually the Junior teams. There is no record of the Juvenile championship games. It would appear that the Juniors and Juveniles were the same thing this time, reported differently, especially as the above teams were later called the junior teams in a match in Nelson.

THE EDMONTON-NELSON CHALLENGE

After the Rossland Carnival, Nelson challenged the Edmonton Senior team, Champions of the Alberta League, and the challenge was eagerly taken up by Fred Whitcroft, who was still hungry for Champion teams to beat, after losing in the Stanley Cup Final. Two games were to be played, and the lineups were as follows:

Nelson		Edmonton
Bishop, H.	goal	Winchester
Patrick, F.	point	Crowley
Dunne, Tim	cover	Ross, Hugh
Patrick, L.	rover	Boulton
Bishop, A	center	Deeton
Thompson, Joe	lw	Whitcroft, Fred
Steel	rw	Miller

Fred Whitcroft had not only captained the Edmonton team which had challenged the Montreal Wanderers for the Stanley cup and lost twice that season, once in December, and once in January, but he had also defended the cup in 1907 with Kenora, even though he had not been with their winning team two months earlier. Unfortunately he chose the wrong month, and helped to just barely lose the cup back to the Wanderers, scoring two goals.[23] This 1909 rendition of the Edmonton Team, however, had won 12 of their last 13 games, mostly important challenge matches, only losing, barely, in the Stanley Cup Final. They had wrested the "Fit-Reform" cup, a challenge cup for the Western Canadian Championship, from the Maple Leafs of Winnipeg in two separate games, played some league games back in Edmonton, and then successfully defended the Fit-Reform cup against Saskatoon. (In 1910 Edmonton was again the champion of the Alberta League, and challenged for the Stanley Cup, only to lose again to Ottawa.)

Fred Whitcroft was well disposed to bringing in ringers to aid his cause, and as he had used Jack Winchester in goal before, in his Stanley Cup

---

[23] In the excellent book, The Trail of the Stanley Cup, on page 761 of the 1st volume, Charles Coleman has given Fred Whitcroft a star for 1907 indicating he won the Stanley cup. This is not correct, and if one studies the lineups given in the text for the Challenge games of Kenora in Mr. Coleman's book, one will find that Whitcroft is not listed with the winning team, on pages 144 and 145, as indeed, he was not there.

challenges, and as Winchester was the winning goalie for Winnipeg in the Manitoba League, he eagerly attached him to his team for this challenge. (Winchester played one season for the Shamrocks of the NHA in 1910, as indicated in the TOTSC.)

Bert Boulton joined Jack Winchester for a year with the Montreal Shamrocks of the NHA. Hugh Ross was a well known player from Manitoba. Harold Deeton and Jack, or John, or (Hay) Millar, were only nominally Edmonton residents, but helped challenge for the Stanley Cup in 1909 and 1910 with Whitcroft's team. Millar was also a member of the great Renfrew team which played for the right to challenge for the Stanley Cup in 1910, but lost its championship series. He had quit hockey for four years before being enticed back by Whitcroft in 1908.

Bill Crowley had been primarily the team's trainer.

It was indeed a formidable team which traveled to Nelson to challenge the British Columbia champions.

The first game was the best hockey seen in Nelson up to that time, and probably the best in British Columbia. The Edmonton seven's teamwork and passing was more precise and practiced than that of Nelson, but Nelson's defense was extremely strong, and the Nelson forwards made a point of back checking. Fred Whitcroft for Edmonton scored first, but it was a see-saw battle after that. Archie Bishop tripped or slipped twice just as he had a chance in front of the goal. Dunne and Whitcroft were both sent off for two minutes for a stick duel. Nelson had a power play, as Joe Thompson was tripped by Whitcroft, but Edmonton then scored a short handed goal. Many of the Nelson players made sensational rushes, including Frank Patrick and Lester Patrick, both scoring two goals. At the end of the first period the score was tied two-two. In the second, the see-saw continued, and Edmonton put the last goal in with 3 minutes to go, winning the game 6-5.

Goals: Deeton, (2); Whitcroft, (2); Ross, (2); Patrick, Lester, (2); Patrick, Frank (2); Bishop, A. (1).

Two days later the second game was played. Both teams went at it "hammer and tongs," and it was just as fast and exciting as the first. The Edmonton team remained the same, but two changes were made in the Nelson lineup. Bawlf, from Moyie, replaced Joe Thompson, and Neil of Rossland replaced Les Steel. There is no explanation for this. Joe Thompson and Steel do not seem to be injured, and they played well in the previous game. It seems highly unfair that they would be replaced by outside players, and they were not even designated spares. In fact, as bizarre as it might seem today, the game was stopped completely several times while the player's injuries were attended to, as was the custom, without spares being inserted. Bawlf sustained a leg injury twice; Frank Patrick had a large gash in his forehead, and also collided with the goal post, causing major delays. In fact, when it became clear that Bawlf could no longer play, they actually removed an Edmonton player, Boulton, to even up the game. No substitutions! The knights of winter played until they dropped.

Once again Lester Patrick was forced to play six man hockey, instead of seven, for roughly fifteen minutes, and his team was not the worse for it.

Edmonton had taken a four to one lead in the first half, but in the second half Nelson began to pick up their game, scoring, it appears, on a few power plays. On one occasion a beautiful combination play was performed by

Archie Bishop, to Lester Patrick to Frank Patrick for a goal. Unfortunately, it was too little, too late, and Edmonton won 8-4.

Goals: Millar, (3); Whitcroft (3), Deeton (2); Patrick, L, (2); Patrick, F. (1); Bishop, A. (1).

As usual, there was much banqueting and toasting afterwards. But these matches ended the season for the Nelson Seniors.

In March, a small article appeared in the Ottawa Free Press, picking an all-star team, as the best possible team in Canada, as follows:

Goal – P. Morton, Quebec
Point – Lester Patrick, Nelson
C-Point – Fred Taylor, Ottawa
Rover – Pud Glass, Wanderers
Centre – Frank McGee, Ottawa
R. Wing – Alf Smith, Senators
L. wing – Tom Phillips, Edmonton

Three of these men later played in the Pacific Coast Hockey League, started in 1911.

BOUNDARY

In the Boundary Hockey League Greenwood, Phoenix and Grand Forks, played 8 games each, until Phoenix and Grand Forks were tied at the end of regularly scheduled games. They then played a tie-breaking total goals, 2 game series, in which Grand Forks won the first game 7-2, and Phoenix won the second 5-4, leaving Grand Forks the Victor of the Boundary League (Intermediate) Championship. They sometimes referred to themselves as Intermediates, but they were actually the best Senior teams available. Phoenix could have clinched the whole championship in its last league game against Greenwood, but they withdrew from the game when it became too rough, after 15 minutes. Then, in their last game, against Grand Forks, they practiced for 3 hours just before the game, and tired themselves out so much they lost 9-2, setting up the playoff. One Phoenix player, R. McDonald, pulled himself out of the hospital, against his doctor's advice, to play.

Those who played for the teams were:

Greenwood		Phoenix	Grand Forks
Watson, W.G.	goal	Lackey, S.	Woodland
Dill, S.	point	McDonald, A.	McAlmond
Russell, C.	cover	Simms, S.	Elliott
Meyer, F.	rover	Grant, J.R.	Read
Swain, J.	centre	McKelvie, L.	Mann
Cameron, R.	rt. Wing	Clark(e), R.	Jost
Madill, J.	lt. Wing	McQueen, A.	Longhurst
		McDonald, R.	Baker
		Clunis, C.	

Games:

	Greenwood	Grand Forks	Phoenix
Wins	2	5	5
Losses	6	3	3
Final playoff		1 win 1 loss	1 win 1 loss

Goals: The only known credited goals in regulation games were four by C. Russell for Greenwood, in a 4-3 win over Grand Forks. He scored 3 with his "rush lifts" in regular play and one in overtime.

In the playoffs the only known credited goals were by McQueen (1); McDonald, A, (1).

OKANAGAN

Vernon and Armstrong played a series of challenge matches. Sawyer, the great Vernon goalie, had jumped to Armstrong, possibly as a move to reduce boredom, as he usually won with Vernon. This resulted in his worst ever goals against average of 4.66.

The results were as follows:

	Vernon	Armstrong
1st game	6	2
2nd game	2	2
3rd game	5	3
4th game	1	7

Vernon therefore won the challenge series.

Vernon		Armstrong
Spencer, H..	goal	Sawyer, W.
Birnie, H..	point	Maundrell, A.
McKinnon, A.	cover	Mills, W
French, P.	rover	?
Middleton, W.	center	Hood, W.
Cary, J.	rw	Morrison, P
Speer, S.	lw	Daykin J.

This appears to be the second year that the Armstrong team did not use a rover, and it's possible that they played with only 6 men against 7.

Armstrong Juniors defeated Enderby Juniors 2-1. (This was reported as the 6th game of hockey for Armstrong, and the first it has won.)

Summerland defeated Kelowna 3-2.

Summerland		Kelowna
Rutherford	goal	Fuller
Phinney, N	point	Copeland
McLean	cover	Nirbey
Agur, A.	rover	Barrows
Tingley	center	Fuller
Scaefer	lw	Munson
Agur, E.	rw	McIntyre

Kelowna then defeated Summerland 2-0 in a return match.

KAMLOOPS and AREA

Nicola played a series of games with Merritt for the Haddad Trophy, which Nicola won. Then they put it up again in a series of games with Middlesboro and Merritt. Nicola lost the first game to Middlesboro, but the rest is unknown. Nicola and Kamloops played no games, and Kamloops played only some intra-city games between the CPR, the banks, the high school and one team called "The Orphans." (see Wind and Ice by Glen Cowley.)

SLOCAN VALLEY

The Cornwall Cup was played for by New Denver, Slocan City, Nakusp and Sandon. (The fellow who donated the Cornwall Cup, T.E. Cornwall, was a resident of New Denver, but moved around this time to Spokane, where he was a manager at the Bank of Montreal there.) The Cup was often a challenge cup, as it was this year, and it was supposed that one would have to play at least a two game series for it. Slocan first won the cup from New Denver, and then Slocan put the cup up to challenge Nakusp and won the two games. Slocan also played one game against Sandon which Sandon won, but apparently did not win the cup.

The Teams involved were basically the following: (Sandon and Nakusp not known.)

New Denver		Slocan
Jacobssen, C.	goal	Laires (& tomes)
Byrnis, J. (or Byrne	point	Pinchbeck, J. (or Pinchback)
Wood	cover	Kachtell, J.E. (or Katchell)
Blumeneaus	rover	Tipping, E.
(or Bleaumener or Blumenear, or Blumenaur)		
Gifford, C.	centre	McMillan, R.
Campbell, F.	rw	Hicks, W
Macdonald, C.	lw	Terrey, J. (or Terry)
Baker	?	

Games:	won	loss
Slocan City	4	1
New Denver		2
Nakusp		2
Sandon	1	

Known goals: Tipping, E. (3); McMillan, R. (3); Wood, (2); Campbell, F. (2); MacDonald, C. (1); Baker (1); Terrey (or Terry) (1)

KASLO

Finally Kaslo organized an official club again, after an absence of many years. They actually had to raise money from the club's members to purchase pucks, sticks, nets, etc, as the previous equipment had disappeared. The Kaslo team attempted to arrange their competiion schedule so that they would play "doubleheaders" to save time and travel costs for all teams involved. They also intended to challenge for the silver cup being offered in the Slocan Valley, presumably the Cornwall Cup.

Women began playing in Kaslo as well, but there is no record of a game's result.

Kaslo considered its team to be Intermediate, and they challenged Nelson's Intermediate team, in Kaslo. (Before the Rossland Carnival).

The Kaslo Intermediates defeated the Nelson Intermediates 7-0, in Kaslo. (The Nelson paper also put the score at 6-0.) This is remarkable, as the Kaslo team had hardly had much time to practise, and hadn't had a serious team at all for about 5 years. It was so remarkable, in fact, that the Nelson papers described it as the Kaslo Senior team defeating the Nelson Juniors, neither of which was strictly true. It was true that some of the Nelson team competed as juniors, and the Kaslo players were the best Kaslo had to offer, but they had clearly competed as Intermediates, and had asked for an intermediate team to attend from Nelson. The Kaslonians thought it was one of the greatest games ever played in Kaslo.

Kaslo Intermediates		Nelson Intermediates
Carney, G (Gussie)	goal	Cummins
Blackwell	point	Riley, or Reilly
Anderson	cover	Bell
Burgess, Billy	rover	Bellrose
Jenkins	centre	Gore
McDonald, (Hughie?)	rw	Miller
Carney, Tom	lw	McDonald
Hutchinson	spare/rover	

Goals scored: Carney, Tom, (2); The rest unknown.

After the Rossland Carnival, Kaslo Juniors played a true Nelson Junior team in Kaslo, and the Nelson juniors won 7-2.

Kaslo Juniors		Nelson Juniors
Larmouth, N.	goal	Boyes, T.
Green, Howard	point	Kinehan, H.
Mackay, W.	cover	Whitehead, R.
White, Clarence	rover	Grant, F.
Zwicky, Everett	centre	Lyonais, D.
Dedolph, Walter	rw	Ogenski, F.
Tapanilla, Arvid	lw	Patrick, G.

Goals: Grant, 4; White, 1; Ogenski 1; Lyonais 1; Whithead 1.

The Nelson Juniors stayed over for a big party, and an impromptu dance was held for the seniors.

Then Kaslo Intermediates met Rossland Intermediates in Kaslo, for what Kaslo called the British Columbia Championship. Rossland did hold the title, after the Rossland Carnival, but they certainly didn't consider this another championship series.. However, they played a double header that was fiercely fought for. In the first match Kaslo defeated Rossland 5-2. In the second match the next day Rossland was leading 4-1 in the second half, when Kaslo poured it on and tied it up in the last minutes, 4-4.

Kaslo Intermediates		Rossland Intermediates
Carney, G	goal	Cosgriff
Blackwell,	point	Staunton
Anderson, A.	cover	Braden
Burgess, Billy	centre	Griffith
Jenkins	rover	Stanaway
McDonald, Hughie	rw	Hamilton
Ware, L.	lw	Demuth

(Goals by on next page)

Goals: FIRST GAME: Hamilton, 1; Burgess, 2; Jenkins, 2; Griffith, 1; McDonald, 1.

Goals: SECOND GAME: Stanaway, 2; Burgess, 1; Jenkins, 2; Griffith, 2; McDonald, 1.

Kaslo Intermediates then travelled to Rossland in March, after the Rosslander's tour was over, and played a return match. The teams were basically the same, except that McDonald was in goal for Kaslo, not Carney, who now played right wing, and Sawyer (?) replaced Blackwell, and Jackson replaced Ware. Rossland was ahead 3-2 at the first half, but Kaslo tied it up in the second, only to see Rossland put the final goal in the net with only one minuite left, ending the game 4-3 for Rossland.

Goals: Jenkins, (2); Demuth, (1); Hamilton, (1); Griffith, (1); Burgess, (1); Stanaway, (1).

A Nelson Junior (or High School) Team travelled to Kaslo and challenged their Junior team, possibly mixed with the Intermediate team. The Nelson Juniors were so overmatched, that the referree began to penalize the Kaslo players for ridiculous infractions, just to try to even things up. At one time he had four Kaslo players off the ice, but it didn't seem to help Nelson much. Kaslo still won 13 to 3. The Nelson paper did not report the game.

REVELSTOKE

In Revelstoke, a City League was started, giving the city their first game of hockey in two years. The YMCA beat the Bankers 5-2. Three players were named, but not the teams they played for: Peterson, Hope, and J.H. Armstrong, who twisted his ankle badly. The CPR was to play games as well, but further results are not known.

JUNIORS

An inter-city Juvenile match took place in Nelson. The Maple Leafs won by a score of 1-0 on a goal by O'Malley.

Maple Leafs		Junior Thistles
Madden, C.	goal	Whitelaw, B.
Fennel, V..	point	Leslie, J.
O'Malley, C.	cover	Mastberg V.
Grant, F.	rover	Wolverton, J.
Lyonnais, D.	center	Whitehead, R.
Madden, T	lw	McQuarrie, D.
Ogenski, F. (or Ogensky)	rw	Gibson, D.

Both teams played another game, won again by the Maple Leafs 3-0, on goals by Grant and Ogensky. Some changes in the lineups included, C. Patrick now playing for the Maple Leafs, as point, and T. Boyes playing goal, instead of Madden, who played left wing; Kinahan playing coverpoint, instead of O'Malley, who didn't play; and for the Junior Thistles, A. Simons now played point, D. McQuarrie played coverpoint, Whitehead was rover, Wolverton was center, Gibson played rw, and J. Leslie replaced Mastberg, playing left wing.

The most significant thing about these games was the inclusion of C. Patrick, playing point. Was this another member of the famous Patrick family? It appears to be so, but not in the way one might expect. Lester and Frank had no children yet, and their children wouldn't be teenagers anyway. The only Patricks listed in Nelson were the famous logging/hockey family, and Joe Patrick did have many other children, but none of the boys had names that started with C. He did, however, have a girl, named Cynda, who was then about 20. Was a girl, a young woman, asked to join the Junior Maple Leafs team?

One would have to have evidence that Cynda actually played hockey, for this supposition to gain further merit. Eric Whitehead's biography of the Patricks never mentions any hockey being played by female Patricks. But the Nelson newspapers do. There had been female games of hockey in Nelson for many years, but in 1910, as will be seen in the next chapter, female hockey expands enormously in Nelson, and Cynda Patrick is listed prominently as one if its mainstays, taking the position of Manager of the Nelson Ladies Hockey Team (or teams), and usually playing point or cover-point, just like her famous brother. In fact, her sister, Dora, about two years younger, was also an active player.

No one thought much about this at the time, but considering that many court cases have taken place in recent decades to allow girls to play on boys teams, one might find this possible historical precedent of interest.

Another possibility is that this was a misspelling of Guy Patrick's first initial, as he had also apparently begun to play hockey, but he was a juvenile at this time, not really a junior, and the Maple leafs were a junior team.

The Nelson Public School and High School played a game, the public school winning 3-1.

High school		Public school
Emory, C.	goal	Whitehead, R.
Grizelle, P.	point	Newitt, M.
Decew, R.	cover	Grizzelle, C.
Graham, a..	rover	Ferguson, J.
Svobodia, H.	center	Ferguson, W.
Gibbs, H.	rw	Grant, F.
Poupore, A.	lw	Garde, F.

Another game took place between these teams, with a tie score, 2-2. The lineup changed somewhat, with Mathew (or Matthew) playing point Pearcey playing centre, B. Grizelle (or Grizzelle) playing centre, and for the Public school, Richardson replaced Grant.

The Nelson Juniors played the Rossland juniors directly after the last Edmonton Game.

Rossland Juniors		Nelson Juniors
Evans.	goal	McLeod
Ellers	point	Brown
McLean	cover	Miller
Keeting	rover	Mathews
Donahue	center	Grant
MacDonald	lw	Boyce
Boyce	rw	Cummins

Ellers broke his skate and had to retire, replaced by Owens. Nelson won 8-4.

Goals: Grant, (3); Keeting (3); Mathew, (2); Cummins, (2); Miller (1), Davidson, (1).

The Juniors then played the high school team, and won 7-0. Hardle replaced Mathews for the Juniors, and the High school team had Hartin in goal, and included Brett, Waters, Mathew, and Newitt.

Goals were scored by: Grant (2); Brown, (2); Boyes, (2); and Hardle (1).

The High School Team then beat the Juniors 5-3. A change of goalies may have served to make the difference, Newburn in for McLeod, of the Juniors.

The Junior Team (Now called the Junior Wanderers) then defeated the public school team 1-0 on a goal by J. Grant.

Public School	Nelson Juniors
Positions unknown	
Richardson, N.	McLeod, N.
Ferguson, J.Ellers	Grant, F. Brown
Ferguson, w.McLean	Grant, J.Miller
Hardle, D.	Pourpore, A.Mathews

The Junior Wanderers then defeated the High school 5-2.

High School		Nelson Juniors
Turner, D..	goal	McLeod, N.
Waters, S.	point	Boyce, G.
Brett	cover	Miller, A.
Newitt	rover	Cummins, T.
Grizzelle	centre	Grant, J..
Mathew	lw	Hardy, D.
Poupore, A.	rw	Brown, R.

The High School Team played one more game against the Public School, winning 4-1.

High School		Public School
Hardy, D.	goal	Whitehead, R.
Svoboda, H.	point	Grizzelle, C.
Poupore, A.	cover	Richardson, N.
Mathew, W.	rover	Garde, F.
Grizzelle, P.	centre	Ferguson, W.
Graham, A.	rw	Ferguson, J.

Left wing not given

(See also KASLO, ROSSLAND CARNIVAL, etc.)

CROW'S NEST

In the Crow's Nest Pass, the following results took place:

Moyie tied Coleman Alberta 3-3.

Moyie defeated Fernie (score unknown).

Moyie defeated Fernie again, 10-5.

Moyie tied Coleman 6-6.

Coleman defeated Fernie, 6-1.

It appears that these games were challenge, or exhibition games, and no one claimed the championship of the Crow's Nest Pass, or at least not in the newspaper reports.

TRAIL

City results were sparse this year. As indicated in ROSSLAND, the City Industrial League might have been discontinued.

The Arlington and Crown Point teams challenged but the result is not available.

The Le Roi and Rocky Mountain Rangers of Rossland tied. Trail was to play the winners. Result is not available.

GOLDEN

No mention of hockey.

VANCOUVER

On January first, New Year's day, 1909, British Columbia had its first hockey fatality. On Trout Lake, in Vancouver, a pickup game of hockey was started on very thin ice. The players included Edward Hughes, who worked at Phillips' Gents Furnishing store in New Westminster; A. Pringle, The Columbian Newspaper city editor, (New Westminster); and W.E. Sinclair, a New Westminster shoe merchant. During the game, Hughes and Pringle collided and a weak part of the ice gave way. Pringle could swim, and dragged himself out, but Hughes could not, and struggled against the ice, which broke at his touch. Pringle jumped back into the lake, trying to save Hughes, while the others threw in boards for them to hang on to, but Hughes was so exhausted, he slipped under the water, and couldn't get back up, drowning. The body was later dredged up.

Several days later, at Trout Lake, another young man severed his own artery with his skates, and lost consciousness from loss of blood, but recovered. Later, one young man received a nasty gash across the face while playing hockey, and another was cut on the wrist by a skate.

The New Westminster Bankers challenged the Vancouver Bankers, with J.A. Motherwell the contact for New Westminster.

Many Eastern Canadian players were now in Vancouver, for various reasons, and they were itching to play hockey during the short cold snap. Harry Bright, formerly of hockey teams in Brandon Manitoba and Pittsburgh, organized a team of Eastern Canadians to play against a New Westminster team. When the day came, the New Westminster team did not show up in time, so Bright's team played a team composed of "scrubs" from the general population at Trout Lake. At first the "Stars" did very well, but soon their lack of conditioning told, and the scrub team defeated them by a wide margin. The score is not known. Presumably one of the Eastern "Stars" was Tom Phillips, who was notoriously short on conditioning, and who smoked heavily.

Harry Bright had been with Lester Patrick when they both were members of the Brandon team that challenged the Ottawa Silver Seven for the Stanley Cup in 1904, when they lost both games. See TOTSC.

Several thousand skaters were on the small ice surface, throughout the day. One estimate was 3,000 over the course of Sunday, January 10.

The Bankers of New West and Vancouver finally met, after the above game, but "goals came so rapidly that the scorer became confused and did not keep the tally. As a result, a tie was the best that either side could claim."

Recreation Park was reported to be flooded by the city to open more skating surfaces, in the evening, and even dressing rooms were provided. This might have been the Recreation Park on Oak street, between 59th and 64th, in South Vancouver, or the Recreation Grounds, on Powell, between Dunlevy and Jackson, just East of Downtown.

Skating was rampant on Burnaby Lake, and challenges between the Banking teams flew, but there is no record of any game.

Then the cold snap ended.

Plate 28. Nelson Senior Men's Team, 1909. (Showing B.C. Championship shield, International or Open cup, the previous B.C. Championship cup, which this team did not win, and the Daily News Cup, which this team did not win. See Trophies) Player's names starting from top left and proceeding clockwise: Harry Bishop, goal; P.A. Dunne, cover point; Lester Patrick, rover; Joe Thompson, l. wing; G.E. Bellrose, r. wing; R.T. Horswill, point; L.R. Steel, r.wing; Frank Patrick, point; centre photo Archie W. Bishop, centre and captain. Credit: Teck Cominco Metals Ltd. Archives.

Plate 29. Nelson Intermediates, 1909. Back row, left to right: George Gore, rover; D. Hardy, spare; W. Riley, point; J. Bell, cover point and Captain; A. McDonell, [corrected by hand from A. McDonald] Middle row: Bellrose, T., right wing; Harry Bishop, Manager; J. Miller, Left Wing.
Front row: T.C. cummings, goal. Credit Nelson Museum.

Plate 30. The new Nelson Rink, 1909, on Hall Mines Road. From a newspaper photo. Credit: Nelson Museum.

1910 SEASON

Halley's comet arrived this year, ushering in many portents of doom. As Mark Twain predicted, he went out with Halley's comet. To the great detriment of B.C. Hockey, both Lester and Frank Patrick also left, signing on to the Renfrew Creamery Kings, (in Ontario), for the entire 1910 hockey season. This was the highest paid club so far in the history of hockey, and M J. O'Brien, the owner of the team, would stop at no expense to win the Stanley Cup. which, by this time, had been reserved by the trustees for challenges between league champions.

Lester was paid the highest sum for hockey at that time, $3,000, and Frank was paid $2,000. Other greats, such as Cyclone Taylor and Newsey Lalonde were signed as well. A Renfrew paper described the two players after seeing them play some practices: "Lester, despite his six feet odd inches, is as nimble as a dancing master, side steps and hurdles with the agility of a stripling. He is a wonderful skater and stick handler. Frank has Lester's style to a certain extent, but gets away a little faster. [i.e. as Sheelah Castle said, he was lower to the ground]. Each can score, and consequently Renfrew will have the same kind of a skating defence as Ottawa." Unfortunately for O'Brien his highly paid squad did not play up to expectations and failed to win the NHA league championship, finishing third, showing that results from an expensive roster were not guaranteed, even then.

But in Nelson, still the home of the Patrick family, the remaining players were just as eager and inspired for their upcoming season. The West Kootenay League was announced, as usual, but not all of the challenge matches took place. Rossland, for reasons which are unclear, failed to field a senior team for any regular games this season, until the Rossland Carnival.

This was a big year for free agency in the Kootenays, as well as Eastern Canada, as the stars of many teams were head-hunted by others.

Joe Thompson, the stalwart of Nelson, appears to have gone into semi-retirement at this point, becoming a vice president of the Nelson team. It's not clear if he was supplanted by fresh recruits, or whether he decided to step aside.

Nelson Seniors played host to Phoenix, and Harry Bishop was now a forward, leaving one of his brothers in goal. Harry had always been an excellent all-round player, and he was needed on the front lines to replace the lost Patrick presence. Harry's brother, Eddie, took over the goaltending chores, and he was very strong. Phoenix had acquired Rossland's star goalie, Jack McCreary. But the speed of Harry and Archie together, along with Eddie's goaltending, helped Nelson to defeat Phoenix 14-4.

Nelson		Phoenix
Bishop, E.	goal	McCreary, J.
Dunn, Tim	point	McDonald, A.
Steele, Les	cover	Clothier, R.
Bishop, Harry	rover	McKelvy
Bishop, A	center	Clark, R.
Balmer, R.	lw	McQueen, A.
Hackling, E.	rw	Neil, H.

Goals: Bishop, Harry, (6); Bishop, Archie, (5); Dunn(e), (1); Hackling, (1); Clark, (2); Neil (2)

This was the only "League" game played before the Rossland Carnival. After the carnival, Moyie challenged Nelson. Eddie Bishop was back at forward, and Charles, "Flukie" Greyerbiehl was in goal. This was a hard fought contest, with Nelson ahead near the the end of the game, by 5-3, but Moyie scored two goals in the final minutes, making it 5-5.

Nelson		Moyie
Gryerbiehl F. (Flukie)	goal	Grady, H..
Dunn (e), Tim	point	Donahue, J.
Steele, Les	cover	Kelly, H.
Bishop, A	rover	Sheldon, W.
Bishop, H.	center	McWha, P.C.
Balmer, R.	lw	Dixon, J.
Bishop, E.	rw	Dimock, R.

Goals: Bishop, A. (1), Bishop, H.(3); McWha, P.C. (3); Dimock (2) Bishop, E., (1)

Unfortunately attendance was down this year in Nelson, to the point that a game scheduled against Grand Forks was cancelled, since they couldn't assure the Grand Forks team enough gate receipts. This then ended the Kootenay Senior League play, leaving Nelson the ostensible victors, though it was not lauded as such in the papers.

<u>Inner-City</u>

Nelson

The Nelson Inner-City Championship teams played one game. The teams were the Thistles, wearing purple and white, and the Victorias, wearing blue and white. The result was a tie, 7-7. Harry Bishop continued to shine as a forward. This was the only game played, so the City championship was left undecided, once again.

Thistles		Victorias
Bishop, Ed	goal	Greyerbiehl, F.
Newitt, N.	point	Dunn(e) , T.
Steel(e), Les	cover	Miller, J.
Bishop, H	rover	Bishop, A.
Riley, W.	center	Nagle, O.
Miller, S.	lw	McDonnell, A.
Perrier, A.	rw	Bell, R.(Bob)

Goals: Bishop, Harry, (4); Bishop, A. (3); Bell, r. (2); McDonnell, A. (1); Perrier, A. (2); Miller, S. (1); Nagle, O. (1)

KASLO and the SLOCAN

A new skating rink was built in Sandon this year, with the labour of its construction donated by the citizens. However, there is no record of hockey games available.

An Intermediate Men's League was organized in the Kootenay-Slocan area, with a cup to be fought for called "The Member's Cup."

Nelson categorized Kaslo's team as Seniors, but they were clearly Intermediate. i.e. they only competed in Intermediate contests, and were generally not considered capable of beating Senior teams. Nelson tended to call them Seniors whenever their own teams lost to the Kaslo Intermediates. Rossland's team, however, was closer to a Senior team.

Rossland first played Kaslo. The Rossland Miner reported a hard fought game, full of spirit and strength, which was evidenced by as many as four players falling to the ice at one time from the strenuous checking. Kaslo was at a slight disadvantage because they were playing on Rossland ice, which was much wider than their own narrow rink. However, the Kaslo men tended to bunch together more when making combination plays, and were hard to break into. Eventually Rossland prevailed 4-3. Initially the Kaslo paper reported this game as being fairly clean, but in later weeks they pointed out that the Rossland players had in fact cheated with tremendous amounts of rough play which had not been called by the Rossland referees.

Kaslo Intermediates (blue and white)		Rossland Intermediates
Hughes, Richard (Dick)	goal	Cosgriff
Blackwell, B.	point	Staunton (or Stanton)
Carney, T.	cover	Braden
Burgess, Billy	rover	Griffith, C.
Jenkins, H.	centre	Griffith, G.
Carney, A.	rw	Demuth
Ware, Louis	lw	Hamilton
Tananilla, O.	spare	

Goals: Griffith, C. (1); Griffith, George, (2); Jenkins, (1); Ware, Louis (2); Hamilton, (1)

Then Kaslo travelled to Nelson, and crushed them 11-1.

Nelson Intermediates		Kaslo Intermediates
Bishop, E.	goal/forward	Hughes, R. (just goal)
Stewart, N. (or S.)	point	Carney, T.
Miller, J.	cover	Blackwell, B.
Nagle, D	rover	Burgess, W.
Bell, J.	center	Jenkins, H.
Riley, W.	rw	Carney, A. (Gussie)
Miller, S.	lw	Ware, L.
Irvine, E.	spare	Anderson, K.
Parks, N.	spare	Tapanilla, Oscar
Grant, S.	spare	
Greyerbiehl, Flukie	goalie (one game)	

Goals: Burgess, B. (4); Ware, L. (2); Jenkins, H. (3) Parks, N. (1) Blackwell, B. (1); Carney, T. (1)

In a return game, in Kaslo, Nelson put up a slightly better fight, but the result was still 14-3 for Kaslo. This was a hard fought game, with many penalties for fighting, and in one case pulling of hair. Billy Burgess was smashed up and had to leave the game.

Return Game:
Goals: Jenkins, H. (7); Carney, A. (1); Ware, L. (2); Riley, W. (1); Bishop, Eddie (1); Burgess, W. (1); Carney, G. (1) ; Miler, J. (1) "Bouncy", (1), (Unknown to whom this nickname is referring, but it might be Riley); One goal unknown, (although it might have been Burgess).

Nelson and Rossland Intermediates then met. This was one of the roughest and dirtiest games ever played in British Columbia. Both teams were guilty of these tactics and the "fence" had many men sent to it. Stanton and Eddie Bishop had a prolonged fight which stopped the game for several minutes, including the time they were rolling around on the ice together. Demuth of Rossland was tripped and slammed the back of his head on the ice and was unconscious for several minutes. The game was delayed until he came to, and was back in the fight. Riley of Nelson was pushed so hard into the fence that he was knocked out. But he was brought back into consciousness and play then resumed. George Griffith and S. Miller started a fight at the end of the game, where all the players tried to pull them off each other, and time then ran out, with the score tied 3-3. (Archie Bishop, the referee, decided not to allow the game to be played off in overtime.)

Goals: Riley, (1); Bishop, E. (1); Demuth, (1); Griffith, (1); Hamilton, (1); one unknown goal for Nelson.

Nelson Intermediates travelled to Salmo, although this was not entirely an official game for the Member's Cup. "Flukie" Greyerbiehl played goal for Nelson. When C. Cummins of Salmo got knocked out by the puck, Eddie

Bishop, who was playing out of goal this time, dropped out from the Nelson team to even up. Nelson won 6-4.

Salmo

Feeney, B.	goal
Mernett, R.	point
Bell, B.B.	cover
Lindow, C.	rover
Cummins, C.	center
McArthur, F.	rw
Ferry, S.	lw
Mascot Hamlet	spare

Kaslo had to wait until after the Rossland Carnival for Rossland to play their return game, and settle the Member's Cup championship. (Intermediate Championship of the Kootenays). There was much grumbling over this, but Kaslo also sent their Intermediate team to compete at the Carnival. (See Rossland Carnival).

A player named Goodwin was a player on a Kaslo "scrub" team.

Finally, after the Carnival, Rossland met Kaslo in the deciding game for the Member's Cup. The referees, (who were not from Rossland), read the "riot act" to the players before hand, and the game was played without much violence. The Rosslanders still used their superior weight to advantage, however, and also revived the vanishing tactic of "lofting" as their defensemen constantly flipped the puck high into the air and down to their opponent's end. They were also still cheating by playing three men, (according to Kaslo), who had played more than two games on the Senior team, in particular Jack Donahue, one of the Rossland Seniors stars, who was also playing for the Moyie Senior team.

The Kaslo team, however, had speed, making many individual rushes. Billy Burgess was again smashed so badly he couldn't play and had to go to the hospital with a severely injured hip. Rossland was well ahead at half time, 6-3. But Kaslo roared back in the second half and evened the score, lost it again, and then tied it up in the last two minutes, leaving the score 8-8. There was no overtime played.

Goals: Jenkins, (2); Davidson,(1); Burgess, (2); 7 unknown goals for Rossland; 1 unknown goal for Kaslo.

The Kaslo team was basically the same as previous games. Rossland had Cosgriff, Stanton, Demuth, Davidson, Griffiths, Ketcheson, and Jack Donahue.

This was the end of the Intermediate circuit games, and no winner was announced in the papers, with Rossland ostensibly winning the Championship, and the "Member's Cup." It could be said that Kaslo and Rossland tied, however, with same number of points. But Rossland had beaten and tied Kaslo.

Final Standings: (As reported by Kaslo)

	W	L	T
Rossland	2	0	1
Kaslo	2	1	1
Nelson	0	3	1

In other games in the area, the Gerrard team played the Trout Lake team, with Trout Lake winning 3-2.

Gerrard		Trout Lake
Madden, Bob	goal	?
Hillman, Lance	?	
Simpson, Jack	?	
Fitzsimmons, "Cap"	?	

Ferguson played a game against Trout Lake, but did not offer their challenge cup, making the game a "friendly" one. Ferguson won 4-2. These two teams then decided to play for a cash prize of five hundred dollars a side, on the Trout Lake rink. Trout Lake then turned the tables and won 3-1.

Trout Lake		Ferguson
Gorrell	?	Cummings
Barber	?	

THE BOUNDARY

The BOUNDARY SENIOR LEAGUE was the most organized, with three teams playing a fairly regular schedule.

Greenwood salted its team this year with very experienced players, including a mysterious, ex-stanley Cup member. He was never named, but it could have been the McDonald who played for Ottawa in 1905, or George Cameron, who played for Montreal from 1904-1908. See TTOTSC.
Greenwood beat Phoenix 4-3.
Greenwood beat Grand Forks 3-1, (2 goals in two five minute overtime periods)
Phoenix beat Grand Forks, 5-1.
Grand Forks beat Phoenix, 5-2.
Phoenix beat Greenwood 2-1.
Phoenix beat Greenwood 4-3.
Grand Forks beat Greenwood 5-1. Greenwood only played under protest, but it's not clear what the protest was.
Then Greenwood defeated Grand Forks 6-1.

Then there was some kind of difficulty and Phoenix didn't play the two games they should have.

In March two final games were played:
Greenwood defeated Phoenix 8-5.
Greenwood defeated Grand forks 3-2.

Greenwood then became the the Boundary Champion.

In the middle of these games, Miller and Lang of Grand Forks went with the Greenwood team to play in the Rossland Carnival.

Greenwood		Phoenix
Watson,	goal	McQuerrie, J. (actually Jack McCreary)
Russell, C.	point	Sims
McDonald	cover	McKelvey, L.
Bloomfield	rover	Clark, Roy
Clerf	center	Clothier, Roy
Cameron	rw	McQueen, A.
Rochon	lw	Neill, H.
Russell, Cliff	spare	

Grand Forks

Lang, Bert	goal
McAlmon	point
Mann, Art	cover
Miller	rover
Reid, Bert	center
Baker	rw
Quinn, (Barney)	lw

(According to Denny Boyd's History of Hockey in B.C., Art Mann and Barney Quinn, were two hockey playing doctors from Toronto.)

ROSSLAND CARNIVAL

Eldon Winn was nowhere in sight. He does not appear this year in any hockey activity, and the Rossland committee did not contain any of the regular members of the Rossland Senior Team. Once again, Nelson was given an unbiased field on which to play.

A judge of play was again added to every game, so that there were two referees on the ice at all times. However, this did not seem to make much difference in terms of roughness.

Spokane once again tried to put together a team to challenge for the carnival, but it did not come to pass. The names E. McGaugherty, T. McGaugherty, Wurtele, Tatro, Trezona, and Deakin were suggested, along with Robertson, Cardiff, and McBurney. However, nothing came of the talk.

Rossland brought in two ringers from Vancouver, Ed Longfellow, who had played left wing in Fort William, (Quebec or Ontario?), the previous winter, and W. Treherne, who was well known in Brandon and Winnipeg. They also had acquired one of the former stars from Spokane, Tom McGaugherty. (It's not absolutely certain that this is Tom, and not his brother Ernest, but it appears likely). Moyie was still employing Rossland's former star defenseman, Jack Donahue, as well as one of their top scorers, Dixon. Rossland was still without their top goaltender, McCreary, who was playing for Phoenix.

Rossland's first game was in the Open competition, against Moyie. Rossland went ahead 3-1 at the end of the first half. Rossland then went up 5-1 in the second half, and it looked like it was all over, but then Moyie began battling back. Moyie overtook Rossland 6-5, and Rossland was barely able to score a tying goal in the last minute. They then played two five minute periods of overtime. There was no score in the first, but then Moyie scored in the second, and that stood as the winner as time ran out, Moyie finishing ahead 7-6.

Rossland Seniors		Moyie Seniors
Cosgriff	goal	Grady, H..
Stanaway, Ed	point	Donahue, J.
McGaugherty	cover	Kelly, H.
Davison	rover	Sheldon, W.
Treherne, W.	center	McWha, P.C.
Longfellow	lw	Dixon, J.
Demuth	rw	Dimock, R.
Keating, A.	spare	Bloomfield
	spare	Sheridan

Goals: Davison, (1); Treherne, (2); Keating, (3); Longfellow, (1); Demuth, (1); McWha, (1); Dimock, (2); one unknown for Rossland; one unknown for Moyie.

Nelson and Phoenix then played an Open game. It was a bit rough, but not unusually so. Nelson was the best at combination plays, while Phoenix was very good at rushing up the ice. In the end, the experience and finesse of Nelson won out, as they won 9-5, advancing to the finals of the Open competition. Nelson seems to have been given one bye, i.e. they had to play one less game than Rossland or Moyie.

Nelson Seniors		Phoenix Seniors
Bishop, E.	goal	McCreary, J.
Dunn, T.	point	Clothier
Steele, L.	cover	Quinn
Bishop, H.	centre	Kelvie
Bishop, A.	rover	Clark
Balmer, R.	rw	McQueen
Hackling, E.	lw	Neill

Goals: Bishop, H. (2); Bishop, A, (2); Neill, (2); 5 goals unknown by Nelson; 3 goals unknown by Phoenix.

Greenwood then played Moyie to see who would advance to play Nelson in the final. This game was particularly rough and bloody. Greenwood smashed up the Moyie team as far as the referees would allow, and the refs didn't seem to care that much. Kelly was bodychecked so hard by Russell that he fell back onto the ice, and the back of his head hit with such a loud bang that it could be heard all over the ice. A doctor immediately administered aid, but it was ten minutes before Kelly came to consciousness, and the game was delayed another 15 minutes before Kelly was ambulatory enough to start playing again. (Apparently concussions were not considered serious.) Russell also checked McWha so hard that he was unable to play for several minutes, and the game was delayed again. Dixon of Moyie was shot in the mouth with the puck and four teeth were knocked out, as well as a lot of blood. Jack Donahue was shot in the face with the puck and knocked out. In all, these interruptions caused the game to last an extra hour. No one seems to have thought of using a spare man. Greenwood's tactics took their toll and they prevailed, eliminating Moyie 4-1.

Greenwood Seniors

Lang, Bert	goal
Russell	point
McDonald	cover
Bloomfield	rover
Miller	centre
Cameron	rw
Rochon	lw

Goals: McWha, (1); Cameron, (2); Russell, (1); Bloomfield, (1).

Nelson then played Greenwood for the Final of the Open Championship. Nelson took a two nothing lead early on two goals by Archie Bishop, but Greenwood came right back, and by the first half, Greenwood had gone ahead 4-3. In the first half, one of the Greenwood men had been hurt and was unable to play. In the second half, they tried to put in a substitute, but, incredibly, the Nelson team refused this. Nelson also refused to drop one of their own men. Greenwood appealed to the committee, who deliberated for a "lengthy interval," and then finally ruled in favor of Nelson. Apparently teams were within their rights to force another team to play shorthanded. Play resumed, and Greenwood played a man down, for what was eventually over thirty minutes. Incredibly, they still won, beating Nelson 7-6, to take the Open championship. One more time, it had been proven that six man hockey was better than seven man hockey, but no one seemed to be taking note.

Goals: Bishop, A. (2); Bishop, H. (1); Bloomfield, (2); Cameron, (1); four goals unknown for Greenwood; 3 goals unknown for Nelson.

In the first game for the B.C. Championships, Rossland played Phoenix. Phoenix jumped out to a 4-0 lead after the first period. Rossland had one goal disallowed for being offside. In the second half Rossland put up a better fight, but they couldn't erase the deficit, and ended up losing 9-5.

Goals: McQueen, (3); Neill, (2); Clark, (1); Demuth, (1); McGaugherty, (1); Stanaway, (1); McKelvey, (1); two unknown goals for Phoenix; two unknown goals for Rossland.

In the next game Nelson played Moyie. At the end of the first half Moyie was ahead 4-3. Nelson went ahead by 7-5 in the second half, but Moyie battled back and tied it up before the game ended. They then played two five minute periods of overtime, and Nelson scored in both, while Moyie did not score, leaving Nelson the victors, 9-7.

Goals: Bishop, A. (2); Dimock, (5); Bishop, H. (1); McWha, (1); Sheridan, (1); six unknown goals for Nelson.

Phoenix then played Greenwood. Both teams were tired, and decided to play only six men a side. Phoenix won out 5-4. (The Nelson paper put the score 6-4).

Goals: Neill, (3); Clark, (2); McQueen, (1); Cameron, (1); Bloomfield, (1)

Then Phoenix played Nelson for the final B.C. Championship game. (Nelson appears to have been given some kind of bye in the semi-finals, only being required to play one game, while Phoenix had to play two.) Phoenix was forced to play this final game in the evening of the same day as their last game against Greenwood, and they were very tired. Nelson won 6-1, retaining the B.C. Senior championship. Harry and Archie Bishop scored the six goals between them, although it is not specified how many each scored.

Goals: Bishop, Archie, (probably) (3); Bishop, Harry, (probably) (3); Russell, Cliffe, (1). Cliff Russell was probably borrowed from Greenwood for the game.

The Nelson Daily News had the results all screwed up and confused. The Vancouver Province and the Rossland Miner agreed in all aspects, and the Rossland paper's correspondent seemed to be at the games, while the Nelson reporter did not.

Rossland Intermediates defeated Trail Intermediates 10-0. According to the Rossland newspaper, Cosgriff, the Rossland goalie had so little to do he almost froze to death.

Trail Intermediates		Rossland Intermediates
Truswell	goal	Cosgriff
Ellis	point	Staunton (or Stanton)
Booth	cover	Braden
Morgan	rover	Griffith, C.
Weir	centre	Griffith, G.
Milligan	rw	Jewell
Swartz	lw	Donahue, P. (Phil)

Goals: Griffith, C. (3); Griffith, G. (2); Donahue, Phil, (4); Jewell, (1)

Rossland then played Kaslo for the final of the Intermediate Championships. Kaslo was ahead 5-3 after the first half. But Rossland battled back, and finally won the game 7-6. This gave Rossland the Intermediate Championships three years in a row.

Kaslo Intermediates (blue and white)

Hughes, Richard (Dick)	goal
Blackwell, Bert	point
Carney, T.	cover
Burgess, Billy	rover
Jenkins, H.	centre
Carney, G.	rw
Ware, L.	lw
McDonald, Hughie	spare

There is no indication of any Junior Championship games being played.

The CROW'S NEST

Moyie defeated Fernie 12-2. (This is probably Senior play.)

The Coleman Alberta team travelled to Moyie, where a close game took place. But after about 3 minutes of the second half, with the score tied 2-2, Coleman withdrew. As one newspaper correspondent from Moyie viewed it: "to the disgust and disappointment of practically all the spectators the game came to an end. The Coleman players were practically all in, and one of them found that he was in no condition to continue, and the wearers of yellow and black wanted Moyie to drop off a man and play six men only. This was declined, although Moyie expressed willingness to allow Hogan, Coleman's spare man, to take White's place, who was sick. The Coleman team would not agree to this, and quit the ice. After waiting the required time the Moyie boys put the puck between the undefended posts and obtained the necessary goal to claim the game."

Coleman	
White	position?
Hogan	spare

There might have been more games in the Crow's Nest, but these records were not found by this author. Presumably Moyie became the League Champions.

SANDON

Sandon challenged Cody to a game in its new rink, and the Sandon Mayor put up a trophy for the series. The score was tied 1-1. Since no further games were reported, it is unknown who won the cup. (There are no known Sandon newspaper archives after 1903).

Sandon		Cody
Kelson, J.	goal	McKaskill, J.
Murphy, D.	point	Hughie, J.
Shelland, A.	cover	Cameron, E.A.
Vucovitch, N.	centre	Fox, T.
Racine, C.	rover	Grant, J.
Holinquest, A.	lw	McFarlane, J.
Foley, J.T.	rw	Trnary, T.

Goals: Fox, T. (1); Holinquest, or Foley, (1);

TRAIL

Trail Intermediates, who were essentially the Trail Seniors, but who normally only played in Intermediate games, played the Rossland Intermediates, who won 8-2.

Rossland Intermediates		Trail Intermediates
Cosgriffe, F.	goal	Chapman, A.
Stanton, H.	point	Mulligan, F.
Braden, A.	cover	Benan, V.
Griffith, C.	rover	Shorey, P.
Griffith, G.	center	Morgan, R.
Demuth, O.	lw	McGlaughlin, R.
Hamilton, R.	rw	Swartz, R.

(Weir was also named as playing goalie at some point for Trail)

Goals: Griffith, George, (1); Griffith, C. (1); Demuth, O. (1); Hamilton, B. (1); Shorey, (1); Swartz (1); 4 goals for Rossland unaccredited.

The Crown Point hotel (boarders) defeated the Arlington Hotel 6-2.

Crown Point	Arlington
Positions not known	
Sinclair, George	Acton, Bill
Ogden, Joe	Williamson, Cliff
Ray, Fred	Scott, Joe

The Central Hotel defeated the Meakin Hotel 8-2.

The Boilermakers defeated the Machinists 2-0.

Trail Juveniles defeated Rossland Juveniles 2-1.

Trail Juveniles tied Nelson Juveniles 4-4. (The Trail Juveniles played seven games this season, winning 3, losing 3 and tieing 1.)

Trail Seniors defeated the Rossland Clerks in an Industrial League game by a score of 5-2. George Milligan of Trail was body checked into the boards so hard he had to leave the game. The game then continued with 6 men a side.

Trail

Chapman	goal
Sullivan	point
Milligan, F.	cover-point
Shorey	rover
Swartz	forward
Morgan	forward
Milligan, George	forward

Rossland then defeated Trail in an "Industrial League" game, 6-0, but it is not known to which of these Rossland and Trail teams this refers.

If there was an official Industrial League this season, there is no indication of who actually won it. There is no mention of the Le Roi, or Centre Star Mine teams, the perrenial favorites.

According to Trail On Ice, in 1910, the Rossland Intermediates beat the Trail Intermediates in 6 straight games. Then Trail went on a barnstorming tour that saw them beat teams in Nelson, Kaslo, Sandon, New Denver and Slocan City.

JUNIOR Competition

In Nelson several Junior teams were formed, including a cream of the crop distillation, made up of the best players from the previous year. This team was first called the Stars, and then later was called the Rovers. However, in its first challenge game, against the previous team called the Juniors, the Rovers were beaten easily by the Juniors, who had had much more weight.

Nelson Rovers (Juniors)		Nelson Juniors
Boyes, T.	goal	Wilkinson
Grizzelle, C.	point	Miller
Svoboda, H.	cover	Brown, R. (Captain)
Mathew, E.	rover	Grizzelle, P.
Grant, J.	center	Boyes, G.
Ferguson, W.	lw	Newitt
Ferguson, John	rw	Cummins
Emory, C.	spare goal	

Goals: Grizzelle, P. or Cummins, (1); Newitt or Cummins, (1); Boyes, G. (1); Ferguson, John, (1);

Note: The score is not known because the page for January 8, 1910, appears to be missing.

The Nelson "Juveniles" then played the Kaslo Juniors. It's not known what the difference was between Juniors and Juveniles in this case, except that Nelson habitually downgraded its team designations so as to seem the underdog. Nelson won 3-2 in overtime.

Nelson "Juveniles"		Kaslo Juniors
Bois, T. (or Boyes)	goal	Vallance, E.
McPhee, G.	point	Woodland, T.
Kinahan, H.	cover	Zwickey, E.
Mathew, E.	rover	White, C.
Grant, Fred.	center	Mackay, W.
Bard, P.	rw	Dedolph, W.
Lyonnaise, D.	lw	Tapanilla, A

Goals: Grant, Fred, (2); Bard, P. (1); the Kaslo goals are unknown.

The Nelson Juveniles then played the Nelson Rovers, and beat them 9-1. There is no indication of who played centre for the Rovers, and it's possible they played 6 against 7.

Nelson Juveniles		Nelson Rovers
Bois, T. (or Boyes, or Boise)	goal	Miller, R..
McPhee, G.	point	Mathews, E.
Kinahan, H. (or Kinnahan)	cover	Svoboda, H.
Grant, F.	rover	Ferguson, J.
Grant, J.	center	?
Bard, P.	rw	Graham, A.
Whitehead, R.	lw	Miller, C.

The Nelson Rovers then played the "Challengers" and finally won a game, 9-1. The roster of these junior teams was an ever changing affair, but the challengers were also later considered the regular Junior team.

Nelson Challengers		Nelson Rovers
Riley, R.	goal	Boyce, T..
Gunn, W..	point	Grizelle, C.
Parks, F.	cover	Svoboda, H.
Cummins, F.	rover	Mathew, E..
Patterson, W.	center	Ferguson, W.
Murphy, E.	rw	Ferguson, J.
McKinnon, L.	lw	Grant, J.

The Nelson Rovers then played the Mic-Macs, and lost 5-1. Despite these generally poor results, the Rovers later went on a tour.

Nelson Mic-Macs		Nelson Rovers
Riley, R.	goal	Boyes J.
Gunn, W..	point	Grizzelle, C..
Cummins, F.	cover	Ferguson, W..
Parks, F.	rover	Svoboda, H..
Patterson, W.	center	Mathew, E.
McKinnon, L.	rw	Ferguson, J.
Murphy, E.	lw	Grant, J.

The Nelson "Juveniles" then played Kaslo again, beating Kaslo 4-1.

Nelson Juveniles		Kaslo Juniors
Bois, T. (or Boyes)	goal	Woodland, George
McPhee, G.	point	Woodland, G.
Wolverton, J.	cover	Zwickey, E. (or Swickey)
Grant, F.	rover	White, C.
Bard, P..	center	Glegrich, H.
Whitehead, R.	lw	Dedolph, W.
Lyonnaise, D.	rw	Tapanilla, A (or Tapinala)

Goals: White, C. (1); Grant, Fred,(3); Whitehead, R. (1)

The Rovers then defeated the "Shamrocks" 2-0. Few details are known.

Goals: Grant, J. (1); Matthew, E. (1).

The Nelson High School formed a league of 3 teams. Division III defeated Division II, 6-5.

Nelson High School Div III		Nelson High School Div. II
Emory, C.	goal	Steele, C..
Whitehead, J.	point	Ferguson, H..
Ferguson, B.	cover	Elliott, A..
Graham, A.	rover	Newitt, S.
Gibbs, H.	center	Pearcy, C.
McQuarrie, D.A.	rw	DeCew, R.
Fletcher, H.	w	Drewry, H.

The High School Teams then seem to have changed their names. A game took place between the Cyclones (Div. II) and Invincibles (Div. III) with the result a tie, 4-4. The teams were exactly the same as above. The Invincibles defeated the Whirlwinds, (Div. I), but the details are unknown.

The Rovers then made a tour of the Boundary area and played two games, against the Intermediate teams of Grand Forks and Greenwood. They played very well against these older teams, but Grand Forks beat them 2-1 and Greenwood beat them 4-3.

Greenwood Intermediates		Nelson Rovers
McMillan, D.	goal	Boyes T.
Russell, C.	point	Grizzelle, C..
McMillan, A.	cover	Svoboda, H..
Oliver, J...	rover	Mathew, E.
McKelvey, W.	center	Grant, J.
McMillan, F.	rw	Ferguson, J..
Summers, G.	lw	Ferguson, w.

The Nelson Juveniles then played the Trail Juveniles in Trail and defeated them 6-2.

The Nelson Rovers then played the Nelson Juniors, achieving a 3-3 tie. The Rovers team was the same as previous, the Juniors were:

cont.

Nelson Juniors

Newburn, W.	goal
Brown, D.	point
Cummins, T..	cover
Grizzell, P...	rover
Newitt, S..	center
Murphy, J.	rw
Boyes, G..	lw

Goals: Newitt, s. (3); Matthew, E. (1); Grant, J. (1);Boyes, G.

At some point the Rovers were able to beat the Juniors, but there is no record of the details. This set up a final confrontation for the Junior championship of Nelson on Feb. 21st. The Newspaper article which describes this battle is completely confusing about who won. The Headline is "Juniors are Champions, Rovers defeated by 5-3." A little further on it again claims that the Rovers lost. But according to the play-by-play, it's clear that the Rovers won the game 5-3. In fact, the correspondent affirms that the Rovers won, at the end of the article. Unfortunately there is no other mention of who won, so it is still unclear. A penalty was actually given in this game for off-side play, the first mention of such an offense receiving 2 minutes against the fence. Body-checking and tripping also were penalties, but a penalty for off-side play was very rare.

Nelson Juniors		Nelson Rovers (black & yellow)
Newburn, W.	goal	Boyes, T. (Fatty)
Brown, R.	point	Grizzelle, C.
Cummins, S. (Taffy)	cover	Svoboda, H.
Grizzelle, P.	rover	Matthew, E.
Newitt, s.	center	Grant, J..
Boyes, G..	rw	Ferguson, J.
Murphy, Ed..	lw	Ferguson, W.

Goals: Boyes, G. (3); Grant, J. (5)

The Rovers were challenge crazy, and they then challenged the Nelson Intermediates, essentially a senior team. The Intermediates crushed the Rovers 12-4. S. Nagle had to drop out as he dislocated his shoulder. Svoboda dropped out of the Rover's side to even things up.

Nelson Intermediates

Greyerbiehl, Flukie	goal
Miller, J.	point
Bell, J	cover
Nagle, S..	rover
Bishop, E.	center
Riley, R.W.	rw
Newitt, S..	lw

Goals: Newitt, S. (6); Grant, J. (4); Matthew, E.(1); Riley (3); Bell, J. (1); Bishop, E. (1); Miller, (1). (There is a discrepancy over the score and the goals scored.)

This ended the Nelson Junior season.

SALMO

Salmo had an inner-city match with two teams called the Hoboes and the Mess. The score was a tie, 1-1. Lindon, and Etter scored.

Salmo Mess		Salmo Hoboes
Watson	goal	Feeney, D.
Archibald.	point	Meran
Bell	cover	Cawley
Murphy	rover	Mifflin
Cummings	center	Lindow (or Lindon)
Donaldson	lw	McArthur
Etter	rw	Feeney, S.

OKANAGAN

Vernon Intermediates and Armstrong Intermediates played a challenge match in Vernon, which was won by Vernon 3-2.

Vernon		Armstrong
Mohr, W.	goal	Johnstone, A.
Reinhard, Gus.F.	point	McCorkendale, J.
Fulmer, Gordon	cover	Barnes, B..
Meyer, B.	rover	Murray, F.
Reinhard, W. E.	center	Maundrell, P.
Owens, A.	rw	Francis, B.
Scribbler, W..	lw	Simington, F.

Goals: Reinhard, W. (2); Meyer, B.; Murray, F.(1)

Vernon then travelled to Armstrong for the return match. Vernon won 10-4. The teams were essentialy the same, however on the Armstrong squad, W. Blackburn replaced B. Barnes, and on the Vernon squad, J. Carey replaced A. Owens.

Goals: Reinhard, W. (4); Carey, J. (2); Fulmer, G. (2); Meyer, B. (1); Reinhard, Gus (1); Murray, F. (2); McCorkindale, J. (1); Francis, B. (1)

Vernon then travelled to Revelstoke for a game and defeated Revelstoke 4-2. The team was quite different, composed of: Spencer, Calhoun, McKinnon, Simms, J.Carey, Elliott, W. Reinhard, and Gus Reinhard and B. Meyer going only as spares. There are no other details.

Vernon then met with defeat at the hands of the Summerland team, 5-4. According to the correspondent, "…the Vernon boys seemed to be considerably off colour, and at times were as languid as if they nwere officiating at a pink tea."

The Vernon team was: Spencer, Calhoun, McKinnon, Simms, W. Reinhard, Carey and Elliott.

The Summerland team was: Johnston, T., McLarne, G. Faulkner, J. Agur, E, Agur, A., Schaefer, K., Church, E.

Summerland then played Kelowna and lost 9-4. It was mentioned that Summerland had thus won 2, lost one and tied one of their last four games, but only the games mentioned above have reported results.

Vernon then defeated Kelowna in Vernon 6-1.

KAMLOOPS

Kamloops had several challenge matches this year, against Nicola and Merritt. One result is available.

Kamloops defeated Nicola in Nicola, 2-1.

Kamloops		Nicola
Rennan, William	goal	Curtin, Doc.
Robb	point	Dancey
McKinnon, Joseph	cover	Charlton.
Hockin	rover	Thomas
Irwin, Fred	center	Richardson
Bauman	rw	Riley, F.
Munn, Thomas	lw	Riley, E.
	spare	Howse

Goals: Munn, Thomas (1); Dancey, (1); Irwin, F. (1)

As Glen Cowley says in "Wind and Ice, "No one knew Nicola and Kamloops would never cross sticks again. The town faded from Hockey and existence but not before earning the right to be Kamloops' first hockey rivals." (Technically Nicola did not fade from existence until about 1960; it was a long, slow fade.)

LADIES

The Nelson Ladies burst into competition this year. With the increase in population and the general increase in hockey experience, there was a surplus of women who wanted to play, seventeen signing up to play on organized teams. An executive of eight was voted in. Cynda Patrick was voted manager. The first newspaper headline announcing it, said: MALES GET OFF THE ICE, Nelson's Charmers Are Taking to Hockey.

The teams were a conglomeration of teenagers and young women. The first inner-city game took place between the Undines and Mermaids. The Undines wore white sweaters and white touques, with green letters straight across their chests. The Mermaids had the same, except their letters were diagonal. Despite the large number of enthusiasts, it was necessary to fill out one team with a man in goal – Jack Grant. This was another gender precedent, but it was only an exhibition game, after all. A newspaper article described this first game thus:

"The Mermaids and the Undines had a slashing hockey practice at the skating rink last night from 7 to 8 o'clock, when they covered themselves with whiteness and glory, incidentally doing the ice some damage, and treating the puck in a way that was positively cruel. At the end of the hour's smart work-out the Undines received the decision from the dazed referee, H. Bishop, the score standing 5-4. The Mermaids were one Mermaid short, and had to play one Merman in goal. Leslie Steel, like an up to date Ulysses, put on smoked glasses and coached the two teams from the fence…"

The goals scored were unknown.

Undines		Mermaids
Elliott, Ida (Captain)	goal	Grant, Jack.
Henders, Lena	point	Grant, Minnie
Patrick, Cynda	cover	Turner, Mrs. Richard
Patrick, Dora	rover	Cavanaugh, Ola (Capt)
Gore, Helen	center	Foote, Winnie
Ellis, Winnie	rw	McLaughlin, Jean
Gigot, Helen	lw	Manhart, Mrs. E.

In the next game, after several practices, the teams changed their names to the Wanderers and the Sterlings. The Wanderers then changed their uniforms to a large green W on white sweaters, with white touques, while the Stirlings had a large white S on green sweaters, with red touques.

The newspaper reporters were fond of hyperbole in reporting the women's games, but hyperbole and romantic metaphor were also found in the reportage of the men's games. The women were not always taken as beginners however, as one reporter said: "the girls know something of hockey. The flashes of speed that some of them could put on and repeat to order, would nearly beat the camera. Every trick of the stick, how to take the puck in mid-career, how to stop a dangerous opposing forward, was displayed to perfection, all but body-checking, and here let it be said that the girl's game was probably the cleanest game ever played in British Columbia....At that the girls stood lots of hard knocks, for they were not shy about hitting the fence, and often an accidental collision would send a pair down....More than once in a whirlwind clash, skates rang sparks, but the maze would unravel, and the puck be coaxed from the melee and a few seconds after winged skates would be pursuing it like Nemesis after the doomed."

If there were any doubt that the women knew how to play, the first goal was scored by Miss Cavanaugh, by lifting it "about twenty feet over a packed mob of players, into the Wanderer's net."

After two half hour periods the game was tied 3-3. They then played two overtime periods of ten minutes each, until the Sterlings scored, again by Ola Cavanaugh.

Wanderers		Sterlings
Elliott, Ida (Captain)	goal	Manhart, Mrs. E..
Patrick, Cynda	point	Foote, Winnifred
Henders, Lena	cover	Goodwin, Belle
Ellis, Winnifred	rover	Gore, Hazel
Patrick, Dora	center	Cavanaugh, Ola
Gilchrist, Lulu	lw	McLaughlin, Jean
Gigot, Helen	rw	Grant, Minnie

Goals: Cavanaugh, Ola, (2); Gigot, Helen (1); Gore, H. (1); Grant, M (1); Gilchrist, Lulu, (1); Henders, L., (1)

Just after the Rossland Carnival, where there were no ladies games, the Grand Forks "Wonders" travelled to Nelson for a challenge match, with the Nelson "All Stars." The Wonders wore red skirts and white sweaters, with red letters, G.F. on their chests, and white touques. The All Stars had dark red skirts, white sweaters, with the letter S on the chest, and red touques.

The Nelson players were faster, but the Grand Forks team was better at "cleverness in handling the puck and combination play." Nelson lost 4-1.

Nelson All Stars		Grand Forks Wonders
Manhart, Mrs. E.	goal	Stendal, Madeleine
Goodwin, Belle	point	Traunweiser, Edna
Henders, Lena (or Leda)	cover	Lursey, Addie (or Livesly)
Cavanaugh, Ola	rover	Haverty, Irene
Ellis, Winnifred	center	Sloan, Helen
Gore, Hazel	lw	Anderson, Marie
Grant, Winnie (Minnie)	rw	Dumuth, (or Du Muth), Lill

Goals: Haverty, I. (1); Anderson, M., (1); Cavanaugh, Ola, (1); Sloan, Helen, (1); DuMuth, L. (1)

A week later Nelson travelled to Grand Forks for the return game, in the excellent, enclosed rink there. There were some changes in Nelson's lineup;

Dora Patrick, who was Lester and Frank's other sister, and Jean McLaughlin, and Winnifred Foote replaced Mrs Manhart, Lena Henders and Winnie Grant. Only one goal was scored, by Grand Forks, winning 1-0. It's not known who scored the goal. The Nelson team was then treated to a banquet, a dance, and then the next day, several sleigh rides and excursions.

Nelson All Stars		Grand Forks Wonders
Foote, Winnifred.	goal	Stendal, Madeleine
Goodwin, Belle	point	Traunweiser, Edna
Cavanaugh, Ola	cover	Lursey, Addie (or Livesly)
Ellis, Winnifred, Ola	rover	Haverty, Irene
Gore, Hazel	center	Sloan, Helen
McLaughlin, Jean	lw	Dumuth, Lill
Patrick, Dora	rw	Anderson, M.

Goals: Haverty, I. (1); Anderson, M., (1); Cavanaugh, Ola, (1); Sloan, Helen, (1); DuMuth, L. (1)

The Nelson women's team had their photo taken at the Nelson studio.

GOLDEN

No mention of local hockey.

VANCOUVER

A Vancouver team of established stars was announced, along with plans to challenge Nelson for top British Columbia hockey honors. The team would be composed of Tom Phillips, the superstar, Si Griffiths (actually Si Griffis), who won the Stanley cup with Tom Phillips in Kenora, "Longboat" Longfellow, "Bones" Allen, the famous Lacrosse player, Mat Brown, Billy West and "Omey" Omah. According to the Vancouver World, these players were skating on Trout Lake during the January cold snap, and were hungry for opposition.

Unfortunately, the team could not be organized and the challenge fell through.

A New Westminster youth, Kenneth McKenzie, was injured while playing hockey on Burnaby Lake. One of his opponents ran his skate through McKenzie's foot. McKenzie was taken to the medical facility in New West by carriage.

Revelstoke defeated the Vancouver CPR team 3-1. It was not reported where this game took place, and there were no other details.

Skaters in North Vancouver were now using Rice Lake.

Plate 31. Nelson Ladies, 1910. Back Row, left to right: Mrs. A.L. McCulloch, President; Mrs. William Waldie, Honorary President; Mrs. W. Rutherford, Vice-President; Middle Row: Jane McLauchlan, l wing; Mabel Manhart, goal; Minnie Grant, sec. and r wing; Isobel Goodwin, cover point; Cynda Patrick, Manager and point; Ida Elliot, Co-Captain, and goal; Minerva Turner, rover; Leda Henders, cover point; Winnifred Foote, point; Helen Gigot, l wing. Front row: Hazel Gore, Treasurer and centre; dora Paterick, rover; Winnifred Ellis, centre; Louise Gilchrist, r wing. Not shown, Ola Cavanah, rover and Co-Captain. Credit: Nelson Museum.

Plate 32. Rossland Senior Men's Team, in Arena, 1910. Credit Rossland Museum.

Plate 33. Moyie Senior Team, 1910. Left to right: J. Donahue; H. Grady; J. Dixon; W. Sheridan; H. Kelly; A. Keating; D. Dimmock; C.O. Foote; C. Messenger. Credit: postcard from author's collection.

Plate 34. Grand Forks Senior Team, 1910. Back row, left to right: E. Miller, (M.P.P.); R. Curran; W. Mills; H.M. Mann; T.S. Watts. Middle row: G. Hay, Defense; r. Quinn, Forward; B. Reid(?), forward; W. Miller, forward. Front row: A.R. Mann, Forward; B. Lang, goal; D.M. McAllman (?), Defence. Credit: Boundary Museum.

1911 SEASON

For the first time the question of payments for amateur players became an open point for discussion and controversy in British Columbia. There had often been discussion about amateur vs professional status, but the issue was more one of the fairness of suddenly salting a team, and whether a team should be forced to have men on it from the actual town they represented. Ringers were almost expected in Stanley Cup challenges, to the consternation of the trustees who tried to stop it, but who were largely ignored by the players. The Rossland Carnival had implemented a rule for several years that demanded players be resident for at least 30 days of the town they played for. (Although that rule had long been found in the Canadian Amateur Hockey League rules.)

However, once the National Hockey Association was formed in Quebec and Ontario, in 1910, which was the precurser to the NHL, the amateur vs professional question began to flare up everywhere.

Although it had occasionally been mentioned in British Columbia that professionals existed, and played there, no one had come right out and admitted that the players were receiving large amounts for simply playing, until 1911.

As a Nelson Daily News correspondent said, "Many black sheep are to be found in amateur ranks, more than the gentlemen who control affairs care to admit. A case in point: Last season, before the campaign was finished, a local hockey impresario arranged a game with an outside team for a holiday night. He undertook to take up a team of all stars to a northern town on a guarantee of expenses. He figured that the 'boys' would like to make the trip for the fun attached to the junket, but he soon found out his mistake. The first question asked by five of the men he approached was, 'What is in it for me?' The engagement was filled, as per agreement, but the manager of the 'all-stars' had to 'dig' pretty deeply before he got his team together. Two of the players who played on the team in question have signed up in the Ontario pro league this winter. Then the story is told of a player in a Northern town who was made a good offer to play professionally, but who replied, when the salary question was broached, 'I make more than that playing amateur.' He didn't get it straight from the club perhaps, but his 'bit' was made up in other ways." (A similar reference was made of a Phoenix player in 1914, Bernie Morris, who notoriously played for money whenever he could. He was kicked out of Saskatchewan in a controversy over his professional status in 1914, and then signed to play with Phoenix that year. It was pointed out by the Nelson Daily News that Morris had earlier been quoted that he could make more money playing amateur hockey than he could in the professional ranks. In 1914 he was acquired by the Pacific Coast League, and played for money ever after, winning the Stanley Cup with Seattle in 1917.)

Bruce Ridpath, the Eastern star, was quoted from an Ottawa paper, saying, " I was offered one hundred dollars to play with a certain team outside of Toronto in a senior OHA match. Another person learned of the offer and asked me to accept $150 more to throw the game. Of course I turned both down, as I do not stoop to that kind of business, and never have." Ridpath also declared that it was generally known one team outside of Toronto, in the senior O.H.A. was practically made up of professionals, but was overlooked as the series would have been broken up, had they been thrown out.

Payments were not always direct, and The Rossland Miner expressed a desire that "work may be found in the city or at the mines for some players of excellent repute whom it has been necessary to bring into the city in order to strengthen the team, and if work can be obtained for these men it will be the means of giving Rossland a really capable hockey team."

The New Denver hockey team wanted to play Nelson, but was afraid there might be disagreements and repercussions regarding the current, or former payments to both their players and the Nelson players. As a result, these two teams did not meet this season.

Even the Junior teams were not immune to this process, and one Nelson correspondent matter-of-factly announced the replacement of one of the Rovers players this season, with a player from the other Junior Nelson team, as: "Cummins was last year one of the strongest defensemen the Juniors possessed, but being offered a larger sum by the Rovers will fill their list."

The controversy was spreading, but there were no regulatory agencies in the "Wild West" to deal with this issue.

NELSON, ROSSLAND and the KOOTENAYS

The Patricks returned.

Despite the Nelson Daily Miner's admiration for the fine showing of their Nelson boys in the big leagues, they had actually failed miserably to attain the goal they had been hired to achieve. The highest paid team in the history of hockey had not finished first in the NHA and therefore had given their employer, the fanatical M.J. O'Brien, no opportunity to play for the Stanley Cup.

However, Lester and Frank Patrick were none the worse for it all. Lester had received $3,000 for his two months in Renfrew, which was the rough equivalent of three year's average salary, and in January 1911, Joe Patrick sold his lumber business and gave Frank and Lester each $25,000. Frank also got another $35,000 from a private land sale, with his father's help. The sum of twenty-five thousand, by the author's calculation, would be the equivalent today of, very roughly, $750,000.

In "The Patricks," Eric Whitehead says, "The brothers did get back into hockey again that winter, but only for a couple of games with the Nelson Team, in token appearances." As will be seen below, this is a gross misrepresentation of the facts.

The Nelson Senior team had a mini-training camp to decide who would be part of the team, inviting several new players, including juniors, to scrimmage with them. These included: Nancarrow, Johnnie Ferguson, Waldo Ferguson, Boyce, Scotty MacDonnell, the two Grant boys, and Jack Miller.

The first senior challenge match was against Grand Forks, who wore red, in Nelson. For the first time, the B.C. teams began playing the new three period format, which was now officially being used in the professional leagues back East. This was great for the players, who had more of a rest, but there were complaints from the spectators, who had to wait twice for play to resume. Lester Patrick was his usual spectacular self, making exciting rushes, while Frank Patrick was apparently out of practise. Nelson pulled away quickly in the first period, with the score 6-2. Then the game see-sawed, but Grand Forks was not able to pull even, losing 7-4. The last two minutes of the second period were played six a side, when Reid smashed into the fence, and Steel went off to even things up. One of the goals Nelson scored was the result of a face off being given only a couple of yards from the Grand Forks net, where all the Nelson players, save the goalie, scrambled madly to smash the puck into the net.

Nelson		Grand Forks
Bishop, E.	goal	Boland, "Baby doll"
Patrick, F.	point	Mann, A.
Patrick, Lester	cover	Quinn
Bishop, A.	rover	Miller (Manager)
Bishop, Harry	center	Demuth
Steel, Les	lw	Reid
Balmer, R.	rw	Mercer

Goals: Bishop, Archie, (3); Bishop, H. (1), Patrick, Lester, (2), Miller, (1), Steel, Les, (1), Reid, (1), Quinn, (1), Demuth, (1)

The Nelson Seniors then travelled to Rossland for their next match. Frank Patrick was kept in the logging camps by his father, and R.M. Balmer had bank business to attend to, so Nelson took along Brown, Waldo and Johnnie Ferguson. Rossland scored first, on a long shot. But Nelson began to take control, and easily won the game, 9-4. Apparently one of the Rossland officials had wagered on the Nelson team which caused the Rossland reporter some indignation.

Nelson		Rossland
Brown	goal	Cosgriff, F.
Patrick, Lester	point	Donahue, J.
Steele	cover	Jopp, V.
Bishop, A.	rover	Jewell, E.
Bishop, Harry	center	Keating, A.
Bishop, E.	lw	Dixon, J.
Ferguson, John	rw	Ames, F.
Greyerbiehl	spare goal	
Ferguson, Waldo	pare	

Goals: Patrick, Lester, (3); Bishop, H. (3); Bishop, A. (3); Dixon, (2); Jopp, (1), Donahue, (1).

Rossland then travelled to Nelson for the return match. Lester Patrick was spectacular again, and Nelson jumped out to a four goal lead after the first period. Lester stepped aside for Johnnie Ferguson half way through the game, and Nelson continued to dominate, eventually winning 10-2.

Nelson	Rossland

Bishop, E.	goal	Cosgriff
Patrick, F.	point	Donahue, J.
Patrick, Lester	cover	Jopp, V.
Bishop, A.	rover	Jewell, E.
Bishop, Harry	center	White
Ferguson, W.	lw	Ames
Steel, Les.	rw	Dixon, J.
Ferguson, Johnnie	spare	

Goals: Bishop, Archie, (3); Patrick, Lester, (3); Ferguson, Waldo (1); Bishop, Harry, (3); Jewell, E. (2);

Nelson then found it difficult to find Senior teams in B.C. willing to take them on. Finally, Cranbrook, the new Champions of the Crows Nest Pass League, accepted the challenge and travelled to Nelson. This team was a tough one, and the game was tied 2-2 after the first period. Balmer received a major gash on his forehead and Jenkins had to be substituted. Frank Patrick continued his scoring slump, but played well on defense as usual. There were many penalties. Eventually Nelson won 6-4.

Nelson		Cranbrook
Bishop, E.	goal	McManus (or McNames)
Patrick, F.	point	Sims
Patrick, Lester	cover	Kelly
Bishop, A.	rover	McWha
Bishop, Harry	center	McGregor
Steel, Les	lw	Thrasher
Balmer, R.M.	rw	Connolly
Jenkins	spare	

Goals: Patrick, Lester (2); Bishop, Archie (1); McWha, (3); Bishop, Harry, (3); McGregor (1).

After the Rossland Carnival, Nelson made a tour of the Crow's Nest. (See CROW's NEST for further Nelson Senior games).

Nelson junior teams: See JUNIOR Games chapter.

The Nelson Intermediates played the Rossland Intermediates in a challenge match in Rossland, which was won by Rossland 4-0 amid much crowing about their superior team, although this was before the Rossland carnival.

Nelson Intermediates		Rossland Intermediates
Glass, P.	goal	Evans
Miller, J.	point	Waring
McDonald, A.	cover	Braden
Bell, R.	rover	Griffith, C.
Grant, J.	center	Griffith G.
Mackay, E.	lw	Ames
Reilly, W.	rw	Hamilton
Swannell	spare (?)	

Goals by: Hamilton, (1), Griffith, G. (1); Griffith, C. (1); Ames, (1)

Before the Rossland Carnival the Nelson Intermediates played the Trail Intermediates in Trail. This was actually the Trail Senior team, since it was the best team that Trail had. Nelson was defeated beaten 6-1 by Trail. (The Trail papers reported this result as 7-1.) Riley and Miller were the best for Nelson, while Trail's best men were Swartz, Morgan, and Truswell in goal. Swartz was the fastest man on the ice, scoring most of Trail's goals, although the exact number is not known.

Nelson Intermediates		Trail Intermediates
(not known)	goal	Truswell
	point	Milligan, George
	cover	Milligan, Fred
	rover	Morgan, Dick
	center	Owen, W. (or Owens)
	lw	Prescott, J. (possibly)
	rw	Swartz, W.R.

Goals by: not known.

After the Rossland Carnival, the Nelson Intermediates played Trail again, (in Nelson ?) The Trail Intermediates were once again actually the Trail Seniors, as they were the best team Trail had. The Nelson team was quite different from their first meeting, having been beefed up. As a result, they defeated Trail easily, 7-3.

Nelson Intermediates		Trail Intermediates
Boyce.	goal	Truswell, Walter
Miller, J.	point	Milligan, George
Bell, J.	cover	Milligan, Fred
Jenkins	rover	Morgan, Dick
Robinson	center	Owen, W.
Bell, Ole.	lw	Prescott, J.
Reilly, W. (or Riley)	rw	Swartz, W.R.(Bobby)

Goals by: Jenkins, (1), Reilly, (2); Robinson (1); Owen, W., (2); Swartz, (1); Bell, Ole (2); Miller, J. (1).

Inner-city Games

Nelson

The Nelson Wood-Vallance team (Hardware) challenged the Bankers team. The Bankers won 6-5.

Wood-Vallance		Nelson Bankers
Reilly, R.	goal	Stevens
Sharp	point	?
Reilly, W.	cover	Appleyard
Etter	rover	Lane
Patterson	center	Swannell
Kettlewell	lw	Swan
Boyce	rw	Whitebread

Goals by: Swan, (2), Swanell (2); Whitebread (1); Sharp, (1); Reilly, W. (3); Kettlewell, (2).

After the Rossland Carnival, an inner-city game in Rossland took place between the Cigarmakers and the Bartenders. Tom Dixon was too fast for the others and was taken out of the game at one point because it wasn't fair. Percy Hunt fell to the ice and lost two teeth. Foster had to leave the game with an injured ankle. Al Keating played goal for one of the teams. A youngster nicknamed, "Blink," scored the Bartenders only goal. The Cigarmakers tied it up 1-1, and that's how the game ended.

Keating, Al	goal	(team unknown)
Belton, J.C.	goal	(team unknown)
Dixon, Tom		(team unknown)
Hunt, Percy		(team unknown)
Foster		(team unknown)
Smith, Alec		(team unknown)
Blink		Bartenders

Goals: "Blink" (1), one goal unknown

ROSSLAND CARNIVAL

Once again, Lester Patrick was in the centre of a fiasco involving his team and the Rossland Team, and the Carnival organizing committee.

The members of the Nelson Senior team felt they would be missing too much work to go to the Carnival on its first day. Or at least, that was the reported situation. In reality, only three players appeared to be unable to take off the whole four days of the carnival. One was R.M. Balmer, who worked as a teller in the Bank of Montreal. One was Frank Patrick, who had to work in the logging camps for an extra day, and the other was, supposedly, Lester Patrick. But Lester had taken the plum job of manager of the Nelson rink. Instead of giving this job to one of the team members who might have needed the extra money, Lester reveled in the prestige it gave him and the glamour of being in charge of the team's various activites. He became the manager and coach of the Nelson Ladies team, and as Lester was very popular with the ladies, he must have found this position too good to give up. It's likely that a full carnival schedule would have meant that Lester would have missed at least one Ladies team practice, but it was, after all, up to him if he stayed or went. An assistant could have run things for a few days.

In any case, three weeks before the carnival the Nelson team informed the Rossland Committee, by letter, dated February 2nd, and also received Feb 2nd by the Rossland Committee, that they would only be competing for the B.C. Championship and not the International Cup, which they believed would be played for at the beginning of the tournament, which was usually the case. The Nelson Daily News said the games for the B.C. championship had always been played off during the latter days of the tournament, which was not strictly true, as indicated below.

Eldon Winn was still missing from the hockey scene, although he appeared to still have a law practise in the city. However, Jack Donahue, the Captain of the Rossland team, was now back on the hockey committee, along with Dan Thomas, who had recently been elected Chairman of the Rossland Hockey Team, as well as Vice Chairman of the Carnival Hockey committee, and who was now basically in charge of running the Carnival.

The Rossland Carnival Committee had a meeting on February 4th to discuss many matters, including the hockey games, where Arthur Perrier's letter was read by Dan Thomas who was now the hockey chairman. Then, as stated in the Rossland Miner, "Some discussion took place as to the advisability of changing the International and B.C. Finals round and having the former on the Saturday night, [i.e. the end of the Carnival], instead of the B.C. Championship as had been the case in former years."

Why would they suddenly discuss changing the order of events, just after reading out Arthur Perrier's letter? Was this good sportsmanship, in trying to accommodate their main rivals? If so, one would expect the change considered to be to Nelson's benefit, but changing the B.C. Championships, so they started earlier, when the Nelson players had said they had to work on the first two days of the Carnival could hardly be helpful to the Nelson team. It would be directly detrimental.

The spirit of Eldon Winn was taking shape, through his former cohorts.

Rossland sent a terse letter (or telegram) to Nelson on February 5th, from Dan Thomas, Chairman of the Hockey committee, which said, "Terms as stated in your letter accepted by Carnival Committee." There was no attempt to clarify further.

Arthur Perrier and Lester Patrick did not read between the lines, and therefore had no inkling, at that time, of the coming reversal of fortune.

In any case, Lester Patrick had spoken, and expected to be heard. He, and brother Frank, were used now to the admiration of the hockey fraternity, and to the deference shown to their wishes in hockey matters. Even Cyclone Taylor, another of the "greats" related that when they played together on the high powered Renfrew team, the Patricks would often begin discussing hockey, and the other members of the team would just sit around and listen to them.

(See, "The Patricks," and, "Cyclone Taylor.") Of course, this was because those two minds together were the brightest of hockey analyzers. Furthermore, Lester was always the life of the party, the one a gathering turned to for a soliloquey, or an idea. But the problem for Lester was that it appeared that he had become so accustomed to this deference that he believed everyone, including his opponents, would take his word as gospel. At the very least, there would have been no team decision made without the express consent of Lester, their Captain, and this team decision was unprecedented. Nelson had always sent a team to compete for the full festival, whether it was their absolute best or not. It was usually understood by employers that this was important for the city. There was no shortage of good players to draw on, who were eager to go. The imperiousness and elitism evidenced by this decision, sounds like one promoted by Lester Patrick. After all, Lester had many championships to his name, and he might feel no need to play for the "International" Cup, since it was the poor cousin of the Carnival, and it was the B.C. Championship which carried the main prestige.

It was true that while the year previous, 1910, the International, or Open, Championship had been played for first, it was not always so. In 1907, its first year, it was played for second; in 1908 played for first, and in 1909, the year Lester Patrick won it, it was played for in the middle of the program, with the Intermediate games first, and the Senior B.C. Championship last.

On February 8th the Committee sent another letter to Arthur Perrier explaining that the drawings for the hockey events would take place at Hunt and Patterson's Store, on the evening of Tuesday the 14th, just after the night train from Nelson would come in. However, there is no mention of the change in expected schedule. Arthur Perrier apparently did not reply, perhaps not carring who was drawn first, as long as there was no B.C. Championship game on the first day.

But whether the Rossland Carnival Committee had deliberately been trying to discommode the Nelson team or not, they still gave Nelson a chance to change its plans accordingly, when the Carnival schedule was announced, and published in the Rossland paper on February 11th, three days before the carnival started. Here it clearly showed, in fine print, that the first game in the B.C, Championships would take place on the first day of the Carnival, Wednesday, February 15th. There was a notice in the Nelson paper, quietly giving the rundown of the events, noting this hockey schedule. Bizarrely, no one on the Nelson team seems to have noticed it.

But to make things clear from Nelson's standpoint, another message was given to Rossland. As it happened, on Monday night, February 13th, Nelson had a challenge match with Cranbrook, in Nelson. Two Rossland players, Scotty Dickson, and Jack Donahue, along with two Phoenix players, Neil and McQueen, attended the game and had been watching, apparently intent on signing up some top Cranbrook talent for the upcoming B.C. Championship game. (Rossland had eliminated the residence qualification this year, hoping to stack its team.)

Members of the Nelson team, most probably including Lester Patrick, since he was their acknowledged leader, and Captain, although his name is not specifically stated, took this opportunity to make it very clear to these two Rossland players that the Nelson team would not be able to play on the first day of the hockey matches. As the Nelson Daily News reporter said, "the fact was impressed strongly upon them that the Nelson boys could not possibly get over to Rossland until Thursday." There is no record of the response of these two men, but one can imagine their amazement. Here they were, trying to gain any advantage they could to knock off the opposition at the upcoming Carnival, and Lester Patrick's men gave them a golden opportunity on a platter. All they had to do was keep their mouths shut until they got back to Rossland, and since that was basically what they did, making no objections, it was assumed by the Nelson players that everything would go according to Nelson's plan.

Jack Donahue was both the Captain of the Rossland team, and a member of the hockey committee. He had to know that the first B.C. Championship game was on the first day of the carnival, regardless of who was drawn. It is clear that he did not point that out to the Nelson players.

On the evening of the drawing, since no Nelson representative had shown up, a citizen of Nelson, Mr. McIntyre, of the Dominion Express Company, was chosen to witness the drawing for the first day's match, and to the surprise of Nelson, they were drawn first against another surprise team—Rossland. A cable was not sent to Nelson until the following morning, however. Why was this? Were the CPR offices closed in the evenings? This is highly unlikely, due to the possible railroad emergencies which might occur at any time. Furthermore, it seems that everyone forgot there had been telephone service between Rossland and Nelson for many years, and the Carnival office itself had had its own telephone since 1903. However, in any case, a cable was sent to the Nelson team's secretary, Arthur Perrier, at 8:00 a.m., Wednesday morning, which he received at 8:30 a.m., explaining that the Nelson team would have to arrive for that evening's start time, or forfeit the game. Unfortunately, as it happened, the day's train would be leaving for Rossland from Nelson in half an hour from the cable's receipt.

Arthur Perrier felt he had no choice but to accept the ignominious defeat and cabled back that there was no time to get everyone together for the game, since they were all expecting to assemble the next morning. Part of his cable included the pathetic lament, "we thought it had been understood by you." The Nelson Daily News professed ignorance of when it was that Rossland changed the usual order of events, showing that no one in Nelson, including the main news source, had been paying attention to their own news, based on their previous assumptions.

Lester Patrick was quoted in the Daily News, "even if we were drawn to play Rossland tonight, and Phoenix and Greenwood were drawn to play tomorrow night, it would have been the actions of genuine sportsmen to have switched the games." He later went on to intimate that Rossland had done this deliberately, which, to all appearances was certainly probable. But they did it because Lester Patrick, guiding his team, had made many foolish assumptions. He assumed that because he had informed the committee of his team's decision, that he would be accomodated in the highest respect for his wishes. He assumed that in receiving an acknowledgment of his team's decision that meant an acceptance by Rossland of his overall plan; and he assumed that by telling two members of the opposing team, that his own team definitely would not be in attendance on the first hockey playing day, that these two head hunters would relay that information to the Carnival committee in aid of helping Nelson to play for the championship as it wished. (Lester's statement in the paper made it clear he was aware that Jack Donahue had come headhunting during the game against Cranbrook.)

Instead, when the game was announced that evening at the Carnival, the Rossland players assembled their team on the ice, put one goal in the Nelson net and declared themselves the winner of the first game, thereby gaining, with a few telegrams, and an empty net goal, a victory, a berth in the Championship final, without playing a game, and the annihilation of the strongest team in B.C.

Typical of Lester Patrick, he did not even consider playing for the International Cup. There was no official protest, no attempt to make a compromise. The Rossland Carnival Committee might have bended to some pressure, after all. But there was no attempt to plead one's case. By the very fact that someone had had the gall to slight the Nelson team, and Lester Patrick's word, there would be no dealing with them.

Later in Lester Patrick's hockey life he became a shrewd strategist, to go along with his honesty, acumen and sense of fair play. But at this young age, these qualities were not always the ones which came to the forefront.

There is some evidence that this, "Patrick," decision did not sit well with the Nelson team. The Carnival committee received several telephone calls from Nelson senior players trying to get themselves placed on other teams, but the other teams refused. Nelson did send a last minute Intermediate team, as requested by the Carnival.

As the Carnival progressed, the Phoenix Seniors played Greenwood. The game was very fast, with both sides getting many scoring chances, but Phoenix went out ahead 3-0. Greenwood came roaring back, and brought the score to 5-4, but then time ran out, leaving Phoenix the victors, with the right to play Rossland in the Final.

Phoenix (orange and black)		Greenwood
Lang	goal	McCarthy, C
Neill	point	Russell, Cliff
McWha	cover	McGaugherty, E.
Saunders	rover	MacDonald, G.
Lynne	centre	McCarthy, F.
Ouillett	lw	MacDonald, D.J.
Thrasher	rw	Clerf, (or Cleft)

Goals: Lynne (2); MacDonald, D. (1); Thrasher, (1); McCarthy, F. (1); Russell, Cliff (1); Saunders (1), Ouillett, (1); McGaugherty, E. (1)

Phoenix then met Rossland for the B.C. Championship. Rossland had lost their best goaltenders to other teams, and they were reduced to employing the best they could get from an outside team, which in this case was "Baby Doll" Boland, from Grand Forks. Rossland also picked up Mercer, another of Grand Fork's players. Rossland jumped out to a two nothing lead, but they could not sustain it. Rossland was a tired team, and Phoenix appeared fresher. (Rossland had actually played an open series match the night before with Greenwood, as seen below.) Ames of Rossland had to be replaced by A. Keating, because he was suffering from a swollen ankle. But it was all Phoenix in the last two periods, the score ending 8-2, thus giving Phoenix the B.C.

Championship gold. The Phoenix players were then swarmed by their fans, who carried them on their shoulders, around the arena.

Goals: Miller, (1); Dixon, (1); eight goals unknown for Phoenix.

In the Open, or International competition, Phoenix met Missoula Montana. The game was close in the first period, and the first half of the second period, when the score was 4-2 for Phoenix, but then Phoenix pulled away, dominating the game, and the score ended 13-5 for Phoenix. The Missoula team was credited with very fair play.

Missoula

Bliss	goal
Safford	point
Stannaway	cover
Clarke, R.	rover
Dorman	centre
English	lw
Lucy	rw

Goals: Dorman, (1); Stannaway, (1); 13 goals unknown for Phoenix; 3 unknown goal for Missoula.

Greenwood and Rossland had met in the other semi-finals of the Open competition. This was possibly the most exciting game of the Carnival. Ames and Mercer of Rossland both hit the post, while Greenwood went ahead 3-1. Ames was hurt and had to be taken to the dressing room, while the game was delayed. Then Ames returned and was a whirlwind, tieing the score with 2 goals. Dixon of Rossland was also hurt, banging his head on the ice, and again there was a delay as they waited for Dixon to regain consciousness. Ames' goals were the last in regulation, and they went into overtime, tied 3-3. In the first ten minute overtime period, both teams scored once. Then they played another ten minute period, and no one scored. Then they played another ten minute period and Ames of Rossland finally scored an unanswered goal, winning 5-4.

Rossland

Boland	goal
Donahue, J. (capt)	point
Jopp	cover
Miller	rover
Ames	centre
Dixon	lw
Mercer	rw

Goals: McDonald, D. (2); Miller (1); Ames, (3); Dixon, (1); two goals unknown for Greenwood;

Phoenix then met Rossland for the finals of the Open Competition. The Rossland team was very sore and tired from its two previous, hard and punishing games, while Phoenix was not, appearing quite fresh. Keating again replaced Ames. But Rossland put up a good fight, and only lost 8-6.

Goals: Saunders, (1); Keating, (2); Dixon, (1); Miller, (1); two goals unknown for Rossland; seven goals unknown for Phoenix.

Phoenix then went home from the Carnival with the Giant Powder Shield for the B.C. Hockey Championship, and the International Hockey trophy, also called the Fraser Cup. Phoenix also received individual medals for seven players, and 20 other individual medals for various other events.

Nelson and Rossland then met for an Intermediate Championship game. The Nelson team had been cobbled together at the last minute, at the request of the Rossland Carnival, when the Nelson Senior team had refused to come. They were allowed to include Stannaway, from Spokane, and Tapanilla from Kaslo. Boyce, Miller and Jenkins were from their junior city teams. Stannaway also played for Missoula in its Senior Open game. Nelson won 2-1 amid much griping from the Rossland players about Nelson's new players.

Rossland		Nelson
Evans	goal	Boyce
Stanton	point	Miller
Braden	cover	Bell
Griffith, C.	rover	Jenkins
Griffiths, G.	center	Robinson
Waring	lw	Tapanilla
Hamilton	rw	Stannaway

The Nelson Daily News was exuberant about beating Rossland in the Intermediate game, but there was no official mention of who won the Intermediate Championship in that paper, or the Rossland paper. This leaves the question open over whether it was awarded, especially after the Nelson Intermediates then played the Missoula team, who thrashed Nelson 12-4.

Nelson		Missoula
		(As above)
Boyce	goal	
Miller	point	
Bell	cover	
Jenkins	rover	
Robinson	center	
Tapanilla	lw	
Stannaway	rw	

A spokesperson for the Missoula Team thanked the carnival committee and mentioned that theirs was the only town in Montana who took any interest in hockey, and therefore they had played no other games except the ones at the Carnival.

There were no Junior games.

There was one Ladies Match. The Rossland Ladies defeated the Grand Forks Ladies 3-1. Madge Keating made her characteristic dashes through the opposing side but only scored one goal.

Grand Forks Ladies		Rossland Ladies
Sloan, Ellen	goal	Blackman, Eva
Traunweiser, Edna	point	Lee, Sera
Livesley, Adeline	cover	Keating, Madge
Haversty, Irene	rover	Forteath, Pearl
Sloan, Helen	centre	McDonald, Tessie
Livesley, Hazel	rw	Fox, Ethel
Hartinger, Ida	lw	Stark, Belle, (or Nellie)

Goals: Sloan, H. (1); Stark, Nellie (1); McDonald, Tena (1), Keating, Madge (1).

Ostensibly this gave Rossland some kind of Ladies Championship, but it was not announced.

THE BOUNDARY LEAGUE

Greenwood built a new skating rink.

Phoenix played in Grand Forks, resulting in a tie 3-3. (No other details)

Phoenix		Grand Forks
Lang	goal	Boland, "Baby doll"
Ellis	point	Quinn
Neil	cover	Miller
Saunders	rover	Mann, A.
Lynne	center	Demuth
Oulette	lw	Mercer
McQueen	rw	Reid

The return match in Phoenix saw Grand Forks defeated 10-4. Presumably the two teams were the same, or similar to the ones above. (No other details).

Phoenix then played Greenwood, dominating the former champions by the score of 10-4.

Phoenix		Greenwood
Lang	goal	McCarthy
McQueen	point	Russell, C.
Neil	cover	McDonald, D.
Saunders	rover	Hood
McKelvie (y)	center	Russell, Cliff
Oulette	lw	Charlton
Lynn	rw	McDonald, G.

Greenwood then played Grand Forks. The Greenwood team was ahead 2-1 with one minute to play in the third period. Then Grand Forks tied it up, and in the ensuing overtime period, scored two more goals, finishing up as 4-2 winners. (The Grand Forks Gazette put the score at 3-2 in overtime.)
Goals by: Mercer, (1); Miller, (1); rest unknown.

Phoenix then defeated Greenwood 4-3.

Grand Forks then played Phoenix again. The game was very fast, with Phoenix generally in the Grand Forks end. Boland in goal, had to stop a large barrage of shots, and kept his team in the game. McKelvey of Phoenix had to go off at one point in the final period, with an injury. He returned, but played poorly due to blood loss, and Grand Forks was able to put a couple of goals in, near the end, but Phoenix won 5-3.

Phoenix		Grand Forks
Lang	goal	Boland, "Baby doll" (or Bowland)
Ellis	point	Mann, A.
Neil	cover	Quinn
Saunders	rover	Miller
McKelvey	center	Demuth
Oulette	lw	Mercer
Lynn	rw	Reid

Goals known: Lynn: (4)

Phoenix then played Grand Forks once more and won, clinching the Boundary Championship, even though there were a couple of games yet to play. (The score is not known).

Greenwood played Grand Forks and won 3-1. Greenwood had brought in two ringers, McGaugherty, possibly from Spokane, and McCarthy, in preparation for their games in the Rossland Carnival, and put them to good use first against Grand Forks. Both these men were considered stars.

Phoenix and Greenwood then played one more game, essentially as a warmup for the Rossland Carnival. Greenwood pulled ahead half way through the game, but Phoenix poured it on and finally won 6-4. Greenwood's ringers did not seem to be playing to their potential, and another ringer was said to be on the way for Greenwood.

Phoenix		Greenwood
?	goal	?
?	point	?
?	cover	Miller
?	forward	McCaugherty
Lynn(e)	forward	McCarthy
?	forward	McDonald
McQueen	forward	?

Goals known : Lynn (1); McDonald, (D or G ?) (1)

An exhibition match was played in the end of February between Grand Forks and Greenwood, with Greenwood winning 6-1.

An inner-city series of matches took place between the three major hotels in Phoenix. The Captains of the teams were: The Brooklyn, William Curley; The King, James Ferris; the Queen, Joseph Pendegrast. The King's hotel won.

Two weeks after the Rossland Carnival, the Phoenix senior team sent the trustees of the Stanley Cup their challenge. They had fulfilled their obligation to be the champions of their respective league, winning the Boundary championship. They also won the B.C. Championship at Rossland, and, as they put it, the Championship of the State of Washington. No team from the State of Washington actually played, but they were referring to the International Cup. Phoenix was also completely undefeated the whole season, studiously avoiding any games against the Nelson senior team, which was actually still the best team in B.C. One can only guess at the motive for declining the huge gate receipts which would have accrued from a game between the undefeated Phoenix team, and the undefeated Nelson team, but perhaps the Phoenix aggregate was trying to make sure their challenge for the Stanley cup would be accepted.

It was not.

CROW'S NEST

After the debacle at the Rossland Carnival, the Nelson Senior Team was eager to defeat more teams, (and possibly make more money on the side). They travelled to the Crow's Nest area and played Cranbrook again. It was a fast game, with the unusual situation of the Nelson team receiving 24 minutes in penalties, and Cranbrook none. Twice, in fact, Cranbrook had a two-man advantage, although it's not known if they scored during those power-plays. Perrier of Nelson received a bad cut across the face. However, Nelson won 7-4.

Nelson		Cranbrook
?	goal	?
?	point	Wallace, Ben (position ?)
Patrick, Lester	cover	?
Bishop, A.	rover	?
Bishop, Harry	center	?
Perrier, A.	lw	?
Steel, Les	rw	?
Miller, Jack	spare	Kottemier, Roy

Then Nelson moved on to Fernie, which put together an allstar team, borrowing Murphy and Millan of McCleod Alberta, and McWha, McGregor and McManus from Cranbrook. (McCleod Alberta had a team that played in the South Alberta-Lethbridge League, and had the distinction of scoring the largest number of goals known in a league game thus far, in a 19-2 win over Lethbridge.) Nelson did not object, but at first it looked like Fernie's strategy was brilliant, since they jumped out to a 4-0 lead after only 15 minutes. McWha, the excellent Cranbrook player was partly to blame, getting two of the four goals. Perrier of Nelson was replaced with Jack Miller, the junior. Nelson got down to working harder, and slowly brought the score back, winning the game by 9-6.

Nelson			Fernie
?	goal	(?)	Murphy
?	point		Millan
Patrick, Lester	cover		Dunlap
Bishop, A.	rover		Thrasher
Bishop, Harry	center		McWha
Steel, Les.	?		McGregor
Miller, Jack	?		McManus
Perrier, A	spare		
Jenkins	spare		

Goals: Bishop, Archie, (4); Bishop, Harry (1); Patrick, Lester, (1); McWha, (2), Thrasher (3), Steel, Les, (2); Dunlap (1); Jenkins, (1)

The Nelson players then returned via the "Crow" steam boat.

As for any Senior B.C. League, all the games played by Nelson had only been challenge games, and no one could claim to be Champion of the regular season, despite the fact that Nelson had been undefeated.

Fernie defeated Cranbrook in their first game. Details not known.

Cranbrook had a city League game between the C.P.R. shops, and the Commercials, but the result is not known.

Commercials (white)		C.P.R. Shops (red)
McManus	goal	Harrison
Graham	point	Welton
Morris	cover	Kettermire
Pye, D.	forward	Bathol
Wallace, B.	forward	Tyler
Whitehead	forward	Hyde
Small	forward	Collins
Strong	spare	
Miln	spare	

In another Cranbrook City League game, the C.P.R. Traffic Department lost to the Ramblers, 1-0.

Cranbrook Intermediates defeated Moyie Intermediates 5-2. Benny of Cranbrook and Nordman of Moyie were singled out.

The Nelson Rovers, a junior team, tied the Cranbrook Intermediates (?) 4-4.
The Nelson Rovers defeated the Fernie juniors 6-2.
The Nelson Rovers tied the Cranbrook Intermediates 2-2.

THE OKANAGAN

Vernon Seniors played Penticton in Vernon, and Penticton won 5-3.

Penticton travelled to Summerland and defeated the Summerland team. (Score not known).

Vernon travelled to Kelowna and was beaten by that team 8-5, on Haug's rink.

Summerland then visited Vernon, and Vernon finally won, 3-2.

Summerland travelled to Penticton for a re-match and lost again, 4-1.

The Coldstream Ranch challenged Lumby, and Lumby won 6-2. A.V. McLean was Lumby's captain, a defenceman. Lumby's first goal was scored by Dennison, at centre. J. Sharp was in goal. McLean had to leave the ice with injuries, including a dislocated finger.

In the return match Lumby was without its Captain, McLean, and the Coldstream Ranch won 3-2. The Denison brothers together scored a goal for Lumby. D. Hardy also played for Lumby. On the Coldstream team were Cowan and Morley.

Vernon travelled to Lumby and defeated Lumby 2-1.

The Coldstream Ranch travelled to Vernon and played Vernon to a 5-5 tie.

The Vernon High school boys defeated the Public school boys 5-1.

The Vernon United School Girls played the High School boys, with the boys wearing skirts. At one point all the boys except their goaltender were on "the fence" with penalties. The girls won 6-5.

The Vernon Banker's played the Megaw's. The Bankers won 6-4.

Vernon Bankers	(positions not known)	Vernon McGaw's
Meyer, R.	?	Stevenson
Wisdom, H.	?	Phinney
Calquoun, F.	?	McKenzie
Dickson, F.	?	Shields
Buchanan, R.	?	Fulton
Burnyeat, D.	?	Eakins
Forrester	?	

In Kelowna the single ladies tied the married ladies.

Many pickup games were played on the various Reservoirs.

TRAIL

The Industrial League, between Rossland and Trail teams, again appeared to be dormant.

Trail Seniors played the Nelson Intermediates in two games, winning the first 6-1 and losing the second 7-3. See NELSON, above, for details.

Other Trail results were not reported in the Trail paper.

KAMLOOPS

According to "Wind and Ice" Kamloops did not venture outside its own city this season, and stayed at home, until the 1914 season. Some of the inner city teams which competed with each other were named, "Harlington's Boarding House," the "Bankers", the "Batchelors", the "Outlaws", and the "Broadway Speed Artists."

GOLDEN

No mention of local hockey.

LADIES HOCKEY

Nelson ladies formed another club this year with twenty members present at their first meeting. Miss Hazel Gore's dog, a wire-haired terrier, named Mike McGinty, was named the club mascot.

Lester Patrick was now the ladies coach. Those who tried out directly for the team were Hazel Gore (the manager), Miss Henders, Miss Greta MacDonald, Miss (Winnie?) Foote, Miss Gladys Foote, Mrs. A. Seaman, Miss Dora Patrick, Miss Jean McLaughlan, Miss Toye, and Miss Graves.

After several practices the Nelson and Rossland ladies met for a match in Nelson. Madge Keating was the youngest member of the Rossland squad, (although her age is not known), and was also the ablest. She handled stick and puck, "as if she had been playing hockey with senior men's clubs for ten years. She is speedy, uses her head and is equally good on the defensive or offensive." (Nelson Daily News). There were no goals scored in the first period. But in the second, Rossland scored three times, and put the game away. Madge Keating scored the third goal, on a dash all the way down the ice from her own end. Final score 3-0.

Nelson		Rossland
Winnie Foote	goal	Blackman, Eva
Goodwin, Belle	point	Lee, Sera
Henders, Leda	coverpoint	Keating, Madge
Patrick, Dora	rover	Forteath, Pearl
Gore, Hazel	centre	McDonald, Tessie
Toye, Hazel	lw	Fox, Ethel
McLachlin, Jean	rw	Stark, Belle, (or Nellie)
McDonald, Greta	spare	Laughlin, Mrs.
Betts, Beatrice	spare	Mitchell, Nellie

Goals: McDonald, Tessie, (1); Fox, Ethel, (1); Keating, Madge, (1)

Later a return match was played in Rossland. The teams were basically the same. But Ruby Stuart was playing point for Nelson, and Beatrice Betts had not traveled with the team. For Rossland, Belle, or Nellie Stark was not playing. Rossland Ladies had a unique and very effective tactic which prevented goals being scored on them; every time the puck was near their goal they lined up all seven members in front of the net and prevented anyone from Nelson shooting directly on it. The Rossland paper called this tactic, "skillful defense of the home side." Madge Keating had two breakaways, but failed to score. Pearl Forteath scored the only goal in a 1-0 win for Rossland.

Goals: Forteath, Pearl, (1)

After the Rossland Carnival, the Rossland Ladies played a game against the city's Grocery Clerks, who had never played before. The Ladies won 2-1.

The Nelson Ladies played an inner-city game between two scrub teams, the Cubs and the Athletics. The score was 2-1 for the Athletics.

Cubs		Athletics
Winnie Foote	goal	Lewis, Miss
O'Shea, Mrs.	point	Seaman, Mrs.
Goodwin, Belle	cover	Stuart, Miss
Patrick, Dora	rover	Toye, Hazel
Toye, Effie	centre	Gore, Hazel
McDonald, Greta	lw	McLauchlan, Miss
Graves, Nettie	rw	Betts, Beatrice, Miss

Goals: Goodwin, Belle (1); Gore, Hazel (1); McLauchlan (1)

The Salmo ladies played an inner-city game between the Red and Greys, and the Black and Whites. The Red and Greys won 3-0.

Black and Whites		Red and Grey
Wortman, Katie	goal	Gray, Mrs. (or Grey)
Dockendorf, B.K.	point	McIntosh, Mrs..
Garvin, V.	coverpoint	Wilde, W.
Mason, Cosy (B)	rover	McCaslin, Lilly
McLeod, O, Miss	centre	Bennet, Rheta
Thompson, Ethel	lw	McAslin, Florence
McCaslin Mabel	rw	Wilde, Rosie
Bennett, Rheta	spare	Hansen, Mrs.

Another game took place between these teams, with some shuffling of players, which resulted in the Black and Whites this time defeating the Red and Greys 2-0.

In Moyie the first Ladies game ever took place, between two local teams, the Stars and the Crescents. The stars won 5-1.

Moyie Stars		Moyie Crescents
Wallace, Mrs.	?	Blackburn, Miss
Conrad, Lillian, Miss	?	Campbell, Miss
Berry, Beatrice	?	Attwood, Nina
Brenton, Miss	?	Vincent, Irene
Lutner, Miss	?	
	forward	Lowes, Mrs.
	defense	Innis, Mrs.

Goals: Conrad, Lillian, (4); Lutner, Miss, (1); Attwood, Nina

The Moyie Ladies travelled to Cranbrook and defeated Cranbrook 1-0.

The New Denver Ladies had a team comprised of:

New Denver Ladies

Geddes, Miss	goal
Harris, Miss	point
McDougall, Miss A.	cover
Grubbe, Mrs, E.H.H.	rover
McDougall, Miss W.	center
Vallance, Miss	lw
McInnes. Miss	rw

There were no records of serious games.

JUNIOR

The Nelson Juniors and the YMCA juniors of Nelson amalgamated to save costs. Their new uniforms were maroon, green and white. Joe Thompson agreed to be coach and manager.

Frank Patrick agreed to manage the Nelson Rovers. They first defeated the YMCA Juniors in a practise game 3-1.

The Nelson Rovers then defeated the Rossland Juniors, 4-3.

Rossland Juniors		Nelson Rovers (black & yellow)
Lynn, Harvey	goal	Boyes, Tommy
Ellers, W. (or Ehlers)	point	Grizzelle, C.
Jewell, E.	cover	Cummins, Taffy
Owen, H.	rover	Grant, Fred
Keating, H.	center	Grant, Jack.
McClean, M.J.	lw	Ferguson, Waldo
Keefe, W.	rw	Ferguson, Johnnie

Goals by: Keefe, (1); Grant, Jack (2); Ferguson, Waldo, (1); Jewell, (1); Grant, Fred, (1); Keating, (1)

The Rovers then beat the YMCA Juniors again, 4-2. There was much roughhousing and many penalties.

Nelson YMCA Juniors (red)		Nelson Rovers (now green and white)
Newburn, W.	goal	Boyce, Tommy
Miller, Jack	point	Grizzelle, C.
Miller, Art	cover	Cummins, Taffy
Newitt, S.	rover	Grant, Fred
Robinson, E.	center	Grant, Jack.
Murphy, Ed.	lw	Ferguson, Waldo
Boyce, George	rw	Ferguson, Johnnie

Goals by: Grant, Fred, (3); Boyes (sic),G. (2); Ferguson, Waldo (1)

In a third game between these two, there was much dirty play, especially on the part of "Shorty" Robinson, who got many penalties, including a seven minute one. The Rovers finally won 5-4.

Nelson YMCA Juniors (red)		Nelson Rovers (now green and white)
Boyce, G.	goal	Boyce, Tommy
Miller, Jack	point	Grizzelle, C.
Miller, Art	cover	Cummins, Taffy
Jenkine	rover	Grant, Fred
Robinson, S. (Shorty)	center	Grant, Jack.
Murphy, Ed.	lw	Ferguson, Waldo
Newitt, S.e	rw	Ferguson, Johnnie

Goals by: Cummins, Taffy (1); Grant, Fred, (2) Jenkins, (1);, Newitt (2); Ferguson, Waldo (1); Ferguson, Johnnie, (1) Robinson, s. (1.

The Rovers went on a tour of the Crow's Nest area. Ed Bishop was announced as a replacement for Fred Grant, who couldn't make it, but it appears he did make the trip after all, as a spare. He got into the series when

Grizzelle had to drop out with a nasty cut in the face. When the Senior Nelson Team decided not to go to the Rossland Carnival, Harry Bishop went with the Rovers as their coach. In their first game they tied the Cranbrook Intermediates 4-4. Then they defeated the Fernie Juniors 6-2. Then they tied the Cranbrook Intermediates once more, 2-2 before returning to Nelson.

The Rovers then challenged the Nelson Intermediates, who had won at Rossland. In one rush on the Rovers net, Tommy Boyce, the goalie, sped out to challenge the shooter, smashing away the puck. He tried it again, later in the game, but this time the opposing player, Jenkins, slammed into him, and the two boys, and the the puck, all crashed into the net, scoring a goal for Jenkins. Waldo Ferguson scored the final goal on an end to end rush. The final score was 3-2 for the Rovers, who remained undefeated for the season. There were a few more challenges but there does not appear to have been more games played. The Rovers declared themselves Champions of B.C.

Nelson Intermediates		Nelson Rovers (now green and white)
Boyce, George	goal	Boyce, Tommy
Miller, Jack	point	Grizzelle, C.
Miller, Art	cover	Cummins, Taffy
Robinson, Sandy	rover	Grant, Fred
Jenkins	center	Grant, Jack.
Riley	lw	Ferguson, Waldo
Bell, O.	rw	Ferguson, Johnnie

Goals by: Grant, Jack (2); Robinson, S. (1); Ferguson, Waldo (1)

The All-Star Junior hockey team from Nelson defeated the Boy Scouts 8-2. R. Whitehead was the star, but the goals were not given.

All-Stars		Nelson Boy Scouts
Boyes, T.	goal	Pitts, H.
Kinhan, H..	point	Johnstone, L.
Wolverton, J.	cover	Brown, R.
Larson, P.	rover	Fletcher, H.
Lyonnais, D.	center	Laughton, J..
Gibson G.	rw	Ferguson, J.
Whitehead, R..	lw	Graham, A.

The YMCA Juniors played the Salmo Intermediates in Nelson. Jenkins was hurt part way through, and had to go off, but the YMCA team refused to use their spare player, and played the rest of the game short-handed.

Nelson YMCA Juniors (red)		Salmo Intermediates (Black)
Newburn, W.	goal	?
Miller, Jack	point	?
Miller, Art	cover	?
Robinson, E.V.	rover	?
Jenkins, H.	center	Newitt, Dosey, (forward).
Boyes, G..	lw	Lindow, Carl (position ?)
Murphy, Ed.	rw	Clark (position ?)
Ladd, F.	spare	

Goals by, not known.

The Phoenix Juniors defeated the Greenwood Juniors 8-4 in Pheonix.

The Rossland Juniors defeated the Trail Boy Scouts 7-3.

The SLOCAN

Sandon travelled to New Denver and lost to their seniors 4-1. J. Tier for Sandon was their best player, while Grubbe and Nelson were the stars for New Denver. Grubbe got a hat trick.

Sandon Seniors		New Denver Seniors
Tams, C.F.	goal	Slaatebreck, C.
Tier, A.	point	Byrnes, Judd.
McLanders, C.	cover	Nelson, Bert
Tipping, E.	rover	Tier, J..
Breeze, A.	center	Grubbe, E.H.
McDuggal, K.	rw	Webster, G.R.
McLanders, R.	lw	Blumenauer, R.

Goals by: Grubbe, E.H. (3). Rest not known.

New Denver then beat Sandon in a return match, 4-2. The lineups were the same, except Breeze for Sandon was replaced by B. McMillan, who used to play for Slocan city. The goals for New Denver were scored by: Tier, J. (2); Blumenauer, (1); Grubbe, E.H. (1). The goals by Sandon not available.

New Denver had a city league where the "A" team played the "B" team.

New Denver "A's"		New Denver "B's"
Jacobsen,	goal	Burkitt, G.
Byrnes	point	Crosbie
Neslon, Bert	cover	Angrignon
Blumenereau	rover	Nelson, C.
Cue	center	Grubbe, E.H.
Nelson, E.	rw	Webster
Burkitt, J.	lw	Kelly

The first match for the CF Nelson cup took place, and Byrne's team won 6-3. It's not stated who the opponents were. The first game of a three game match, total goals to determine the winner, took place, and E.H. Grubbe's team won 4-1. Again, the opponent was not named. Other games not reported.

SALMO

Ymir and Salmo men played a game in Salmo. The Salmo team was intended to be al married men, but some were not. Salmo won 3-2.

Ymir		Salmo
O'Neil, Hugh	goal	McCarthur, E.
Van de Bogart, M.	point	Clark, J.
Clark, A.E.	cover	Fair, C.G.
Clark, Alfred	rover	McArthur, F.
Turner, W.	center	Cummins, T.C.
Blake, W. C.	lw	McDonald, C.
Stewart, W.	rw	McArthur, A.
	spare	Watkins, Angus

Goals by: Cummins, (2), the rest not available.

Several more inter-city games were played at Salmo. (Results not available).

OTHER GAMES

At Fort George (beside Prince George), skating and pick-up hockey matches began. But it wasn't until the next season that an official hockey match took place.

VANCOUVER

In January, Thomas Neil Phillips, the greatest left winger in the game, according to Lester Patrick, married Ella Gertrude Kilgour in Hamilton Ontario.

He appears to have had one child, but she died early on. Phillips himself died of tooth poisoning in 1923.

Good skating was to be had at Trout Lake and Stanley Park Lake. (Beaver Lake, or Lost Lagoon?) Nelson street in the West End (downtown), became a sled and bobsled run for children.

However there were no reports of local hockey games this year.

Plate 35. Nelson Rovers Junior Team, 1911. "Junior, and Intermediate Champions, 1910-11" Top row (l-r): N.B Cummins (cover point); H.J. Bishop (manager); W.W. Ferguson (left wing). Middle row (l-r): J.A. Ferguson (right wing, captain); T. Boyes (goal); H.C. Grizzelle (point). Bottom row (l-r): F. Grant (rover); J. Grant (centre). Credit: B.C. Sports Hall of Fame and Museum.

EPILOGUE

1912 and later

The end of 1911 was truly a transitional period for B.C. hockey. In March of 1911, the Patrick brothers, and their father, Joe Patrick, decided to pool all their resources and build a professional league on the Pacific Coast. Joe Patrick's logging business had made enough capital to build three new, artificial ice arenas, one each in Vancouver, Victoria and New Westminster. This league lasted in various forms until 1926, and brought the Stanley Cup to the West several times.

The three Bishop brothers also left Nelson that year. Archie, Harry and Eddie were all lured away to play for Bassano Alberta in the Southern Alberta League. They all played forward, and they managed to win that league's championship. Harry returned to Nelson the next year, and usually captained the Nelson team, from 1913 to 1917, but, as he was now wont to do, he played out as a forward most of the time. He played goal in 1918, but that year he was already becoming a spare player, fading from glory. After 1912 he never won another B.C. championship as a player, and retired before the 1919 season. In 1924 he was killed on a train, in the same dynamite explosion that assassinated Peter Veregin, the doukhabor King. Eddie Bishop returned in 1914, and played off and on for the Nelson team, but does not show up after that as a player. He became an electrician and worked at the Trail Smelter. Archie Bishop returned in 1916 and played a full season for Nelson. He switched to defense in order to direct the team, and concentrated on setting up the other members, including his brother Harry. He took them to the final game of the B.C. Championship, but they lost to Rossland.

This same year one of the Pacific Coast League Teams, Seattle Metropolitans, finally fulfilled a long held invitation to the PCL by the Kootenay teams to play some exhibition games. (The Portland Rosebuds, who had won the PCL that year, had traveled to Montreal to play for the Stanley Cup.) Seattle first played Nelson. Archie Bishop played point, directing his team. Harry Bishop was back in goal, but he hadn't played that position in four or five years, and it showed. Seattle won 8-4.

Seattle then defeated Trail 8-3, defeated Rossland, the B.C. Champions, 3-1, and then defeated Phoenix 5-2.

Archie Bishop might have played a few games in 1917, but he seems to have retired that year from hockey. He moved back East, eventually to Ottawa.

William Howarth, the great B.C. hockey player, who married his lady love from the Rossland Ladies team he coached, ended his life tragically young, when he caught a cold playing hockey in Anaconda Montana, and died soon after of pneumonia in February of 1913. He was about 33 yrs old.

The Rossland Carnival continued as the emblem of amateur hockey supremacy in British Columbia, but after the 1917 season, it was discontinued.

Two new trophies were played for starting in 1913, which began to erode the importance of the Rossland Carnival. The first was the Nelson Daily News cup, which was offered to the Nelson Hockey committee, (originally in 1908), to be played for as they considered best. It was decided in 1913 to make this the championship of the West Kootenays, with a playoff of respective leagues, i.e. the West Kootenay League and the Boundary League, which were both now branches of the West Kootenay and Boundary Hockey League.

The second trophy was a silver cup offered in 1913 by the former Premier, Richard McBride, to be called the McBride Cup, and to be used as a challenge cup for the Interior Championship of British Columbia.

At first, these two trophies were played for simultaneously by the Kootenay teams, since no one had actually won them yet. The McBride Cup was sent to Grand Forks when it looked like that city had won the Boundary Championship, and the team posed with the trophy for their 1913 team photo. However, through a protest which negated this result, Grand Forks was forced to play a two game play-off series against Phoenix and lost the championship to that city, losing at once the right to the Boundary Championship, the McBride Cup, and the right to play for the Daily News cup, all to Phoenix.

Another trophy, the Savage Trophy, was played for by Vancouver and Victoria amateur teams for the championship of the Northwest Pacific Coast, starting in 1912, although technically it was to be a challenge cup for league champions. The Coy cup was played for by Victoria teams for that city's supremacy.

Golden formed a team again in 1913, with H.G. Parson and Doctor J.N. Taylor once again two of the chief officers, just as they had been 18 years previously.

Sandon started a resurgence and became a strong team once again, winning the Cornwall cup, for the Slocan Hockey League in 1913 and 1914. But Sandon was fighting a losing battle against becoming a ghost town, and one of the final nails in its coffin was when the roof of its arena collapsed under a weight of snow in 1920.

Phoenix was also a ghost town by the 1920's, and Moyie, Greenwood and New Denver were vastly reduced in population.

Technically, after 1917, there was not a series played for the B.C. Championships, and therefore, no B.C. champion, until 1923. At that time the B.C. Amateur Hockey Association, which was formed in 1919, and which had already annexed the Savage Trophy, convinced the interior teams to become part of the organization. The Interior champion, Nelson, then played the Vancouver Young Liberals for what was essentially the B.C. Championship, with Vancouver winning. (See A History of the B.C. Amateur Hockey Association by Leo Atwell.)

Several players from the B.C. interior tried out for the new professional teams in the PCHA, (or PCL), and a few actually made it, including Bernie Morris, Jack Ulrich, Mickey Mackay, etc. The rest were made up of some of the best in Canada, stolen out from under the NHA. This set up a rivalry which saw the winners of these two leagues playing for the Stanley Cup each March, from 1913 onwards. The Victoria Aristocrats won the cup in 1913, although Quebec Bulldogs reneged on their promise to hand over the cup; Vancouver Millionaires won it in 1915; the Seattle Metropolitans won it in 1917; and the Victoria Cougars won it in 1925.

By 1911 all the elements of organized hockey had now been applied in British Columbia. The NHA, back East, was becoming a model for professional and amateur organizations. It would call itself the NHL in 1917, and the winner of this league had already become the possessor, at least temporarily, of the Stanley Cup. In 1920, teams began to align their defensive positions across the rink, as left and right defence, as the new rules of forward passing, pioneered by the Patricks, in 1912, began to require differences in tactics. (Although forward passing had already been used in Nova Scotia since before the Montreal Rules in 1870.) In 1921 most of British Columbia finally switched to playing six man hockey, as they had already been doing in the East for a decade. But although Lester Patrick, and the Pacific Coast Hockey Association, experimented with six man hockey in 1913, Lester and Frank Patrick refused to adopt it until the 1923 season.

There were many great contests to come in the PCHA and the B.C. interior, but those stories must wait for another book.

Plate 36. Rossland Ladies 1912. Top row, left to right: Ethel Fox; Eva Blackman; Madge Keating; Tess MacDonald; Sarah Lee; L. Conrad; V. Laughlin. Bottom row: N. Mitchell; Mrs. H. Shorlmer; Ethel Stephens. Most of these players, including Madge Keating, Sarah Lee, Eva Blackman, Ethel Fox, V. Laughlin, Nellie Mitchell, and Tessie McDonald, were playing in 1911. Credit: Rossland Museum.

Plate 37. Greenwood Senior Team, 1912. Trophy on the left: "International Championship", Trophy on the right: "BC Championship." Players: Top row (l-r): G. Clerf; C. Russell; B. Russell. Middle row (l-r): Mr. E. Russell (manager); A. Davidson (point); B. Reid (left wing); E. Bloomfield (spare); C.A. Russell (cover point); J. Redden (right wing). Bottom row (l-r): R. Lynne, (center); G. McDonald (goal, captain); J. Ulrich (rover). Sitting: Unknown. Credit B.C. Sports Hall of Fame and Museum.

Appendix one to Prologue:

Many historians have pointed out that the native North American Indians played a game similar to hockey, at least as far back as the seventeen hundreds. In fact, the Society of North American Hockey Historians and Researchers, (not SIHR, which is the Society for International Hockey Research), has made extensive research in this area to prove that Native Indians were the first to play a form of ice hockey in Canada. Unfortunately this theory does not hold up to scrutiny. Many eye-witness reports of the games the Indians played have been found, including those referred to by SONAHHR on their web site. None refer to the Indians in the seventeen hundreds wearing skates. In fact the major source cited by SONAHHR, is in the book, Halifax, Warden of the North, written by Thomas Raddall. According to SONAHHR, Raddall refers to a military diary from 1749, when he (Raddall) states, "the garrison officers found the Indians playing a primitive form of hurley on the ice, adopted and adapted it, and later put the game on skates. When they were transferred to military posts along the Saint Lawrence and the Great Lakes they took the game with them and for some time afterwards continued to send to the Dartmouth Indians for the necessary sticks." Firstly, hurley is not very similar to hockey, since the ball is in the air much of the time, but the issue of skates is a more important one for hockey. Leaving aside the grave issue of the 1749 date for a moment, how can a game be called the precursor to ice hockey without a ball, a stick and skates? SONAHHR reports a dictionary compiled in *1888*, by Silas Tertius Rand, a Priest who studied the Mic-Macs, which shows that they had a word for skates and for skating, as well as many words for the various facets of their competitive games. This may be so, but it does not prove that the Indians used skates themselves in the seventeen hundreds, especially as early as 1749. After all, as SONAHHR points out, the Indians had contact with Europeans, some of whom had skates, and it would be unlikely that the Indians would not come up with a word to describe this, by the eighteen hundreds. They also had names for European priests, but they generally didn't use the priests. More pointedly, however, all pictorial representations known to this author, of the Indians playing their games on the ice, and there are many, show no skates. Furthermore, these games were often played with fifty to *five hundred or more* combatants a side. Did the Indians even have that many skates? In the mid seventeen hundreds, which is the time frame to which SONAHHR refers, there were probably not one hundred pairs of skates in all of Nova Scotia. But didn't the Scots bring their skates with them when they colonized Canada? Not in 1749 they didn't, because they weren't colonizing Canada then. The census of 1767 lists 13,374 people in Nova Scotia, including Cape Breton. Of those, there were 6,913 Americans, 2,165 Irish, 1,946 Germans and other foreigners, 1,265 Acadians, or French, 912 English, and 173 Scots. In Halifax there were only 52 Scots out of 3022 people. (The History of Nova Scotia Web Site, world wide web).

But the Mic-Mac Indians *were* playing hockey in the 1860's because a Colonel Byron Weston remembered playing with them and told this to an early sportswriter, as related in Bill Fitsell's, "Captains, Colonels and Kings." Bill Fitsell also relates a quote from 1943 from Timothy Graham of Dartmouth, who was a speed skater in the 1880's, that he played scrub hockey with the Indians, who would play on moccasins or wood skates.

So it's possible that the Mic-Mac Indians made their own skates. It's also possible, theoretically, that they were making these skates in the middle seventeen hundreds, before hockey was born. But then where have they all disappeared to? According to Ted Pappas, of West Coast Estates, who is, and has been, a renowned dealer in Native artifacts for over 30 years, he has never heard of Indian skates, whether East or West. According to the Bata Shoe Museum in Toronto, to their knowledge, they have never seen ice skates manufactured by native Indians, although they did make sled runners.

But perhaps this is not what SONAHHR meant. Perhaps SONAHHR is only referring to the influence of a game played on ice, in the seventeen hundreds. Unfortunately the games described by SONAHHR clearly had very little influence on the development of ice hockey, (as opposed to lacrosse, for which the Indian games were the direct forerunner, and which are superbly chronicled by SONAHHR.) The Indians were playing a game similar to hurley, not exactly field hockey, but whatever it was, British soldiers of the seventeen hundreds had seen forms of hurley, and other stick and ball games being played all over the place, and it clearly has very ancient origins. Furthermore, the Indians also played dry land games with sticks and balls, which were known by European settlers. The fact that they played some of them on the ice is not particularly significant. The best that can be said, is that the Indian game might have given the soldiers the idea to try hockey, or hurley, on the ice with skates. But that doesn't make the Indian game the forerunner of Canadian Hockey. This is especially clear when one examines the military influence on the Canadian game. Despite the various diaries about playing hockey on the ice, in most of these cases the military outpost did not inspire the general population to take up the game. The soldiers left, and the citizens did what they already had been doing. While the soldiers themselves might have migrated and shown off the sport here and there, it was the civilians who played these games in their mother country, England, Scotland, etc.,who forced the early game of hockey into the public consciousness when they came to Canada.

But more damning still is SONAHHR's assertion that Raddall said this was happening in 1749. *Raddall never wrote anything like that.* He refers to no diary, and no source when he makes that comment, totally unrelated to the chapter in which it is found, which is the 1918-1928 period. It's almost as if someone, an editor, perhaps, has inserted this anomalous passage because he thought it might be true. Can SONAHHR have been referring to another source? Unfortunately, notwithstanding the discussion above, the whole idea is ludicrous, since in 1749 the Mic-Macs were the dread enemies of the English. As Raddall himself relates, bounties were paid for Mic-Mac scalps, and the British soldiers and the Mic-Macs were scalping each other every time they met. The English soldiers would have shot every Mic-Mac they saw on the ice, and the Mic-Macs would have attacked the soldiers with their, "hurlies." This went on for at least 14 more years, until the various chiefs signed another peace treaty. But even then, there is no sign that the Mic-Macs at this time, with three quarters of them dead from disease, and many of the rest dead from combat, would have been quick to cooperate with the British troops.

And what of the British troops? Who among this group of ex-convicts and drunks would bother to carry skates in the seventeen hundreds in Canada? Anything not needed in their packs would be discarded, or more likely sold for extra rum.

So who did have skates? Mostly the upper class, and mostly these would be brought into Halifax after peace had finally reigned there, which was well after the American Revolution, which means after 1783. In fact, Raddall does make one reference to skates from the period when Prince Edward basically ruled Nova Scotia, although he does not date the quote or source: "Skating, [says Raddall], was the popular pastime. Crowds went to the Northwest arm, where, [and here is the quote from an unnamed source], 'judges, lawyers, high officials, rectors, curates, and the dignified Bishop Inglis himself joined hands with the crowd. Colonels, majors, captains, middies were all on skates, and the fair sex were out in full force.'"

This was probably from the late 1790's, as Raddall was describing that period when he said this, and it was supposed to reflect what it was like during Prince Edward's tenure. (1794-1800).

And yet, according to books like "Hockey's Home, Halifax-Dartmouth," by Martin Jones, and, "Captains Colonels and Kings," there is documented, oral, evidence that the Mic-Macs were playing ice hockey in the mid to late *eighteen hundreds*, and even manufacturing and selling the best hockey sticks of that time in Halifax and Dartmouth. So on the one hand we have Mic-Mac indians playing several different types of games on the ice in the seventeenth hundreds, but *not* hockey, and then we have evidence that in the mid-eighteen hundreds, after hockey has started its initial genesis, they are playing hockey type games with the European settlers, and selling sticks to the surrounding inhabitants. Logically the obvious, objective conclusion is that the Mic-Macs were influenced by the settlers, *not the other way around.* The Mic-Macs were good at making wooden implements, and no doubt found a niche for their talents. They were good at all kinds of games, as well. But the evidence actually shows that they were taught to play ice hockey once it was introduced by the English settlers. History is replete with "effect," being mistaken for, "cause."

Unfortunately when it comes to information from Thomas Raddall's book, he has purposely, according to his preface, not given references because that would, "bore the average reader."

In any case, one is led to the conclusion, and it is hoped that the reader who is still awake will agree, that this "branch" of hockey history is not what it has originally been supposed.

Appendix Two to Prologue:

Garth Vaughn has a different viewpoint. Garth Vaughn was one of the first writers to exploit the new research being unearthed by hockey scholars in the 1980's and 1990's in his excellent book, "The Puck Stops Here," Goose Lane Editions, 1996. Unfortunately he does not often give credit to historians like Bill Fitsell or Leslie Loomer, etc., who were among the first to uncover some of the important references used by Mr. Vaughn, so it is difficult to see where his research has come from, or whether it is his own. SONAHHR does not offer references either, whether for credit of discovery, or information source. Garth Vaughn makes a somewhat uncompromising case that Hurley was the overriding direct link for the development of Canadian ice hockey, first in Nova Scotia, and then in the rest of Canada. Unfortunately this is misleading. Firstly, it is true that the name of hurley is used many times by those trying to describe what they see, or what they are doing on the ice, and it is clear that hurley sticks were often used in the beginning of this sport, but hurley is not very similar to hockey. It is perhaps, 20 % similar to early hockey. If the children were actually playing only hurley on the ice, then ice hockey would never have been invented. (In hurley you snatch the ball up with your stick, carry it in front of you on your stick, and then crack it in the air down a very long field, trying to score past a football-like set of uprights. There is no net.) Aspects of Hurley were no doubt used. But each aspect was tried, used for awhile, and then discarded, as it lost its efficacy, in relation to the ice, the skates, the ball, the goals, etc. First the playing field of hurley, which was normally twice the size, or more, of a hockey rink, was reduced. Then the goal size was reduced, then a goalie was introduced, then it became more common to push the ball along the ice, rather than carry it on the stick, especially when a rule was introduced to allow only goals to score which did not leave the ice. In a sense, hurley is less a missing link to hockey than it is an offshoot that didn't survive on Canadian ice. In Nova Scotia, what the Canadian English and Scottish children were playing was a new form of shinty, or shinny, or break-shins, with hurley sticks, which were familiar to them, or sticks that looked like hurley sticks. (Once one uses a hurley stick to bat the ball along the surface, instead of in the air, one is essentially playing shinty, or bandy anyway, not hurley.) There was as yet no name for this new game, though, unless they chose to call it by an older name, i.e. hurley, or, shinty, or hockey on the ice. After a few decades, there *were* new names invented, such as wicket, or ricket, i.e. rock-wicket, which got their names, as Garth Vaughn relates, as did Bill Fitsell before him, from the stones making up the small goal, which was a gigantic departure from hurley. Garth Vaughn says in, The Puck Stops Here, that hurley was used interchangeably with all the other names. However, again, this only proves that the player or onlooker had no firm grasp of what to call the game. But was it even used interchangeably? If one examines Garth Vaughn's index of chronology, one will find that each time the game is described as something other than hurley, Garth Vaughn himself inserts the word [hurley] after it in his own brackets. In this way, wicket, ricket, break-shins, and "playin' ball on the ice," are all made to appear to be hurley, to fit Mr. Vaughn's theory. It is true that Thomas Haliburton himself refers to the use of a hurley being used on Long Pond once, and another man also mentions hurley, once, from the same place, but even if they were actually playing hurley proper, rather than a new hybrid game, they could not have been playing it long, or they would not have started on the path to ice hockey's evolution. In fact, if one looks at the famous 1829 quote from the Pictou Colonial Patriot, discovered by Bill Fitsell, and/or his wife, it does not actually say the boys are playing hurley, as indicated before, it says that they "turn out on skates with hurley in hand and *play the delectable game of 'break-shins'* without regard for the law." If one looks at this objectively, it is clear that a new game is played with a hurley stick, but not hurley. In fairness to Garth Vaughn, the Boston Evening Gazette article from 1859, to which he refers on page 46 of The Puck Stops Here, describes how a hockey player in Nova Scotia will "take the ball at the point of his hurley, and carry it around the pond and through the crowd which surrounds him trying to take it from him; until he works it near his opponent's ricket and then comes the tug of war, both sides striving for the mastery…"

The above quote does seem to indicate that the ball is often still carried on the stick. However, the author of the Boston article admits earlier that no one calls the stick a hurley anymore; it is a hockey. So, yes, there are still reporters who call the sticks hurley's up until 1859, and yes, there is still enough of a remnant in the minds of adults to think of the game as hurley, but those who played the actual game were far ahead of the reporters, although there seems to be still some cases where the ball is possibly carried, rather than pushed or batted along the ice. Martin Jones, in his book, "Hockey's Home, Halifax-Dartmouth," published in 2002, also relates this development.

Perhaps the point being made here is that Garth Vaughn prefers to allow only hurley the honour of being hockey's ancestor. I prefer to allow other ancestors their due.

In fact, while hurley only resembled the ice hockey of the mid to late eighteen hundreds superficially, there were three other games that were already being played, which resembled ice hockey much further; one was field hockey, which, although ancient, was not played much in England at this time, and had no codified rules yet; shinty, which was played almost exclusively in Scotland and resembled ice hockey somewhat, but wasn't played on the ice; and bandy, which resembled the early ice hockey of the late eighteen hundreds by perhaps 75 percent, including its use on ice, with skates. In fact, although organized bandy games required fairly large goals with posts, when played informally, according to Tebbutt, it only required *two stones placed on the ice*, just like ricket, although that name, ricket, was never used in English bandy as far as is known by this author. Hurley could not, and did not use such a goal, and shinty, as far as I know, did not use such a goal either. Another similarity is the word, "doubling," which has been found to be used several times in Nova Scotian newspaper reports of ricket, and was also used in bandy to describe one of the moves. The Nova Scotian references are not explicated, but Martin Jones, in his book, "Hockey's Home," postulates, as did Bill Fitsell before him, that doubling probably meant stick-handling. However, as reported by Tebbutt, in 1892, in bandy, doubling referred to the action on one's skates of darting first one way, and then doubling back, as if a hare were trying to shake a bobcat, or "two greyhounds," as Tebbutt says. The word used to describe stickhandling in bandy was usually dribbling, just as in field hockey.

Another word used in hockey and bandy is, "lofting," which means essentially the same in both, i.e., shooting the puck far into the air, with various methods. However, the references for this word in both sports go back only to the 1890's, as far as I have been able to discover, so it is difficult to say if one has influenced the other.

It is possible, then, that bandy had some influence in Nova Scotia, while it was also drifting up into Ontario. Was it a bandy player who pointed out that the game could use stones on the ice for goals, because that was what they often did? We will probably never know.

(Please see Appendix Three for further discussion of this issue).

Appendix Three to Prologue:

Early Authors on the Origins of hockey

J. MacDonald Oxley, in 1895: From a book called, My Strange Rescue, and other Stories of Sport and Adventure in Canada," by J. Macdonald Oxley, 1895, Thomas Nelson and Sons. New York, London and Edinburgh. The book was reprinted at least until 1903. The passages below were from an eight page chapter called, "The Game of Rink Hockey," which was probably published earlier in a Youth Magazine, but had to be between 1887 and 1895. Oxley did actually play the game. He was born in 1855 in Halifax and died in Toronto in 1907. His early life and schooling took place in Halifax, and he practiced law there until about 1883, when he moved variously to Ottawa, Montreal and Toronto. Joseph Strutt, referred to by Oxley, lived from 1749-1802, but the earliest copy of his book, The Sports and Pastimes of the English People, I could find listed, was 1810.

"The most ancient account of hockey is to be found in that delightful old book, Strutt's 'Sports and Pastimes of the English People', where it figures under the name of 'bandy ball'—what is now called the hockey stick being then known as the, 'bandy,' and there is attached to the description a comical little woodcut representing two boys in short frocks, each wielding bandies almost as big as themselves, playing with a ball half the size of their heads.

"As first played in Canada, hockey went by various names, some of which were apparently merely local—hurley, shinty, rickets, and so forth. It was played only upon the ice in winter time and there was not much pretense to rules, each player taking part as best he knew how. No effort towards systematizing the game appears to have been made until the year 1875, when the members of the Montreal Football Club, in search of some lively athletic amusement for their long winter months, recognized in hockey the very thing they wanted."

[Oxley goes on to describe the game, and even what it was like to play goal.]

Arthur Farrell, in 1899: From "Hockey, Canada's Royal Winter Game," 1899, Montreal, which was the first manual written on ice hockey, by Arthur Farrell, two time Stanley cup winner.

"Daniel Webster's definition of hockey reads as follows: "A game in which two parties of players, armed with sticks or clubs, curved or hooked at the end, attempt to drive any small object, (as a ball or a bit of wood), towards opposite goals.

"The Learned lexographer must, of course, refer to the game as played in Canada in the good old days when anything from a broom handle to a shilalah was used as a hockey stick, and a tin can rendered service as a puck.

"....Truly it is a fact, though, that the foundation of our glorious scientific game was laid on, "any small object and a curved stick," for the remotest recollections of the oldest players bring them back to the time when these formed the materials of the sport.

"....It is difficult to precisely say from which particular sport, "shinny," and hockey are directly sprung. The warlike Romans enjoyed a peculiar game that is most likely the precursor of hockey in England, "hurly," in Ireland, and, "shinty," in Scotland, which, in point of fact, are now one and the same." [Farrell is probably referring to the fact that the Hurley and Shinty associations play inter-discipline challenge matches with alternating rules.]

"....The original Scotch, "shinny," resembled it more closely than did "hurley," or English hockey, but savored a trifle more of Canada's winter sport...Of all the games that developed from the old Roman sport the British hockey alone shaped the destiny of ours. There can be but little doubt, but that, "shinny," the forerunner of our scientific hockey, is the Canadian interpretation of the game played across the water, adapted in its application to the climate of the country. Hockey in England as played in the winter is played on the frozen ground. It consists in driving a ball from one point to another by means of a hooked stick. The players are divided into two teams, each of which has its goals, which are fixed towards either end of a tolerably spacious ground. The goals are two upright posts, about six feet apart, with a cross pole placed at the height of four feet. Through these the ball must be driven in order to score a point. As regards the playing of the game, it is unnecessary further to speak, because it bears little reference to hockey as played in Canada. Suffice it to say that in the shape of the sticks, not limited in their proportions, in the nature of the object that was used as a ball, in the unlimited numbers of the players, and in its principles, it is the parent of, "shinny on the ice."

Farrell goes on to describe the wild shinny games that were played in Canada before the refinements of rules. However he seems to be mixing up a few things in the above passages. He does not mention bandy, with regard to the English game, but he is in fact, at one point, describing organized bandy. The size of the goal posts are the exact size for those of a bandy game before the 1890's, which were doubled in size after that, not a field hockey or shinty game, and the bandy players were encouraged to play bandy on the flat ground during times when the ice wasn't available. He then makes the leap of talking about non-limited shapes of sticks, pucks, etc, and the unlimited numbers of players, which is a distinctly Canadian development, although it seems to have been transplanted back into England that way in the 1880's and 1890's. He then describes the first organized games of hockey in Canada, but he seems unaware of Creighton, and concentrates on the 1880's, mostly in Quebec. He is totally unaware of any historical development in Nova Scotia.

Thomas K. Fisher, in 1929: From an article in Saint Nicholas Magazine in January 1929, New York, by Fisher, who also published the first hard cover book on hockey in 1926.

"When we speak of the game of hockey today in the North of this country, or in Canada, there is no misunderstanding in any one's mind; it does not mean the original bandy, and it does not mean field-hockey; it is ice hockey, a game that has secured a happy stronghold in the hearts of the sporting public…As sixteenth and seventeenth century paintings will testify, hockey—or bandy as it was then called—has an ancient history and in its ancient form has even come into modern times under the sponsorship, forinstance, of the National Bandy Association of England. [What paintings is Fischer talking of!?] About the only resemblances to our ice hockey to be found in bandy are that the game is played on ice; the players wear skates, the bandies are not unrelated in appearance to our hockey sticks; the ball, of solid India rubber is not far removed from the rubber puck; there are goals at either end of the playing surface; and the referee starts the game by throwing up the ball in the centre of the field. The more obvious differences from hockey are that in bandy the playing surface is far larger, six hundred by three hundred feet; the goal posts are higher and wider, seven by twelve feet, joined only by a lath without netting; the team consists of eleven players instead of six, and the rules of necessity differ widely…[and relating to its development in America and Canada)…Rules were becoming more thorough and complex, and the game was following the genius of its own development without thought of the parent game, bandy."

The reference to a goal length of 12 feet was an introduction into Bandy around the eighteen-nineties, when the goal size was doubled, because goaltenders were lying on the ice and preventing any goals from being scored. Fisher makes the playing field a bit larger than normal, however.

Appendix Four to Prologue:

Early references to hockey in Ontario:

1839: Bill Fitsell says in his acknowledgements in Hockey's Captains, Colonels and Kings, that the Kingston Whig-Standard, "along with its predecessors, has been recording the game in this hockey hub since 1834." However, after I asked him about this, and he believes that this was an editorial error, and he believes now, or at least as of 1996, when I phoned him, that the earliest reference he has seen to any kind of shinty game in Kingston was actually around 1839.

1843: The Arthur Henry Freeling Diary. Freeling was an officer stationed in either Kingston or Napanee, Ontario, from 1839-1844. His diary, in January 1843, states, "Began to skate this year, improved quickly and had great fun at hockey on the ice.: This diary is found in the Public Archives of Canada Material in Ottawa. (Ref. MG24 F72).

1844: Approximate date, give or take one year, referred to by George Stanley in his book, Life In The Woods, published in England in 1864, in which he describes life in Toronto, including a type of shinny which he does not name. "The ice was covered by one restless throng from morning to night…the games of different kinds played between large numbers were very exciting. Scotchmen with their curling, others with balls, battering them hither and thither, in desperate efforts to carry them to a particular boundary." How many were playing with skates is not known.

1847: The Horsey Diary. This is a reference discovered by the Canadian Amateur Hockey Association, and is a report by a Mr. Horsey, an early Kingston historian, in his diary, that, "in 1847, most of the soldier boys were quite at home on skates. They could cut the figure eight and other fancy figures, but shinney was their first delight…"

Appendix 5: List of Players 1895-1911

(Many players with no first name, or with an initial appear to be listed more than once here. But unless I could be absolutely certain that they were the same man, I left many of the listings as I found them. I have also repeated names when different teams are involved. The year given represents the final part of the season, as very few games took place in December. Therefore, a date given like this: 1907-08, means two separate years, 1907 and 1908. This is also expressed as 1907, 1908 where applicable. A date like this: 1898-1907, would mean the player was on that team for all the years between 1898 to 1907, inclusive.)

Name	position	team	date
Acorn, A.L.	lw	Le Roi (Rossland)	1906-07
Acton, Bill		Arlington Hotel (Trail)	1910
Adams	goal	Coldstream Hotel (Vernon)	1908
Adams, H.A.	point/rw	Kamloops Seniors	1902-03
Adams.	point	The Rossland Victorias	1900
Agur, A.	rover	Summerland Seniors	1909-10
Agur, E.	rw	Summerland Seniors	1909-10
Aldice		Smithers Seniors	1910
Allan (named in photo as W.C. Allan)	cover	Rossland Seniors	1908
Allan	left wing	Revelstoke Seniors	1904
Allan	cover	Rossland Seniors	1908
Allen	point	Rossland Seniors	1908
Allen	cover	Rossland Bankers	1906
Allen	rover	Rossland Intermediates	1907
Allen (named in photo as K.C. Allen) spare		Le Roi (Rossland)	1907
Allen, KC. (possibly same man as W.C. Allan) cover		Rossland Seniors	1909
Allen, (or Allan), J.	lw	Revelstoke Seniors	1904
Allen, Bones		Vancouver Allstar team (no known opponents)	1910
Bones Allen was a famous lacrosse player in Vancouver			
Allen, J.	lw	Revelstoke Seniors	1907
Allsion, W.		Kaslo Bankers	1898
Allum, E. M.	goal	Revelstoke Seniors	1903
Ames	rw/centre	Rossland Seniors	1911
Ames	lw	Rossland Intermediates	1911
Anderson		Vancouver scrub team	1905
Anderson, Allen	centre	Kaslo Intermediates	1908

Anderson, J.	left wing	Bank of Montreal (Rossland)	1903
Anderson, John	forward	Le Roi Mine (Rossland Industrial League)	1904
Anderson, K.	spare/cover	Kaslo Seniors	1909-10
Anderson, Robert H.	tried out for team	Le Roi Mine (Rossland Industrial League)	1904
Andrews, R.	center	Hunter Brothers (Rossland)	1903
Angrignon	cover	New Denver "B"s	1911
Angus, Johnny	cover	Palace and Filbert Hotels (Sandon)	1901
Appleyard	cover	Nelson Bankers	1911
Archibald	point	Salmo Mess (inner-city)	1910
Archibald, Barney	spare	Nelson Seniors	1899
Archibald, Barney	point	Nelson Lacrosse-Hockey Seniors	1900
Archibald, Barney	point	Nelson Wholesalers	1903
Archibald, Cyril, I. (or J.) "Barney"	point	Nelson Seniors	1899, 1901-5, 07

Cyril, Issac, (sometimes written as a J.), "Barney" Archibald was the equivalent of one of the top "Goons" from the 1970's in the NHL. He was the roughest player, and some intimated he was the dirtiest, in his league. One team refused to play if Archibald was playing against them. He was, however, very effective for his team, Nelson, sometimes acting as Captain. He worked as an accountant for the Sayward Lumber company, and reached a position of management.

Armitage	goal	Royal Hotel (Vernon)	1908
Armitage	right wing	Fernie Seniors	1906
Armitage, A. (or Armytage)	rw	Nelson Seniors	1905
Armstrong (capt.)	forward	Rossland Junior Victorias	1899
Armstrong, Captain Frank P.	Honorary Vice President	Golden Seniors	1895

Captain Armstrong was one of the founders of hockey in British Columbia. See his biography in the first chapter.

Armstrong, J.H.		Revelstoke City League Team (unnamed)	1909
Armytage, A. (or R.)	rw	Nelson Seniors	1905
Arnold, C.M.		Kaslo Hotel	1898
Atherton, J.J.	manager	Lardeau Hockey Club (top of Kootenay Lake)	1905
Ault, Z.	forward	Nelson Tramway	1901
Ayres	rover/centre	Trail Seniors	1902
Ayres	centre	Trail Seniors	1902
Babington, A.R.	spare	Trail smelter	1907
Bailey	cover	Vancouver Seniors	1901
Bailey (same as Beyley?)	tried out	Vancouver Terminals	1907
Bailey, W.		Enderby Seniors	1901
Bain(s)	cover	Silverton Seniors	1903-4
Baker	rw	Rossland Intermediates	1905
Baker	centre	Nelson Seniors	1904
Baker	lw	Rossland Seniors	1905
Baker	rw	Grand Forks Seniors	1910
Baker	centre	Coleman Seniors	1908
Baker	spare (?)	Grand Forks Seniors	1909
Baker	spare	New Denver Seniors	1909
Baker	forward	Grand Forks Seniors	1905
Baker	forward	Nelson Intermediates	1903
Baker	forward (lw)	Grand Forks Senior	1902
Baker, B.	center	Boundary combined team	1906
Baker, B.	center	Boundary Seniors	1906
Baker, C., (or A)	forward /centre	Nelson Seniors	1903-05
Baker, R.	goal	Vernon Juniors	1907
Baker, W.		Grand Forks Seniors try-out	1905
Ball	forward	Nelson West Ward ("Hand-Warmers")	1907
Ball, R.	center/rw	Diamond A-Ashdowns (Nelson hardware)	1906-7
Balmer, R.	rw	Nelson Seniors	1910
Balmer, Robert.M.	rw/lw	Nelson Seniors	1910-11

Robert M. Balmer was a teller at the Bank of Montreal.

Name	Position	Team	Year
Bamfield	goal	Nelson Bankers	1903
Banning, W.	forward	Nelson Seniors	1898
Barber		Trout Lake Seniors	1910
Barber	point	Slocan City Seniors	1903
Barber	center	Revelstoke Seniors	1904
Barber	forward (?)	Ferguson Seniors	1908
Barber, G.		Kamloops Seniors	1905
Barber, W.J.	rover	Revelstoke Seniors	1907
Barber, W.J. (capt)	rover	Revelstoke Seniors	1904
Bard, P.	rw	Nelson Juveniles	1910
Barnes, .F.	point	Armstrong Juniors	1907
Barnes, B.	cover	Armstrong Intermediates	1910
Barrett, Charles E.	goal	West Kootenay Power & Light Co. (Rossland Ind. League)	1904
Barrough	rover	Trail Seniors	1902
Barrows	rover	Kelowna Seniors	1909
Bathol	forward	C.P.R. Shops (Cranbrook)	1911
Bauman	rw	Kamloops Seniors	1910
Bawlf	centre	Moyie Seniors	1909
Bawlf	(one game against Edmonton)	Nelson Seniors	1909
Baxter	f	Sandon Seniors	1898
Baynton, K. (or Bayntun)	centre/rover	Kamloops Seniors	1902-3
Bayntun, E.		Kamloops Picked Town Team	1903
Beacher	forward	Hodder's Hill Team (Kaslo)	1900
Beasley	forward	Nelson Juniors	1901
Beasley, C.E.	tried out for team	Nelson Seniors	1901
Beattle, G.A.	f	Ashcroft Seniors	1901
Becher, A. Lorne	forward /goal	Rossland Victorias	1899-1900
Becker	point	Rossland Seniors	1898
Beecher or Becher	forward	Rossland Seniors	1898
Beecher or Becher	forward	Rossland Seniors	1898
Beer		Nelson Militia	1901
Beer, Lieut. G.S.	point	Nelson Hardware	1901
Bell		Salmo Mess (inter-city)	1910
Bell	rover	Nelson Intermediates	1909
Bell	center	Nelson Invincibles (Junior)	1905
Bell	cover	Wood-Vallance (Nelson hardware)	1907
Bell	cover	Nelson Juniors	1907
Bell	cover	Nelson Juniors	1909
Bell	cover	Nelson West Ward ("Hand-Warmers")	1907
Bell	center	Nelson Invincibles (Junior)	1905
Bell	cover	Nelson Intermediates	1911
Bell	forward	Nelson Grocers	1907
Bell	centre	Nelson Intermediates	1906
Bell, B.B.	cover	Salmo Seniors/Intermediate	1910
Bell, F.	cover	Nelson East Ward ("Stick-Arounds")	1907
Bell, G.	goal	Nelson Seniors	1899

(George Bell was the manager of the Nelson Senior team in 1901)

Name	Position	Team	Year
Bell, J.	cover	Nelson Juniors	1908
Bell, J.	rover	Nelson Mountains	1908
Bell, J.	tried out	Nelson Intermediates	1908
Bell, J.	center/cover/goal	Nelson Intermediates	1910-11
Bell, O.	rw /lw	Nelson Intermediates	1911
Bell, Ole	centre	Nelson Seniors	1907
Bell, Ole (might be R. Bell)		Nelson West Ward	1906
Bell, R.	rw	Victorias (Nelson inter-City)	1910

Bell, R.	over	Nelson "Fossils"	1908
Bell, R.	rover	Thistles (Nelson City League)	1909
Bell, R.	tried out	Nelson Intermediates	1908
Bell, R. (Bob)	sub/spare/rover	Nelson Seniors	1906-09
Bell,R.	lw	Nelson Rivers	1908

(At one time, prior to 1907, R. Bell, who was also a Nelson hockey player, was the Champion skater of the Central United States. A Robert Bell was listed in the 1907 B.C. directory as a teamster, with the Bell Trading company, who were grocers on Stanley St.)

Bellrose		Nelson Intermediates	1909
Bellrose	coverpoint	Nelson Intermediates	1906
Bellrose	spare/lw/rw/rover	Nelson Seniors	1906-08
Bellrose,	rw	Nelson Mountains	1908
Belrose	spare	Nelson West Ward	1906
Belrose, G.	lw	Victorias (Nelson City League)	1909
Belrose, J.	lw	"Fossils" (Nelson)	1908
Belrose, T.	rw	Thistles (Nelson City League)	1909

(It's probable that some of the above named Bellrose's are one and the same. However, the 1910 city directory lists two men named Bellrose, Gilbert E., who worked as an express messenger for Dominion Express, and Theophilus, who worked as a driver for Dominion Express.)

Belton, J.C.	goal	Rossland Cigarmakers, or Bartenders	1911
Benan, V.	cover	Trail Intermediates	1910
Benedict	cover	Nelson Wholesalers	1903-04
Benedict, C. E.	forward	Nelson Grocers	1901
Bennett,	cover	Vernon Bankers	1907
Bennett, C.	goal	Nelson Diamond A-Ashdown Hockey Club (Hardware)	1906
Benny		Cranbrook Intermediates	1911
Berger, Charles	cover	Hurricanes (Rossland junior)	1901
Bergman	rover /f	Nelson Juniors	1907
Berry, Robert	forward	Slocan City Seniors	1899
Besner	goal	Phoenix Intermediates	1907
Bews, W.	rw	Revelstoke Seniors	1903-04
Beyley (this might actually be Bailey – see above)	cover	Vancouver Terminals	1907
Biglen, F.	forward	Cyclones (Rossland juniors)	1901
Biner	goal	Phoenix Intermediates	1908
Biner, A.		Phoenix Juniors	1903
Biner, G.		Phoenix Juniors	1903
Bingay	rover	Trail Seniors	1902
Bingay	centre	Trail Smelter	1906
Bingay, T.W.	rover	Trail Smelter	1905-07
Bingay, T.W.	rover	Trail Smelter Team	1905
Birbeck		Grand Forks Juniors	1903
Birchall	goal	Sandon Seniors	1899
Birchall	goal	Sandon Seniors	1898
Birchall, E.		Vancouver Seniors practise	1902
Birchell	f	Sandon Seniors	1901
Birnie, H.	cover	Vernon High School	1903
Birnie, H..	point	Vernon Seniors	1908-09
Birnie, W.J.	cover	Grand Forks Seniors	1905
Bishop, Archie		Nelson East Ward	1906
Bishop, Archie	rover	Victorias (Nelson inner-City)	1910
Bishop, Archie	center	"Fossils"(Nelson)	1908
Bishop, Archie	center	Nelson Mountains	1908
Bishop, Archie	centre	Thistles (Nelson City League)	1909
Bishop, Archie	centre/rover	Nelson Seniors	1905-11

Archie Bishop was probably born in Niagara-on-the-Lake Ontario. He played for the Niagaras and the Lakes, before moving to Nelson in 1905. He scored the most goals by far of anyone in British

Columbia, and led the province unofficially five times in season's goals. He was a member of several championship teams in Nelson, (and Bassano Alberta). His hockey playing brothers were Harry and Eddie, (and possibly Bob). He was also a champion trap shot, and won tournaments in Canada and the U.S. After leaving Nelson in 1912, he returned to play for them one more year, in 1916, and then moved back East permanently.

Name	Position	Team	Year
Bishop, Eddie	goal	Thistles (Nelson inner-City)	1910
Bishop, Eddie	spare	Nelson Lakes	1908
Bishop, Eddie	spare	Nelson rovers (Junior)	1911
Bishop, Eddie	center/rover/goal	Nelson Intermediates	1908, 10
Bishop, Eddie	lw /rw/goal/rover	Nelson Seniors	1907, 10-11

Eddie Bishop played in Niagara, Buffalo, New York and Pittsburgh before arriving in Nelson in 1906, (for the 1907 season). He was one of the hockey playing Bishop brothers. He didn't normally play goal, but when he took over the goaltending position from his brother Harry in 1910 and 1911, on the Senior team, he had a total of 8 wins, one loss and one tie. He left with his brothers in 1912 to play for Bassano Alberta, but returned to Nelson in 1914 to play there for one more year. It was said in Douglas Jerome's memoirs that Eddie became an electrician at the Trail Smelter, but in the 1914 city directory for Nelson he was listed as a brakeman for the CPR. It appears he lived on Josephine St. in Nelson, but he settled later in Trail.

Name	Position	Team	Year
Bishop, Harry	lw	Nelson Mountains	1908
Bishop, Harry	goal	"Fossils" (Nelson)	1908
Bishop, Harry	goal	Nelson Seniors	1905
Bishop, Harry	rover	Nelson Lakes	1908
Bishop, Harry	rover	Thistles (Nelson inner-City)	1910
Bishop, Harry	goal	Victorias (Nelson City League)	1909
Bishop, Harry	forward	Kaslo Hill Juniors	1901
Bishop, Harry	forward	Kaslo Hill Juniors	1901
Bishop, Harry	goal/forward	Nelson Seniors	1903-11

Harry Bishop was born in Niagara-on-the-Lake, Ontario, about 1882. He had several hockey playing brothers. He played for a Senior team in London Ontario. Then he moved to British Columbia in 1901, first playing on a Kaslo junior team. Then he moved to Nelson in 1902. Right from the start of his career he was recognized as a superlative goaltender, and he soon won a perennial spot on the Nelson Senior team, in 1903. He won many championships with this team, between 1903 and 1911. In 1912 he left Nelson, and captained the Bassano Alberta team to the Southern Alberta Championship, along with his brothers Archie and Eddie. He returned to Nelson in 1913, and continued playing until 1917. He was primarily a goaltender, and he had the most wins as a goalie in B.C. (See the stats) In one game against Rossland he stopped 27 shots in ten minutes. When he began playing also as a forward in 1910, in the center and rover positions, he racked up impressive numbers of goals, alongside his brother, Archie. Both Harry and Archie were competitive rowers, and marksmen, and they loved duck hunting. Harry played many other sports, including lacrosse, and baseball. He married Jenny Midgley of Nelson and had four sons. He was a traveling salesman, first for the Thorpe bottling works, and later for Swift's meat packers. While he was traveling on the CPR line, outside Castlegar, he was killed in the same explosion on the train which assassinated Peter Veregin, the Doukhabor King, on Oct. 29, 1924. He was forty-two.

Name	Position	Team	Year
Black		Banff Alberta Seniors	1899
Blackburn, W.	cover	Armstrong Intermediates	1910
Blackie		Ferguson Seniors	1908
Blackwell	point	Kaslo Intermediates	1908
Blackwell	cover	Nelson West Ward ("Hand-Warmers")	1907
Blackwell	point	Kaslo Seniors	1909
Blackwell	cover	Nelson West Ward ("Hand-Warmers")	1907
Blackwell, A.E.	center	Nelson Diamond A-Ashdown Hockey Club (Hardware)	1906
Blackwell, B.	cover	Kaslo Seniors	1910
Blackwell, Bert	point/cover	Kaslo Intermediates	1908-10
Blackwell, R.	rover	Nelson Ashdowns (Hardware)	1906-7
Blackwood,	forward	(at Rossland Carnival) Nelson Lacrosse-Hockey Seniors	1900

Blackwood, B.	point	Sandon	1898
Blackwood, C.D.	forward (team Captain)	Nelson Seniors	1903
Blackwood, C.D.	tried out	Nelson Seniors	1905
Blackwood, C.D. (capt)	?	Nelson Real Estate Team	1908
Blackwood, C.D. (Dudley)		Sandon Seniors	1897-99
Blackwood, D. (probably Dudley)	point	Sandon Seniors	1897

(This is Clarence D. Blackwood, who was named in the 1914 Nelson city directory as being employed by Procter and Blackwood, real estate, mining and insurance agents. In any case, the C.D. Blackwood shown above was nicknamed Dudley.)

Blain, C.	goal	Victoria, Daniel's team,	1899
Blair, Clifford	goal	Kamloops Seniors	1903
Blake, W. C.	lw	Ymir Seniors	1911
Blanchard, E.J. (capt)		Coeur D'Alene Idaho Seniors	1908
Blaylock	point	Trail Seniors	1902
Blaylock	point	Trail Intermediates	1906
Blaylock	point	Trail Smelter	1905-06
Blaylock	point	Trail Smelter	1906
Blaylock, S.G.	point	Trail Smelter Team	1905
Blink		Rossland Bartenders	1911
Bliss	goal	Missoula (Montana) Seniors	1911
Blomfield	forward	Silverton Seniors	1904
Bloomfield	rover	Greenwood Seniors	1910
Bloomfield	rw	Rossland Interrmediates	1906
Bloomfield	forward	Kaslo Seniors	1901
Bloomfield, E.	goal	Sandon Seniors	1902
Bloomfield, E.V.		Kaslo seniors	1901
Bluer	goal	Phoenix Intermediates	1906
Blumenaur, R	rover	New Denver Seniors	1909
Blumenaur, R.	lw	New Denver Seniors	1911

Blumenaur, R. (or Blumeneaus, Bleaumener, Blumenear, Blumenaur, Blumenereau)

Blumenaur, R.	rover	New Denver "A"s	1911
Bois, T. (or Boyes) ("Fatty") see Boyce	goal	Nelson Juveniles	1910
Boland	goal	Rossland Seniors	1911
Boland, "Baby doll"	goal	Grand Forks Seniors	1911
Bonter	forward	Victorias (Rossland seniors)	1901
Bonter, C.	forward	Rossland Seniors	1901
Bonter, C. (Charles ?)	forward	Rossland Seniors (scratch team)	1901
Booth	cover	Trial Intermediates	1910
Borck	goal	Trail Seniors	1902
Bordeille, L.	cover	Kaslo	1898
Borradaile, A.L.T.		Kaslo Bankers	1898
Borradiale	point	Kaslo Seniors	1898

(The above three names are probably the same player with different spellings)

Boss, W.A.		Kaslo Hotel	1898
Boultbee	lw	Rossland Stars (Juvenile)	1906
Bower	forward	Hoboes (Grand Forks)	1903
Bowers, A.E.	goal	Le Roi Mine (Rossland)	1905
Bowers, A.E.	goal	Le Roi Mine (Rossland Industrial League)	1904
Bowes	rover	Silverton Seniors	1904
Bowes	goal	Silverton Seniors	1903
Bows, (or Bews), H.	rw	Revelstoke Seniors	1904
Boyce	rw	Nelson Wood-Vallance	1911
Boyce	rw	Rossland Juniors	1909
Boyce	goal	Nelson Intermediates	1911
Boyce	tried out	Nelson Seniors	1911
Boyce (or Boyes)		Nelson Juniors	1909

Boyce, G.	point	Nelson Junior Warriors (formerly Nelson Juniors)	1909
Boyce, G.	goal	Nelson YMCA Juniors	1911
Boyce, G. (or J.)	rw	Nelson Juniors	1908
Boyce, George	goal	Nelson Intermediates	1911
Boyce, George	rw/goal	Nelson YMCA Juniors	1911
Boyd, J.P.	lw	Lardeau Seniors	1905
Boyd, J-P	centre	Revelstoke Seniors	1903
Boyes		Nelson Juveniles	1909
Boyes	rw	Nelson Juniors	1909
Boyes, G.	centre	Nelson Juniors	1910
Boyes, G..	lw	Nelson YMCA Juniors	1911

(The name Boyes and Boyce has been used interchangeably by the reporters for the same player. However G. Boyes is not necessarily George. At one time, George, and another G. Boyce were playing on the same team.)

Boyes, G..	lw	Nelson YMCA Juniors	1911
Boyes, Tommy	goal	Maple Leafs (Nelson Juvenile)	1909
Boyes, Tommy	goal	Nelson All-Stars (juniors)	1911
Boyes, Tommy	goal	Nelson Rovers (Junior)	1910-11
Braden	rw	Rossland Juveniles	1905
Braden	point	Rossland Intermediates	1906
Braden	cover	Rossland Juniors	1908
Braden	cover	Rossland Intermediates	1911
Braden	goal	Nickel Plate Flat (Rossland Juvenile)	1906
Braden	lw	Grocery Clerks (Rossland)	1906
Braden	rw	Rossland Juniors	1908
Braden	point	Rossland Intermediates	1906
Braden	goal	Nickel Plate Flat (Rossland Juvenile)	1906
Braden, A.	lw	Rocky Mountain Rangers (Rossland)	1907
Braden, A.	center	Rossland Juniors	1904
Braden, A.	cover	Rossland Intermediates	1910
Braden, A.	forward	Hurricanes (Rossland juniors)	1901
Braden, Alf	rw	Rossland Juniors	1905
Braden, E.	rw	Rocky Mountain Rangers (Rossland)	1907
Bradshaw, Reggie	goal	Rossland Juniors	1905
Brandon brothers	tried out for team	Spokane Amateur Athletic Club	1906
Breedon, F.W.	point	Armstrong Seniors	1907
Breeze, A.	center	Sandon Seniors	1911
Bremner, J.A.	point	Ashcroft Seniors	1901
Brennan, William	goal	Kamloops Seniors,	1908
Brett	cover	Nelson High School	1909
Brew	lw	Trail Seniors	1902
Brewster		Banff Seniors	1899
Brewster, W.	forward	Revelstoke Seniors	1901
Bride, Roy	goal	Nelson Grocers	1901
Bright, Harry	capt.	Vancouver's Eastern Canadians "Stars"	1909

Harry Bright had played hockey in Brandon and Pittsburgh. His 1909 team was in poor condition and a Vancouver "scrub" team beat them. Harry Bright was with Lester Patrick when they both were members of the Brandon team that challenged the Ottawa Silver Seven for the Stanley Cup in 1904. They lost both games. (see TOTSC)

Broadhead, R.E.		Broadhead's Boarders challenge team, (Vancouver)	1905
Brock	goal	Trail Seniors	1902
Brown	lw	Fernie Seniors	1904
Brown	goal	Nelson Juniors	1901
Brown	goal	Kaslo Seniors	1901
Brown	centre	Rossland Seniors	1907
Brown	cover	Trail Juniors	1907

Brown	goal	Ashdowns (Nelson hardware)	1907
Brown	goal	Nelson Seniors	1911
Brown	goal	Le Roi (Rossland)	1906
Brown	point	Nelson Juniors	1909
Brown	point	Trail Juniors	1906
Brown	point	Rocky Mountain Rangers (Rossland)	1907
Brown	cover	Rossland Intermediates	1908
Brown	cover	Rocky Mountain Rangers (Rossland)	1906
Brown	forward	Slocan City seniors	1903
Brown	forward	Fernie Seniors	1904
Brown	coverpoint	Rossland Intermediates	1906
Brown,	rover	Grand Forks Senior	1902
Brown, A.	goal	Kaslo Seniors	1897
Brown, A.H.		Kaslo seniors	1901
Brown, C.	l. wing	Fernie Seniors	1904
Brown, C.C.	rw	Rossland Intermediates	1907
Brown, C.C. (or T.D.)	point	Rocky Mountain Rangers (Rossland)	1907
Brown, C.M.	point	Bank of Mon./ Can. Bank of Com. (Rossland)	1901
Brown, D.	point	Nelson Juniors	1910
Brown, D.	point	Trail Juniors	1908
Brown, G.	f	Hunter Brothers (Rossland Ind. League)	1904
Brown, G.	centre	Hunter Brothers (Rossland)	1905
Brown, George	spare	Nelson Wholesalers	1908
Brown, Mat		Vancouver Allstar team (no known opponents)	1910
Brown, R.	lw	Nelson Juniors	1908
Brown, R.	rw	Nelson Junior Warriors (formerly Nelson Juniors)	1909
Brown, R.	cover	Nelson Boy Scouts	1911
Brown, R. (capt)	cover	Nelson Juniors	1910
Brown, Ted		Vancouver scrub team	1905
Bruce, Douglas	goal	Kaslo Hill Juniors	1901
Buchanan	goal	Trail Intermediates	1906
Buchanan	goal	Trail Smelter Team	1905
Buchanan	rover	Centre Star/War Eagle (Rossland)	1906
Buchanan	forward	Phoenix Seniors	1905
Buchanan	rover	Centre Star/War Eagle (Rossland)	1906
Buchanan J.	lw	Trail Smelter	1908
Buchanan, J.	rw	Trail Intermediates	1907
Buchanan, J.	goal	Trail Smelter Team	1905
Buchanan, J.	rw	Trail smelter	1907
Buchanan,R.		Vernon Bankers	1911
Buggins	rw	Trail Seniors	1902
Bull	lw	Slocan City Seniors	1903
Bull	forward	Silverton Seniors	1903
Bullock, L.N.B.	forward	Victoria, Captain Langley's team	1899
Bunyan	manager	Nelson Seniors	1906
Bunyan	Trainer	Nelson East Ward	1906
Burceill, S (probably Burchell) goal		(see also Birchall) Sandon Seniors	1898
Burchell, C.O. (or Birchall) point		Kaslo Seniors	1897
Burchell, E.		Kaslo Hotel	1898
Burde, Frank	manager	Vancouver Seniors practise	1902
Burden, F.	forward	New Westminster Seniors	1901
Burgess, Billy	rover	Kaslo Intermediates	1910
Burgess, w.	rover	Kaslo Seniors	1910
Burke, W.G.	tried out for team	Hunter Brothers (Rossland Ind. League)	1904
Burkitt, J.	lw	New Denver "A"s	1911
Burkitt, G.	goal	New Denver "B"s	1911

Burnette, C.	rover	Vernon Seniors	1907
Burnette, C.	forward	Vernon Town team	1907
Burns, Ernie P.	point	Palace and Filbert Hotels (Sandon)	1901
Burns, F.	goal	Cyclones (Rossland juniors)	1901
Burnyeat, D.		Vernon Bankers	1911
Burnyeat, D.	goal/rover	Armstrong Seniors	1907-08
Bush, W.	goal	Revelstoke Seniors	1907
Bustin	rw	Royal Hotel (Vernon)	1908
Byers, H.		Kaslo Hotel	1898
Byram, H.	cover	Rossland Centre Star	1907
Byrnes, Judd	point	New Denver "A"s	1911
Byrnes, Judd	point	New Denver Seniors	1911
Byrnis, J. (or Byrne)	point	New Denver Seniors	1909
Byrons	point	Silverton Seniors	1903
Calhoun		Vernon Intermediates	1910
Callaghan		Trail Juniors	1904
Callahan	lw	Trail Juniors	1905
Callahan	rw	Trail Intermediates	1906
Callahan	rover	Trail Juniors	1904
Callahan	rw	Trail Intermediates	1906
Callahan	centre	Trail Intermediates	1906
Callahan, John	left wing	Trail Juniors	1905
Calquoun, F.		Vernon Bankers	1911
Cambell, Edwin	secretary	Rossland Seniors	1897
Cameron	rw	Greenwood Seniors	1910
Cameron	point/rover	West Kootenay Power and Light (Rossland)	1906
Cameron, E.A.	cover	Cody Seniors	1910
Cameron, H.D.	forward	Sandon Seniors	1897
Cameron, J	forward	Sandon Seniors	1898
Cameron, Jack	cover	Merchants (Sandon)	1901
Cameron, R.	rw	Greenwood Seniors	1909
Cameron, W.	forward	Ashcroft Seniors	1901
Campbell	point	Rossland Seniors	1897
Campbell	forward	Heroes (Grand Forks)	1903
Campbell, F.	rw	New Denver Seniors	1909
Campbell, K.		Vancouver scrub team	1905
Campbell, K.A.		Vancouver CPR	1901
Campbell, L	forward	Victoria, Captain Langley's team	1899
Campbell, L.A. tried out for team		West Kootenay Power & Lt Co. (Ross Ind. Lg)	1904
Campbell, Lorne A.	goal	West Kootenay Power and Light Company (Rossland)	1903
Campbell, W.J.	centre	Vancouver Bankers	1907
Capt. Langley,	point	Victoria, Captain Langley's team	1899
Cardiff		Spokane Seniors (suggested for team)	1910
Cardiff	lw	Spokane Seniors	1908
Cardiff	lw	Spokane Seniors	1908
Carey, J.	rw	Vernon Intermediates	1910
Carey, J.	centre	Vernon Juniors	1903
Carey, J.	r. wing	Commonage Intermediates (Vernon)	1904
Carlington, A.R.	forward	Nicola Lake Seniors	1902
Carmichael		Rosslands	1903
Carmichael	cover	Rossland Seniors	1902
Carmichael	f	Rossland Victorias	1901
Carmichael	cover	Rossland Victorias	1903
Carmichael	f	Rossland Seniors	1901
Carmichael	point	Archer's Flat Team (Kaslo)	1900
Carmichael	rover	Hunter Brothers (Rossland)	1905

Carmichael	cover	Victorias (Rossland)	1902
Carmichael	cover	Rossland Junior Victorias	1902
Carmichael	cover	Rossland Intermediates	1905
Carmichael	lw	Wood's Independents (Spokane)	1907
Carmichael, Charles	f	Merchants (Sandon)	1901
Carmichael, D.J.	cover	Saloons (Sandon)	1901
Carmichael, Duncan J.	f	Palace and Filbert Hotels (Sandon)	1901
Carmichael, G.	cover	Rossland Seniors	1901
Carmichael, G.	forward	Rosslands (senior)	1901
Carmichael, G.	cover	Bank of Montreal (Rossland)	1903
Carmichael, G.A.	forward	Rossland Seniors	1901
Carmichael, G.M.	cover	Phoenix Seniors	1904
Carmichael, R.	forward	Phoenix Seniors	1904
Carney	forward	Kaslo Seniors	1901
Carney	goal	Kaslo Seniors	1909
Carney, Augustus (Gustie)	forward	Kaslo Hill Juniors	1901
Carney, C.		Sandon Juniors	1899
Carney, G (?)		Kaslo Intermediates	1908
Carney, G.	rw	Kaslo Intermediates	1910
Carney, H.		Kaslo Seniors	1901
Carney, H.	point	Kaslo Seniors	1910
Carney, Hiram (brother of Thomas)		Kaslo Juniors	1899
Carney, T.	cover	Kaslo Intermediates	1910
Carney, Thomas	forward	Kaslo Hill Juniors	1901
Carney, W.		Sandon Juniors	1899
Carpenter, W.	centre	Bank of Montreal (Rossland)	1903
Carruthers	goal	Rossland Seniors	1909
Cary, J.	rw	Vernon Seniors	1908-09
Cawley	cover	Salmo Hoboes (inter-city)	1910
Chalk, "Chick" (or Chic)	rover	Fernie Seniors	1906
Chalmers, F.W.	forward	Rossland Victorias	1899
Chambers	rw	Arlington Hotel "Shin-Peelers" (Trail)	1907
Chambers, W.	lw	Revelstoke Seniors	1903
Champion, W.	goal	Nelson Tramway	1901
Channer	tried out for team	Spokane Amateur Athletic Club	1906
Chapman		Trail Juniors	1904
Chapman		Trail Seniors	1910
Chapman	goal	Trail Intermediates	1909
Chapman	goal	Trail Intermediates	1906
Chapman	centre	Trail Juniors	1904
Chapman, A.	goal	Trail Intermediates	1907
Chapman, A.	goal	Trail Smelter	1907
Chapman, A.	goal	Trail Smelter	1908
Chapman, A.	goal	Trail Intermediates	1910
Chapman, Arthur	right wing	Trail Juniors	1905
Charbonneau, F.	centre	Sandon Intermediates	1908
Charlton		Nicola Seniors	1908
Charlton	lw	Greenwood Seniors	1911
Charlton	cover	Nicola Seniors	1910
Chave, (E.J. ?)	rover	Nelson Mountains	1908
Chene, L.	point	New Westminster (Royals)	1907
Chester (prob. Chesterton)	cover	Rossland Seniors	1898
Chesterton		Rossland Senior	1898
Chesterton	lw	Phoenix Seniors	1902
Chesterton	forward	Rossland Bank team	1897
Chesterton,	centre	Greenwood Seniors	1902

Name	Position	Team	Year
Chesterton, CW.	Forward	Rosslands	1899
Cheyne	goal	New Westminster Seniors	1901
Cheyne, R.H.		New Westminster (Royals)	1907
Chisolm, J.A.		Sandon Seniors	1913
Christian, C.		Vernon Seniors	1901
Christian, L.	rover	Armstrong Juniors	1907
Christie, H.R.		Slocan City Seniors	1899
Christien, H.	goal	Vernon High School	1903
Chubb	cover	Rossland Bankers	1907
Church	cover	Phoenix Seniors	1903
Church, E.		Summerland Seniors	1910
Clarence		Vancouver scrub team	1905
Clark		Salmo Intermediates	1911
Clark	centre	Trail Seniors	1902
Clark	lw	Phoenix Intermediates	1906
Clark	cover	Phoenix Intermediates	1907
Clark	rover	Phoenix Seniors	1910
Clark(e)		Phoenix Seniors	1903
Clark(e), R.	rw	Phoenix Seniors	1909
Clark, A.E.	cover	Ymir Seniors	1911
Clark, Alfred	rover	Ymir Seniors	1911
Clark, H.	point	Phoenix Intermediates	1908
Clark, J.	point	Salmo Seniors	1911
Clark, R.	rw	Phoenix Intermediates	1908
Clark, R.	centre	Phoenix Seniors	1910
Clark, Roy	rover	Phoenix Seniors	1910
Clark, W.	center	Associated Banks (Rossland)	1903
Clark, X.	rw	Rosslands	1903
Clarke, A.	forward	Phoenix Seniors	1904
Clarke, R.	rover	Missoula (Montana) Seniors	1911
Clerf	center	Greenwood Seniors	1910
Clerf (or Cleft)	rw	Greenwood Seniors	1911
Cleveland	f	Rossland Seniors	1898
Cliff(e), W.	f	Sandon Juniors	1901
Cliff(e), W. (Billy)	forward	Sandon Juniors	1899, 1901
Cliffe		Sandon Seniors	1899
Cliffe		Sandon Seniors	1900
Cliffe	f	Sandon Seniors	1901
Cliffe	point	Printers of Sandon (Dec. 1901)	1902
Cliffe	spare	Sandon Seniors	1902
Cliffe	forward	Sandon Juniors	1901
Cliffe, B.	f	Merchants (Sandon)	1901
Cliffe, W.	cover	Kaslo Intermediates	1908
Cliffe, W. (probably Walter)	f	Printers of Sandon (Dec. 1901)	1902
Cliffe, Walter		Sandon Juniors	1899
Cliffe, William (capt.)		Sandon Juniors	1899
Cliffe, Wm	centre	Lardeau Seniors	1905
Cliffe, Wm.	f	Printers of Sandon (Dec. 1901)	1902
Cliffe, Wm.	forward	Sandon Seniors	1903

(William Cliff was listed in the 1904 B.C. directory for Sandon as a millman.)

Name	Position	Team	Year
Clothier		Rossland Seniors	1903
Clothier	lw	Rossland Seniors	1902
Clothier	rover	Rossland Seniors	1904
Clothier	lw	Rossland Victorias	1903
Clothier	lw	Rossland Junior Victorias	1902
Clothier	rw/centre	Moyie Seniors	1909

Name	Position	Team	Year
Clothier	rover	Rossland Seniors	1904
Clothier	point	Phoenix Seniors	1910
Clothier, George	cover	Le Roi Mine (Rossland Industrial League)	1904
Clothier, Roy	f	Sandon City (Dec. 1901)	1902
Clothier, Roy	centre/cover	Phoenix Seniors	1910
Clunis	rw	Nelson Rivers	1908
Clunis	spare	Victorias (Nelson City League)	1909
Clunis, C.	spare	Phoenix Seniors	1909
Clunis, M.	lw	Nelson Intermediates	1906
Clunis, M.	spare/lw/centre	Nelson Seniors	1907
Cochrane		Vernon Single Men	1906
Cochrane	goal	Vernon Seniors	1904
Cochrane, A.O.		Vernon Seniors	1900-01
Cochrane, A.O.	goal	Grand Forks Seniors	1902-03
Cody	forward	Archer's Flat Team (Kaslo)	1900
Cody, E.	forward	Nelson Seniors	1905
Cody, E. D.	spare	Nelson Seniors	1905
Cody, L.		Kaslo Seniors	1900
Cole	lw	Rossland Intermediates	1908
Cole	goal	Phoenix Seniors	1903
Cole, Arthur A.	tried out for team	War Eagle Mine (Rossland Industrial League)	1904
Cole, H.	lw	Centre Star (Rossland)	1908
Coleman		Trail Juniors	1904
Coleman, H.	goal	Trail Juniors	1904
Coleman, H.	goal	Hurricanes (Rossland junior)	1901
Coles	spare	Phoenix Seniors	1902
Collings (probably Collins, below)	point	Phoenix Seniors	1907
Collins	point	Phoenix Seniors	1904
Collins	cover	Phoenix Seniors	1905
Collins	forward	C.P.R. Shops (Cranbrook)	1911
Collins, Jack	point	Phoenix Seniors	1907
Collins, T.	point	Nelson Seniors	1902
Colpitts	point	Reilly Club of Nelson	1904
Colton	forward	Phoenix Seniors	1903
Conklin	goal	Trail Seniors	1902
Connell	rw	West Kootenay Power and Light (Rossland)	1906
Connelly	forward	Kaslo Seniors	1899
Conolly	rw	Cranbrook Seniors	1911
Conroy	cover	Rossland Seniors	1905
Conroy	point	Rossland Intermediates	1905
Cook, P.	cover	Phoenix Seniors	1903
Cook, W.	point	Phoenix Seniors	1903
Cooke, R.F.	forward 1 game	Nelson City Seniors	1900
Cooper	rw	Le Roi (Rossland)	1906
Cooper, W.		Nelson Seniors	1897
Copeland	point	Kelowna Seniors	1909
Cornwall, H.A.	lw/cover	Kamloops Seniors	1902-03
Cosgriff	rw	Rossland Juniors	1908
Cosgriff	goal	Rossland Seniors	1910
Cosgriff(e)	goal	Rossland Intermediates	1909-10
Cosgriff(e)	goal	Rossland Seniors	1910-11
Cosgriff, F.	lw	Rossland Juniors	1908
Cosgriffe	lw	Rossland Juniors	1907
Cosgriffe, F.	goal	Rossland Intermediates	1910
Cosgro, John, P.	goal	War Eagle Mine (Rossland Industrial League)	1904
Costello	centre	Hunter Brothers (Rossland Ind. League)	1904

Costello	goal	Rossland Junior Victorias	1899
Coulson (or Colton)		Grand Forks Seniors	1903
Coulton	rw	Phoenix Seniors	1902
Coulton	forward	Phoenix Senior	1904
Cowan		Coldstream Ranch Seniors	1911
Cowan, Sandy		Vancouver Seniors practise	1902
Cowan, Sandy	forward	Vancouver Seniors	1901
Cowan, Sandy	forward	Vancouver CPR	1901
Cowan, T. (or C.)	forward	Nelson Seniors	1899
Coxhead, pte.	forward	Nelson Militia	1901
Cram, James, K.	f	War Eagle Mine (Rossland Industrial League)	1904
Crandel		Smithers Seniors	1910
Crawford		Sandon Seniors	1900
Crawford	rw	Rossland Seniors	1906
Crawford	rw	Rossland Victorias Alberta Challenge Team	1906
Crawford	forward	Sandon Seniors	1899
Crawford	forward	Sandon Seniors	1900
Crawford	forward (1 game)	Sandon Juniors	1901
Crawford		Sandon Juniors	1899
Crawford, Ernie	f	Sandon City (Dec. 1901)	1902
Crawford, Ernie	cover	Sandon Juniors	1899, 1901
Crawford, Ernie	rover	Sandon Seniors	1902
Crawford, Ernie	rover	Lardeau Seniors	1905
Crawford, Ernie	forward	Sandon Seniors	1900,02-03
Crawford, Ernie		Sandon Juniors	1899
Crawford, Ernie	cover	Sandon Juniors	1901

(In the 1899 Sandon city directory, Ernie Crawford is listed as a bell boy).

Crawford, J	point	Sandon Seniors	1900, 1902-03
Crawford, J.	point	Sandon Juniors	1901
Crawford, J.	point	Sandon Seniors	1902
Crawford, J.	point	Sandon City (Dec. 1901)	1902
Crawford, J.	cover	Sandon Seniors	1903
Crawford, J.	point	Sandon Juniors	1899-1901
Crawford, Jack		Sandon Juniors	1899
Crawford, Jack		Slocan City Seniors	1899
Crawford, Jack	point	Lardeau Seniors	1905
Crawford, Jack	point	Sandon Seniors	1901
Crawford, W.	cover	Sandon Seniors	1902
Crawford, W.	cover	Sandon City (Dec. 1901)	1902
Crawford, W. Jack (Rusty)		Sandon Juniors	1899
Crawford, W.J.		Sandon Juniors	1901
Crawford, W.J. (Rusty) cover (capt. in 1902)		Sandon Seniors	1900-01-02-03
Crawford, William	f	Sandon Juniors	1901

(There was also a Willam James Crawford listed in Sandon in the 1904 B.C. directory as a packer, as well as a John A.. who was a packer at S.F. Colla.)

Crawford, Wm.	cover	Lardeau Seniors	1905
Cropp, Rev.	goal	Nicola Lake Seniors	1902
Crosbie	point	New Denver "B"s	1911
Cross	lw	Hunter Brothers (Rossland)	1905
Cross, Floyd	cover	Cyclones (Rossland juniors)	1901
Crosse, D.	cover	Nelson Intermediates	1904
Crough, J.E.	cover	Nelson Seniors	1901
Crow	cover	Nelson Juniors	1901
Crowell, T. Jr.		Vernon Seniors	1900
Crowell, T.E.	spare/or manager	Vernon Seniors	1904

Name	Position	Team	Year
Crowell, Thomas E.	rover (capt. in 1900)	Vernon Seniors	1900-01-02-03
Cruikshank, G.	tried out for team	War Eagle Mine (Rossland Industrial League)	1904
Cue	center	New Denver "A"s	1911
Cummings	center	Salmo Mess (inter-city)	1910
Cummings	goal	Nelson Juniors	1907
Cummins	goal	Nelson Juniors	1907
Cummins	goal	Nelson Juniors	1909
Cummins	rw	Nelson Juniors	1910
Cummins, (also Cumming)T.	goal/cover	Nelson Juniors	1908
Cummins, C.	goal	Nelson Intermediates	1908
Cummins, C.	center	Salmo Seniors/Intermediates	1910
Cummins, F.	rover	Nelson Challengers (Junior)	1910
Cummins, F.	cover	Nelson Mic-Macs (Junior)	1910
Cummins, N.	goal	Nelson Lakes	1908
Cummins, T.	rover	Nelson Junior Warriors (formerly Nelson Juniors)	1909
Cummins, T..	cover	Nelson Juniors	1910
Cummins, T.C.	centre	Salmo Seniors	1911
Cummins, T.C.	(from photo)	Nelson Intermediates	1909
Cummins, Taffy	cover	Nelson Rovers (junior)	1911
Cunnigham, P.	centre	Trail Juniors	1907
Cunningham		Trail Juniors	1904
Cunningham	lw	Trail Intermediates	1906
Cunningham	centre	Trail Juniors	1908
Cunningham, Jimmy	point	Meakin Hotel "Never-Sweats" (Trail)	1907
Cunningham, P.	lw	Meakin Hotel "Never-Sweats" (Trail)	1907
Curley, William (capt)		Brooklyn Hotel (Phoenix)	1911
Curran	cover	Nelson Intermediates	1903
Curran, J.	cover	Rossland Intermediates	1904
Curran, Joe.W.	cover	Nelson Juniors	1902
Curtin, Doc.	Goal	Nicola Seniors	1910
Curtis, C.	forward	Nicola Seniors	1908
Dalmage	point	Fernie Seniors	1906
Dalmage, F.	point	Fernie Seniors	1905
Dancey	point	Nicola Seniors	1910
Daniels, F.J.	point	Victoria, Daniel's team,	1899
Daniels, P.R.	forward	Victoria Daniel's team,	1899
Darling, F.	goal	Rossland Juniors	1904
Darragh	cover	Trail Seniors	1902
Davidson	rover	Rossland Intermediates	1909
Davidson	rw	Rossland Juniors	1909
Davidson, (Davison), W.		Nelson Seniors (as sub)	1906
Davidson, (Davison), W.	cover	Nelson West Ward ("Hand-Warmers")	1907
Davidson, (Davison), W.	spare	Nelson East Ward	1906
Davidson, (or Davison)	lw	Nelson Juveniles	1905
Davidson, W.	goal	Nelson Juniors	1902
Davis	rover	Rossland Seniors	1902
Davis, A.W.	forward	Rosslands	1899
Davis, Carl R.	point	War Eagle Mine (Rossland Industrial League)	1904
Davison		Rossland Seniors	1910
Davison	rover	Rossland Seniors	1910
Davison (or Davidson)		Rossland Juveniles	1909
Davison, Billy	point	Nelson East Ward	1907
Dawson	lw	Trail Intermediates	1909
Daykin, J.	centre/rover/lw	Armstrong Seniors	1907-08-09
Dayton, George (capt)	cover	Commonage Intermediate Team (Vernon)	1904
Dayton, H.	goal	Commonage Intermediates (Vernon)	1904

De Voin	forward	Rossland Junior Victorias	1899
Deacon	point	Nelson Seniors	1908
Deacon	cover	Nelson Mountains	1908
Deacon	cover	Reilly Club of Nelson	1904
Deacon, F., (or W.H.)	point	Nelson Seniors	1905
Deacon, W.H.		Nelson West Ward	1906
Deacon, W.H.	cover	Rossland Seniors	1907
Deacon, W.H.	cover/point	Nelson Seniors	1904-06
Deacon, W.H.	point	Nelson "Fossils"	1908
Dean, D.W. (or S.W.)	point	Kamloops Seniors	1903
DeCew, R.	rw	Nelson Cyclones (high school)	1910
Decew, R.	cover	Nelson High School	1909
Dedolph, W.	rw	Kaslo Juniors	1910
Demock	lw	Moyie Seniors	1909
Demuth	rover	Rossland Juniors	1908
Demuth	centre	Rossland Invincibles (Juniors)	1906
Demuth	centre	Grand Forks Seniors	1911
Demuth	l. wing	Rossland Juniors	1905
Demuth	rover	Rossland Juniors	1907
Demuth	rw	Rossland Seniors	1910
Demuth	center	Rossland Juveniles	1905
Demuth (or Demouth)	lw	Rossland Intermediates	1909
Demuth B.	rw	Rossland Invincibles (Juniors)	1905
Demuth,	rover	Rossland Juniors	1908
Demuth, J.	centre	Rossland Invincibles (Junior)	1905
Demuth, O.	lw	Rossland Intermediates	1910
Demuth, O.	rover	Rossland Juniors	1904
Denison (brothers)		Lumby Seniors	1911
Dennings, T.	goal	Kamloops Seniors	1902
Dennison or Denison	centre	Lumby Seniors	1911
Dewdney	lw	Rossland Bankers	1906
Dewdney	lw	Rossland Bankers	1907
Dewdney, (possibly E.E.L.)	lw	Bank of Montreal (Rossland)	1905
Dewdney, E.E.	f	Bank of Montreal (Rossland Industrial League)	1904
Dewdney, E.L.	forward	Bank of Mon./Can Bank of Com. (Rossland)	1901
Dewry, H.	lw	Nelson Cyclones (high school)	1910
Dickson	lw	Rossland Seniors	1908
Dickson, F.		Vernon Bankers	1911
Dickson, J.	forward	Cyclones (Rossland juniors)	1901
Dickson, J.	forward	Rossland Juniors	1901
Dickson, J.	forward	Rossland Cyclones (Junior)	1901
Dickson, J.	forward	Cyclones (Rossland juniors)	1901
Dill	lw	Greenwood Seniors	1902
Dill	cover	Kaslo Seniors	1899
Dill	forward	Hodder's Hill Team (Kaslo)	1900
Dill,	cover	Kaslo Seniors	1901
Dill, (Bert)		Kaslo seniors	1899-1900
Dill, A.J.	point	Nelson Diamond A-Ashdown Hockey Club (Hardware)	1906
Dill, B	forward	Kaslo Seniors	1897-98
Dill, E.B.	point	Boundary Seniors	1906
Dill, E.B. (or E.P.)	point	Boundary combined team	1906
Dill, J.	cover	Kaslo Seniors	1900
Dill, S.	point	Greenwood Seniors	1909
Dill, A.	forward	Nelson Wholesalers	1904
Dimmock (or Dimock)	lw	Moyie Seniors	1909
Dimock, R.	lw/rw	Moyie Seniors	1910

Name	Position	Team	Year
Dinmore (?) D.		Moyie Seniors	1910
Dion(?) J.		Moyie Seniors	1910
Dixon	lw	Rossland Intermediates	1905
Dixon	lw	Rossland Seniors	1909
Dixon	lw	Rossland Seniors	1911
Dixon	rw	Rossland Seniors	1909
Dixon	rw	Rossland Seniors	1907
Dixon	rw	Rossland Intermediates	1906
Dixon	forward	Rossland Intermediates	1903
Dixon	rw	Rossland Intermediates	1906
Dixon	centre	Le Roi Mine (Rossland)	1905
Dixon	lw	Rossland Intermediates	1906
Dixon, E.	rover	Rossland Juniors	1902
Dixon, J.	rw	Moyie Seniors	1910
Dixon, J.	lw	Rossland Seniors	1911
Dixon, J.	forward	Nelson Intermediates	1904
Dixon, J.	lw/rw	Moyie Seniors	1910
Dixon, J.A.	centre	Le Roi Mine (Rossland)	1905
Dixon, James	rw	Rossland Seniors	1907
Dixon, James	rover	Rossland Juniors	1902
Dixon, S.	rw	Rossland Seniors	1907
Dixon, Scotty	rw	Rossland Seniors	1908
Dixon, Tom		Rossland Cigarmakers, or Bartenders	1911
Donahoe (or Donahue)	point	Moyie Seniors	1909
Donahue		Rossland Juveniles	1909
Donahue		Rosslands	1903
Donahue	point	Rossland Seniors	1904
Donahue	point	Rossland Seniors	1906
Donahue	centre	Rossland Juniors	1909
Donahue	cover	Rosslands (senior)	1901
Donahue	center	Rossland Juniors	1909
Donahue	rw (one game)	Rossland Intermediates	1910
Donahue	spare	Rossland Victorias Alberta Challenge Team	1906
Donahue (Donohue), Jack	point/cover	Rossland Seniors	1904-05-06-07-08,11
Donahue, J.	forward	Columbias (Rossland junior)	1901
Donahue, J. (capt)	point	Rossland Seniors	1911
Donahue, Jack	goal	Rossland Juniors	1899
Donahue, Jack	point	Moyie Seniors	1910
Donahue, Jack	point	Rossland Seniors	1908
Donahue, John (Jack)		Rossland Juniors, IXL	1899
Donahue, John (Jack) (capt)	point	Rossland Seniors	1907
Donahue, Phil	lw	Rossland Intermediates	1910
Donahue, Phil	rover	Rossland Stars (Juvenile)	1906
Donaldson	lw	Salmo Mess (inner-city)	1910
Donaldson, John	goal	Hoboes (Grand Forks)	1903
Donnelly	forward	Kaslo Seniors	1897
Donnelly, J.	coverpoint	Kaslo Seniors	1897
Donohoe	spare	Victorias (Rossland)	1902
Donohoe	point	Rossland Citizen Team	1903
Donohue	rover	Rossland Junior Victorias	1902
Donough, Charles		Nelson Seniors	1897
Dorman	centre	Missoula (Montana) Seniors	1911
Douglas	cover	Hodder's Hill Team (Kaslo)	1900
Douglas (capt)		Banff Seniors	1899
Douglas, K.	forward	Nelson West Ward ("Hand-Warmers")	1907
Douglas, R. (capt)	rover	Revelstoke Seniors	1903

Name	Position	Team	Year
Douskue (?) J		Moyie	1910
Downey, M	forward	Nelson Hardware	1901
Downey, pte	forward	Nelson Militia	1901
Driscoll	centre	Meakin Hotel "Never-Sweats" (Trail)	1907
Dumoulin	cover	Nelson Bankers	1903
Driscoll	Forward	Trail Juniors	1907
Driscoll	cover	Grocery Clerks (Rossland)	1906
Duncan	lw	Coldstream Hotel (Vernon)	1908
Duncan, J.H.	f	Nicola Lake Seniors	1902
Duncan, Thomas	forward	Nelson Seniors	1897,99-1900

It appears that Thomas Duncan became a mining developer, being at one time the local director of Duncan Mines, ltd.

Name	Position	Team	Year
Duncan, Wm	point	Nelson City Seniors	1900
Duncan, Wm.	Point	Nelson Seniors	1897-98-99
Dunlap		Fernie Seniors	1911
Dunn		Vancouver CPR	1901
Dunn	forward (?)	Camborne Alberta Seniors	1908
Dunn (e), Tim	point	Nelson Seniors	1909-10
Dunn(e), Tim	cover	Thistles (Nelson City League)	1909
Dunn(e), Tim	point	Victorias (Nelson inter-City)	1910
Dunn, Nelson		Vancouver Seniors practise	1902
Dunn, Nelson	goal	Vancouver Seniors	1901
Dunn, P.	centre	Revelstoke Seniors	1907
Dunn, T.	point	Nelson Seniors	1910
Dunne, C.	forward	Nelson Tramway	1901
Dunne, W.	f	War Eagle Mine (Rossland Industrial League)	1904
Duthie, E.	tried out for team	Bank of Montreal (Rossland Industrial League)	1904
Eakins		Vernon Megaws	1911
Eden	forward	Nelson Bankers	1903
Edmonds, W.H.	Manager/coach	Kamloops Picked Town Team	1903
Edwards, E.	cover	Revelstoke Seniors	1904
Edwards, E.	point	Revelstoke Seniors	1901
Edwards, J.		Vernon Seniors	1900
Eede	lw	Spokane Amateur Athletic Club	1907
Egan	goal	Rossland bank team	1897
Egan, Charlie	goal	New Westminster (Royals) (Lent by Vancouver)	1907
Ehlers	point	Rossland Juniors	1909
Ehlers, W.	point	Rossland Juniors	1911
Ellers	point	Rossland Juniors	1909
Ellers, W.	point	Rossland Juniors	1911
Elliott		Vernon Intermediates	1910
Elliott	cover	Royal Hotel (Vernon)	1908
Elliott	cover	Grand Forks Seniors	1909
Elliott	forward	Silverton Seniors	1903
Elliott, (Elliot) P. (capt)	cover	Vernon Seniors	1907-08
Elliott, (Elliot) P.	cover	Vernon Town team	1907
Elliott, A.	cover	Nelson Cyclones (high school)	1910
Ellis	goal	Nelson Invincibles (Junior)	1905
Ellis	point	Phoenix Seniors	1911
Ellis	point	Trial Intermediates	1910
Ellis, E.	goal	Nelson Juveniles	1905
Elwood	point	Vancouver Seniors	1901
Elwood, J.B.	cover	Rosslands	1899
Elwood, J.B.	cover	Rossland Seniors	1900
Elworthy, Edward (or Ellworthy) (capt)	cover	Vernon Seniors	1902-03-04
Emery, A.B.	cover	War Eagle Mine (Rossland Industrial League)	1904

Name	Position	Team	Year
Emory, C.	goal	Nelson Invincibles (high school)	1910
Emory, C.	goal	Nelson High School	1909
Emory, C.	spare goal	Nelson Rovers (Junior)	1910
England	goal	Spokane Amateur Athletic Club	1907
English	lw	Missoula (Montana) Seniors	1911
Erickson, Al	forward	Hurricanes (Rossland junior)	1901
Estey		Revelstoke seniors	1899
Etter	rw	Salmo Mess (inter-city)	1910
Etter	rover	Nelson Wood-Vallance	1911
Evans	goal	Rossland Intermediates	1911
Evans	goal	Rossland Juniors	1909
Evans	goal	Rossland Intermediates	1911
Evans.	Goal	Rossland Juniors	1909
Ewing	f	Phoenix Seniors	1901
Ewing	lw/rw	Phoenix Seniors	1902
Ewing, George, (capt)	cover	Grand Forks Seniors	1903
Fair, C.G.	cover	Salmo Seniors	1911
Falding	rover	Rossland Bankers	1906
Falding, H.	right wing	Associated Banks (Rossland)	1903
Falding, Homer	point	Bank of Montreal (Rossland Industrial League)	1904
Farrell	spare	Grand Forks Senior	1902
Faulkner, J.		Summerland Seniors	1910
Feeney		Grand Forks Juniors	1903
Feeney, B.	goal	Salmo Seniors/Intermediates	1910
Feeney, D.	goal	Salmo Hoboes (inner-city)	1910
Feeney, S.	rw	Salmo Hoboes (inner-city)	1910
Feill (probably Neill	cover	Spokane Amateur Athletic Club	1907
Felion	rover	Rossland Victorias	1903
Felion	forward	Rossland Seniors	1903
Fennel, V..	point	Maple Leafs (Nelson Juvenile)	1909
Ferguson		Imperial Bank (Nelson)	1908
Ferguson	cover	Nelson Lakes	1908
Ferguson,	spare	Nelson Wholesalers	1904
Ferguson, B.	cover	Nelson Invincibles (high school)	1910
Ferguson, H.	point	Nelson Cyclones (high school)	1910
Ferguson, Johnnie	spare	Nelson Seniors	1911
Ferguson, Johnnie	rover	Nelson Public School	1909
Ferguson, Johnnie	rw	Nelson Boy Scouts	1911
Ferguson, Johnnie	rw	Nelson Rovers (Junior)	1910
Ferguson, W.	cover	Nelson Seniors	1907

W. Ferguson played in Vancouver, before moving to Nelson. Before that he played in Cincinatti, Houghton Michigan, and Portage La Prairie.

Name	Position	Team	Year
Ferguson, Waldo		Nelson Public School	1909
Ferguson, Waldo	lw	Nelson Seniors	1911
Ferguson, Waldo	lw/rw	Nelson Rovers (Junior)	1910-11
Ferrier	f	Rossland Victorias	1901
Ferrier	point	Rossland Seniors	1902
Ferrier	point	Rosslands (senior)	1901
Ferrier	point	Victorias (Rossland)	1902
Ferrier	point	Rossland Junior Victorias	1902
Ferrier	goal	Rossland Juniors	1901
Ferrier (probably Roy)	point/goal	Spokane Seniors	1907-08

Ferrier was a Canadian who played for Spokane Seniors.

Name	Position	Team	Year
Ferrier,	point	Spokane Seniors	1908
Ferrier, E.	point	Columbias (Rossland junior)	1901
Ferrier, Elgin		Rossland IXL Juniors,	1899

Ferrier, Elgin	point	Rossland Juniors	1899
Ferrier, R.	cover	Spokane Seniors	1907
Ferrier, R.	goal	Columbias (Rossland junior)	1901
Ferrier, Roy	forward	Rossland Juniors	1899
Ferrier, Roy	goal	Spokane Seniors	1907
Ferrier, Roy	cover	Wood's Independents (Spokane)	1907
Ferrier, Roy	spare	Spokane Amateur Athletic Club	1906
Ferrier, Roy	cover/point	Spokane Seniors	1907-08
Ferrier, Roy (Capt)	cover	Eagles (Spokane)	1906
Ferris, James (capt)		King Hotel (Phoenix)	1911
Ferry, S.	lw	Salmo Seniors/Intermediates	1910
Ferteath	rw	Rossand Juniors	1905
Field		Golden Senior	1899
Fife, F.	rover	Nelson East Ward ("Stick-Arounds")	1907
Fife, F.	tried out	Nelson Intermediates	1908
Finerty	point	Nelson Invincibles (Junior)	1905
Fisher, H. G.	forward	Bank of Mon./Can Bank of Com. (Rossland)	1901
Fisher, S.	cover	Armstrong Juniors	1907
Fleming	goal	Nelson Bank Team	1907
Fleming	tried out	Moyie Seniors	1909
Fleming George	spare	Bell Trading Company (Nelson grocers)	1906
Fletcher, Archie	officer	Kaslo Seniors	1897
Fletcher, H.	lw	Nelson Invincibles (high school)	1910
Fletcher, H.	rover	Nelson Boy Scouts	1911
Fletcher, H.R.		Kaslo Bankers	1898
Flood, Billy		Vancouver Seniors practise	1902
Foley, J.T.	rw	Sandon Seniors	1910
Foote	tried out	Moyie Seniors	1909
Foote, C.O.		Moyie Seniors	1910
Ford, J.	point	Nelson Tramway	1901
Forrester		Vernon Bankers	1911
Forrester.	center	Coldstream Hotel (Vernon)	1908
Forteath	rw	Rocky Mountain Rangers (Rossland)	1906
Forteath, D.	lw	Rossland Juniors	1905
Forteath, D.	r. wing	Rossland Juniors	1904
Forteath, D.	rover	Rocky Mountain Rangers (Rossland)	1907
Forteith, D.	rw	Nelson Intermediates	1908
Forteith, D.	forward	Nelson West Ward int	1907
Fortin, F. D.	cover	West Kootenay Power & Light Co. (Ross Ind. League)	1904
Foster		Rossland Cigarmakers, or Bartenders	1911
Foster	goal	Bank of Mon./Can Bank of Com. (Rossland)	1901
Foster	Honorary President	Golden Seniors	1895
Fotheringham, Billy (?)	goal/trainer	Nelson East Ward ("Stick-Arounds")	1906-07
Fotheringham, W.	goal	Nelson Lakes	1908
Fox	cover	Rossland Invincibles (Juniors)	1905
Fox	cover	Rossland Invincibles (Juniors)	1906
Fox	cover	Rossland Juveniles	1905
Fox, T.	centre	Cody Seniors	1910
Francis, A.	goal	Armstrong Juniors	1907
Francis, B.	rw	Armstrong Intermediates	1910
Franier, George	forward	Phoenix Seniors	1904
Fraser		Vancouver scrub team	1905
Fraser	forward	Nelson Wholesalers	1903
Fraser (or Frazer)	spare/centre	Phoenix Seniors	1907
Fraser, George	point	Le Roi Mine (Rossland Industrial League)	1904
Fraser, J.	rover	Phoenix Seniors	1907

Fraser, J.	centre	Phoenix Intermediates	1907
Fraser, J.	center	Fernie Seniors	1905
Fraser, J.S.C.	goal	Associated Banks (Rossland)	1903
Fraser, J.S.C.	tried out for team	Bank of Montreal (Rossland Industrial League)	1904
Frazer, E.W.	cover	Vancouver Bankers	1907
Fred	rover	Royal Hotel (Vernon)	1908
French, G. (capt)	l wing	Vernon High School	1903
French, P.	rover	Vernon Seniors	1908-09
French, P.	r wing	Vernon High School	1903
French, S.	lw	Vernon Juniors	1907
Friez	rover	Trail Intermediates	1906
Friez	lw	Trail Intermediates	1906
Frieze	rover	Trail Intermediates	1906
Frost		Banff Senior	1899
Frost	forward	Rosslands Seniors	1900
Frost, C.E.		Kaslo Seniors	1899
Frost, S. (capt)	forward	Kaslo Seniors	1898-99
Fuller	goal/centre	Kelowna Seniors	1909
Fulmer, Gordon	cover	Vernon Intermediates	1910
Fulton		Vernon Megaws	1911
Funk	center	Rossland Juniors	1902
Funk	centre	Rossland Intermediates	1905
Funk, Ed	centre	Rossland Juniors	1902
Funk, Ed.	forward	Hurricanes (Rossland junior)	1901
Funk, Eddie	forward	Nelson Intermediates	1904

Edward Funk was the son of Mr. and Mrs. William Funk of Rossland. He was an all-around athlete, playing baseball and lacrosse as well. He traveled to McGill in 1905 to study, and apparently went into medicine.

Futcher	goal	Rocky Mountain Rangers (Rossland)	1906
Gagnon, Louis	goal	Saloons (Sandon)	1901
Galbraith	lw	New Westminster (Royals)	1907
Gallon	forward	Rossland Intermediates	1904
Gallon, T.	forward	Reilly Club of Nelson	1904
Gamble, C.	forward	Victoria, Daniel's team,	1899
Garde, F.	rw/rover	Nelson Public School	1909
Gardner, Martin	f	Saloons (Sandon)	1901
Garrett, "Rusty"	forward (?)	Ferguson Seniors	1908
George	point	Coldstream Hotel (Vernon)	1908
Gerrard, G.B.		Kaslo Bankers	1898
Gibbs, H.	center	Nelson Invincibles (high school)	1910
Gibbs, H.	rw	Nelson High School	1909
Gibbs, M.	left wing	Associated Banks (Rossland)	1903
Gibson G.	rw	Nelson All-Stars (juniors)	1911
Gibson, D.	rw	Junior Thistles (Nelson Juvenile)	1909
Gichrist, L.	forward	Nelson Juniors	1901
Gifford, C.	centre	New Denver Seniors	1909
Gifford, T.	(Probably goal)	New Westminster (Royals)	1907
Gigot	lw	Phoenix Intermediates	1907
Gigot	rw	Nelson Intermediates	1906
Gilchrist, Lance	center	Nelson Juniors	1902
Gilchrist, P.	forward	Nelson Juniors	1901
Gill	goal	Hunter Brothers (Rossland)	1905
Gill	goal	Grocery Clerks (Rossland)	1906
Gill, B.	goal	Rocky Mountain Rangers (Rossland)	1907
Gill, H.B.	goal	Rocky Mountain Rangers (Rossland)	1907
Gillard, J.	rw	Bank of Montreal (Rossland)	1903

Gilman		Kaslo Seniors	1897
Gilmour	forward	Vancouver Seniors	1901
Gininan (probably Goninan)	forward	Rossland Intermediates	1903
Glass, P..	rover	Nelson Intermediates	1911
Glegrich, H.	centre	Kaslo Juniors	1910
Glencross	rover	Grocery Clerks (Rossland)	1906
Glover, G.	defense	Trail Juniors	1904
Godlich, E.	point	Nicola Lake Seniors	1902
Goninan	goal	Rossland Seniors	1900
Goninan	goal	Phoenix Seniors	1907
Goninan, B.	goal	Centre Star (Rossland)	1908
Goninan, D.	goal	Rossland Centre Star	1907
Goninan, D.	lw/rw	Rossland Juniors	1902
Goninan, Dick	goal	Rossland int.	1907
Goninan, Dick	goal	Rossland Intermediates	1907
Goodeve	rw	Rocky Mountain Rangers (Rossland)	1906
Goodeve	rw	Rossland Bankers	1906
Goodeve	point	Rossland Stars (Juvenile)	1906
Goodeve	centre/rw	Rocky Mountain Rangers (Rossland)	1906
Goodeve, H.	rw/lw	Rocky Mountain Rangers (Rossland)	1907
Goodeve, H. (probably Harry)	lw/rw	Rossland Bankers	1906-07

(An H.T. Goodeve was listed in the 1907 Rossland Telephone directory as a clerk at the Bank of British North America.)

Gore	rw	Nelson Lakes	1908
Gore	rover	Nelson Intermediates	1909
Gore	centre	Nelson Juniors	1909
Gore	rw	Nelson Juniors	1907
Gore	forward	Nelson Juniors	1907
Gore,	rw	Nelson Juniors	1908
Gore, G.	tried out	Nelson Intermediates	1908
Gore, G.	cover	Nelson Juveniles	1905
Gore, George	left wing	Nelson Invincibles (Junior)	1905
Gore, George	spare	Nelson Seniors	1909
Gore, George	centre	Victorias (Nelson City League)	1909
Gormely	f	Sandon Seniors	1898
Gormley	cover	Slocan Seniors	1904
Gorrell		Trout Lake Seniors	1910
Grady, H.	goal	Moyie Seniors	1909-10
Grady, H..	goal	Moyie Seniors	1910
Graham	point	Commercials (Cranbrook)	1911
Graham	rover	Revelstoke Seniors	1904
Graham	lw	West Kootenay Power and Light (Rossland)	1906
Graham	point	Le Roi (Rossland)	1907
Graham, A	rover	Nelson High School	1909
Graham, A.	lw	Nelson Boy Scouts	1911
Graham, A.	rw	Nelson Rovers (Junior)	1910
Graham, A.	rover	Nelson Invincibles (high school)	1910
Graham, C.	centre	Revelstoke Seniors	1904
Graham, D.	rw	Armstrong Seniors	1907
Graham, D.	center	Vernon High School	1903
Graham, J.	forward	Revelstoke Seniors	1901
Granger, H.	spare, or manager	Revelstoke Seniors	1904
Grant		Golden Seniors	1899
Grant		Nelson Juveniles	1909
Grant	point	Grand Forks Seniors	1905
Grant	centre	Nelson Juniors	1909

Name	Position	Team	Year
Grant	point/cover	Grand Forks Seniors	1902-03
Grant, F.		Grand Forks Seniors try-out	1905
Grant, F.		Nelson Junior Warriors (formerly Nelson Juniors)	1909
Grant, F.	rover	Maple Leafs (Nelson Juvenile)	1909
Grant, F.	rover	Nelson Juniors	1909
Grant, Fred	rover	Nelson Rovers (junior)	1911
Grant, Fred(?)	tried out	Nelson Seniors	1911
Grant, Fred.	center	Nelson Juveniles	1910
Grant, G.P.	cover	West Kootenay Power and Light Company (Rossland)	1903
Grant, Garnet, P.	centre	West Kootenay Power & Light Co. (Ross Ind. League)	1904
Grant, J.		Nelson Junior Warriors (formerly Nelson Juniors)	1909
Grant, J.	rover	Nelson Juniors	1908
Grant, J.	center	Nelson Intermediates	1911
Grant, J.	center	Nelson Rovers (Junior)	1910
Grant, J.R.	rover	Phoenix Seniors	1909
Grant, Jack	centre	Nelson Rovers (junior)	1911
Grant, Jack	tried out	Nelson Seniors	1911
Grant, James, (capt)	cover	Nelson Invincibles (Junior)	1905
Grant, S.	Spare	Nelson Intermediates	1910
Grant. J.	rover	Cody Seniors	1910
Grassie, Charlie		Vancouver Seniors practise	1902
Grearson, Andy		Slocan City seniors	1899
Greatix, A.		Kamloops Seniors	1903
Greatrix, Alf		Kamloops Picked Town Team	1903
Green, Howard	point	Kaslo Juniors	1909
Green, R.F	officer	Kaslo Senior	1897
Greenflield, W.	coverpoint	Victoria, Captain Langley's team	1899
Greenless	forward	Nelson Juniors	1901
Greenley (or Greenlees)	forward	Nelson Lacrosse-Hockey Seniors	1900
Gresack, F.	rw	Coleman Seniors	1908
Grey	spare	Thistles (Nelson inter-City)	1910
Greyerbeihl (possibly Charles)	goal	Nelson Seniors	1905
Greyerbiehl	goal	Nelson Seniors	1902
Greyerbiehl (possibly Charles)	forward	Rossland Intermediates	1904
Greyerbiehl (possibly Charles)	goal	Nelson Intermediates	1903
Greyerbiehl (possibly Charles)	goal	Nelson Seniors	1907
Greyerbiehl (possibly Charles)	goal	Nelson Mountains	1908
Greyerbiehl (possibly Charles)	goal	Nelson Intermediates	1909
Greyerbiehl (possibly Charles)	goal	Thistles (Nelson City League)	1909
Greyerbiehl, (possibly Charles)	point	Nelson Juniors	1902
Greyerbiehl, Charles, "Flukie"	goal	Nelson East ward int	1906
Greyerbiehl, Charles	Sub goal	Nelson Seniors	1906-07, 1910
Greyerbiehl, F.	goal	Victorias (Nelson inner-City)	1910
Greyerbiehl, F.	goal	Nelson Intermediates	1906
Greyerbiehl, F.	tried out	Nelson Intermediates	1908
Greyerbiehl, Flukie	goal	Nelson Intermediates	1910

Charles, "Flukie," Greyerbiehl was an excellent Goaltender. Born in Springfield Missouri. He came to Nelson in 1899 as a boy. He played with the Juniors, and then Intermediates, before jumping to the Senior team in 1906, (and possibly 1905), as a sub for Harry Bishop. (Newspaper reports showing him as F. Greyerbiehl are referring to his nickname, Flukie. There are also many misspellings of his name, and he has often been mistaken for his brother Paul, including by me.)

Name	Position	Team	Year
Greyerbiehl, P.	lw	Nelson Intermediates	1904
Greyerbiehl, P.	cover	Nelson Wholesalers	1904
Greyerbiehl, Paul	goal	Nelson Seniors	1902

Paul Greyerbiehl was probably the brother of Charles.

Name	Position	Team	Year
Greyerbiel	point	Nelson Seniors	1905

Grierson	f	Sandon Seniors	1901
Grierson	lw	Rossland Seniors	1905
Grierson	f	Sandon Seniors	1898
Grierson	f	Sandon Seniors	1901
Grierson	r wing	Rossland Seniors	1904
Grierson	cover	Archer's Flat Team (Kaslo)	1900
Grierson	forward	Sandon Seniors	1903
Grierson , Andy		Kaslo Seniors	1900
Grierson, A.	f	Sandon City (Dec. 1901)	1902
Grierson, A.	forward/lw	Sandon Seniors	1901-02
Grierson, A. W. (capt)	forward/cover	Sandon Seniors	1897-98-99
Grierson, Andy	rw	Rossland Seniors	1905
Griffis, C. (Or Griffith)	point	Rossland Seniors	1909
Griffis, Si (spelled Griffiths in newspaper)		Vancouver Allstar team	1910

Si Griffis was one of the great players of his era, and is a member of the Hall of Fame. Although he had very little occasion to play hockey in Vancouver prior to 1912, (there were no known opponents to his 1910 Allstar team), he had previously won the Stanley Cup with Kenora in 1907, and became a stalwart for the Vancouver Millionaires in the Pacific coast League between 1912 and 1919. He was born in Kansas, U.S.A. in 1883 and died in 1950. (See Trail of the Stanley Cup)

Griffith	cover	Rossland Juniors	1905
Griffith	point	Rossland Juniors	1907
Griffith	point	Rocky Mountain Rangers (Rossland)	1906
Griffith	centre	Rossland Intermediates	1908
Griffith	goal	Rocky Mountain Rangers (Rossland)	1906
Griffith	goal	Rossland Invincibles (Juniors)	1906
Griffith	l. wing	Rossland Juveniles	1905
Griffith	cover	Rossland Intermediates	1906
Griffith(s), G.	center	Rossland Intermediates	1909
Griffith, C.	cover	Rossland Juniors	1904
Griffith, C.	rover	Rossland Intermediates	1911
Griffith, C.	rover	Rossland Intermediates	1910
Griffith, C.	centre	Le Roi (Rossland)	1908
Griffith, C.	rover	Rossland Intermediates	1910-11
Griffith, Charles	cover	Rossland Juniors	1905
Griffith, Charles	point/cover	Rocky Mountain Rangers (Rossland)	1907
Griffith, F.	point	Centre Star (Rossland)	1908
Griffith, F.E.	rw	Rossland Centre Star	1907
Griffith, G.	cover	Rossland Juniors	1908
Griffith, G.	center	Rossland Intermediates	1910
Griffith, G.	centre	Rossland Intermediates	1910-11
Griffith, G.	lw	Rossland Juniors	1908
Griffith, George	forward	Rossland Invincibles (Junior)	1905
Griffiths	centre	Rossland Intermediates	1910
Griffiths, G.	center	Rossland Intermediates	1911
Grizzelle, (ell), (zzelle) (zelle) P.	point/centre	Nelson High School	1909
Grizzelle, C.	cover	Nelson Public School	1909
Grizzelle, C.	point	Nelson rovers (Junior)	1910-11
Grizzelle, P.	rover	Nelson Juniors	1910
Grosvenor	rw	Trail Smelter Team	1905
Grosvenor	rover	Trail Smelter	1906
Grosvenor, F.	spare	Nelson Seniors	1907
Grosvenor, F.E.	r wing	Trail Smelter Team	1905
Grotie, R.	forward	Kaslo Town Juniors	1901
Grubbe, E.H.	centre	New Denver Seniors	1911
Guay	rover	Nelson Seniors	1904
Guay, A.	?	Nelson East Ward	1906

Guay, A.	cover/rover	Nelson Seniors	1904, 1906
Guay, A.	cover	Nelson Seniors	1906
Guerson, A.	centre	Sandon Seniors	1903
Guest, H	goal	Slocan City Seniors	1899
Gunn, W..	point	Nelson Challengers (Junior)	1910
Gunn, W..	point	Nelson Mic-Macs (Junior)	1910
Gusty	cover	Sandon Seniors	1899
Gusty, J.	f	Sandon City (Dec. 1901)	1902
Hacker, A.	spare	Nelson Seniors	1903
Hackling, (or Hacking) Ernie	lw/rw	Nelson Seniors 1910 Ernie	

Hacking, (or Hackling) was born in Listowell Ontario. He played as a teammate of "Cyclone" Taylor on the Listowel team from 1900-1904, when they were the champions of the Northern League. In 1905 he was in Thesalon. In 1909 he began playing for the Nelson team, and continued on that team at least until 1914. The 1914 city directory for Nelson lists Ernest G. Hacking as a despatcher for the CPR.

Haddock, A.	forward	Ashcroft Seniors	1901
Hale, A.E.	point	Enderby Seniors	1904
Haller		Vancouver scrub team	1905
Hamberger	goal	Slocan City seniors	1903
Hamilton	rw/lw	Rossland Intermediates	1910-11
Hamilton	rw	Rossland Intermediates	1911
Hamilton, B.	rw	Centre Star (Rossland)	1908
Hamilton, B.	rw	Rossland Intermediates	1909
Hamilton, R.	rw	Rossland Intermediates	1910
Hamilton, W.R.	Secretary treasurer/cover	Golden Seniors	1895

W.R. Hamilton was one of the first hockey players in B.C. He was also an avid curler, and a well known business man in Golden.

Hammond	point	Sandon Seniors	1898
Hammond, Robert	goal	Sandon Seniors	1897-99

One of the best goalies ever to play in B.C., we only have a record of a few of his games. He was probably the R. Hammond who joined the Lord Strathcona's Horse battalion and was killed in South Africa in the Boer War in 1899. He probably worked at the Hammond Livery Stable in Sandon.

Hancock, C.	lw	Enderby Seniors	1904
Hankinson	forward	Heroes (Grand Forks)	1903
Hannah, H.	forward	Nelson West Ward ("Hand-Warmers")	1907
Hanson, Charlie	f	Saloons (Sandon)	1901
Hanson, Chas.	cover	Miner's and Kootenay Hotels (Sandon)	1901
Hardie, (or Hardy), D.	point	Nelson Juniors	1908
Harding, H.	goal	"Tenderfeet" (Nelson)	1908
Hardle		Nelson Juniors	1909
Hardle, D.		Nelson Public School	1909
Hardy		Nelson Juveniles	1909
Hardy	lw	Nelson Juniors	1909
Hardy, D.	point	Nelson Intermediates	1909
Hardy	cover	Nelson Juniors	1909
Hardy, D.		Lumby Seniors	1911
Hardy, D.	goal	Nelson High School	1909
Hardy, D.	lw	Nelson Junior Warriors (formerly Nelson Juniors)	1909
Harrington, C.	goal	Nelson Seniors	1898
Harris	centre	Rossland Seniors	1902
Harris	cover	Rossland Intermediates	1903
Harris	rw	Rossland Victorias	1901, 1903
Harris	rw	Rossland Intermediates	1908
Harris	point	Rossland Juniors	1905
Harris	spare	Nelson West Ward ("Hand-Warmers")	1907

Harris	centre	Rossland Seniors	1902
Harris	centre	Rossland Junior Victorias	1902
Harris	forward	Rossland Seniors	1898
Harris	forward	Rossland Juniors	1901
Harris	point	Centre Star/War Eagle (Rossland)	1906
Harris	rover	Le Roi (Rossland)	1908
Harris	forward	Victorias (Rossland seniors)	1901
Harris, A.	forward	Columbias (Rossland junior)	1901
Harris, Al		Rossland Juniors	1899
Harris, Al	forward	Rosslands (seniors)	1901
Harris, E.	cover	Rossland Cyclones (Junior)	1901
Harris, E.	cover	Rossland Juniors	1901-02
Harris, E.	rover	Rossland Centre Star	1907
Harris, E.	point	Nelson Intermediates	1904
Harris, Edgar	point	Rossland Juniors	1905
Harris, Edgar	cover	Rossland Juniors	1902
Harris, Edgar	point	Cyclones (Rossland juniors)	1901
Harris, W.C. (or W.S.) "Duke"	forward	The Rossland Victorias	1899-1900
Harris, W.S.	forward	Rossland Seniors	1901
Harris, Al, (capt)		Rossland Juniors, IXL	1899
Harris, E.	point	Rossland Intermediates	1907
Harrison	goal	C.P.R. Shops (Cranbrook)	1911
Hartin		Imperial Bank (Nelson)	1908
Hartin	goal	Nelson High School	1909
Hartin, D.	goal	Nelson Juniors	1908
Hatrup	rw	Hunter Brothers (Rossland)	1905
Hattrup, E. H.	rover	Hunter Brothers (Rossland Ind. League)	1904
Hault, W.	forward	Revelstoke Seniors	1901
Haverty	goal	Phoenix Seniors	1904
Haverty, G.		Grand Forks Seniors try-out	1905
Haverty, John	goal	Phoenix Seniors	1904
Hawkins	forward	Nelson City Seniors	1900
Hawkins, J.	forward	Nelson Tramway	1901
Hawman, J.		Vancouver scrub team	1905
Hay		Grand Forks Juniors	1903
Hay	forward	Grand Forks Seniors	1905
Hedley	forward	Nelson Bankers	1903
Hemphill, O.	Manager	The New Ramblers, Vancouver,	1907
Henderson		Sandon seniors	1898
Henderson	Forward	Nelson Seniors	1899
Henderson	f	Sandon Seniors	1898
Henderson, G.	forward	Nelson Seniors	1899
Henderson, J.		Sandon Seniors	1897
Henderson, T	forward	Sandon Seniors	1898
Henderson, T.	point	Slocan City Seniors	1899
Hering, W.	point	Rossland Juniors	1904
Herman, Charlie		Vancouver Seniors practise	1902
Herman, Charlie	cover	Herman's Champions, Vancouver	1907
Herman, Charlie (Captain)	cover	Vancouver Terminals	1907
Herr, E..	centre	Rossland Centre Star	1907
Hetherington		Banff Seniors	1899
Hiams	forward/spare	Reilly Club of Nelson	1904
Hickinbottom, E.	forward	Cyclones (Rossland juniors)	1901
Hicks	cover	Slocan City seniors	1903
Hicks	rover	Slocan Seniors	1904
Hicks, W.	rw	Slocan Seniors	1909

Hicks, W. G.	point	Hunter Brothers (Rossland)	1905
Hicks, W. G.	point	Hunter Brothers (Rossland Ind. League)	1904
Higgins	rw	Rossland Seniors	1902
Higgins	goal	Coleman Seniors	1908
Higinbotham, F.	goal	Rossland Cyclones (Junior)	1901
Higinbotham, F. (or Hickinbottom)	goal	Rossland Juniors	1901
Hill	forward	Kaslo Seniors	1898
Hill, F. Jim		Kaslo Bankers	1898
Hilliard		Vernon Single Men	1906
Hilliard	goal	Phoenix Seniors	1905
Hilliard, W.B.	point	Vernon Seniors	1907
Hilliard, W.B.	point	Vernon Town team	1907
Hillman, Lance		Gerrard Seniors	1910
Hipperson	forward	Nelson Wholesalers	1903
Hipperson, A.E.		Nelson Ashdowns	1907
Hipperson, B.	cover	Nelson Hardware	1901
Hipperson, C.	cover	Nelson Ashdowns (hardware)	1907
Hipperson, Charles		Nelson Senior	1897

Charles Hipperson was a tinsmith with J.H. Ashdown, Hardware.

Hipperson, W.	rw	Ashdowns (Nelson hardware)	1907
Hipperson, W.	point	Nelson West Ward ("Hand-Warmers")	1907
Hipperson, W.	centre	Nelson Ashdowns (hardware)	1907
Hipperson, W.	forward	Nelson Wholesalers	1904
Hipperson, W.J.	rover	Nelson Diamond A-Ashdown Hockey Club	1906

William John Hipperson was a driver with Lawrwence Hardware in 1898, and later a clerk at J.H. Ashdown, Hardware.

Hobbs	point	Rossland bank team	1897
Hockin	rover	Kamloops Seniors	1910
Hogan	goal	Sandon Seniors	1900
Hogan	sparc	Coleman Alberta Seniors	1910
Hogan,	goal	Sandon Seniors	1902
Hogan, G.	goal	Sandon Juniors	1901
Hoggan, G.		Sandon Seniors	1901
Hoggan, Geo.	goal	Sandon Seniors	1903
Hoggan, I.G.	goal	Sandon Seniors	1903

George Hogan was one of the best goalies in B.C. during his short career. His name was given many different ways. It's still not clear whether it should be spelled with one g, or two.

Holinquest, A.	lw	Sandon Seniors	1910
Holmes	point	Ashdowns (Nelson)	1907
Holmes, J.	forward	Nelson CPR	1901
Holmes, J.C.	f	Kamloops Seniors	1902
Holmes, J.W.	cover	Nelson Diamond A-Ashdown Hockey Club	1906
Holmes, Joe	point	Nelson Wholesalers	1904
Holmes, W.J.		Nelson Ashdown Hockey Club	1906-07
Hood		Sandon Seniors	1900
Hood	goal	Sandon Seniors	1899
Hood(s)	centre	Rossland Seniors	1904-05
Hood	rover	Greenwood Seniors	1911
Hood	centre	"Tenderfeet" (Nelson)	1908
Hood (s)	centre	Rossland Victorias Alberta Challenge Team	1906
Hood(s), W.R.	centre/rover	Phoenix Seniors	1907
Hood(s), W.R.	centre	Rossland Seniors	1906
Hood, Robertson	f	Sandon Seniors	1901-03
Hood, R.	f	Printers of Sandon (Dec. 1901)	1902
Hood, R.	centre	Sandon Seniors	1902
Hood, Robertson	f	Sandon Juniors	1899-00-1901

Hood, W.	centre	Armstrong Seniors	1908-09
Hoods	centre	Nelson Rivers	1908
Hoods, R.	forward	Sandon Juniors	1901

(All of the above players named Hood or Hoods, are probably the same man. Robertson Hood was one of the best forwards in B.C. and played first for Sandon, winning many championships as a junior, and then for Rossland and other teams as a Senior. It's not known what happened to him after 1909, although he could be the Hood who played for Greenwood in 1911. He was often referred to as W.R. or R. or W. Hood.)

Hope		Revelstoke City League Team (unnamed)	1909
Hope, G.	rw	Sandon Intermediates	1908
Hope, T.	centre	Revelstoke Seniors	1907
Horswill	point	Victorias (Nelson City League)	1909
Horswill	point	Nelson Retailers	1908
Horswill, Al	point	Nelson Lakes	1908
Horswill, Al	point	Nelson Seniors	1909

(In the 1914 city directory for Nelson there were 3 Horsewill's listed: Alfred S., a bookkeeper; Algernon, S., and Algernon, T., manager, who all worked at A.S. Horswill, a grocers.)

Howard	forward (possibly Howarth)	Victorias (Rossland)	1900
Howarth, William	lw	Rossland Victorias Alberta Challenge Team	1906
Howarth, W.	f	Printers of Sandon (Dec. 1901)	1902
Howarth, William	lw/rw	Sandon Seniors	1901-03
Howarth, William	lw/rover	Rossland Seniors	1904-07
Howarth, William ("Weary Willie")		Grand Forks Seniors	1903

William, "Weary Willie" Howarth, was one of the top forwards in B.C. He started playing in Sandon, then moved to Rossland and became one of their stars. He worked as a printer, starting at the Sandon Paystreak. He died in 1913, after catching pneumonia while playing hockey in Anaconda Montana, where he worked. He was about 33 years old. He had coached the Rossland Ladies team, and in 1907 married one of those ladies, Reba Demuth.

Howden	cover	Nelson City Seniors	1900
Howden (capt)		Golden Seniors	1899
Howell	right wing	Nelson Invincibles (Junior)	1905
Howell, P.	point	Nelson Juveniles	1905
Howse	spare	Nicola Seniors	1910
Hudson		Phoenix Juniors	1903
Hughes, B.	goal	Kaslo Seniors	1910
Hughes, Edward		New Westminster pick-up team	1909

Edward Hughes was the first hockey player to die in a hockey game in British Columbia. He fell through the ice at Trout Lake in Vancouver, during a pick-up game. He could not swim, and the other players could not pull him out before he sank and drowned. He worked at Phillip's Gents Furnishings in New Westminster

Hughes, Richard (Dick)	goal	Kaslo Intermediates	1910
Hughes, W.G.	forward	Bank of Toronto/Royal Bank (Rossland)	1901
Hughie, J.	point	Cody Seniors	1910
Hulten, Fred	2nd cover	Miner's and Kootenay Hotels (Sandon)	1901
Hunt, Percy		Rossland Cigarmakers, or Bartenders	1911
Hunter,	forward	Archer's Flat Team (Kaslo)	1900
Hunter, pte	forward	Nelson Militia	1901
Hunter, Bert		Rossland Tigers	1899
Hunter, J. (Capt)	forward	Nelson Hardware	1901
Hunter, Robert	goal	Hunter Brothers (Rossland Ind. League)	1904
Hunter, Robert	goal	Hunter Brothers (Rossland)	1903
Hunter, Sam	cover/forward	Kaslo Seniors	1897-1900

Sam Hunter was a mining property developer.

Hurley, J.	cover	Nelson CPR	1901
Hutchinson	rover	Kaslo Seniors	1909
Hyatt, A.	point	Revelstoke Seniors	1903

Name	Position	Team	Year
Hyde	forward	C.P.R. Shops, Cranbrook,	1911
Inches	goal	Rossland Intermediates	1905
Inches	centre	Rossland Intermediates	1907
Inches	centre	Rossland Juniors	1907
Inches	goal	Le Roi (Rossland)	1908
Inches	rover	Rossland Juveniles	1905
Inches	goal	Rossland Intermediates	1906
Inches	rover	Rocky Mountain Rangers (Rossland)	1906
Inches	point	Rossland Intermediates	1903
Inches	rover	Rossland Invincibles (Juniors)	1906
Inches	centre	Rossland Juniors	1908
Inches, B.	centre/lw	Le Roi (Rossland)	1907
Inches, B.	goal	Rossland Intermediates	1908
Inches, Bob	point	Rossland Cyclones (Junior)	1901
Inches, Bob	point	Rossland Juniors	1901
Inches, J.	centre	Rossland Juniors	1908
Inches, Jack, (Jimmy) (capt)	rover	Rossland Invincibles (Juniors)	1905
Inches, R.	point	Rossland Juniors	1902
Inches, R.	goal	Nelson Intermediates	1904
Inches, R.	forward	Cyclones (Rossland juniors)	1901
Irvine, E.	spare	Nelson Intermediates	1910
Irvine, H,T.	manager	Nelson Seniors	1897
Irving, A	spare	Nelson Grocers	1906
Irving, A.	spare	Bell Trading Company (Nelson grocers)	1906
Irwin, F.L		Kaslo Bankers	1898
Irwin, Fred		Kamloops city teams	1903
Irwin, Fred	center	Kamloops Seniors	1908, 1910
Isley		Trail Juniors	1904
Isley	point/rover	Trail Intermediates	1906
Isley, C.	cover	Trail Juniors	1904
Isley, Claude	point	Trail Juniors	1905
Isley, Matt	cover	Trail Juniors	1905
Jackson		Vernon Single Men	1906
Jackson	lw	Kaslo Intermediates	1909
Jackson	rw	Wood-Vallance (Nelson hardware)	1907
Jackson	cover	Sandon Seniors	1901
Jackson	lw	Nelson Retailers	1908
Jackson	cover	Sandon Seniors	1901
Jackson	point/rw	Nelson Juniors	1907
Jackson	center	Vernon Seniors	1905
Jackson	center	Vernon Seniors	1904
Jackson	forward	Nelson Seniors	1898
Jackson	point	Heroes (Grand Forks)	1903
Jackson,	point	Grand Forks Seniors	1902
Jackson, B.	forward	Vernon Seniors	1902
Jackson, Bert,		Vernon Seniors	1900
Jackson, E.A. (or E.S.)	centre	Vernon Seniors	1905
Jackson, E.R.		Vernon Seniors	1901
Jackson, E.S.	center	Vernon Seniors	1903
Jackson, E.S.	centre	Vernon Seniors	1904
Jackson, E.S.	point	Vernon Seniors	1908
Jackson, H.		Sandon Seniors	1901
Jackson, Harry	point	Grand Forks Seniors	1903
Jackson, R.		Vernon Seniors	1900
Jackson, R.	cover	Vernon Seniors	1902
Jackson, W.	forward	Kaslo Seniors	1897

Jacobssen	goal	New Denver "A"s	1911
Jacobssen, C.	goal	New Denver Seniors	1909
Jameison	rover	Phoenix Seniors	1907
Jameison, H.	rover	"Tenderfeet" (Nelson)	1908
Jameson	cover	Rossland Seniors	1905
Jamieson	rover	Rossland Victorias Alberta Challenge Team	1906
Jamieson	rover	Coleman Seniors	1908
Jamieson, H.	rover	Rossland Seniors	1906
Jamieson (or Jameson)	cover	Rossland Seniors	1905
Jamieson, A	rw	Rossland Seniors	1905
Jamieson, H.	cover	Rossland Seniors	1905
Jamieson, Harry	rover	Phoenix Seniors	1907
Jardeau		Smithers Seniors	1910
Jarvis, W.		Kamloops Seniors	1902
Jeffs	cover	Nelson Seniors	1902
Jeffs	forward	Rossland bank team	1897
Jeffs, A.	spare/ goal	Nelson Seniors	1898
Jeffs, A.	cover	Nelson Lacrosse-Hockey Seniors	1900
Jeffs, Alf	cover	Nelson Seniors	1899

Alf Jeffs was a former member of the "Brants" of Paris Ontario, which was a championship team. He was a stalwart on the Nelson Senior defence for a few years. It's probable that he was the Alfred Jeffs listed in the 1898 B.C. Directory as Alfred Jeffs, of Ball and Jeffs, tinsmiths and plumbers, in Nelson.

Jeffs, C.	point	Nelson Seniors	1907
Jeffs, C.	cover	Nelson Seniors	1901
Jeffs, Charlie	cover	Nelson Seniors	1903
Jenkins	center	Kaslo Seniors	1909
Jenkins	rover	Nelson YMCA Juniors	1911
Jenkins	spare	Nelson Seniors	1911
Jenkins	center	Nelson Intermediates	1911
Jenkins	rover	Nelson Intermediates	1911

Jenkins, Charles V. tried out for team War Eagle Mine (Rossland Industrial League) 1904

Jenkins, H.	centre	Kaslo Intermediates	1910
Jenkins, H.	center	Nelson YMCA Juniors	1911
Jenkins, H.	spare/centre/rover	Kaslo Intermediates	1908-09-10-11
Jewell	rw	Rossland Intermediates	1910
Jewell, E.	cover	Rossland Juniors	1911
Jewell, E.	rover	Rossland Seniors	1911
Johns	goal	Rossland Intermediates	1903
Johns, B.	goal	Rossland Juniors	1902
Johns, D.	goal	Rossland Juniors	1902
Johns, D.	goal	Rossland Intermediates	1904
Johns, H		Nelson Intermediates	1903
Johns, Steve	goal	Nelson Juniors	1901
Johnson	rw	Rossland Stars (Juvenile)	1906
Johnson, A.	rw	Enderby Seniors	1904
Johnson, C.	rw	Armstrong Seniors	1908
Johnson, C.	rover	Commonage Intermediates (Vernon)	1904
Johnson, H.	goal	Enderby Seniors	1904
Johnson, J.D.	forward	Revelstoke Seniors	1901
Johnston, A.		Enderby Seniors	1901
Johnston, C.E.	spare, or manager	Revelstoke Seniors	1904
Johnston, T.		Summerland Seniors	1910
Johnstone	goal	Armstrong Intermediates	1910
Johnstone, L.	point	Nelson Boy Scouts	1911
Joiner	forward	Hunter Brothers store Rossland	1899

Joiner, P.	rover	Hunter Brothers (Rossland)	1903
Jones	cover	Le Roi (Rossland)	1906
Jones	point	Grocery Clerks (Rossland)	1906
Jones, Stanley	lw	Rossland Invincibles (Juniors)	1905
Jopp, V.	cover	Rossland Seniors	1911
Jost	rw	Grand Forks Seniors	1909
Jost	cover	Phoenix Intermediates	1908
Jost	point	Rossland Seniors	1909
Jost, J.M.	cover	Boundary Seniors	1906
Jost, J.M. (or J.S.)	cover	Boundary combined team	1906
Joy, R.G	spare	Nelson Grocers	1906
Joy, R.G.	spare	Bell Trading Company (Nelson grocers)	1906
Kachtell, J.E (or Katchell)	cover	Slocan Seniors	1909
Kamm	tried out	Moyie Seniors	1909
Kane, C	cover/goal	Kaslo Seniors	1897-98
Kastner	cover	Fernie Seniors	1904
Kastner	cover	Fernie Seniors	1905
Kastner	cover	Fernie Seniors	1906
Kastner, M.	cover	Fernie Seniors	1904
Kearns	cover	Coldstream Hotel (Vernon)	1908
Keating		Rossland Juveniles	1909
Keating	rover	Rossland Seniors	1907
Keating	rover	Rossland Intermediates	1905
Keating	center	Rossland Seniors	1909
Keating	centre	Rossland Seniors	1911
Keating	centre	Rossland Intermediates	1906
Keating	rover	Le Roi Mine (Rossland)	1905
Keating	rover	Rossland Juniors	1909
Keating	centre	Rossland Seniors	1908
Keating	centre	Rossland Intermediates	1906
Keating A.	f	Rossland Juniors	1901
Keating, A		Moyie Seniors	1910
Keating, A.	forward	Rossland Cyclones (Junior)	1901
Keating, A. (capt.)	forward	Nelson Intermediates	1904
Keating, A.K.	centre	Rossland Seniors	1909
Keating, Al	rover	Le Roi Mine (Rossland)	1905
Keating, Al	rw	Rossland Juniors	1902
Keating, Al		Rosslands	1903
Keating, Al	forward	Le Roi Mine (Rossland Industrial League)	1904
Keating, Al	centre	Rossland Seniors	1907
Keating, Al	goal	Rossland Cigarmakers, or Bartenders	1911
Keating, Al	center	Rossland Seniors	1908
Keating, H.	center	Rossland Juniors	1911
Keatings	forward	Rossland Intermediates	1903
Keddy		Smithers Seniors	1910
Keefe	goal	Rossland Juniors	1908
Keefe	goal	Rossland Invincibles (Junior)	1905
Keefe	goal	Rossland Juniors	1907
Keefe	goal	Rossland Juveniles	1905
Keefe, E.	goal	Rossland Juniors	1908
Keefe, W.	rw	Rossland Juniors	1911
Keefe, Willie	centre	Rossland Stars (Juvenile)	1906
Keeting	rover	Rossland Juniors	1909
Kelly	lw	New Denver "B"s	1911
Kelly	cover	Cranbrook Seniors	1911
Kelly	goal	Phoenix Seniors	1907

Kelly	cover	Moyie Seniors	1909
Kelly	point	Rocky Mountain Rangers (Rossland)	1906
Kelly	cover	Phoenix Intermediates	1906
Kelly, C.	goal	Phoenix Seniors	1907
Kelly, E.	centre	Eagles (Spokane)	1906
Kelly, E. (capt)	rw	Wood's Independents (Spokane)	1907
Kelly, H.	cover	Moyie Seniors	1910
Kelson, J.	goal	Sandon Seniors	1910

(This is possibly Jacob Kelsen, who ran a cigar, fruit and pool room in Sandon, according to the 1901 B.C. Directory).

Kelvie	centre	Phoenix Seniors	1910
Kemp	lw	Nelson Seniors	1908
Kemp	centre	Fernie Seniors	1908
Kennedy	point	Royal Hotel (Vernon)	1908
Kennedy, G.	point	Commonage Intermediates (Vernon)	1904
Kent	point	Fernie Seniors	1908
Kent, B.	rw	"Tenderfeet" (Nelson)	1908
Kerr, C..	point	Kaslo Seniors	1897
Ketcheson	lw	Rossland Intermediates	1910
Kettermire	cover	C.P.R. Shops (Cranbrook)	1911
Kettlewell	lw	Nelson Wood-Vallance	1911
Kinahan	cover	Maple Leafs (Nelson Juvenile)	1909
Kinahan, H.	cover	Nelson Juveniles	1910
Kinehan, H.	point	Nelson Juniors	1909
King	lw	Centre Star/War Eagle (Rossland)	1906
Kingsmill	forward	Rossland Junior Victorias	1899
Kinhan, H..	point	Nelson All-Stars (juniors)	1911
Kirby, E.B.	tried out for team	War Eagle Mine (Rossland Industrial League)	1904
Kirvin, J.	forward	Sandon Seniors	1897
Knight, G.	rw	Revelstoke Seniors	1907
Knott	point	Nelson Grocers	1907
Knowlton		Golden Seniors	1899
Koster, M.		Crow's Nest Senior Team	1903
Kottemier, Roy	spare	Cranbrook Seniors	1911
Kydd D.M.	spare	Reilly Club of Nelson	1904
Kydd, N.	forward	Reilly Club of Nelson	1904
La Fortune (or Lafortunee)	rw	Fernie Seniors	1904
Lackey, S.	goal	Phoenix Seniors	1909
Ladd, F.	spare	Nelson YMCA Juniors	1911
Laeler, John		Rossland Juniors, IXL	1899
Lafferty, H.	cover	Rossland Seniors	1906
Lafferty	cover	Rossland Victorias Alberta Challenge Team	1906
Lafferty	cover	Rossland Seniors	1906
Lafferty	cover	Phoenix Seniors	1907
Lafferty, T.	cover	Phoenix Seniors	1907
Lafferty, Thomas	cover	Phoenix Seniors	1907
Lafortune	r. wing	Fernie Seniors	1904
Lafortune, (or Lafontane), D.	r. wing	Fernie Seniors	1904
Lahey	forward	Rosland Seniors	1898
Lahey, Mike	point	Rosslands (seniors)	1899-1900
Laidlaw	lw	Herman's Champions, Vancouver,	1907
Laidlaw	lw	Vancouver Terminals	1907
Laires	goal	Slocan Seniors	1909
Lake, J.	Vice-President	Golden Seniors	1895
Lamont	rover	Bank of Montreal (Rossland)	1905
Lamont	point	Rossland Bankers	1906

Name	Position	Team	Year
Lamont, N.	cover	Bank of Mon./ Can. Bank of Com. (Rossland)	1901
Lamont, R.	cover	Bank of Montreal (Rossland Industrial League)	1904
Lamont, Robert	cover	Associated Banks (Rossland)	1903
Lane	rover	Nelson Bankers	1911
Lang, Bert	goal	Greenwood Seniors	1910
Lang	goal	Phoenix Seniors	1911
Lang, Bert	goal	Grand Forks Seniors	1910
Lang	forward	Vernon Bankers	1907
Lang, J.	rw	Vernon Seniors	1907
Langille	rw	Moyie Seniors	1909
Lapointe		Kamloops Seniors	1908
Lapointe, J.		Kamloops Seniors	1905
Larmouth, N.	goal	Kaslo Juniors	1909
Larson, C.	forward	Nelson East Ward ("Stick-Arounds")	1907
Larson, P.	rover	Nelson All-Stars (juniors)	1911
Laughlin, M.	rover	Nelson grocers	1906
Laughton, J.	centre	Nelson Boy Scouts	1911
Lavasser	center	Nelson Wholesalers	1908
Lavasser	right wing	Nelson Grocers	1906
Lavasser	rw	Bell Trading Company (Nelson grocers)	1906
Lavasseur, T.	lw	Hunter Brothers (Rossland Ind. League)	1904
Lawe	spare	Rossland Victorias	1902
Lawes, F.R.	center	Enderby Seniors	1904
Lawes, T.		Enderby Seniors	1901
Lawler	forward	Hunter Brothers store Rossland	1899
Lawler, G.	left wing	Hunter Brothers (Rossland)	1903
Lawrence		Imperial Bank (Nelson)	1908
Lawson, A.		Grand Forks Seniors try-out	1905
Layton (probably Leighton)	goal	Rossland Seniors	1904
Lee	centre	Bank of Montreal (Rossland)	1905
Lee	centre	Rossland Bankers	1906
Lee (capt)	centre	Rossland Bankers	1907
Lee, J.	rw	Hunter Brothers (Rossland Ind. League)	1904
Leighton	cover	Bank of Montreal (Rossland)	1905
Leighton	goal	Rossland Seniors	1902
Leighton	goal	Rossland Seniors	1904
Leighton	goal	Rossland Seniors	1906
Leighton	goal	Victorias (Rossland)	1902
Leighton	goal	Rossland Citizen Team	1903
Leighton	goal	Rosslands	1903
Leighton	goal	Rossland Seniors	1906
Leighton, A	point	Rossland Seniors	1901
Leighton, Art	goal	Rosslands (senior)	1901
Leighton, A.G.		Rossland Victorias	1901
Leighton, A.G. (Art)	goal	Bank of Montreal (Rossland)	1903
Leighton, A.G. (Art)	goal	Rossland Seniors	1901
Leighton, G.	cover	Rossland Seniors	1901
Leighton, G.A.	forward	Bank of Toronto/Royal Bank (Rossland)	1901
Leighton, Art	goal	Wood's Independents (Spokane)	1907

(Art Leighton was one of the best goalies in B.C. It's not clear if another Leighton, with the first initial G was another man, or whether the newspaper was sometimes using his middle initial. Players sometimes gave either their first or second name to reporters.)

Name	Position	Team	Year
Leitch	goal	Wood Vallence, Nelson, Hardware	1907
Lemrise, O.	forward	Hurricanes (Rossland juniors)	1901
Leslie, A.		Kaslo Bankers	1898
Leslie, H.E.	cover	Ashcroft Seniors	1901

Leslie, J.	point	Junior Thistles (Nelson Juvenile)	1909
Lewer, C.E.	point	Bank of Montreal (Rossland)	1903
Lewis	lw	Coleman Seniors	1908
Lewis	rw	Centre Star/War Eagle (Rossland)	1906
Lewis, R.	forward	Hurricanes (Rossland junior)	1901
Lindow (or Lindon)	centre	Salmo Hoboes (inner-city)	1910
Lindow, C.	rover	Salmo Seniors/Intermediates	1910
Lindow, Carl		Salmo Intermediates	1911
Lindquist	rw	Rossland Invincibles (Juniors)	1906
Lindsay		Banff Seniors	1899
Lindsay, B.	forward	Kaslo Town Juniors	1901
Lindsay, J.	goal	Kaslo Town Juniors	1901
Linquist	lw	Rocky Mountain Rangers (Rossland)	1906
Linton	point	Silverton Seniors	1904
Little, C.		Vernon Seniors	1901
Livingstone, W.M.	spare	Nelson Seniors	1898
Livingstone.	Cover	Nelson Seniors	1898
Lockhart, H.	f	Rossland Juniors	1901
Lockhart, H.	forward	Rossland Cyclones (Junior)	1901
Lockhart, H.	point	Hurricanes (Rossland junior)	1901
Logan, Gordon	point	West Kootenay Power and Light Company (Rossland)	1903
Longfellow, "Longboat"		Vancouver Allstar team no known opponents)	1910
Longfellow, Ed		Rossland Seniors	1910

Longfellow was a ringer from Vancouver, brought in for the Rossland Carnival. He played the previous winter in Fort William (Quebec or Ontario?).

Longfellow, Ed	lw	Rossland Seniors	1910
Longhurst	lw	Grand Forks Seniors	1909
Longhurst	rw	Nelson Wholesalers	1908
Longhurst	lw	Phoenix Intermediates	1908
Longhurst, A.	forward	Nelson Grocers	1901
Lovatt	goal	Kaslo Seniors	1899
Lucy	rw	Missoula (Montana) Seniors	1911
Luff	cover	Rossland Stars (Juvenile)	1906
Lynch	centre	Trail Seniors	1902
Lynch F.	forward	New Westminster Seniors	1901
Lynch, Fred		New Westminster challenge team	1905
Lynch, Fred		New Westminster (Royals)	1907
Lynn(e), R. (Rusty)	centre	Phoenix Seniors	1911

Rusty Lynn(e) played for Greenwood in 1912 when they won the International, or Open B.C. Championships. Jack Ulrich was also on that team, and Ulrich was already the spare player for the Vancouver Millionaires, in 1912, (and then the Victoria Aristocrats in 1913 and 1914.) Ulrich and Lynne seemed to follow each other around. For some reason, Ulrich was allowed time off from Vancouver to play in the 1912 championship series in Rossland, on the Greenwood Team. Lynne soon became a hot property, and he was head-hunted by the Grand Forks team in 1913, but for the Rossland Carnival, and the B.C. Championships, Lynne, along with the peripatetic Jack Ulrich, were both employed by the Rossland team. Rossland won the International, or Open Cup that year, with Ulrich and Lynne instrumental in its victory. Later, Lynn(e) went back to Grand Forks, who won the 1913 Boundary Championship. Lynn(e) was then noticed by the Pacific Coast League, and he later played as a spare with the New Westminster Team in 1914, and there is photographic evidence that he also played as a spare, or tried out for the Vancouver Millionaires around 1915.

Lynn, Harvey	goal	Rossland Juniors	1911
Lyon(s)	point	Phoenix Seniors	1902
Lyonnais, D.	center	Maple Leafs (Nelson Juvenile)	1909
Lyonnais, D. (or Lyonais, or Lyonnaise)	center	Nelson All-Stars (juniors)	1911
Lyonnaise, D.	lw	Nelson Juveniles	1910

Lyons	cover	Phoenix Seniors	1901
Lyons	point	Phoenix Seniors	1902
Lyons	cover/goal	Phoenix Seniors	1903
Mabee		Vernon single Men	1906
Mabee	lw	Vernon Seniors	1904
Mabee	lw	Vernon Seniors	1905
Mabee,	forward	Vernon Bankers	1907
Mabee, O. St. C.	lw	Vernon Seniors	1904
Mabee, C.	lw	Vernon Seniors	1903
Mabee, O. St. C.		Vernon Seniors	1905
Mabee, Oliver St.-Clair	lw	Vernon Seniors	1905, 1908

It's never been totally clear whether this player's last name was St. Clair-Mabee, or part of his first name was St. Clair, and his last name was Mabee. There were two other people with this name: Mabee, St.Clair, Gilfred, and Ernest, so it can not be assumed that all of the above Mabees were Oliver. Photographic evidence, however, shows that Oliver was the one who won the B.C. Championships in 1904. (He was listed as a clerk in 1898)

MacAdams	cover	Printers of Sandon (Dec. 1901)	1902
MacCormick, Alf.		Kamloops Picked Town Team	1903
MacDonald	lw	Rossland Juniors	1909
MacDonald	rw	Kaslo Seniors	1909
MacDonald	rover	Nelson Juniors	1909
MacDonald	centre	Nelson Intermediates	1909
MacDonald	2nd cover	Palace and Filbert Hotels (Sandon)	1901
Macdonald, C.	lw	New Denver Seniors	1909
Macdonald, C.	lw	New Denver Seniors	1909
MacDonald, D.		Greenwood Seniors	1911
MacDonald, D.J.	lw	Greenwood Seniors	1911
MacDonald, G.	rover	Greenwood Seniors	1911
MacDonell, Scotty	tried out	Nelson Seniors	1911
Machin		Combined Banks (Nelson)	1908
Machin	goal	Rossland Bankers	1907
Mackay, W. (Billy)	cover/centre	Kaslo Juniors	1909-10
Mackintosh, E.C.	goal	Rossland Victorias	1899
Madden, Bob	goal	Gerrard Seniors	1910
Madden, C.	goal	Maple Leafs (Nelson Juvenile)	1909
Madden, T	lw	Maple Leafs (Nelson Juvenile)	1909
Madill, J.	lw	Greenwood Seniors	1909
Mair	forward	Golden Seniors	1895
Malcomson	point	New Westminster Seniors	1901
Malcomson, Sid		New Westminster (Royals)	1907
Malsley	lw	Trail Juniors	1904
Manhart	cover	Nelson Grocers	1907
Manhart	point	Nelson East Ward ("Stick-Arounds")	1907
Manhart, C	point /cover	Nelson Grocers	1906-7
Manhart, C.	point	Bell Trading Company (Nelson grocers)	1906
Manhart, H.	tried out	Nelson Intermediates	1908
Manly	cover	Grand Forks Seniors	1905
Mann	centre	Grand Forks Seniors	1909
Mann, A.	point/rover	Grand Forks Seniors	1911
Mann, Art	cover	Grand Forks Seniors	1910

(According to Denny Boyd, Art Mann was a doctor from Toronto.)

Marpole, Clarence		Vancouver Seniors practise	1902
Marrin	spare at Rossl. Crn.	Nelson City Seniors	1900
Marshall	rover	Le Roi (Rossland)	1906
Marshall, C.	goal	Golden Seniors	1895
Marten		Camborne Seniors	1908

Martin, M.	spare	Sandon Seniors	1898
Martin, W.	l. wing	Fernie Seniors	1905
Martiu	forward	Hunter Brothers store Rossland	1899
Mascot Hamlet	spare	Salmo Seniors/Intermediates	1910
Mason, A.V.	cover	Nelson Tramway	1901
Mason, G.R.		Kamloops Seniors	1903
Mason, G.R.		Kamloops Picked Town Team	1903
Mastberg, V.	cover	Junior Thistles (Nelson Juvenile)	1909
Mather		Banff Seniors	1899
Mathew		Nelson High School Team	1909
Mathew (or Matthew)		Nelson High School	1909
Mathew, (s) E.	lw	Nelson High School	1909
Mathew, E.	rover	Nelson Juveniles	1910
Mathew, E.	rover	Nelson Rovers (Junior)	1910
Mathews		Nelson Juveniles	1909
Mathews	rover	Nelson Juniors	1909
Mathews	point	Nelson Juniors	1909
Mathews, E.	point	Nelson Rovers (Junior)	1910
Maundrell, .F.	lw	Armstrong Juniors	1907
Maundrell, A.	point	Armstrong Seniors	1909
Maundrell, P.	centre	Armstrong Intermediates	1910
Maundrell, S.	goal	Armstrong Seniors	1908
Maxwell, G.	rw	Vernon Juniors	1907
May	goal	Vernon Bankers	1907
Maybee, O.St.C.	see Mabee		
McAlman	rover	Nelson Bank Team	1907
McAlman	forward	Nelson Grocers	1907
McAlmon	point	Grand Forks Seniors	1910
McAlmond	point	Grand Forks Seniors	1909
McAnn	cover	Revelstoke Seniors	1904
McArthur	lw	Salmo Hoboes (inner-city)	1910
McArthur	rover	Phoenix Seniors	1902
McArthur	cover	Phoenix Seniors	1902
McArthur F.	rover	Salmo Seniors	1911
McArthur, A.	rw	Salmo Seniors	1911
McArthur, F.	rw	Salmo Seniors/Intermediates	1910
McArthur, P.C.	f	Phoenix Seniors	1901
McAstocker, C.	forward	Nelson CPR	1901
McAuliffe		Phoenix Juniors	1903
McAvoy, C.	forward	Columbias (Rossland junior)	1901
McBeath, H.	lw	Phoenix Seniors	1907
McBeath, Les	point	Nelson Juniors	1901
McBeth	rw	Phoenix Seniors	1907
McBride	cover	Rossland Seniors	1898
McBride	goal	Rossland Seniors	1898
McBride (capt)	forward	Rossland Seniors	1897
McBride, (R. ?)	goal	Wood-Vallance (Nelson hardware)	1907
McBride, C.	f	War Eagle Mine (Rossland Industrial League)	1904
McBride, C.R.	forward	Rosslands	1899
McBride, C.R.	forward	Rossland Seniors	1897
McBride, C.R. (capt.)	forward	Rosslands Seniors	1900
McBride, R.	point	Wood-Vallence, Nelson, Hardware	1907
Mcbride, W.	cover	Wood-Vallence, Nelson, Hardware	1907
McBurney	tried out for team	Spokane Amateur Athletic Club	1906
McCabe, A.E.	centre	Nelson Intermediates	1904
McCallum	lw	Grand Forks Seniors	1905

McCallum	forward	Phoenix Seniors	1905
McCandlish	point	Nelson Bank Team	1907
McCandlish, L. (capt.)		Nelson Amateurs (Junior)	1904
McCandlish, M.	rw	Nelson Juveniles	1905
McCandlish, s.	forward	Nelson East Ward	1907
McCandlish, S.	forward	Nelson East Ward ("Stick-Arounds")	1907
McCann, Barney	spare, or manager	Revelstoke Seniors	1904
McCarthur	rover	Phoenix Seniors	1902
McCarthur, E.	goal	Salmo Seniors	1911
McCarthur, P.C.		Phoenix Seniors	1901
McCarthy		Greenwood Seniors	1911
McCarthy	goal	Greenwood Seniors	1911
McCarthy	spare	Rossland Seniors	1908
McCarthy, C.	goal	Greenwood Seniors	1911
McCarthy, Ernest (erroneously named for Ernest McCaugherty)	pt	Spokane Seniors	1907
McCarthy, F.	centre	Greenwood Seniors	1911
McCaugherty, Ernest	point/rw	Spokane Seniors	1907-08

In 1909 Ernest McCaugherty was in Cleveland Ohio. It appears he returned and played for Greenwood in 1911. It's unknown which McCaugherty brother, (or McGaugherty, as it was sometimes spelled), played for Rossland in 1910. My guess is Tom.

McCaugherty, Tom	point	Rossland Seniors	1908
McCaugherty, Tom	cover	Spokane Seniors	1908

In 1909, Tom McCaugherty was in Vancouver B.C., and he was probably the McCaugherty, or McGaugherty who played for Rossland in 1910.

McClean	lw	Rossland Juniors	1911
McClean, A.V. (capt)	defense	Lumby Seniors	1911
McCleod, D.		Enderby Seniors	1901
McCluskey, J.	goal	Vernon Juniors	1903
McClusky, F.	cover	Vernon Juniors	1907
McColl	forward	Golden Seniors	1895
McConnan, D.G.	spare	Victoria, Captain Langley's team	1899
McCorkendale, J.	point	Armstrong Intermediates	1910
McCormick, W.H.	cover	Enderby Seniors	1904
McCoy, O.	point	Vernon High School	1903
McCreary	f	Rossland Seniors	1898
McCreary	goal	Rossland Victorias	1903
McCreary	goal	Rossland Seniors	1905
McCreary	goal	Rossland Seniors	1909
McCreary	goal	Rossland Seniors	1905
McCreary	goal	Phoenix Seniors	1910
McCreary	point	Rossland Intermediates	1906
McCreary, John (Jack)	goal	Rossland Seniors	1907
McCreary, J.	goal	Rossland Seniors (scratch team)	1901
McCreary, J.	goal	Rossland Victorias	1900-01
McCreary, J.	goal	Rosslands	1899
McCreary, J.	goal	Rossland Seniors	1901
McCreary, J.	goal	Rossland Seniors	1901
McCreary, J.	goal	Phoenix Seniors	1910
McCreary, J.	goal	Rosslands	1899
McCreary, J.	goal	Rossland Seniors	1901
McCreary	goal	Rossland Juniors	1901
McCreary, Jack	goal	Eagles (Spokane)	1906
McCreary, Jack	goal	Rossland Seniors	1908
McCreary, Jack	goal	Rossland Seniors	1906

Jack McCreary was one of the best goalies in B.C. His name was often misspelled in many different ways.

McCreary, W.	goal	Rossland Seniors	1898
McCullouch, Luther	centre	Nickel Plate Flat (Rossland Juvenile)	1906
McDonald		Rossland Juveniles	1909
McDonald	cover	Greenwood Seniors	1910
McDonald	center	Nelson Juniors	1908
McDonald	cover	Nelson grocers	1906
McDonald	cover	Bell Trading Company (Nelson grocers)	1906
McDonald	lw	Nelson Lakes	1908
McDonald	rover	Nelson Invincibles (Junior)	1905
McDonald	wing	Spokane Seniors,	1907 (?)
McDonald	rover	Kaslo Intermediates	1908
McDonald	cover	Greenwood Seniors	1910
McDonald	goal	Rossland Victorias	1906
McDonald	lw	Rossland Juniors	1909
McDonald	centre	Nelson Juniors	1907
McDonald	goal	Rossland Victorias Alberta Challenge Team	1906
McDonald	forward	Nelson Juniors	1907
McDonald	rover	Phoenix Intermediates	1908
McDonald,	wing	Spokane Seniors	1908(?)

Canadian who it was said played played for Spokane at the Rossland Carnival, (1908), but might not have.

McDonald, A	rover	Rocky Mountain Rangers (Rossland)	1907
McDonald, A.	point	Phoenix Seniors	1910
McDonald, A.	point	Phoenix Seniors	1909
McDonald, A.	center	Nelson Intermediates	1908
McDonald, A.	rover	Nelson Juveniles	1905
McDonald, A.	lw	Rossland Intermediates	1907
McDonald, A.S.	cover	Rocky Mountain Rangers (Rossland)	1907
McDonald, C.	lw	Salmo Seniors	1911
McDonald, C.D.		Grand Forks Seniors try-out	1905
McDonald, D.	cover	Greenwood Seniors	1911
McDonald, D.	cover	Nelson Grocers	1901
McDonald, D.	lw	West Kootenay Power and Light Company (Rossland)	1903
McDonald, G.	rw	Greenwood Seniors	1911
McDonald, Hughie	lw/spare	Kaslo Intermediates	1908, 1910
McDonald, J.	forward	Nelson Grocers	1901
McDonald, J.A.	spare	Nelson Wholesalers	1908
McDonald, John D.	lw	West Kootenay Power & Light Co. (Ross Ind. League)	1904
McDonald, R.	spare	Phoenix Seniors	1909
McDonald, W.	cover	Revelstoke Seniors	1901
McDonald, W.A.		Nelson Seniors	1903
McDonell, A. (misidentified on photo as A. McDonald)		Nelson Intermediates	1909
McDonell, F.	cover	Sandon Intermediates	1908
McDonnell, A.	lw	Victorias (Nelson inter-City)	1910
McDonough	centre	Fernie Seniors	1905
McDougal, J.	cover	Nelson Juniors	1901
McDougall	spare	Rossland Intermediates	1904
McDougall	forward	Grand Forks Seniors	1903
McDougall, C.	lw	Rossland Centre Star	1907
McDougall, F.	rover	Sandon Intermediates	1908
McDougall, G.	rw	Le Roi (Rossland)	1907
McDougall, N.	spare	Rossland Intermediates	1904
McDuggal, K.	rw	Sandon Seniors	1911
McFarland	centre	Nelson Juniors	1902
McFarland	centre	Trail Intermediates	1906
McFarland	cover	Trail Intermediates	1906

Name	Position	Team	Year
McFarland	forward	Nelson Juniors	1901
McFarland	forward	Nelson Bankers	1903
McFarlane	cover	Trail Intermediates	1906
McFarlane	centre	Trail Juniors	1905
McFarlane, F.	rover	Trail Juniors	1905
McFarlane, J.	lw	Cody Seniors	1910
McGaugherty	cover	Rossland Seniors	1910
McGaugherty	f/cover (see McCaugherty)	Spokane Seniors	1907
McGaugherty, Ernest	cover (see McCaugherty)	Greenwood Seniors	1911
McGaugherty, Ernest	rw (see McCaugherty)	Spokane Seniors	1908
McGaugherty, Ernest	cover (see McCaugherty)	Spokane Amateur Athletic Club	1907
McGaugherty, Tom	cover (see McCaugherty)	Spokane Seniors	1908
McGlaughlin	lw	Rosslands	1903
McGlaughlin		Trail Seniors	1910
McGlaughlin, G.E.	Manager	Nelson SeniorTeam	1903
McGlaughlin, R.	lw	Trail Intermediates	1910
McGregor		Fernie Seniors	1911

(McGregor was from Cranbrook, and was borrowed for one game with Fernie.)

Name	Position	Team	Year
McGregor	goal	Trail Smelter	1906
McGregor	centre	Cranbrook Seniors	1911
McHardy, C.	forward	Nelson Hardware	1901
McHardy, pte.	forward	Nelson Militia	1901
McInnis	point	Hunter Brothers store Rossland	1899
McIntosh	point	Wood-Vallance (Nelson hardware)	1907
McIntosh	center	Nelson Seniors	1905
Mcintosh,	point	Nelson Seniors	1906
McIntosh, A.	forward	Kaslo Seniors	1901
McIntosh, G.		Kaslo Seniors	1901
McIntosh, J.	forward/point	Nelson Seniors	1905-06
McIntosh, J. (or G.)	spare/manager	Nelson Seniors	1905
McIntosh, R.		Nelson West Ward	1906
McIntosh, R.	point	Nelson Seniors	1906
McIntosh, R.		Nelson West Ward ("hand warmers")	1906
McIntosh, R.	point	Nelson Seniors	1906
McIntosh, R.M.		Kaslo seniors	1901
McIntyre	rw	Kelowna Seniors	1909
McIntyre	cover	Rossland Bank Team	1897
McIntyre	forward	Rossland Junior Victorias	1899
McIntyre,		Nelson Seniors	1897
McIntyre, R.J.	point	Sandon Seniors	1903

(R.J. McIntyre was formerly minister of the Methodist church at Enderby and was also a pitcher for the base-ball team of that distsrict.)

Name	Position	Team	Year
McKanday, Jack		Nelson Seniors	1897
McKasill, J.	goal	Cody Seniors	1910
McKelvey		Phoenix Juniors	1903
McKelvey	forward	Phoenix Seniors	1905
McKelvey, L.	cover	Phoenix Seniors	1910
McKelvey, W.	center	Greenwood Intermediates	1910
McKelvie	rw	Phoenix Intermediates	1906
McKelvie	centre	Phoenix Intermediates	1908
McKelvie (y)	center	Phoenix Seniors	1911
McKelvie, L.	centre	Phoenix Seniors	1909
McKelvy	rover	Phoenix Seniors	1910
McKenzie		Vernon Megaws	1911
McKenzie, Erl	forward	Kaslo Hill Juniors	1901
McKenzie, J.K.	rover	Bank of Montreal (Rossland)	1903

McKenzie, Kenneth		New Westminster pick-up team player	1910
McKibbin, R.S.	centre	West Kootenay Power and Light Company (Rossland)	1903
McKibbin, Robert S.	rw	West Kootenay Power & Light Co. (Ross Ind. League)	1904
McKibbon	cover	West Kootenay Power and Light (Rossland)	1906
McKinney, R.	forward	Kaslo Town Juniors	1901
McKinnon		Vernon Intermediates	1910
McKinnon	spare	Greenwood Seniors	1902
McKinnon	forward	Sandon Seniors	1902
Mckinnon	forward	Silverton Seniors	1904
McKinnon F.	rover	Boundary Seniors	1906
McKinnon,	centre	Slocan City Seniors	1903
McKinnon, A	center (3rd game)	Vernon Seniors	1908
McKinnon, A.	cover	Vernon Seniors	1909
McKinnon, A.	cover	Vernon Seniors	1908
McKinnon, Bob	forward	Sandon Seniors	1898
McKinnon, F.	goal	Sandon City (Dec. 1901)	1902
McKinnon, F.	rover	Boundary combined team	1906
McKinnon, F.	rover	Boundary Seniors	1906
McKinnon, Frank		Sandon Juniors	1899, 1901
McKinnon, J.	forward	Sandon Juniors	1901
McKinnon, John	f	Sandon Juniors	1901
McKinnon, Joseph	cover	Kamloops Seniors	1910
McKinnon, L.	lw	Nelson Challengers (Junior)	1910
McKinnon, L.	rw	Nelson Mic-Macs (Junior)	1910
McLachlan	forward	Fernie Seniors	1904
McLachlin	forward	Reilly Club of Nelson	1904
McLanders, C.	cover	Sandon Seniors	1911
McLanders, R..	lw	Sandon Seniors	1911
McLane	cover	Rossland Juniors	1909
McLane	rw	Trail Juniors	1905
McLarne, G.		Summerland Seniors	1910
McLaughlan	forward	Nelson Bank Team	1907
McLaughlin (also McGlaughlin)		Rossland Seniors	1903
McLaughlin	rw	Nelson Retailers	1908
McLaughlin	center	Fernie Seniors	1904
McLaughlin	forward	Nelson Grocers	1906-7
McLaughlin	forward	Nelson Grocers	1907
McLaughlin	rover	Nelson West Ward ("Hand-Warmers")	1907
McLaughlin	goal	Nelson Rivers	1908
McLaughlin, J.	center	Fernie Seniors	1904
McLaughlin, J.	right wing	Hunter Brothers (Rossland)	1903
McLaughlin, J.	tried out for the team	Nelson Seniors	1901
McLaughlin, J.	goal	Vernon Seniors	1902
McLean	cover	Rossland Juniors	1909
McLean	cover	Summerland Seniors	1909
McLean	rover	New Westminster (Royals)	1907
McLean, A.	rw	Nickel Plate Flat (Rossland Juvenile)	1906
McLean, Homer	rw	Nelson Juniors	1901-02
McLean, M.J.	lw	Rossland Juniors	1911
McLean, Milton	point	Nickel Plate Flat (Rossland Juvenile)	1906
McLean, W.	forward	Nelson Hardware	1901
McLennan (or McLellan)	forward	Rossland Seniors	1901
McLeod		Nelson Juniors	1909
McLeod	goal	Nelson Juniors	1909
McLeod	left wing	Nelson Grocers	1906
McLeod	lw	Bell Trading Company (Nelson grocers)	1906

McLeod, Ed.	goal	Miner's and Kootenay Hotels (Sandon)	1901
McLeod, N.		Nelson Junior Warriors (formerly Nelson Juniors)	1909
McLeod, Wm.	f	Miner's and Kootenay Hotels (Sandon)	1901
McMahon, P.J.	Manager	Moyie Seniors	1901
McManus		Fernie Seniors	1911
McManus	goal	Commercials (Cranbrook)	1911
McManus (or McNames)	goal	Cranbrook Seniors	1911

McManus was from Cranbrook, and was borrowed for one game for Fernie.

McMillan	rw	Phoenix Intermediates	1907
McMillan	rw	Grand Forks Seniors	1905
McMillan	cover	Slocan City Seniors	1903
McMillan	centre	Phoenix Intermediates	1906
McMillan	forward	Phoenix Seniors	1905
McMillan	forward	Slocan Seniors	1904
McMillan W.	left wing	Boundary Seniors	1906
McMillan, A.	cover	Greenwood Intermediates	1910
McMillan, B.	centre	Sandon Seniors	1911
McMillan, D.	goal	Greenwood Intermediates	1910
McMillan, F.	rw	Greenwood Intermediates	1910
McMillan, R.	centre	Slocan Seniors	1909
McMillan, W.	left wing	Boundary combined team	1906
McMillan, W.	goal	Nelson CPR	1901
McMillan, W.	lw	Boundary Seniors	1906
McNab	cover	Trail Intermediates	1906
McNabb	cover	Trail Smelter Team	1905
McNabb	cover	Trail Smelter	1906
McNabb, A.J.	cover	Trail Intermediates	1907
McNabb, A.J.	cover	Trail Smelter Team	1905
McNabb, A.J.	cover	Trail Smelter	1907
McNabb, J.	cover	Trail Smelter	1908
McNaughton, A.E.	practised with	Vancouver CPR	1901
McNaughton, W.	point	Bank of Toronto/Royal Bank (Rossland)	1901
McNeish, William	President	Golden Seniors	1895

(The B.C. Directory for Golden in 1899 lists William McNeish as a hotelkeeper, and in 1901, the proprietor of Columbia House.)

McNichol, D.	Manager	Nelson Seniors	1904
MCosh	point	Bank of Montreal (Rossland)	1905
McPhee, G.	point	Nelson Juveniles	1910
McPherson		Rossland Seniors	1903
McPherson	centre	Rossland Victorias	1903
McPherson	point	Phoenix Seniors	1901
McPherson	point	Greenwood Seniors	1902
McPherson	point	Phoenix Seniors	1901
McPherson, W. (Happy)	cover	Meakin Hotel "Never-Sweats" (Trail)	1907
McQuade	cover	Centre Star/War Eagle (Rossland)	1906
McQuade, E.M.	point	Rossland Centre Star	1907
McQuaig	goal	Rossland Seniors	1905
McQuarrie	goal	Rossland Junior Victorias	1902
McQuarrie	manager	Nelson Seniors	1907
McQuarrie, D.	lw	Junior Thistles (Nelson Juvenile)	1909
McQuarrie, D.A.	rw	Nelson Invincibles (high school)	1910
McQuarrie, James,	President	Commonage Intermediate Team (Vernon)	1904
McQuarrie, M.R.	manager	Nelson Seniors	1908
McQuarrie, W.G.,	goal	Ashcroft Seniors	1901
McQueen	lw	Phoenix Seniors	1907
McQueen	lw/rw	Rossland Seniors	1909

McQueen	rw	Phoenix Seniors	1911
McQueen	goal	Vancouver Terminals	1907
McQueen	rw	Phoenix Seniors	1907
McQueen	goal	Herman's Champions, Vancouver	1907
McQueen	rw	Phoenix Seniors	1910
McQueen	forward	Grand Forks Seniors	1902
McQueen	forward/rw	Grand Forks Seniors	1903
McQueen A.	rw	Boundary Seniors	1906
McQueen, A.	rw	Vernon Seniors	1904
McQueen, A.	lw/rw	Phoenix Seniors	1909-10
McQueen, A.	rw	Vernon Seniors	1905
McQueen, A.	right wing	Boundary combined team	1906
McQueen, A. (capt)		Vernon Intermediates	1905
McQueen, T.	lw	Vernon Juniors	1903
McQuerrie, J. (or McCreary)	goal	Phoenix Seniors	1910
McRae	forward	Slocan City Seniors	1903
McTavish, H.		Revelstoke Seniors	1899
McVichie	center//point	Sandon Seniors	1897-99
McVichie	cover	Sandon Seniors	1898
McVichie, J	forward	Sandon Seniors	1898
McVickie J. A.	cover	Sandon Seniors	1897
McVickie, D. (capt)	cover	Sandon Seniors	1897
McWha	rover	Cranbrook Seniors	1911
McWha	centre	Fernie Seniors	1911
McWha was from Cranbrook, and was borrowed for one game with Fernie.			
McWha	cover	Phoenix Seniors	1911
McWha, P.C.	centre	Moyie Seniors	1910
McWha, P.C.	rover	Moyie Seniors	1910
Mead	forward	Phoenix Seniors	1903
Mearn	forward	Vancouver Seniors	1901
Meegan	rover	Trail Seniors	1902
Megans, F.	f	Sandon Juniors	1899
Melligan (or Milligan), Winter	goal	Trail Juniors	1907
Meran	point	Salmo Hoboes (inner-city)	1910
Mercer	rw	Rossland Seniors	1911
Mercer	rw/lw	Grand Forks Seniors	1911
Mernett, R.	point	Salmo Seniors/Intermediates	1910
Merritt	forward	Vancouver Seniors	1901
Merritt (capt.)	point	Rossland Seniors	1898
Merritt, J.	point	Sandon Seniors	1897
Merritt, J.N.	point	Rossland Victorias	1899
Messenger, C.		Moyie Seniors	1910
Meyer, B.	rover	Vernon Intermediates	1910
Meyer, F.	rover	Greenwood Seniors	1909
Meyer, H.F.	rover	Vernon Seniors	1908
Meyer, R.		Vernon Bankers	1911
Meyer, R. (capt)	rw	Vernon Juniors	1903
Michner		Grand Forks Juniors	1903
Middleton	lw	Wood-Vallance (Nelson hardware)	1907
Middleton, W.	center	Vernon Seniors	1908-09
Mifflin	rover	Salmo Hoboes (inner-city)	1910
Miggins	rw	Rossland Junior Victorias	1902
Millan	point	Fernie Seniors	1911
Millan was from McCleod Alberta, and was borrowed for one game for Fernie.			
Millar, E.	tried out	Nelson Intermediates	1908
Miller	lw	Nelson Wholesalers	1908

Miller	point	Fernie Seniors	1904
Miller	lw	Nelson Juniors	1907
Miller	point	Nelson Juniors	1910
Miller	point	Nelson Intermediates	1911
Miller	point	Fernie Seniors	1904
Miller	rover	Rossland Seniors	1911
Miller	cover	Grand Forks Seniors	1911
Miller	goal	Fernie Seniors	1906
Miller	lw	Nelson Intermediates	1909
Miller	lw	Nelson Juniors	1909
Miller	point	Nelson Intermediates	1911
Miller	centre	Greenwood Seniors	1910
Miller	rover	Grand Forks Seniors	1910
Miller	rover	Nelson Juniors	1909
Miller	forward	Archer's Flat Team (Kaslo)	1900
Miller	forward	Nelson Juniors	1907
Miller	rover/ manager	Grand Forks Seniors	1911
Miller	forward	Nelson Juniors	1907
Miller	goal	Heroes (Grand Forks)	1903
Miller, A.	forward	Hodder's Hill Team (Kaslo)	1900
Miller, Alex	forward	Heroes (Grand Forks)	1903
Miller, Art	cover	Nelson Intermediates	1911
Miller, Art	cover	Nelson YMCA Juniors	1911
Miller, C.	lw	Nelson Rovers (Junior)	1910
Miller, J.	lw	Nelson Intermediates	1908
Miller, J.	forward	Nelson Juniors	1907
Miller, J.	goal	Fernie Seniors	1905
Miller, J.	point/cover	Nelson Intermediates	1911
Miller, J.	cover	Victorias (Nelson inner-city)	1910
Miller, J.	point/cover	Nelson Intermediates	1910
Miller, Jack	spare	Nelson Seniors	1911
Miller, Jack	point	Nelson Intermediates	1911
Miller, Jack	point	Nelson YMCA Juniors	1911
Miller, Jack	spare	Thistles (Nelson City League)	1909
Miller, Jack	lw	Nelson Juniors	1908
Miller, R.	point	Fernie Seniors	1904
Miller, R.	goal	Nelson Rovers (Junior)	1910
Miller, S.	lw	Thistles (Nelson inner-city)	1910
Miller, S.	lw	Nelson Intermediates	1910
Miller, S.	cover	Nelson Intermediates	1908
Miller, S.	rover	Nelson Juniors	1908
Miller. A.	cover	Nelson Junior Warriors (formerly Nelson Juniors)	1909
Milligan	rw	Trial Intermediates	1910
Milligan	cover	Trail Intermediates	1909
Milligan, F.	rover	Trail Juniors	1908
Milligan, F.	cover	Trail Seniors	1910
Milligan, Fred	cover	Trail Intermediates	1911
Milligan, George		Trail Seniors	1910
Milligan, George	point	Trail Intermediates	1911
Mills	point	Rossland Bankers	1907
Mills	forward	Silverton Seniors	1904
Mills, W.	cover	Armstrong Seniors	1908-09
Miln	spare	Commercials (Cranbrook)	1911
Milne	forward	Slocan City Seniors	1903
Milne	forward	Slocan Seniors	1904
Milne, Jack	f	Miner's and Kootenay Hotels (Sandon)	1901

Mitchell	lw	Vancouver Bankers	1907
Mitchell	goal	Phoenix Seniors	1901
Mitchell	goal	Phoenix Seniors	1902
Mitchell	rw	Nickel Plate Flat (Rossland Juvenile)	1906
Mitchell, W	forward	Grand Forks Seniors	1903
Moe	goal	Nelson Juniors	1902
Moe	rover	Grand Forks Seniors	1905
Moe, C.E.	forward	Grand Forks Seniors	1905
Moe, R.S.	forward	Nelson CPR	1901
Moe, Roy	rover	Nelson Juniors	1902
Moffatt, S	forward	Victoria, Captain Langley's team	1899
Mohr	forward	Vernon Town team	1907
Mohr, W.		Vernon Seniors	1907
Mohr, W.	cover	Vernon Juniors	1903
Mohr, W.	goal	Vernon Intermediates	1910
Moir, J.	cover	Revelstoke Seniors	1903
Monk	f	Phoenix Seniors	1901
Monk	lw	Phoenix Seniors	1902
Monk (capt)	centre	Phoenix Seniors	1902
Monk, E.W.	1 game	Rossland Victorias	1900
Montgomery, H.P.A.		Kaslo Hotel	1898
Moodie, J.	tried out	Nelson Intermediates	1908
Moody	lw	Nelson Rivers	1908
Moore	goal	Trail Smelter	1906
Moore	point	Kaslo Seniors	1899
Moore, "Maggie"	goal	Meakin Hotel "Never-Sweats" (Trail)	1907
Moore, C.	forward	Kaslo Seniors	1901
Moran, J.	point	Trail Juniors	1904
Morgan		Trail Seniors	1910
Morgan	rover	Trial Intermediates	1910
Morgan	centre	Trail Juniors	1906
Morgan	forward	Trail Juniors	1907
Morgan, "Capt."	Coach	Trail Smelter Team	1905
Morgan, D.	centre	Trail Juniors	1908
Morgan, Dick	rover	Trail Intermediates	1911
Morgan, J.	coach	Trail Smelter Team	1905
Morgan, R.	rw	Meakin Hotel "Never-Sweats" (Trail	1907
Morgan, R.	centre	Trail Intermediates	1910
Morkill, A.B.	forward	Bank of Toronto/Royal Bank (Rossland)	1901
Morkill, D.B.	f	Le Roi Mine (Rossland Industrial League)	1904
Morkill, D.B.	forward	Rossland Seniors	1901
Morley		Coldstream Ranch Seniors	1911
Morris	cover	Commercials (Cranbrook)	1911
Morris	point	Hodder's Hill Team (Kaslo)	1900
Morrison	goal	Fernie Seniors	1908
Morrison, E.	point	Hunter Brothers (Rossland)	1903
Morrison, P.	rw	Armstrong Seniors	1908-09
Morrison, R.S.	center	Vernon Seniors	1908
Morrison, R.	forward	Vernon Town team	1907
Morrow	rw	Trail Juniors	1906
Morrow	forward	Trail Juniors	1907
Morrow, C.	rw	Trail Juniors	1908
Morrowson		Smithers Seniors	1910
Motherwell, J.A.	contact for the team	New Westminster Bankers	1909
Muller, H.G. (capt)		Coldstream Hotel (Vernon)	1904
Mulligan, F.	point	Trail Intermediates	1910

Name	Position	Team	Year
Munn		Kamloops City Team	1904
Munn		Kamloops Seniors	1905
Munn,		Kamloops city teams	1903
Munn, Thomas		Kamloops Seniors	1908, 1910
Munroe, A.	wing	Eagles (Spokane)	1906
Munroe, A.	centre	Spokane Amateur Athletic Club	1907
Munson	lw	Kelowna Seniors	1909
Murat, Jack C.	f	Palace and Filbert Hotels (Sandon)	1901
Murphy	rover	Salmo Mess (inner-city)	1910
Murphy	goal	Fernie Seniors	1911

Murphy was from McCleod Alberta, and was borrowed by Fernie for one game.

Name	Position	Team	Year
Murphy, D.	point	Sandon Seniors	1910
Murphy, E.	rw	Nelson Challengers (Junior)	1910
Murphy, E..	lw	Nelson Mic-Macs (Junior)	1910
Murphy, Ed.	rw	Nelson YMCA Juniors	1911
Murphy, J.	rw	Nelson Juniors	1910
Murphy, Paddy	f	Saloons (Sandon)	1901
Murray		Nicola Seniors	1908
Murray, F.	rw	Armstrong Juniors	1907
Murray, F.	rover	Armstrong Intermediates	1910
Murray, J.	forward	Nicola Lake Seniors	1902
Murray, W.	forward	Nicola Lake Seniors	1902
Musselman, Frank	Manager	Nelson Seniors	1904
Myers, B	forward	Vernon Bankers	1907
Myers, B.	rover	Vernon Seniors	1908
Myers, R.	rover	Vernon Bankers	1907
Nace, O.	forward	Nelson Seniors	1901
Nagle	forward	Nelson Grocers	1907
Nagle, D	rover	Nelson Intermediates	1910
Nagle, O.	center	Victorias (Nelson inner-city)	1910
Nagle, S..	rover	Nelson Intermediates	1910
Nagle.	point	Nelson Intermediates	1911
Nancarrow	tried out	Nelson Seniors	1911
Nase	rw	Nelson Seniors	1902
Nash	goal	Rossland Seniors	1897
Nash, George R.	point	Rossland Seniors	1897
Neal		Nicola Seniors	1908
Neal	rw	Rossland Seniors	1908
Neelands (or Newlands) P.N.	f	Rossland Seniors	1901
Neelands, Sam	goal/manager	Nelson Seniors	1899-1901

Sam Neelands first tried out, and didn't make the team, but later he became a regular, playing goaltender and becoming manager. In 1900 he decided to discontinue his boat and shoe business and devote his attention to other business.

Name	Position	Team	Year
Neil	lw	Rossland Seniors	1908
Neil	centre	Centre Star/War Eagle (Rossland)	1906
Neil	cover	Phoenix Seniors	1911
Neil	point	Spokane Amateur Athletic Club	1907
Neil (from Rossland)?	(one game against Edmonton)	Nelson Seniors	1909
Neil, H.	lw/rover	Rossland Seniors	1907-1910
Neil, H. (or Neill)	lw	Phoenix Seniors	1910
Neill	lw	Phoenix Seniors	1910
Neill	centre	Le Roi (Rossland)	1906
Neill	point	Phoenix Seniors	1911
Neill, H.	centre	Centre Star/War Eagle (Rossland)	1906
Neill, Herb	lw	Rossland Seniors	1907
Neilson		Vancouver scrub team	1905

Neilson, O.	point	Vancouver Terminals	1907
Neilson, Oscar	point	Herman's Champions, Vancouver	1907
Neilson, Oscar,	spare (and manager)	Vancouver Terminals	1907
Nelson, A.		Enderby Seniors	1901
Nelson, Angus (capt)	rover/forward	Kamloops Seniors	1902-03, 05, 08
Nelson, Angus,		Kamloops City teams	1903-04
Nelson, Bert	cover	New Denver "A"s	1911
Nelson, Bert	cover	New Denver Seniors	1911
Nelson, C.	rover	New Denver "B"s	1911
Nelson, E.	rw	New Denver "A"s	1911
Newburn		Nelson Juniors	1909
Newburn	goal	Nelson Juniors	1909
Newburn, W.	goal	Nelson Juniors	1910
Newburn, W.	goal	Nelson YMCA Juniors	1911
Newell, Wm	goal	Palace and Filbert Hotels (Sandon)	1901
Newitt	rover	Nelson High School	1909
Newitt	lw	Nelson Juniors	1910
Newitt, Dosey	forward	Salmo Intermediates	1911
Newitt, M.	point	Nelson Public School	1909
Newitt, N.	point	Thistles (Nelson inner-city)	1910
Newitt, S.	rover	Nelson YMCA Juniors	1911
Newitt, S.	rover	Nelson Cyclones (high school)	1910
Newitt, S..	lw	Nelson Intermediates	1910
Newitt, S..	center	Nelson Juniors	1910
Newlands (or Neelands) P.N.	f	Rossland Seniors	1910
Newport, J	point	Nelson CPR	1901
Newton	spare	Nelson Mountains	1908
Newton	spare	Nelson Rivers	1908
Newton, C.R.B.	lw	"Tenderfeet" (Nelson)	1908
Niblett	centre	Spokane Seniors	1907
Niblett	rw	Wood's Independents (Spokane)	1907
Niblitt, J.	centre	Spokane Seniors	1907
Nicholls	lw	Wood's Independents (Spokane)	1907
Nichols, Russell	cover	Slocan City Seniors	1899
Nickerson Brothers		Combined Banks (Nelson)	1908
Niles	f	Phoenix Seniors	1901
Niles	rover	Grand Forks Seniors	1902
Niles, C.H.	rover	Grand Forks, Seniors	1903
Nirbey	cover	Kelowna Seniors	1909
Nixon		Combined Banks (Nelson)	1908
Noble	rw	Trail Smelter	1906
Nordman		Moyie Seniors	1911
North, C.	centre	Kaslo Intermediates	1908
Nott, Frank	tried out	Nelson Seniors	1908
Nunn	goal	Nelson Wholesalers	1903
Nunn	goal	Nelson Wholesalers	1908
Nunn	goal	Nelson Wholesalers	1903, 1908
Nunn, G	goal	Nelson Grocers	1901, 1906
Nunn, George	goal	Nelson Wholesalers	1904
Nunn, George	goal	Bell Trading Company (Nelson grocers)	1906
Nunn, George (capt)	cover/goal	Nelson Seniors	1898-99, 1905
Nunn, George.	goal	Nelson Lacrosse-Hockey Seniors	1900
O'Brien	f	Rossland Seniors	1898
O'Brien	cover	Rossland Victorias	1901
O'Brien	cover	Nickel Plate Flat (Rossland Juvenile)	1906
O'Brien (capt)	cover	Rossland Seniors	1898, 1901

Name	Position	Team	Year
O'Brien, Ed. M. (capt)	cover	Rossland Victorias	1899-1901
O'Brien, Eddie	cover	Rossland Seniors	1901
O'Brien, R.	rw	Rossland Stars (Juvenile)	1906
O'Connor	cover	Nelson Wholesalers	1908
O'Connor	cover	Nelson Bank Team	1907
O'Hearn	rover	Victorias (Rossland)	1902
O'Hearn, E.	forward	Columbias (Rossland junior)	1901
O'Hearn, E.	forward	Rossland Juniors	1901
O'Malley		Vancouver scrub team	1905
O'Malley, C.	cover	Maple Leafs (Nelson Juvenile)	1909
O'Neil, Hugh	goal	Ymir Seniors	1911
Ogden, Joe		Crown Point Hotel (Trail)	1910
Ogenski, F. (or Ogensky)	rw	Maple Leafs (Nelson Juvenile)	1909
Oliver	rover	Vernon Seniors	1905
Oliver	goal	Hodder's Hill Team (Kaslo)	1900
Oliver	forward	Nelson Bank Team	1907
Oliver	goal	Sandon Seniors	1901
Oliver, Bert	rover	Vernon Seniors	1905
Oliver, E.		Enderby Seniors	1901
Oliver, H.G.	tried out for team	War Eagle Mine (Rossland Industrial League)	1904
Oliver, J.	rover	Greenwood Intermediates	1910
Omah, "Omey"		Vancouver Allstar team (no known opponents)	1910
Orr		Camborne Seniors	1908
Orr, J.	rover	Vancouver Bankers	1907
Ouillett	lw	Phoenix Seniors	1911
Oulette	lw	Phoenix Seniors	1911
Owen	lw	Rossland Invincibles (Juniors)	1906
Owen	rover	Rossland Juniors	1911
Owen	rw	Rossland Juniors	1907
Owen, H.	rw	Rossland Juniors	1908
Owen, W. (or Owens)	centre	Trail Intermediates	1911
Owens	rw	Rossland Bankers	1907
Owens	point	Rossland Juniors	1909
Owens	rover	Nickel Plate Flat (Rossland Juvenile)	1906
Owens, A.	rw	Vernon Intermediates	1910
Owens.	rover	Rossland Intermediates	1909
Padden, A.E.	f	Bank of Montreal (Rossland Industrial League)	1904
Page	point	Nelson Wholesalers	1908
Palmer (or Balmer)	spare	Victorias (Nelson City League)	1909
Palmer, S.	forward	Hodder's Hill Team (Kaslo)	1900
Parker, J. W.	point	West Kootenay Power & Light Co. (Rossland Ind. League)	1904
Parks, F.	rover	Nelson Mic-Macs (Junior)	1910
Parks, F.	cover	Nelson Challengers (Junior)	1910
Parks, N.	spare/centre	Nelson Intermediates	1910
Parr	spare	Vancouver Seniors	1901
Parry	lw	Ashdowns (Nelson hardware)	1907
Parry (or perry), F.	right wing	Nelson Ashdowns (hardware)	1907
Parsons		Kamloops city teams	1903
Parsons		Kamloops City team	1904
Partington	centre	Nelson Retailers	1908
Partington, C. T.	centre	Nelson Grocers	1906
Partington, C.T.	centre	Bell Trading Company (Nelson grocers)	1906
Party, C.D.	defense	Nelson Retailers	1908
Patrick, C.	point	Maple Leafs (Nelson Juvenile)	1909

This was possibly Cynda, the sister of Lester and Frank Patrick, who played a lot of hockey. (See Ladies, below).

Patrick, Frank	point	Thistles (Nelson City League)	1909
Patrick, Frank	point/lw	Nelson Seniors	1909, 1911

Frank Patrick was one of the greatest players in the history of hockey, as well as one of its most important builders. Born in Ottawa 1886, died 1960. He usually played defense, and made a huge difference to any team he played with. With his brother Lester, and his father, Joe, he started the Pacific Coast League in 1911, and went on to win the Stanley cup in 1915 with the Vancouver Millionaires. (He played for the cup directly several times.) See, "The Patricks," by Eric Whitehead, and the, "Trail of The Stanley Cup, by Coleman," for more info.

Patrick, G.	lw	Nelson Juniors	1909

This was possibly Guy Patrick, one of the youngest brothers of Lester and Frank, who would have been about ten.

Patrick, Lester	cover	"Tenderfeet" (Nelson)	1908
Patrick, Lester	point	Nelson Rivers	1908
Patrick, Lester	rover	Victorias (Nelson City League)	1909
Patrick, Lester	cover/point/rover	Nelson Seniors	1908-09, 1911

Lester Patrick was one of the greatest players in the history of hockey, as well as an important builder and coach. Born in Drummondville, Quebec in 1883, died 1960. He usually played defence, but also played rover. He was the premier player of any team he was on, and helped to make the Nelson team a powerhouse while he was there. He won the Stanley cup twice in 1905 and 1906 with the Montreal Wanderers. He played for it several times after that, and won it again in 1913 with the Victoria Aristocrats of the Pacific Coast League, but the Quebec Bulldogs reneged on giving up the trophy. (They did so just before the contest took place, making the games a challenge series with no trophy). Lester won the cup as a coach of the Victoria Cougars in 1925, and again as a coach with the New York Rangers in 1928, 1933, and 1940. Lester won the B.C. Championships with Nelson in 1909. With his brother Frank, and Father Joe, Lester started the Pacific Coast League in 1911. See, "The Patricks," by Eric Whitehead, and the "Trail of The Stanley Cup," by Coleman, for more info.

Patterson	center	Nelson Wood-Vallance	1911
Patterson, W.	center	Nelson Mic-Macs (Junior)	1910
Patterson, W.	center	Nelson Challengers (Junior)	1910
Patterson, W. (or Paterson)	center	Nelson Juniors	1908
Patton	cover	West Kootenay Power and Light (Rossland)	1906
Pawnell, V.	wing	Eagles (Spokane)	1906
Paxton, A.	goal	Reilly Club of Nelson	1904
Pearcey		Nelson High School	1909
Pearcy, C.	centre	Nelson Cyclones (high school)	1910
Peck, Bill	f	Palace and Filbert Hotels (Sandon)	1901
Pelly, R.	rover	Armstrong Seniors	1908
Pemberton	goal	West Kootenay Power and Light (Rossland)	1906
Pendegrast, Joseph, (capt)		Queen Hotel (Phoenix)	1911
Penrose	rw	Grocery Clerks (Rossland)	1906
Penrose	point	Le Roi (Rossland)	1908
Penrose	point	Rossland Intermediates	1908
Penrose, B. (or W.)	point/ rw	Le Roi (Rossland)	1907
Percell	point	Phoenix Intermediates	1907
Perrier	rw	Nelson Rivers	1908
Perrier	rw	Nelson Seniors	1904
Perrier	centre	Grand Forks Seniors	1903
Perrier	rover	Nelson Seniors	1902
Perrier	forward	Nelson Lacrosse-Hockey Seniors	1900
Perrier	forward	Nelson Bank Team	1907
Perrier, (or Ferrier)	rover	Nelson Intermediates	1906
Perrier, A.		Nelson West Ward	1906
Perrier, Arthur	lw/ rw	Thistles (Nelson inner-City)	1909-10
Perrier, Arthur, A.	lw/rw/cent/spare	Nelson Seniors	1899-1907, 1911

Arthur Perrier was born in Prescott, and played in Eastern Canada before moving to Nelson. He was a bookkeeper at Ferland and Company. Later, in 1914, he was listed as an employee of Poole Drug Co. He played on the Nelson Senior team for many years, winning several championships, although in later years he was often a sub. He left for a few years, to parts unknown, then returned. He was French Canadian, with a thick accent.

Name	Position	Team	Year
Perry	forward	Rosslands Seniors	1900
Perry, Fred	forward	Nelson West Ward ("Hand-Warmers")	1907
Peters	cover	Le Roi Mine (Rossland)	1905
Peters, F.S.	cover	Le Roi Mine (Rossland)	1905
Petersen, R.	forward	Nelson East Ward ("Stick-Arounds")	1907
Peterson		Revelstoke City League Team (unnamed)	1909
Peterson, Ralph	forward	Nelson East Ward	1907
Petrie	cover	Heroes (Grand Forks)	1903
Pever	rover	Fernie Seniors	1908
Phillips, G.	point	Nelson Grocers	1901
Phillips, Tom		Vancouver Allstar team (no known opponents)	1910

Tom Phillips came to Vancouver after winning the Stanley cup in 1907 with Kenora Thistles. He was eager to play hockey, but there were few opportunities in Vancouver. Although I haven't listed it above, he probably was a member of Harry Bright's Eastern, "Stars," who played a Vancouver scrub team in 1909 and lost, largely due to poor conditioning. Tom Phillips was a very heavy smoker, and was typically out of shape and out of breath. He married, and might have had one daughter, who died very young. Phillips died in 1923 from an infected tooth. He had recently been made a manager in a Vancouver Lumber business. He is a member of the Hockey Hall of Fame. He started his career at McGill university where he was a star, then moved to various teams in Ontario and Quebec, finally achieving immortality by defeating the Montreal Wanderers for the Stanley Cup in 1907 with Kenora Thistles. Lester Patrick called him the greatest left winger in the game. He broke his foot in a challenge match for the Stanley cup in 1908, with Edmonton, and was never really the same after that. He was still living in Vancouver when Lester Patrick coaxed him out of retirement for the first year of the Vancouver Millionaires team in 1911-1912, in the new Pacific Coast League, but he could only stand one year, and then retired permanently, being addicted to cigarettes.

Name	Position	Team	Year
Phinney		Vernon Megaws	1911
Phinney, N	point	Summerland Seniors	1909
Phipps	lw	Victorias (Rossland)	1902
Phipps, (or Fipps) W.H.G.	forward	Bank of Mon./Can Bank of Com. (Rossland)	1901
Phipps, W.G.H.	f	Bank of Montreal (Rossland Industrial League)	1904
Phipps, W.H.G.	forward	Rossland Seniors	1901
Phipps, W.H.G.	rover	Associated Banks (Rossland)	1903
Phipps, W.H.G.	rw	Bank of Montreal (Rossland)	1905
Pierce		Phoenix Juniors	1903
Pierce	rover	Phoenix Intermediates	1906
Pinchbeck	point	Slocan Seniors	1904
Pinchbeck	forward	Silverton Seniors	1903
Pinchbeck, J. (or Pinchback)	point	Slocan Seniors	1909
Pindle,	point	Vancouver Terminals	1907
Pinkham	forward	Nelson Bankers	1903
Pinkham, H.		Revelstoke Seniors	1899
Pinkham, W.		Revelstoke Seniors	1899
Pitts, H.	goal	Nelson Boy Scouts	1911
Poff, G.	cover	Victoria Daniel's team	1899
Pollett.	goal	Hunter Brothers store Rossland	1899
Pool	cover	Nelson Retailers	1908
Potter	goal	Printers of Sandon (Dec. 1901)	1902
Poupore, A.	lw	Nelson High School	1909
Pourpore, A.		Nelson Junior Warriors (formerly Nelson Juniors)	1909
Power	centre	Royal Hotel (Vernon)	1908

Name	Position	Team	Year
Powers	cover	Rossland Seniors	1904
Powers, Richard		Penticton Seniors	1908
Pownell, R.	forward	Rossland Seniors	1901
Pownell, V.	cover	Rossland Juniors	1899
Pownell, Virgie		Rossland Juniors, IXL	1899
Prescott	goal	Trail Juniors	1905
Prescott, J.	lw	Trail Intermediates	1911
Prest	forward	Rossland Seniors	1897
Prest, W.J.	forward	Rossland Seniors	1897
Preston	forward	Rossland Intermediates	1903
Preston	rover	Rosslands	1903
Preston	rover	Rossland Intermediates	1906
Preston, J.	lw	Rossland Juniors	1902
Preston, J.	forward	Nelson Intermediates	1904
Preston, John	point	Rossland Juniors	1902
Pringle	rover	Vancouver Terminals	1907
Pringle	rover	Herman's Champions, Vancouver	1907
Pringle, A.		New Westminster pick-up team	1909

Pringle was the City Editor at the Columbian Newspaper, in New Westminster. He fell through the ice in a game at trout lake, and tried to save another player, as he got out, but was unsuccessful, and the other player drowned.

Name	Position	Team	Year
Prior, B.G.	forward	Kamloops Senior	1902
Proudfoot, D.	point	Nelson Grocers	1901
Pullen	rw	Nelson Juniors	1902
Pullen	forward	Nelson Juniors	1901
Pullen	forward	Nelson Seniors	1902
Pullen	forward, 2 games	Nelson City Seniors	1900
Pullen, F.	forward	Nelson Tramway	1901
Putnam	goal	Nickel Plate Flat (Rossland Juvenile)	1906
Pye, D.	forward	Commercials (Cranbrook)	1911
Quigley	manager	Vancouver Seniors practise	1902
Quinn	cover	Phoenix Seniors	1910
Quinn	cover	Grand Forks Seniors	1911
Quinn	point	Grand Forks Seniors	1911
Quinn, Barney	lw	Grand Forks Seniors	1910
Racine, C.	rover	Sandon Seniors	1910
Rae	rw	Victorias (Rossland)	1902
Rae	cover	Rossland Seniors	1897
Rae	goal	Rossland Seniors	1898
Rae	forward	Rossland Seniors	1900
Rae, Jack	f (see also Rea and Ray)	Sandon Juniors	1899
Rae (or Rea), J.E.	goal	Spokane Amateur Athletic Club	1906-07
Rae, T.R.	forward	Rosslands	1899
Rason	rover	Nelson Wholesalers	1908
Rawlings, Beecher	forward	Cyclones (Rossland juniors)	1901
Ray	forward	Rossland Bank team	1897
Ray, Edmund E. (or Rae)	cover	Rossland Seniors	1897
Ray, Fred		Crown Point Hotel (Trail)	1910
Ray, J.	cover	Rosslands	1903
Raymer	centre	West Kootenay Power and Light (Rossland)	1906
Rea	rw	Rossland Seniors	1902
Rea	cover	Rossland Citizen Team	1903
Rea	forward	Rossland Victorias	1901
Rea	point	Grand Forks Seniors	1905
Rea	point	Rossland Victorias	1901
Rea, J. (or Rae)	point	Rossland Seniors	1901

Name	Position	Team	Year
Rea, T.H.	cover	Rossland Seniors	1897
Read	rover	Grand Forks Seniors	1909
Reed	point	Centre Star/War Eagle (Rossland)	1906
Reid (also named as W.H. Read in photo)	goal	Le Roi (Rossland)	1907
Reid	lw	Grand Forks Seniors	1911
Reid	rw	Grand Forks Seniors	1911
Reid, Bert	center	Grand Forks Seniors	1910
Reid, J.	cover	Armstrong Seniors	1907
Reilly	point	Nelson Juniors	1909
Reilly, Misses	mascots	Reilly Club of Nelson	1904
Reilly, R.	goal	Nelson Wood-Vallance	1911
Reilly, W. (or Riley)	cover	Nelson Wood-Vallance	1911
Reilly, W. (or Riley)	rw	Nelson Intermediates	1911
Reinhard, F.	point	Vernon Juniors	1907
Reinhard, Gus.F.	point	Vernon Intermediates	1910
Reinhard, W	rover	Vernon Juniors	1907
Reinhard, W. E.	center	Vernon Intermediates	1910
Rennan, William	goal	Kamloops Seniors	1910
Reynolds, F.L.	forward	Ashcroft Seniors	1901
Rhodes	rw	Vancouver Bankers	1907
Rich, A.J.	tried out for team	West Kootenay Power & Lt Co. (Ross Ind. Lg)	1904
Richards, Bert	rw	Lardeau Seniors	1905
Richards, Billy	f	Saloons (Sandon)	1901
Richardson		Nelson Public School	1909
Richardson	centre	Nicola Seniors	1910
Richardson, N.		Nelson Public School	1909
Richie, (Or Ritchie) A.B. (Bruce)	centre	Trail smelter	1907
Riddle, R.	lw	Commonage Intermediates (Vernon)	1904
Ried	goal	Centre Star/War Eagle (Rossland)	1906
Rilance	rw	Fernie Seniors	1908
Riley	lw	Nelson Intermediates	1911
Riley	point	Nelson Mountains	1908
Riley	point	Nelson Juniors	1908
Riley	rover	Nelson West Ward ("Hand-Warmers")	1907
Riley	cover	Nicola Lake Seniors	1902
Riley	cover	Nelson Intermediates	1909
Riley	rover	Wood-Vallance (Nelson hardware)	1907
Riley (or Reilly)	point	Nelson Intermediates	1908
Riley, E.	lw	Nicola Seniors	1910
Riley, F.	rw	Nicola Seniors	1910
Riley, R.	goal	Nelson Mic-Macs (Junior)	1910
Riley, R.	goal	Nelson Challengers (Junior)	1910
Riley, R.W.	rw	Nelson Intermediates	1910
Riley, W.	rw	Nelson Intermediates	1910
Riley, W.	center	Thistles (Nelson inner-city)	1910
Riley, W.	centre	Nelson Juveniles	1905
Riley, W. (capt.)		Nelson Champions (Junior)	1904
Riliance (or Rillance)	rover	Rossland Seniors	1908
Rillance	rover	Rossland Seniors	1908
Ringquist	lw	Rocky Mountain Rangers (Rossland)	1906
Rinquist	rw	Le Roi (Rossland)	1908
Rinquist, A.	lw/centre	Le Roi (Rossland)	1907
Ritchie	goal	Merchants (Sandon)	1901
Ritchie, B.	rover	Trail Intermediates	1907
Rob, W.		Arlington Hotel Shin-Peelers (Trail)	1905
Rob, W.	point	Arlington Hotel "Shin-Peelers" (Trail)	1907

Name	Position	Team	Year
Robb	point	Kamloops Seniors	1910
Robb, E.	point	Trail Intermediates	1907
Robb, Herb.	Cover	Arlington Hotel "Shin-Peelers" (Trail)	1907
Robb, W.	point	Trail Smelter	1907-08
Robbins, F.	rover	Vernon High School	1903
Robbins, J.	tried out for team	Le Roi Mine (Rossland Industrial League)	1904
Roberston	point	Rossland senior team	1906 (played for Fernie in 1905)
Roberts	point	Nelson Seniors	1904
Robertson		Golden Seniors	1899
Robertson		Spokane Seniors (suggested for team)	1910
Robertson	cover	Nelson Seniors	1905
Robertson	point	Nelson Seniors	1905
Robertson	point	Vernon Seniors	1905
Robertson	rw	Phoenix Seniors	1907
Robertson, R.H.	point	Vernon Seniors	1904
Robertson	point	Rossland Seniors	1906
Robertson, "Mary"	point	Rossland Victorias Alberta Challenge Team	1906
Robertson, Charles E.	goal	Spokane Seniors	1907-08
Robertson, Charles E.	goal	Wood's Independents (Spokane)	1907
Robertson, I.G.	cover	Nelson Seniors	1906
Robertson, J.	cover	Nelson Seniors	1905-06
Robertson, I.G.	right wing	Nelson Seniors	1904
Robertson, J. (or I.G.)	cover	Nelson Seniors	1905
Robertson, R.H.	point	Vernon Seniors	1904-05
Robertson, R.H.	lw/point	Phoenix Seniors	1907
Robertson, R.W. (or H.)	point	Vernon Seniors	1903
Robinson	goal	Trail Juniors	1906
Robinson	point	Phoenix Seniors	1907
Robinson	center	Nelson Intermediates	1911
Robinson	point	Rossland Junior Victorias	1899
Robinson	point	Phoenix Seniors	1907
Robinson	center	Nelson Intermediates	1911
Robinson, C.	goal	Trail Juniors	1908
Robinson, E.V.	rover	Nelson YMCA Juniors	1911
Robinson, Sandy	rover	Nelson Intermediates	1911
Robinson, E. ("Shorty")	center	Nelson YMCA Juniors	1911
Rochon, Joel	lw	Greenwood Seniors	1910
Rodgers	lw	Centre Star/War Eagle (Rossland)	1906
Rollins, A.	cover	Centre Star (Rossland)	1908
Rose, B.	rw	Nelson Seniors	1907
Ross	centre	Grand Forks Seniors	1905
Ross	rover	Nelson Juniors	1902
Ross	cover	Wood's Independents (Spokane)	1907
Ross, Albert	f	Merchants (Sandon)	1901
Ross, Dr S.A.	forward	Rossland Victorias	1900
Ross, H.	forward	Grand Forks Seniors	1905
Routh, Cliff,	forward	Victoria, Captain Langley's team	1899
Rowlings, B.	f	Rossland Juniors	1901
Rowlings, B.	forward	Rossland Cyclones (Junior)	1901
Runell, Cleft		Greenwood Seniors	1911
Russel, R.	cover	Trail Juniors	1907
Russell	point	Spokane Seniors	1907
Russell	rover	Phoenix Intermediates	1907
Russell, C.	point	Greenwood Intermediates	1910
Russell, Cliff(e)	spare/centre/point/cover	Greenwood Seniors	1909-11
Rutherford	goal	Summerland Seniors	1909

Name	Position	Team	Year
Rutherford	goal	Fernie Seniors	1904
Rutherford	point	Nelson Juniors	1901
Rutherford	point	Nelson Juniors	1902
Rutherford	point	Rossland Stars (Juvenile)	1906
Rutherford	forward	Nelson Seniors	1903
Rutherford	forward	Nelson Seniors	1898
Rutherford, C.	goal	Fernie Seniors	1904
Rutherford, D,	point	Nelson Seniors	1902
Rutherford, Dave	forward	Nelson City Seniors	1900
Ryall, H.		New Westminster (Royals)	1907
Ryall, H.	cover	New Westminster Seniors	1901
Ryall, Herb	manager	New Westminster practise	1902
Safford	point	Missoula (Montana) Seniors	1911
Saint-Clair Mabee, Oliver (see Mabee, O. St.C.)		Vernon Seniors	1904-05
Sanderson, C.B.	wing/centre	Spokane Amateur Athletic Club	1906
Sangster	rw	Herman's Champions, Vancouver,	1907
Sangster	center	Vancouver Terminals	1907
Sangster	forward	Rossland Citizen Team	1903
Saunders	rover	Phoenix Seniors	1911
Saunders	position	Phoenix Seniors	1911
Savage	cover	Hoboes (Grand Forks)	1903
Sawyer, H.	point	Revelstoke Seniors	1904
Sawyer	point	Kaslo Intermediates	1909
Sawyer, J.	point	Revelstoke Seniors	1907
Sawyer, W.	goal	Vernon Seniors	1902-05, 07-08
Sawyer, W.	goal	Armstrong Seniors	1909
Sawyer, W.	goal	Vernon Town Team	1907
Sawyer, W. (capt)	goal/point	Revelstoke Seniors	1899, 1901

One of the greatest goalies in the game, W. Sawyer won the B.C. Championship in 1904, but when his team lost in 1905, he never returned to the B.C. championships, or played outside the Okanagan again, during this book's period. His first name was probably William, and it was probably he who was listed in Revelstoke between 1902-1904 in the B.C. directories as owning a sash and door factory. He appears to have closer ties to Revelstoke than Vernon, but played for Vernon more often. It's not known what happened to him after 1909. His first name was never given in any published source related to hockey. It appears, from the photographic evidence, that H. Sawyer, who played for Revelstoke, might have been his twin brother.

Name	Position	Team	Year
Scaefer	lw	Summerland Seniors	1909
Scanlan, T. J	spare	Nelson Grocers	1906
Scanlan, T.J.	spare	Bell Trading Company (Nelson grocers)	1906
Schaefer, K.		Summerland Seniors	1910
Schaeffer, W.	rw	Spokane Seniors	1907
Schaeffer, W.	lw/point/cover	Spokane Amateur Athletic Club	1906-07

W. Schaeffer had his name also spelled Schafer, Schaefer, and Schaefer. He appeared to be one of the true Americans on the Spokane team, as he had the same last name of the owners of the Star Shingle artificial rink, and was never named as one of the many Canadians who played there. It's possible that he was the son of either Jacob Schaeffer, or E. M. Schaeffer, the co-owners.

Name	Position	Team	Year
Schofield. J.H.	goal	Crow's Nest Combined SeniorTeam	1903

Normally J.H. Schofield played for Pincher Creek Alberta. He was one of the older members of the team, and before he became a business man in Pincher Creek, he was a member of the North West Mounted Police for many years. He was the nephew of Judge Schofield of Rossland.

Name	Position	Team	Year
Schulfer, J.	tried out for team	West Kootenay Power & Lt Co. (Ross Ind. Lg)	1904
Schultz, Sam,	goal	Victoria, Captain Langley's team	1899
Schultz, W.G.	goal	Lardeau Seniors	1905
Schwartz (see also Swartz)	tried out	Vancouver Terminals	1907
Schwartz, B.	lw	Trail Juniors	1908
Schwartz, R.	rw	Trail Smelter	1908

Name	Position	Team	Year
Scott		Revelstoke Seniors	1899
Scott	rw	Le Roi Mine (Rossland)	1905
Scott, Joe		Arlington Hotel (Trail)	1910
Scott, O.N.	rw	Le Roi Mine (Rossland)	1905
Scott, W.	point	Vernon Juniors	1903
Scribbler, W.	lw	Vernon Intermediates	1910
Seatle, W. R.	goal	Imperial Bank (Nelson)	1908
Senoith	rover	Nickel Plate Flat (Rossland Juvenile)	1906
Seukler, S. (probably the same as Senkler, below)		Nelson Senior Team	1897
Sharp	cover	Nelson Seniors	1906
Sharp	point	Nelson Wood-Vallance	1911
Sharp	centre	Wood-Vallance (Nelson hardware)	1907
Sharp	forward	Rossland Intermediates	1904
Sharp(e)	cover	Nelson Seniors	1905
Sharp, J.	goal	Lumby Seniors	1911
Sharp, R.		Nelson Seniors	1907
Sharp, R.		Nelson East Ward	1906

This R. Sharp played hockey originally in Sandon, and it is probable that this is actually Roy Sharpe, as seen below.

Name	Position	Team	Year
Sharpe	spare	Thistles (Nelson City League)	1909
Sharpe	forward	Nelson Wholesalers	1903
Sharpe	forward	Nelson Intermediates	1903
Sharpe, R	cover/point	Nelson Seniors	1906-7
Sharpe, Roy	rover	Nelson Seniors	1904
Sharpe, Roy	centre	Nelson Juniors	1902
Sharpe, Roy	forward	Nelson Wholesalers	1904

Roy Sharpe, or Sharp, was often a member of the Nelson Senior team. It was never clear if his last name should be spelled with an "e" or not. It is assumed that most, if not all, of the above listings of R. Sharp are all Roy Sharp(e).

Name	Position	Team	Year
Shatford, S.A.	forward	Vernon Seniors	1900, 1902-03
Sheldon, W.	rover/spare	Moyie Seniors	1910
Shelland, A.	cover	Sandon Seniors	1910
Sheridan (possibly the same as Sheldon)	rover	Moyie Seniors	1910
Sheridan, H.		Moyie	1910
Sherman	rover	Moyie Seniors	1909
Sherman, Edward	center	Fernie Seniors	1906
Sherrey (or Shorey)		Trail Seniors	1910
Sherwood, F.P.		Kaslo Hotel	1898
Shields		Vernon Megaws	1911
Shields, R.	goal	Nelson Hardware	1901
Shoemaker	lw	Trail Seniors	1902
Shorey	rover	Trail Intermediates	1909
Shorey, M.	centre	Trail Smelter	1908
Shorey, P.	rover	Trail Intermediates	1910
Simington, F.	lw	Armstrong Intermediates	1910
Simm	rover	Arlington Hotel "Shin-Peelers" (Trail)	1907
Simms		Vernon Intermediates	1910
Simms	cover	Coleman Seniors	1908
Simms	point	Wood's Independents (Spokane)	1907
Simms	point	Spokane Amateur Athletic Club	1907
Simms	tried out	Moyie Seniors	1909
Simms, S.	cover	Phoenix Seniors	1909
Simons, A.	point	Junior Thistles (Nelson Juvenile)	1909
Simpson, C.E.	tried out for team	Le Roi Mine (Rossland Industrial League)	1904
Simpson, Jack		Gerrard Seniors	1910
Simpson, V.	goal	Hurricanes (Rossland junior)	1901

Name	Position	Team	Year
Sims (see also Simms)	lw	Spokane Seniors	1907
Sims	point	Cranbrook Seniors	1911
Sims	point	Phoenix Seniors	1910
Sinclair, George		Crown Point Hotel (Trail)	1910
Sinclair, W.E.		New Westminster pick-up team	1909
He was a New Westminster shoe merchant.			
Sissons, C.B.	cover	Revelstoke Seniors	1907
Siwash, Alec		Enderby Seniors	1901
Slaatebreck, C.	goal	New Denver Seniors	1911
Slinger, Steve	f	Miner's and Kootenay Hotels (Sandon)	1901
Sloper		Grand Forks Juniors	1903
Small	forward	Commercials (Cranbrook)	1911
Smiley, Oliver	forward	Hurricanes (Rossland junior)	1901
Smith	rw	Slocan City Seniors	1903
Smith, E.	rover	Vernon Seniors	1904
Smith	center	Herman's Champions, Vancouver,	1907
Smith	point	Vernon Bankers	1907
Smith	cover	Centre Star/War Eagle (Rossland)	1906
Smith	forward	Vernon Town team	1907
Smith	forward	Nelson Seniors	1898
Smith, (Doc), Frank	forward	Victoria, Daniel's team,	1899
Smith, "Dutch"	forward (?)	Camborne Seniors	1908
Smith, A.	rover	Vernon Seniors	1904
Smith, A..	goal	Kaslo	1897
Smith, Alec		Rossland Cigarmakers, or Bartenders	1911
Smith, F.	rover	Nelson Juniors	1908
Smith, F. E. W.	forward	Nelson Seniors	1898
Smith, Frank		Nelson Seniors	1897, 1899
Smith, George		Vernon Seniors	1901
Smith, H.	point/cover	Spokane Amateur Athletic Club	1906
Smith, Y.	rover	Fernie Seniors	1905
Smyth(e), Plum	goal	Nelson West Ward ("Hand-Warmers")	1906-7
Somers, C.	rover	West Kootenay Power and Light Company (Rossland)	1903
Somes, T. (Capt)		Kamloops Seniors	1908
Soucie		Vancouver scrub team	1905
Southon, H.	forward	New Westminster seniors	1901
Spearman	manager	Vancouver challenge team	1900
Speer, S.	lw	Vernon Seniors	1908-09
Speers	lw	Coldstream Hotel (Vernon)	1908
Speers, S.J. (or S.H.)	rw	Vernon Seniors	1908
Spencer		Vernon Intermediates	1910
Spencer	rover	Coldstream Hotel (Vernon)	1908
Spencer, H..	goal	Vernon Seniors	1908-09
Spier	forward	Hoboes (Grand Forks)	1903
Spring, J.W.		Rossland Lions	1899
Springs, F.H.		Ashcroft Seniors	1901
Sprye	cover	Nelson Juniors	1902
St. C. Mabee, O. (Listed as such)	lw	Vernon Seniors	1908
Stanaway	centre	Rocky Mountain Rangers (Rossland)	1906
Stanaway	centre	Grocery Clerks (Rossland)	1906
Stanaway	lw	Rossland Intermediates	1906
Stanaway	rover	Rossland Intermediates	1908
Stanaway	rover	Rossland Intermediates	1909
Stanaway	center	Rossland Juniors	1905
Stanaway, A.	centre	Trail Intermediates	1907
Stanaway, E.	centre	Rossland Bankers	1907

Stanaway, E.	centre	Centre Star (Rossland)	1908
Stanaway, E.	centre	Rocky Mountain Rangers (Rossland)	1907
Stanaway, E.	goal	Cyclones (Rossland juniors)	1901
Stanaway, E.	l wing	Rossland Juniors	1904
Stanaway, Ed	point	Rossland Seniors	1910
Stanaway, Edgar		Trail Smelter Team	1907
Stanaway, Edgar	rover	Rossland Juniors	1905
Stanaway, Edgar	centre	Rocky Mountain Rangers (Rossland)	1907

Ed Stanaway was the best player on the Rossland Rockey Mountain Rangers, but was head-hunted by the Trail Smelter team, given a position at the smelter, and added to the Trail Team from February 1907 onward. His name was also spelled Stannaway.

Stanaway, H.	point	Rossland Juniors	1908
Stannaway	rw (one game)	Nelson Intermediates	1911
Stannaway	cover	Missoula (Montana) Seniors	1911
Stanton	point	Rossland Intermediates	1909
Stanton	cover	Rossland Juniors	1907
Stanton	point	Rossland Juniors	1908
Stanton	point	Rossland Intermediates	1911
Stanton	cover	Rossland Juniors	1908
Stanton (or Staunton)	point	Rossland Intermediates	1910-11
Stanton, H.	point	Rossland Intermediates	1910
Starkey, F	spare	Nelson Grocers	1906
Starkey, F.	spare	Bell Trading Company (Nelson grocers)	1906
Starkey, Fred	spare	Nelson Wholesalers	1908
Starr		Combined Banks (Nelson)	1908
Steed, W.B.	lw	Nelson Juniors	1902
Steel(e), L.		Nelson West Ward	1906
Steel(e) Les	rw	Victorias (Nelson City League)	1909
Steel(e), (Les?)	forward	Phoenix Seniors	1904
Steel(e), Les	cover	Thistles (Nelson inner-City)	1910
Steel,	lw	Nelson Mountains	1908
Steel, Les	cover	"Fossils" (Nelson)	1908

It was never clear whether Les Steele's name should be spelled with or without an e. He also played with the Fernie team.

Steele	forward	Nelson Intermediates	1903
Steele, C.	goal	Nelson Cyclones (high school)	1910
Steele, L.	point	Nelson Juniors	1902
Steele, L.	r wing	Fernie Seniors	1905
Steele, L.	cover	Nelson Seniors	1910
Steele, Les	cover	Nelson Seniors	1910
Steele, or Steel, Les	rw/point/cover/spare	Nelson Seniors	1906-11

Les Steel, or Steele, was one of the regular members of the Nelson team. He is probably the Leslie R. Steel(e) who was listed in the 1910 B.C. Directory as working as a foreman for the Nelson City Light Department.

Steer	rw	Greenwood Seniors	1902
Stenaway (probably Stanaway)	lw	Rossland Seniors	1909
Stenson, G.		Kaslo Seniors	1900
Stephensen, J.	forward	Kaslo Town Juniors	1901
Steub (or Stubb)	spare/point	Nelson Seniors	1908
Stevens	goal	Nelson Bankers	1911
Stevens	lw	Nickel Plate Flat (Rossland Juvenile)	1906
Stevens	point	Le Roi (Rossland)	1906
Stevens	rover	Nelson Retailers	1908
Stevens	rover	Fernie Seniors	1904
Stevens, J.	rover	Fernie Seniors	1904
Stevenson		Vernon Megaws	1911

Stewart	point	Rossland Intermediates	1904
Stewart	goal	Archer's Flat Team (Kaslo)	1900
Stewart	point	Nelson Intermediates	1903
Stewart	point	Nelson Intermediates	1906
Stewart	goal/point	Nelson Seniors	1906
Stewart	forward	Hoboes (Grand Forks)	1903
Stewart, C	lw	Armstrong Seniors	1907
Stewart, J.	spare	Nelson Juniors	1908
Stewart, J.	center	Armstrong Seniors	1907
Stewart, L.	rw	Nelson Seniors	1906

The B.C. Directory for 1907 lists a Lorne Stewart as a clerk in the Bell Trading Company, in Nelson, who were grocers, and avid hockey players.

Stewart, N.	cover	Nelson Juniors	1902
Stewart, N.	point	Nelson Intermediates	1910
Stewart, N.	goal	Nelson Seniors	1906
Stewart, N.C.		Nelson West Ward	1906
Stewart, N.C.	goal	Nelson Seniors	1906
Stewart, S.	point	Nelson Intermediates	1910
Stewart, W.	rw	Ymir Seniors	1911
Stinson	forward	Archer's Flat Team (Kaslo)	1900
Stow		Phoenix Seniors	1902
Stowe	goal	Greenwood Seniors	1902
Strather	cover	Kaslo Seniors	1898
Strathern, O.	officer	Kaslo Seniors	1897
Stretzel	cover	Phoenix Seniors	1902
Strickland, A.	point	Associated Banks (Rossland)	1903
Stroeger, A.		Kamloops Picked Town Team	1903
Strong	spare	Commercials (Cranbrook)	1911
Strutzel (Struzel)	forward	Phoenix Seniors	1903
Stuart, J. (or stewart)	goal	Kaslo Seniors	1900
Stutzel	cover	Phoenix Seniors	1902
Sullivan	lw	Trail Smelter	1906
Sullivan	point	Trail Seniors	1910
Sullivan	lw	Trail Smelter Team	1905
Sullivan	lw	Trail Smelter	1906
Sullivan	point	Trail Intermediates	1909
Sullivan, M.	lw	Trail Intermediates	1907
Sullivan, M.	rover	Trail Smelter	1908
Sullivan, M.H.	lw	Trail smelter	1907
Sullivan, M.H.	l wing	Trail Smelter Team	1905
Summers, Charles E.	rover	West Kootenay Power & Light Co. (Ross I. League)	1904
Summers, G.	lw	Greenwood Intermediates	1910
Sutherland	rw	New Westminster (Royals)	1907
Sutherland, E.G.	f	Bank of Montreal (Rossland Industrial League)	1904
Svoboda, H.	cover	Nelson Rovers (Junior)	1910
Svoboda, H.	point/centre	Nelson High School	1909
Swain, J.	centre	Greenwood Seniors	1909
Swan		Imperial Bank (Nelson)	1908
Swan	centre	Nelson Lakes	1908
Swan	lw	Nelson Bankers	1911
Swan	rover	Nelson Rivers	1908
Swannell		Imperial Bank (Nelson)	1908
Swannell	lw	Nelson Intermediates	1911
Swannell	centre	Nelson Bankers	1911
Swartz		Trail Seniors	1910
Swartz	lw	Trial Intermediates	1910

Name	Position	Team	Year
Swartz	rover	Trail Juniors	1906
Swartz	forward	Trail Juniors	1907
Swartz	spare	Vancouver Bankers	1907
Swartz	centre	Trail Intermediates	1909
Swartz	forwards	Trail Juniors	1907
Swartz, W.R. (Bobby)	rw	Trail Intermediates	1911
Symmington, F.	center	Armstrong Juniors	1907
Symonds, W. (or Simmons)	forward	Kaslo Seniors	1897
Tait, W.	lw/centre	Vancouver Terminals	1907
Tams	goal	Slocan Seniors	1904
Tams, C.F.	goal	Sandon Seniors	1911
Tapanilla	lw (one game)	Nelson Intermediates	1911
Tapanilla, Arvid	lw	Kaslo Juniors	1909-10
Tapinalla, Oscar	spare	Kaslo Intermediates	1908
Tapanilla, Oscar	spare	Kaslo Seniors	1910

After 1911 Oscar Tapanilla played for the Sandon Seniors.

Name	Position	Team	Year
Tascett		Smithers Seniors	1910
Tatro, Oliver U.	rw/centre	Spokane Amateur Athletic Club	1907-06
Tattrie, W.D.	goal	Sandon Intermediates	1908
Taylor		Grand Forks Juniors	1903
Taylor, A.E.		Enderby Seniors	1906
Taylor, Doctor J.N.	player	Golden pick-up team	1905
Taylor, Doctor J.N. (capt)	forward	Golden Seniors	1895

James Norman (Doc) Taylor was one of the founding fathers of hockey in British Columbia. Essentially the town's doctor for many years, he ran the hospital and served on many committees. He was an avid curler, as well. He married Captain Armstrong's daughter and had two daughters of his own.

Name	Position	Team	Year
Taylor, F.G.S.	cover	Vernon Seniors	1905
Taylor, K.		Vernon Seniors	1900
Taylor, K.		Vernon Seniors	1901
Taylor, S.S.		Vernon Seniors	1905
Taylor, S.S. (or F.G.S.)	cover	Vernon Seniors	1905
Teague	goal	Nelson Grocers	1907
Teague	goal	Nelson Retailers	1908
Teazona	rover	Spokane Seniors	1908
Tees, R.	lw	Nickel Plate Flat (Rossland Juvenile)	1906
Ternan, W. G.	cover	Hunter Brothers (Rossland)	1905
Ternan, W. G.	cover	Hunter Brothers (Rossland Ind. League)	1904
Ternan, W.G.	cover	Hunter Brothers (Rossland)	1903
Terneau (capt)	forward	Hunter Brothers store Rossland	1899
Terrey, J. (or Terry)	lw	Slocan Seniors	1909
Terry	forward	Slocan Seniors	1904
Therin	lw	Fernie Seniors	1908
Thomas	rover	Nicola Seniors	1910
Thomas, Dan	manager	Rossland Seniors	1906
Thomas, Dan	manager	Rossland Victorias Alberta Challenge Team	1906
Thomas, J.	rover	Vernon Juniors	1903
Thompson		Vancouver scrub team	1905
Thompson	rover	Nelson Rivers	1908
Thompson	point	Phoenix Seniors	1905
Thompson	point	Phoenix Intermediates	1906
Thompson, Crawford	forward	Victoria, Daniel's team,	1899
Thompson, F. (or Thomson)	spare	Nelson East Ward	1906
Thompson, Frank, V.	rover	Nelson Seniors	1906
Thompson, H.V.	cover	Nelson Seniors	1905
Thompson, H.V. (or F.V.)	rover	Nelson Seniors	1905

Name	Position	Team	Year
Thompson, Joe		Nelson East Ward	1906
Thompson, Joe	cover	Victorias (Nelson City League)	1909
Thompson, Joe	right w	"Fossils" (Nelson)	1908
Thompson, Joe	Manager	Nelson Juniors	1911
Thompson, Joe	forward	Nelson Lacrosse-Hockey Seniors	1900
Thompson, Joe, (F.)	rover/cover/lw/rw	Nelson Senior	1898-99-00-1-2-3-4-5-6-7-8-9

Joe Thompson was one of the greatest hockey players in British Columbia. From the second year of hockey in Nelson, (1898), to 1909, he was never absent from the Senior Team, (except for a few games here and there). He scored the second largest number of goals overall in B.C. He and Lester Patrick were often paired together on defense in 1908 and 1909. But he also played forward positions, where he became one of the province's leading scorers. He essentially retired from hockey in 1910, although he still played recreationally and coached. He was a partner in a sign painting company called Thompson and Douglas.

Name	Position	Team	Year
Thompson, R. (Not Joe)	forward	Nelson City Seniors	1900
Thomson, F.V.	rover	Nelson Seniors	1906
Thomson, Frank		Revelstoke Seniors	1907
Thomson, Frank V. (capt.)	rover	Nelson Seniors	1906
Thomson, Frank V.		Nelson East Ward ("Stick arounds")	1906

Frank H.V. Thompson, (or Thomson), was a regular on the Nelson Senior team in 1905 and 1906. His name was spelled several different ways, with different initials, always a combination of H.V. and F. He was transferred from Nelson to Revelstoke in 1907, although it looks like this was job related.

Name	Position	Team	Year
Thorburn	goal	Silverton Seniors	1904
Thrasher	lw	Cranbrook Seniors	1911
Thrasher	rw	Phoenix Seniors	1911
Thurman, William		Nelson Seniors	1897
Tier	forward	Slocan City Seniors	1903
Tier, A.	point	Sandon Seniors	1911
Tier, J.	rw	Sandon Seniors	1903
Tier, J.	rover	New Denver Seniors	1911
Tingley	center	Summerland Seniors	1909
Tipping, E.	rover	Sandon Seniors	1911
Tipping, E.	rover	Slocan Seniors	1909
Tomes	goal	Slocan Seniors	1909
Tonkin	lw	Le Roi Mine (Rossland)	1905
Tonkin, G.	f	Le Roi Mine (Rossland Industrial League)	1904
Tonkin, S.G.	lw	Le Roi Mine (Rossland)	1905
Towl, J.	lw	Armstrong Seniors	1908
Townley	goal	Vancouver Bankers	1907
Townsend	goal	Rossland Stars (Juvenile)	1906
Townsend	point	Le Roi Mine (Rossland)	1905
Townsend	forward	Rossland Seniors	1898
Townsend	forward	Rosslands (seniors)	1901
Townsend, A.F.	point	Le Roi Mine (Rossland)	1905
Townshend	f	Rossland Victorias	1901
Townshend	forward	Rossland Victorias	1900
Townshend, F. (or Townsend)	f	Rossland Seniors	1901
Townshend, G.E. (or Townsend)	forward	Rossland Victorias	1900
Townshend, J.	forward	Rossland Seniors	1901
Trainer		Phoenix Juniors	1903
Trainer	centre	Spokane Seniors	1908
Trainer	centre	Wood's Independents (Spokane)	1907
Trainer	centre	Spokane Seniors	1908
Trainer, G.	lw	Spokane Seniors	1907
Trainer, G.	centre	Wood's Independents (Spokane)	1907
Trainer, George	lw	Spokane Seniors	1907

Name	Position	Team	Year
Trainner	forward	Phoenix Seniors	1904
Traunweiser		Grand Forks Juniors	1903
Treherne, W.	center	Rossland Seniors	1910

Treherne was a ringer from Vancouver, brought in for the Rossland Carnival. He had played previously in Brandon and Winnipeg.

Name	Position	Team	Year
Trezona		Spokane Seniors (suggested for team)	1910
Trezona	cover	Rocky Mountain Rangers (Rossland)	1906
Trezona	point	Rossland Juveniles	1905
Trezona	point	Rossland Invincibles (Junior)	1905
Trezona	point	Rossland Invincibles (Juniors)	1906
Trezona	rover	Spokane Seniors	1907
Trezona	rover	Rossland Intermediates	1906
Trezona	rover	Rossland Intermediates	1906
Trezona Frank (?)	rover	Spokane Seniors	1907
Trezona (? brother of Jim)	point	Wood's Independents (Spokane)	1907
Trezona,	rover	Spokane Seniors	1908
Trezona, J.	centre	Rossland Juniors	1905
Trezona, J	rover	Spokane Seniors	1907
Trezona, J.	rover	Centre Star (Rossland)	1908
Trezona, Jim	rover	Wood's Independents (Spokane)	1907
Trezona, Jim	rover	Eagles (Spokane)	1906
Trezona, Jim	rover	Spokane Seniors	1907
Trezonna (or Trezona)	rover	Rossland Juniors	1905
Trnary, T. (as reported)	rw	Cody Seniors	1910
Truswell	goal	Trial Intermediates	1910
Truswell	cover	Trail Juniors	1906
Truswell	point	Trail Juniors	1907
Truswell, D.	cover	Trail Juniors	1908
Truswell, Walter	goal	Trail Intermediates	1911
Turnbull	center	Trail Smelter Team	1905
Turnbull	forward	Fernie Seniors	1904
Turnbull, A.	forward	New Westminster Seniors	1901
Turnbull, A.T.	forward	Rossland Seniors	1897
Turnbull, Alex		New Westminster challenge team	1905
Turnbull, Alex		New Westminster (Royals)	1907
Turnbull, C.	?	Fernie Seniors	1904
Turnbull, H.	lw	Royal Hotel (Vernon)	1908
Turnbull, J.M.	center	Trail Smelter Team	1905
Turner	centre	Spokane Seniors	1908
Turner, Alf		New Westminster (Royals)	1907
Turner, D..	goal	Nelson High School	1909
Turner, M.R.	point	Eagles (Spokane)	1906
Turner, Reynolds		Rossland Junior IXL	1899
Turner, W.	center	Ymir Seniors	1911
Tuttle, Jay	f	War Eagle Mine (Rossland Industrial League)	1904
Tyler	forward	C.P.R. Shops (Cranbrook)	1911
Tyson		Trail Juniors	1904
Tyson	center	Trail Juniors	1905
Tyson	rw/centre/rover	Trail Intermediates	1906
Tyson	rover	Trail Juniors	1905
Tyson, C.	lw	Arlington Hotel "Shin-Peelers" (Trail)	1907
Unwin, E.		Kamloops Seniors	1902
Unwin, J.M.		Kamloops Picked Town Team	1903
Vahey	spare	Grand Forks Seniors	1902
Vallance, E.	goal	Kaslo Juniors	1910
Van de Bogart, M.	point	Ymir Seniors	1911

Viets	cover	Trail Seniors	1902
Vincent	forward	Golden Seniors	1895
Vucovitch, N.	centre	Sandon Seniors	1910
Wadds	cover	Rossland Junior Victorias	1899
Wadds, Sergeant J.	goal	Nelson Militia	1901
Wade	goal	Phoenix Seniors	1907
Wade, M. P.	goal	Boundary Seniors	1906
Wade, M.P. (or W.C.)	goal	Boundary combined team	1906
Waide, James	rw	West Kootenay Power and Light Company (Rossland)	1903
Walker	f	Rossland Victorias	1901
Walker	centre	Victorias (Rossland)	1902
Walker, C.C.	forward	Rossland Seniors	1901
Walker, C.C.	rover	Spokane Amateur Athletic Club	1906
Walker, F.A.		Sandon Seniors	1897-99
Walker, J.	f	Rossland Seniors	1901
Walker, J.	forward	Sandon Seniors	1897
Wallace		Smithers Seniors	1910
Wallace	point	Nelson Bankers	1903
Wallace	forward	Rossland Intermediates	1904
Wallace	forward	Nelson Intermediates	1903
Wallace, A.H.	lw	Nelson Juniors	1902
Wallace, A.N.	rover	Nelson Juniors	1902
Wallace, B.	forward	Commercials (Cranbrook)	1911
Wallace, Ben		Cranbrook Seniors	1911
Wallace, Bert	forward	Nelson Juniors	1901
Wallace, Bert	forward	Rossland Intermediates	1904
Walmsley	point	Saloons (Sandon)	1901
Walmsley, Chas.	point	Miner's and Kootenay Hotels (Sandon)	1901
Walter, R.	goal	Kaslo Intermediates	1908
Walters	goal	Centre Star/War Eagle (Rossland)	1906
Ware, Louis, (Butch)	lw	Kaslo Intermediates	1908-10
Waring	lw/point	Rossland Intermediates	1911
Waring	cover	Le Roi (Rossland)	1908
Waring (Werring)	cover	Le Roi (Rossland)	1907
Warren	point	Phoenix Seniors	1902
Warren	coverpoint	Greenwood Seniors	1902
Warren, A.	cover	Rossland Intermediates	1907
Warren, Charles A.	possibly played with	Golden Seniors	1895

(Charles A. Warren was an associate of the first hockey players in Golden, he did a lot of curling, and in 1901 he was listed in the Golden city directory as the president of the Golden rink company. He was also the postmaster and a general merchant.)

Warren, E.	forward	Rossland Victorias	1899
Warren, E.G.	point	Rossland Seniors	1901
Warren, E.J.	point	Rossland Seniors	1901
Waters		Nelson High School Team	1909
Waters, S.	point	Nelson High School	1909
Watkins, Angus	spare	Salmo Seniors	1911
Watson	goal	Greenwood Seniors	1910
Watson	goal	Salmo Mess (inner-city)	1910
Watson	forward	Rossland Seniors	1897
Watson	forward	Rossland Bankers	1906
Watson, J, (or W.J. Wayson)	goal	Rossland Seniors	1897
Watson, J.H.	forward	Bank of Toronto/Royal Bank (Rossland)	1901

(J.H. Watson had apparently played hockey in Eastern Canada.)

Watson, W.G.	goal	Greenwood Seniors	1909
Webster	rw	New Denver "B"s	1911

Webster, G.R.	rw	New Denver Seniors	1911
Weir	rw	Trail Intermediates	1909
Weir	goal	Trails Seniors	1910
Weir	lw	Trail Juniors	1906
Weir	centre	Trial Intermediates	1910
Weir, A.	goal	Kaslo Intermediates	1908
Weir, B.	cover	Kaslo Intermediates	1908
Weir, Jimmy	f	Merchants (Sandon)	1901
Welton	point	C.P.R. Shops (Cranbrook)	1911
West, Billy		Vancouver Allstar team (no known opponents)	1910
Wetmore	centre	Nelson Seniors	1902
Wetmore, A.	forward	Nelson Seniors	1902
Wetmore, M.	forward	Nelson Seniors	1899
Wetmore, M.	forward	Nelson Lacrosse-Hockey Seniors	1900
Wetmore, M. (or A)	forward	Nelson Seniors	1901
Wheatley	point	Golden Seniors	1895
Wheeler	rover	Vancouver Terminals	1907
White		Coleman Alberta Seniors	1910
White	centre	Rossland Seniors	1911
White	point	Coleman Seniors	1908
White	forward	Hoboes (Grand Forks)	1903
White	left wing	Fernie Seniors	1906
White, Clarence	rover	Kaslo Juniors	1909-10
Whitebread	rw	Nelson Bankers	1911
Whitehead	forward	Commercials (Cranbrook)	1911
Whitehead, J.	point	Nelson Invincibles (high school)	1910
Whitehead, R.	lw	Nelson Juveniles	1910
Whitehead, R.	goal	Nelson Public School	1909
Whitehead, R.	centre	Junior Thistles (Nelson Juvenile)	1909
Whitehead, R.	lw	Nelson Juveniles	1910
Whitlaw. B.	goal	Junior Thistles (Nelson Juvenile)	1909
Whittet, E.	forward	Nelson CPR	1901
Wilkinson	goal	Nelson Juniors	1910
Williams		Vancouver scrub team	1905
Williamson, Cliff		Arlington Hotel (Trail)	1910
Williamson, Cliff	centre	Arlington Hotel "Shin-Peelers" (Trail)	1907
Williamson, Jim.	goal	Arlington Hotel "Shin-Peelers" (Trail)	1907
Willing, Ed		Kamloops Picked Town Team	1903
Willis, J.B.	cover	Armstrong Seniors	1908
Wilson		Golden Seniors	1899
Wilson	goal	Grand Forks Seniors	1905
Wilson	rover	Rossland Seniors	1905
Wilson	cover	Nelson Rivers	1908
Wilson	lw	Le Roi (Rossland)	1908
Wilson	spare	Nelson Rivers	1908
Wilson, D.	forward	Nelson Grocers	1901
Wilson, G.		Nelson Ashdowns	1907
Wilson, G.	lw	Nelson Diamond A-Ashdown Hockey Club	1906
Wilson, George (capt)		Armstrong Seniors	1906
Wilson, Pte. G.	cover	Nelson Militia	1901
Wilson, W.	point	"Tenderfeet" (Nelson)	1908
Winn		Golden Seniors	1899
Winn, Eldon S.H.	point/f/centre	Victorias (Rossland)	1900-03
Winn, Eldon S.H. (or Wynn) (capt)	f/rover	Rossland Seniors	1901-03

Eldon S.H. Winn was a stalwart player for Rossland. He gave up playing after 1903 and became the referee of choice for Rossland's important matches from 1905-1908. He was often vilified by the Nelson team and generally aided the Rossland team in crucial games. He was a lawyer, who first articled in Nelson, and then had his own firm, of McDonald and Winn, and in later years appears to have been on his own. His name was also mistakenly spelled Wynn at times.

Name	Position	Team	Year
Winter	goal	Rossland Bankers	1906
Winter, (or Winters), C.B.	goal	Bank of Montreal (Rossland)	1905
Winter, C.B.	goal	Bank of Montreal (Rossland Industrial League)	1904

(C.B. Winter was an accountant at the Bank of Montreal.)

Name	Position	Team	Year
Winters	cover	Hunter Brothers store Rossland	1899
Winters	point	Merchants (Sandon)	1901
Winters, A.	cover	Kamloops Seniors	1903
Wisdom, H.		Vernon Bankers	1911
Wolverton, J.	cover	Nelson All-Stars (juniors)	1911
Wolverton, J.	rover	Junior Thistles (Nelson Juvenile)	1909
Wolverton, J.	cover	Nelson Juveniles	1910
Wood		Phoenix Seniors	1902
Wood	cover	New Denver Seniors	1909
Wood, (or Woods), W.	goal	Revelstoke Seniors	1904
Woodland	goal	Grand Forks Seniors	1909
Woodland	forward	Heroes (Grand Forks)	1903
Woodland, G.	point	Kaslo Juniors	1910
Woodland, George	goal	Kaslo Juniors	1910
Woodland, H.E.	goal	Grand Forks Seniors	1905
Woods	goal	Revelstoke Seniors	1904
Woods, G.	center	Commonage Intermediates (Vernon)	1904
Woods, W.	rover	Enderby Seniors	1904
Worth, Dick		Vancouver Seniors practise	1902
Wright	lw	Nelson Juniors	1902
Wright	cover	Fernie Seniors	1908
Wright	forward	Reilly Club of Nelson	1904
Wright, H.K. (capt)		Vernon Bank Employees	1906
Wright, P.	forward	Nelson Grocers	1901
Wright, Perry	forward	Nelson Wholesalers	1903
Wurtele, Hunter, (capt)	rover/wing	Spokane Amateur Athletic Club	1906-07

Wurtele was one of the fastest skaters for Spokane Washington, and he had played for the Montreal Victorias. (He does not show up, however in TTOTSC.) He had also played two seasons for the Spokane Amateur Athletic club teams on the artificial ice surface at the Star Shingle company arena, on the North side of Spokane. It was intended that Wurtele would play on the Spokane Senior teams when they competed at the Rossland Carnival in 1907 and 1908, but both times he couldn't get away from work. He was the Assistant Superintendent of light and power of the Washington Water Power company.

Name	Position	Team	Year
Wynn, E.S.H. (sometimes used for Winn. See above)	f	Rossland Seniors	1901
Yelmer	centre	Nelson Juniors	1907
York, J.	rover	Slocan City Seniors	1903
York, L.	goal	Slocan City Seniors	1903
Yorke	forward	Silverton Seniors	1903
Young	goal	West Kootenay Power and Light (Rossland)	1906
Young, D.J.		Kaslo Hotel	1898
Young, D.J. (capt)	forward	Kaslo Seniors	1897, 1900-01
Young, Jack,	rover	Meakin Hotel "Never-Sweats" (Trail)	1907
Zimmerman	forward, 1 game only	Nelson City Seniors	1900
Zithen, C.	f	Trail Juniors	1904
Zwickey, Everett (or Zwicky)	centre/cover	Kaslo Juniors	1909-10

Appendix 6: List of Ladies

Players	Postion	Team	Year
Aconite, (or Aconitt), Joanna	point/goal	Rossland Blues	1904
Aconite, Johanna	goal	Rossland Ladies 2nd team	1904
Aconite, Johanna	point	Rossland Ladies	1906
Aconite, Miss	goal	Rossland Blues	1905
Adams, Dot	f	Rossland Blues	1904
Adams, Dot	r wing	Rossland Ladies 2nd team	1904
Adams, Dot (capt)	forward	Rossland Whites	1904
Agnew, Effie	cover/point	Rossland Reds	1905
Agnew, Effie		Possibly Rossland Ladies	1900
Agnew, Effie, Miss	point	Rossland Crescents	1900-01
Agnew, Effie, Miss	cover	Crescents (Rossland)	1907
Agnew, Miss W.	point	Rossland Blues	1905
Anderson, Marie	lw	Grand Forks Wonders	1910
Attwood, Nina		Moyie Crescents	1911
Baldwin, Wilhelmina, Miss		Nelson Ladies	1905
Barclay, Miss	rover	Silverton Ladies	1904
Barton, Ona, Miss	rw	Rossland Crescents	1901
Barton, Ona, Miss	rw	Crescents (Rossland)	1907
Batho, Miss	lw	Armstrong Ladies	1907
Bell, Dora, Miss	point	Vernon Ladies	1907
Bennet, Rheta	centre	Salmo Red and Greys	1911
Bennett, Rheta	spare	Salmo Black and Whites	1911
Berry, Beatrice		Moyie Stars	1911
Betts, Beatrice	spare	Nelson Ladies	1911
Betts, Beatrice, Miss	rw	Nelson Athletics	1911
Blackburn, Miss		Moyie Crescents	1911
Blackman, E.		Possibly Rossland Ladies	1900
Blackman, Ethel	rover	Rossland Ladies	1906
Blackman, Ethel	r. wing	Rossland Reds	1905
Blackman, Ethel, Miss	cover	Rossland Blues	1905
Blackman, Eva	goal	Rossland Ladies	1911
Blackman, Eva	goal	Rossland Ladies	1906
Blackman, Evelyn	point	Rossland Blues	1904
Blackman, Hazel	rw	Rossland Ladies	1906
Blackman, Hazel	l. wing	Rossland Reds	1905
Blackman, Hazel, Miss	lw	Rossland Blues	1905
Blackman, Miss, E.	point	Rossland Ladies	1904
Blackman, Miss, E.	point	Rossland Whites	1904
Blackman, Miss, E.	point	Rossland Reds	1905
Blakemore, Barbara, Miss		Nelson Ladies	1905
Blakemore, Gladys	rw	Nelson Ladies	1906
Blakemore, Miss C.		Nelson Ladies	1906
Blakemore, Miss Teenie	lw	Nelson Ladies	1906
Blakemore, MissG.		Nelson Ladies	1906
Bogart, Eva	rover	Rossland Ladies 2nd team	1904
Bogart, Eva	point	Rossland Whites	1904
Bogart, Eva	forward	Rossland Blues	1904
Bogart, Eva	tried out for team	Rossland Reds	1905
Bogart, Eva,	tried out for team	Rossland Reds	1905
Bogart, Miss	goal	Rossland Ladies	1901
Bogart, Miss	goal	Crescents (Rossland)	1907
Bogart, Miss	cover	Rossland Blues	1905

Name	Position	Team	Year
Brenton, Miss		Moyie Stars	1911
Buck, A.	forward	Revelstoke Ladies	1904
Buck, Adelaide C., Miss	secretary	Revelstoke Ladies	1905
Bull, N	forward	Slocan Ladies	1904
Bull, N.		Slocan City Ladies	1904
Burnet, Mrs.	goal	Rossland Stars	1900
Byers, Miss (capt)		Vernon Ladies	1905
Campbell, Miss		Moyie Crescents	1911
Cavan, Miss	cover	Slocan Ladies	1904
Cavanaugh, Ola	centre	Sterlings, (Nelson)	1910
Cavanaugh, Ola	rover	Nelson All Stars	1910
Cavanaugh, Ola (capt)	rover	Mermaids (Nelson)	1910
Christie, P.		Slocan City Ladies	1904
Coburn, Miss	forward	Silverton Ladies	1904
Coburn, Miss	forward	Silverton Ladies	1904
Coleman, M.V.	cover	Revelstoke Ladies	1904
Conrad, Lillian, Miss		Moyie Stars	1911
Cooper, Alice		Possibly Rossland Ladies	1900
Corley, M.	forward	Revelstoke Ladies	1904
Cosgriff, Ella	rover	Rossland Blues	1905
Cosgriffe, Ella	spare	Rossland Blues	1904
Cummins, Miss D.		Nelson Ladies	1906
Cummins, Miss Dorothy	cover	Nelson Ladies	1906
Daykin, Miss	rw	Armstrong Ladies	1907
Demuth, Lilly	lw	Rossland Blues	1905
Demuth, E.	forward	Rossland Ladies	1904
Demuth, Lilly	f	Rossland Blues	1904
Demuth, Lilly	l wing	Rossland Reds	1905
Demuth, Lily	centre	Rossland Ladies 2nd team	1904
Demuth, Lily	forward	Rossland Whites	1904
Demuth, Reba	lw	Rossland Ladies	1906
Demuth, Reba	rw	Rossland Blues	1905
Demuth, Reba	cover	Rossland Whites	1904
Demuth, Reba	r. wing	Rossland Reds	1905
Demuth, Reva	cover	Rossland Ladies 2nd team	1904
Demuth, Selma	forward	Rossland Blues	1904
Demuth, Selma	l wing	Rossland Ladies 2nd team	1904
Demuth, Selma, Miss	point	Rossland Blues	1905
Dockendorf, B.K.	point	Salmo Black and Whites	1911
Donahue, Flossie	forward	Rossland Blues	1904
Donahue, Flossie	forward	Rossland Whites	1904
Donahue, Flossie	rw	Rossland Blues	1905
Dumuth, (or Du Muth), Lill	rw	Grand Forks Wonders	1910
Dunne, M.N.	goal	Revelstoke Ladies	1904
Elizabeth Ellison, Miss	cover	Vernon Ladies	1907
Elliott, Ida (Captain)	goal	Undines (Nelson)	1910
Elliott, Ida (Captain)	goal	Wanderers (Nelson)	1910
Ellis, Winnie	rw	Undines (Nelson)	1910
Ellis, Winnifred	rover	Wanderers (Nelson)	1910
Ellis, Winnifred	center	Nelson All Stars	1910
Ellison, E. Miss	cover	Vernon Junior Ladies	1907
Evans, Kate, Miss		Nelson Ladies	1905
Falding, Helen, Miss	cover	Rossland Blues	1904
Few, Miss	goal	Slocan Ladies	1904
Fielding, Miss	coverpoint	Rossland Stars	1900
Findlay, Miss	cover	Silverton Ladies	1904

Name	Position	Team	Year
Foote, Winnie	centre	Mermaids (Nelson)	1910
Foote, Winnie, Miss		Nelson Ladies	1911
Foote, Winnifred	goal	Nelson All Stars	1910
Foote, Winnifred	point	Sterlings, (Nelson)	1910
Forteath, Pearl	rover	Rossland Ladies	1911
Fox, Ethel	lw	Rossland Ladies	1911
Francis, Misss	point	Armstrong Ladies	1907
Garvin, V.	coverpoint	Salmo Black and Whites	1911
Geddes, Miss	goal	New Denver Ladies	1911
Gibbs, Ethel, Miss	point	Vernon Junior Ladies	1907
Gigot, Helen	lw	Undines (Nelson)	1910
Gigot, Helen	rw	Wanderers (Nelson)	1910
Gigot, Miss D.		Nelson Ladies	1906
Gigot, Miss D.	spare	Nelson Ladies	1906
Gigot, Rose	goal	Nelson Ladies	1906
Gilchrist, Lulu	lw	Wanderers (Nelson Ladies Team)	1910
Goninan, M.	cover	Rossland Whites	1904
Goninan, Minnie	cover	Rossland Blues	1904
Goninan, Minnie	cover	Rossland Ladies	1904
Goodwin, Belle	point	Nelson Ladies	1911
Goodwin, Belle	cover	Sterlings, (Nelson)	1910
Goodwin, Belle	point	Nelson All Stars	1910
Goodwin, Belle	coverpoint	Nelson Cubs	1911
Gore, Hazel	lw	Nelson All Stars	1910
Gore, Hazel	rover	Sterlings, (Nelson)	1910
Gore, Hazel	centre	Nelson Ladies	1911
Gore, Hazel	centre	Nelson Athletics	1911
Gore, Hazel, Miss		Nelson Ladies	1905
Gore, Helen	center	Undines (Nelson)	1910
Gran(t), Winnie (Minnie)	rw	Nelson All Stars	1910
Grant, Jack	goal	Mermaids (Nelson)	1910
Grant, Minnie	rw	Sterlings, (Nelson)	1910
Grant, Minnie	point	Mermaids (Nelson)	1910
Graves, Greta, Miss		Nelson Ladies	1905
Graves, Miss	tried out	Nelson Ladies	1911
Graves, Nettie	rw	Nelson Cubs	1911
Gray, Mrs. (or Grey)	goal	Salmo Red and Greys	1911
Grubbe, Mrs, E.H.H.	rover	New Denver Ladies	1911
Hamill, Miss	cover	Armstrong Ladies	1907
Hamilton, Kit	forward	Rossland Whites	1904
Hamilton, Kittie	forward	Rossland Ladies	1904
Hansen, Mrs.	spare	Salmo Red and Greys	1911
Harding, Miss	point	Armstrong Ladies	1907
Harris, Kittie	point	Rossland Ladies 2nd team	1904
Harris, Miss	point	New Denver Ladies	1911
Harris, Miss Mae, (capt)	forward	Rossland Stars	1900
Harvey, Miss,	goal	Nelson Ladies	1900
Haskins, Miss	goal	Rossland Crescents	1900
Hattrup, Edna, Miss	goal	Rossland Reds	1905
Hattrup, Mrs. E.H.	rover	Rossland Reds	1905
Haverty, Irene	rover	Grand Forks Wonders	1910
Henders, L (or Benders)	coverpoint	Nelson Ladies	1911
Henders, Lena	point	Undines (Nelson)	1910
Henders, Lena	cover	Wanderers (Nelson)	1910
Henders, Lena (or Leda)	cover	Nelson All Stars	1910
Henders, Miss	tried out	Nelson Ladies	1911

Name	Position	Team	Year
Herchmer, Miss	forward	Rossland Stars	1900
Hewing, Eva, Miss	cover	Rossland Crescents	1901
Hewing, Miss Eva	point	Crescents (Rossland)	1907
Hicks, Mrs.	forward	Slocan Ladies	1904
Hill, L. Miss	goal	Armstrong Ladies	1907
Honey, Edna	spare	Rossland Blues	1904
Honey, Edna	forward	Rossland Whites	1904
Honey, Edna	forward	Rossland Ladies	1904
Honey, F.	forward	Rossland Ladies	1904
Honey, Frances (capt)	center	Rossland Reds	1905
Honey, Francis	centre	Rossland Ladies	1906
Honey, Francis	forward	Rossland Blues	1904
Honey, Francis	forward	Rossland Whites	1904
Hook, Ruby	forward	Rossland Whites	1904
Horton, Miss	forward	Silverton Ladies	1904
Hudson, Miss F.	forward	Nelson Ladies	1900
Husband, Miss	point	Rossland Stars	1900
Inches, Bella, Miss	cover/f	Rossland Crescents	1900-01
Inches, Bella, Miss	f	Crescents (Rossland)	1907
Inches, B., Miss	forward	Rossland Stars	1900
Inches, Nellie		Possibly Rossland Ladies	1900
Inches, Nellie, Miss	Secretary	Rossland Crescents	1901
Innis, Mrs.	Defense	Moyie Crescents	1911
Jacques, Hazel, Miss	lw	Vernon Junior Ladies	1907
Johnson, Miss,	forward	Nelson Ladies	1900
Keating, Madge	cover	Rossland Ladies	1911
Kennedy, Jessie, Miss	rw	Vernon Junior Ladies	1907
Kenny, R. Mrs.	point	Vernon Ladies	1907
Lalonde, C.O. Mrs.	President	Rossland Crescents	1901
Laughlin, Mrs.	spare	Rossland Ladies	1911
Lawson, Miss	point	Silverton Ladies	1904
Lawson, Miss	forward	Silverton Ladies	1904
Lee, Sera	point	Rossland Ladies	1911
Lewis, Miss	goal	Nelson Athletics	1911
Lillywhite, Miss,	cover	Nelson Ladies	1900
Lockhart, Miss	forward	Rossland Crescents	1900
Lowes, Mrs.	forward	Grand Forks Wonders	1910
Lutner, Miss		Moyie Stars	1911
Macdonald, H., Miss		Nelson Ladies	1906
MacDonald, G., Miss		Nelson Ladies	1906
MacDonald, Greta	centre	Nelson Ladies	1906
MacDonald, Greta	spare	Nelson Ladies	1911
MacDonald, Greta, Miss		Nelson Ladies	1905
MacDonald, H., Miss		Nelson Ladies	1906
MacDonald, Helen, Miss	point	Nelson Ladies	1906
MacFarlane, Miss, (capt)	forward	Rossland Crescents	1900
Manhart, Mrs. E.	lw	Mermaids (Nelson)	1910
Manhart, Mrs. E.	goal	Nelson All Stars	1910
Manhart, Mrs. E.	goal	Sterlings, (Nelson)	1910
Marshall. Miss	forward	Rossland Stars	1900
Mason, Cosy (B)	rover	Salmo Black and Whites	1911
McAllister, Miss	spare	Vernon Ladies	1907
McAslin, Florence	lw	Salmo Red and Greys	1911
McCaslin Mabel	rw	Salmo Black and Whites	1911
McCaslin, Lilly	rover	Salmo Red and Greys	1911
McDermott, Miss	forward	Nelson Ladies	1900

Name	Position	Team	Year
McDonald, Greta	lw	Nelson Cubs	1911
McDonald, Greta	spare	Nelson Ladies	1911
McDonald, Tena		Rossland Ladies	1911
McDonald, Tessie	centre	Rossland Ladies	1911
McDougall, Miss A.	cover	New Denver Ladies	1911
McDougall, Miss W.	center	New Denver Ladies	1911
McInnes. Miss	rw	New Denver Ladies	1911
McIntosh, Mrs.	point	Salmo Red and Greys	1911
McIntyre, A. Mrs.	rw	Vernon Ladies	1907
McLachlin, Jean (or McLaughlan)	rw	Nelson Ladies	1911
McLaughlin, Jean	lw	Sterlings, (Nelson)	1910
McLaughlin, Jean	lw	Nelson All Stars	1910
McLaughlin, Jean	rw	Mermaids (Nelson)	1910
McLeod, O, Miss	centre	Salmo Black and Whites	1911
Milne, Mary	goal	Rossland Whites	1904
Milne, Mary	goal	Rossland Ladies	1904
Milne, Mary	cover	Rossland Ladies	1906
Milne, Mary	goal/cover	Rossland Reds	1905
Mills, Lena	goal (formerly Lena Vetterhaus)	Silverton Ladies	1904
Mitchell, Nellie	spare	Rossland Ladies	1911
Morrison, Mrs. E.		Possibly Rossland Ladies	1900
Morkill, Joyce, Miss	point	Vernon Ladies	1907
Morkill, Joyce, Miss	centre	Vernon Junior Ladies	1907
Murray, Miss	rover	Armstrong Ladies	1907
Nagorssen, Mabel, Miss		Nelson Ladies	1905
Northy, Alice		Possibly Rossland Ladies	1900
Northey, Miss	forward	Rossland Crescents	1900
O'Shea, Mrs.	point	Nelson Cubs	1911
Palmer, R.E., Mrs.	president	Rossland Crescents	1901
Patrick, Cynda	cover	Undines (Nelson)	1910
Patrick, Cynda	point	Wanderers (Nelson)	1910
Patrick, Dora	rw	Nelson All Stars	1910
Patrick, Dora	center	Wanderers (Nelson)	1910
Patrick, Dora	rover	Undines (Nelson)	1910
Patrick, Dora	rover	Nelson Ladies	1911
Patrick, Dora	rover	Nelson Cubs	1911
Periard, Miss	centre	Armstrong Ladies	1907
Pettipiece, E.	point	Revelstoke Ladies	1904
Polson, O. Miss	rover	Vernon Ladies	1907
Preston, Ella	goal	Rossland Blues	1904
Raymer, Mrs. Frank	goal	Rossland Blues	1905
Reagh, Jeannie, Miss	lw	Crescents (Rossland)	1907
Reagh, Jeannie, Miss	forward	Rossland Crescents	1900-01
Robertson, Miss		Nelson Ladies	1906
Robertson, Miss		Nelson Ladies	1906
Robertson, Miss	spare	Nelson Ladies	1906
Sawyer, B.	forward	Revelstoke Ladies	1904
Seaman, Mrs.	point	Nelson Athletics	1911
Seaman, Mrs. A.	tried out	Nelson Ladies	1911
Shrapnel, Miss	goal	Rossland Ladies	1903
Sloan, Helen		Grand Forks Ladies	1911
Sloan, Helen	centre	Grand Forks Wonders	1910
Smith, Mary	centre	Rossland Blues	1905
Smith, A. Miss	center	Vernon Ladies	1907
Smith, K, Miss	goal	Vernon Ladies	1907
Smith, K. Miss	goal	Vernon Junior Ladies	1907

Name	Position	Team	Year
Smith, Mary, (or May)	centre	Rossland Blues	1905
Spellman, Mrs.	f (capt)	Crescents (Rossland)	1907
Spellman, Mrs.	f	Rossland Crescents	1901
Stanaway, Olive	f	Rossland Blues	1904
Stanaway, Olive	forward	Rossland Whites	1904
Stark, Belle	rw	Rossland Ladies	1911
Stark, Nellie		Rossland Ladies	1911
Stendal, Madelaine	goal	Grand Forks Wonders	1910
Stuart, Ruby	point	Nelson Ladies	1911
Stuart, Miss	cover	Nelson Athletics	1911
Tamblyn, Miss L.O.	forward	Nelson Ladies	1900
Tamblyn, Miss S,	point	Nelson Ladies	1900
Thompson, Ethel	lw	Salmo Black and Whites	1911
Tipping, Miss	rover	Slocan Ladies	1904
Toye, Effie	centre	Nelson Cubs	1911
Toye, Hazel	lw	Nelson Ladies	1911
Toye, Hazel	rover	Nelson Athletics	1911
Traunweiser, Edna	point	Grand Forks Wonders	1910
Turner, Mrs. Richard	cover	Mermaids (Nelson)	1910
Vallance, Miss	lw	New Denver Ladies	1911
Vetterhaus, Miss Lena	goal	Silverton Ladies	1904

(Miss Vetterhaus, or Wetterhaus, married Billy Mills and became Lena Mills)

Name	Position	Team	Year
Vincent, Irene		Moyie Crescents	1911
Wallace, Mrs.		Moyie Stars	1911
Webb, Miss	point	Slocan Ladies	1904
Welton, J.R. Mrs.	lw	Vernon Ladies	1907
Wilde, Rosie	rw	Salmo Red and Greys	1911
Wilde, W.	cover	Salmo Red and Greys	1911
Foote, Winnie	goal	Nelson Ladies	1911
Foote, Winnie	goal	Nelson Cubs	1911
Wortman, Katie	goal	Salmo Black and Whites	1911
Wragge, Mrs.	rover	Nelson Ladies	1906

(Also possibly, for Nelson, Miss Poppie MacDonald, Miss M. Blakemore. And Mrs. W.A. MacDonald)

Appendix 7: Teams (Men)

S = Senior Team
J = Junior Team
I = Intermediate Team
c = City Team, which did not challenge outside teams

Name	place	colours	level	year
Arlington Hotel Shin-peelers	Trail		S	1905, 1907-1910
Armstrong Int.	Armstrong		I	1910
Armstrong Seniors	Armstrong		S	1906-09
Arrowhead	Arrowhead (Near Rossland)		S	1905
Ashcroft	Ashcroft		S	1901, 1909
Ashdowns	Nelson		S	1907
Associated Banks	Rossland		S, c	1903
B.C. Sugar Refinery	Vancouver		S, c	1899

Team	Location	Type	Year
Bank Clerks	Vancouver	S,c	1908
Bank Clerks	Rossland	S	1906
Bank of Montreal	Rossland	S,c	1903-05
Bank of Montreal	Trail	S	1904
Bankers	New Westminster	S,c	1909
Bankers	Kamloops	S,c	1911
Bankers	Vancouver	S,c	1907, 1909
Bankers	Rossland	S	1905
Bankers	Kaslo	S	1898
Bankers	Revelstoke	S,c	1909
Bankers	Enderby	S,c	1906
Bankers	Nelson	S	1903
Batchelors	Kamloops	S,c	1911
Bell Trading Co. Nelson (Grocers)		S	1906
Blacks	Sandon	S,c	1897
Boilermakers	Trail	S	1910
Boundary combined	Boundary area	S	1906
Boundary Hockey club	essentially Greenwood	S	1900
Boy Scouts	Nelson	J	1911
Bright's Stars	Vancouver	S,c	1909
Broadhead's Boarders	New Westminster, or Vancouver	S,c	1905
Broadway Speed Artists	Kamloops	S,c	1911
Brooklyn Hotel	Phoenix	S,c	1911
Business Men	Kaslo	S	1901
Camborne	Camborne	S	1908
Camp McKinney	Camp McKinney	S	1900
Canadian Foresters	Nelson	S	1904
Captain Langley's team	Victoria	S,c	1899
Central Hotel	Trail	S	1910
Centre Star Mine(s)	Rossland	S,c	1905
Centre Star Team	Rossland	S,c	1906, 1908
Centre Star/War Eagle	Rossland	S,c	1906
Challengers	Nelson	J	1910
City team	Revelstoke	S,c	1901
Clerks	Kaslo	S,c	1901
Cody	Cody	S	1910
Coeur D'Alene	Idaho	S	1908
Coldstream Hotel	Vernon	S,c	1904, 1908
Coldstream Ranch	Coldstream	S	1911
Coldstream Valley	Coldstream	S	1905-07
Coleman	Alberta yellow and black	S	1907-08, 1910
Columbias	Rossland	J	1901
Combined banks	Nelson	S	1908
Commercials	Cranbrook white	S	1911
Commonage Int.	Vernon	I	1904
Cowley	Cowley	S	1908
CPR	Revelstoke	S,c	1909
CPR Nelson	Nelson	S	1901-02-03
CPR Seven	Vancouver	S,c	1901
CPR shops	Cranbrook red	S	1911
CPR traffic Department	Cranbrook	S	1911
Cranbrook Intermediates	Cranbrook	I	1911
Cranbrook Seniors	Cranbrook	S	1904, 1911
Crow's Nest Combined	Crow's nest towns	S	1903
Crown Point Hotel	Trail	S,c	1908-09-10
Cyclones	Nelson (high school)	J	1910

Team	Location		Level	Years
Cyclones	Rossland		J	1901
Daniel's Team	Victoria		S,c	1899
Diamond A Ashdown	Nelson (Hardware)		S	1906
(They were also called the Ashdowns, in 1907)				
Eagles	Spokane Washington		S,c	1906
Enderby Int.	Enderby		I	1904
Enderby Juniors	Enderby		J	1907-09
Enderby Seniors	Enderby		S	1899, 1906-07, 1909
Fats	Sandon		S,c	1897
Ferguson Seniors	Ferguson		S	1908, 1910
Fernie Juniors	Fernie		J	1911
Fernie Seniors	Fernie		S	1903-09, 1911
Fire Brigade	Nelson		S	1899
Fossils	Nelson		S,c	1908
Gerard (town)	Gerard		S	1910
Go-Go's	Nelson		S,c	1898
Golden pick up team	Golden		S,c	1905
Golden Seniors,	Golden		S	1895, 1899
Grand Forks Juniors	Grand Forks		J	1903
Grand Forks Seniors	Grand Forks	red and white (or just red)	S	1902-03, 1909-10
Greenwood Int.	Greenwood		S	1903, 1908
Greenwood Juniors	Greenwood		J	1911
Greenwood Seniors	Greenwood		S	1900-1911
Grocers	Nelson		S	1907
Grocery Clerks	Rossland		S,c	1906
Harlington's Boarding House	Kamloops		S,c	1911
Herman's Champion's	Vancouver		S	1907
Heroes	Grand Forks		S, c	1903
High School	Nelson		J	1909-1910
Hoboes	Grand Forks		S,c	1903
Hoboes	Salmo		S,c	1910
Hudson's Bay Company	Vancouver		S,c	1905
Hudson's Bay Stores	Nelson		S,c	1900
Hunter Bros. Store	Rossland		S,c	1899
Hunter Brothers	Rossland		S,c	1903-05
Hurricanes	Rossland		J	1901
Independents	Spokane (Changed their names to the Eagles)		S,c	1906
Imperial Bank	Nelson		S	1908
Invincibles	Nelson (high school)		J	1910
Invincibles	Rossland		J	1905-06
Invincibles	Nelson		J	1905
Junior Thistles	Nelson		J	1909
Junior Victorias	Rossland		J	1899
Kamloops Banks	Kamloops		S,c	1909
Kamloops College	Kamloops		S,c	1903-04
Kamloops CPR	Kamloops		S,c	1903-1904, 1909
Kamloops High School	Kamloops		J,c	1909
Kamloops Lumber company	Kamloops		S,c	1906
Kamloops Seniors	Kamloops		S	1898, 1902-05, 1908-10
Kaslo Downtown	Kaslo		S,c	1899
Kaslo Flat	Kaslo		S,c	1900
Kaslo Hill	Kaslo		J	1901
Kaslo Hill	Kaslo		S,c	1899-1900
Kaslo Hotel	Kaslo		S,c	1898
Kaslo Intermediates	Kaslo		I	1908-1910
Kaslo Seniors	Kaslo	red, white and green in 1900		1897-1911

Team	Location	Notes	Class	Years
Kaslo Town	Kaslo		S	1901
Kaslo Town	Kaslo		J	1901
Kelowna Dramatic club	Kelowna		S,c	1898
Kelowna High School	Kelowna		J	1908
Kelowna Juniors	Kelowna		J	1908
Kelowna Public School	Kelowna		J	1908
Kelowna Seniors	Kelowna		S	1898, 1908-1911
King Hotel	Phoenix		S,c	1911
Lakes	Nelson		S,c	1908
Lardeau Hockey Club	Trout Lake (Near Rossland)		S	1905
Leans	Sandon		S,c	1897
Le Roi Mine	Rossland		S,c	1904-05-06, 1909
Lions	Rossland	red jerseys and yellow belts	S,c	1899
Lumby	Lumby		S	1911
Machinists	Trail		S,c	1910
Maple Leafs	Nelson		J	1909
Marysville	East Kootenay town		S	1902
McGaw's (or Megaws)	Vernon		S,c	1911
McLellan-McFeeley and Co.	Vancouver		S,c	1899, 1905
Meakin Hotel Never sweats	Trail		S,c	1905, 1907-1908, 1910
Medicine Hat	Alberta		S	1903
Merchants	Sandon		S, c	1901
Merritt Seniors	Merritt		S	1909-10
Mess	Salmo		S,c	1910
Mic-Mac's	Vernon		J	1904
Mic-Macs	Nelson		J	1910
Middlesboro	Middlesboro		S	1909
Miner's and Kootenay Hotels	Sandon		S,c	1901
Missoula	Montana		S	1911
Mountains	Nelson		S,c	1908
Moyie Int.	Moyie		I	1911
Moyie Juniors	Moyie		J	1899
Moyie Seniors	Moyie		S	1901, 1909-10
Nakusp	Nakusp		S	1909
Nelson East Ward	Nelson	black and white	S,c	1906-07
Nelson Electric Tramway company	Nelson		S,c	1901
Nelson Grocery	Nelson		S,c	1901
Nelson Hardware	Nelson		S,c	1901
Nelson Intermediates	Nelson		I	1903, 1906-1911
Nelson Juniors	Nelson	Maroon, green and white, in 1911	J	1900-01-02, 07-11

In 1909 the Nelson Juniors became the Junior Wanderers. They changed back the next year, but there were many junior teams in Nelson by that time.

Team	Location	Notes	Class	Years
Nelson Juveniles	Nelson		J	1909-1910
Nelson Lacrosse-Hockey	Nelson		S	1900
Nelson Militia Company	Nelson		S,c	1901
Nelson Seniors	Nelson	green and white	S	1897-19

In 1900 the Nelson team split into two teams, the first called the Nelsons, or the Nelson City Hockey Team, the second team called the Nelson Lacrosse-Hockey Team. They did not reform for the Rossland Carnival. In 1905 the Nelson Seniors were again split into two for challenge matches, both teams called the Nelson Senior Team. They then combined the team once more for the Rossland Carnival.

Team	Location	Notes	Class	Years
Nelson West Ward	Nelson	red and yellow	S,c	1906-07
Nelsons, or Nelson City	Nelson		S	1900
New Denver A	New Denver		S,c	1911
New Denver B	New Denver		S,c	1911
New Denver Seniors	New Denver		S	1906, 1909, 1911

Team	Location	Notes	Type	Years
New Ramblers	Vancouver		S,c	1907
New Westminster Royals	New Westminster	crimson	S	1907
New Westminster Seniors	New Westminster		S	1901
Nickel Plate Flat	Rossland		J	1906
Nicola Lake	Nicola Lake		S	1898, 1908-10
Northport	Washington State		S	1905
Orphans	Kamloops		S, (?) c	1909
Palace and Filbert Hotels	Sandon		S, c	1901
Peachland	Peachland		S	1908
Penticton	Penticton		S	1908, 1911
Phoenix Int.	Phoenix		I	1904, 06-07-08
Phoenix Juniors	Phoenix		J	1903, 1911
Phoenix Seniors	Phoenix	white, then orange and black	S	1902, 1909-10-11
Pincher Creek	Pincher Creek Alberta		S	1903, 1909
Prairie Valley	Prairie Valley		S	1905
Printers	Sandon		S,c	1901
Public School	Nelson		J	1909
Queen Hotel	Phoenix		S,c	1911
Ramblers	Vancouver	possibly existed	S,c	1900
Ramblers	Cranbrook		S	1911
Ramblers (mining)	Sandon		S	1898
Ramblers, (The New)	Vancouver		S,c	1907
Rawhides	Sandon		S	1903
Real Estate Team	Nelson		S,c	1908
Reco's (Hotel)	Sandon		S,c	1898
Reilly Hockey Team	Nelson		S,c	1903
Retail Clerks	Nelson		S,c	1902
Retail Clerks	Nelson		S,c	1904
Retailers (Grocers)	Nelson		S,c	1908
Revelstoke Int.	Revelstoke		I	1904
Revelstoke Seniors	Revelstoke	initially white suits and stockings	S	1899-1906, 1909-11
Revelstoke YMCA	Revelstoke		S,c	1909
Rivers	Nelson		S,c	1908
Rocky Mountain Rangers	Nelson		S,c	1902-03
Rocky Mountain Rangers	Rossland		S,c	1905-1909
Rossland Bank Team	Rossland		S,c	1897
Rossland Bankers	Rossland		S,c	1906
Rossland Citizen Team	Rossland		S	1903
Rossland Clerks	Rossland		S,c	1910
Rossland Intermediates	Rossland		I	1903, 1905, 1907-1911
Rossland IXL	Rossland		J	1899-1890
Rossland Juniors	Rossland		J	1901-02, 1904-05, 08, 09
Rossland Juveniles	Rossland		J	1909
Rossland Seniors	Rossland	normally red, they also wore blue	S	1897-1911

This team was split from 1899-1903 into the Rossland Hockey Team, also called The Rosslands, and the Rossland Victorias. They amalgamated once again in 1904.

Team	Location	Notes	Type	Years
Rossland Stars	Rossland		J	1906
Rossland Victorias Alberta Challenge Team	Rossland		S	1906

Team colours were: red and white sweaters, white pants, and red stockings.

Team	Location	Notes	Type	Years
Rovers	Nelson	black and yellow, then green and white	J	1910-1911
Royal Hotel	Vernon		S,c	1908
Salmo	Salmo		I	1910-11
Saloons	Sandon		S,c	1901
Sandon city	Sandon		S,c	1902
Sandon Juniors	Sandon		J	1899-1901

Team	Location	Notes	Level	Years
Sandon Seniors	Sandon	black in 1900/red & white in 1903	S	1897-1911
Shamrocks	Nelson		J	1910
Silverton Seniors	Silverton		S	1901-04
Slocan City Seniors	Slocan City		S	1898-1903, 1909
Spokane High School	Spokane, Washington		J	1900
Spokane Juniors	Spokane		J	1900, 1902
Spokane Seniors	Spokane, Washington		S	1907-08
Spokane Amateur Athletic Club	Spokane, Washington		S & c	1906-07-08
St. Pancras Inn	Kaslo		S	1901
Stars	Nelson	(they became the Rovers)	J	1910
Summerland	Summerland		S	1905, 1908-11
Tenderfeet	Nelson		S,c	1908
Thistles	Nelson	red and white, then purple and white	S,c	1909-1910
Tigers	Rossland	white jerseys	S	1899
Trail Intermediates	Trail		I	1909-1910
Trail Juniors	Trail		J	1904-1908, 1910
Trail Juveniles	Trail		J	1906, 1908, 1910
Trail Seniors	Trail		S	1899, 1904, 1908, 1910-1911
Trail Smelter	Trail		S,c	1906
Trail Smelter Team	Trail		S	1904-1907
Trout Lake (town)	Trout Lake		S	1910
Vancouver CPR	Vancouver		S	1910
Vancouver Lacrosse Club	Vancouver		S	1899
Vancouver pick-up team	Vancouver		S	1899, 1901
Vancouver Seniors	Vancouver	white	S	1907
Vancouver Terminals	Vancouver (same team as the Van. Seniors)		S	1907
Vernon Bank employees	Vernon		S,c	1906
Vernon Bankers	Vernon		S,c	1905, 1907, 1911
Vernon High School	Vernon		J	1903-04, 1911
Vernon Int.	Vernon		I	1905, 1910
Vernon Juniors	Vernon	blue	J	1903, 07-08
Vernon Married Men	Vernon		S,c	1906
Vernon Public School	Vernon		J	1911
Vernon Seniors	Vernon	blue and white	S	1898-99, 1903-05, 1908-09, 1911
Vernon Single Men	Vernon		S,c	1906
Victoria Hotel	Vernon		S,c	1904
Victorias	Nelson	blue and white	S,c	1909-1910
Victorias	Rossland		S	1899-1903
Wah-Wah's	Nelson		S,c	1898
War Eagle Mine	Rossland		S,c	1906
West Kootenay Power and Light Company	Rossland		S,c	1903-04-05-06
Whirlwinds	Nelson (high school)		J	1910
Whites	Sandon		S,c	1897
Wholesalers	Nelson		S	1900-01, 03-04, 08
Wigwam	Revelstoke		S,c	1901
Wilmer Seniors	Wilmer (near Windermere)		S	1905
Wood-Vallance	Nelson		S,c	1907
Woods Independents	Spokane Washington		S,c	1907
Ymir Seniors	Ymir		S	1911

Appendix 8: Teams: Ladies

Team	Location	Description	Year
Allstars	Nelson	Dark red skirts, white sweaters with the letter S on the chest and red toques	1910
Athletics	Nelson		1911
Blues	Rossland	Blue sweaters	1904
Blues	Rossland	Blue blouses with sailor collars trimmed with white braid, blue skirts, dark hose, black shoes, shining skates and white toboggan caps.	1905
Cranbrook Ladies	Cranbrook		1911
Crescents	Moyie		1911
Crescents	Rossland	Black and red	1900
Cubs	Nelson		1911
Grand Forks Ladies	Grand Forks		1911
Mermaids	Nelson	White sweaters, white toques with green letters diagonally across their chests.	1910

After one game, the Mermaids changed their names to the Sterlings.

Team	Location	Description	Year
Nelson Ladies	Nelson	Green jerseys trimmed with white, and dark skirts with no head coverings	1906
Nelson Ladies	Nelson		1911
New Denver Ladies	New Denver		1911
Reds	Rossland	Red blouses with sailor collars, trimmed in white, with blue short skirts, and lots of black hose underneath. Also, toboggan caps and dark little shoes and nickel plated skates.	1905
Revelstoke Ladies	Revelstoke		1904
Rossland Ladies	Rossland		1903
Rossland Ladies	Rossland	Red sailor waists, trimmed with white, and red skirts, trimmed with white, and white toques	1906
Rossland Ladies	Rossland		1900, 1904-06, 1911
Sandon Ladies	Sandon	(practicing)	1897
Silverton Ladies	Silverton		1904
Slocan City Ladies	Slocan City		1904
Stars	Moyie		1911
Stars	Rossland	Black and gold	1900
Sterlings	Nelson	Large White S on green sweaters, with red touques.	1910
Undines	Nelson	White sweaters, white toques, with green letters straight across their chests.	1910

After one game, the Undines changed their names to the Wanderers

Team	Location	Description	Year
Vernon Junior Ladies	Vernon		1907
Vernon Ladies	Vernon		1905-07
Vernon United School Girls	Vernon		1911
Wanderers	Nelson	Large green W on white sweaters, with white toques	1910
Whites	Rossland	White sweaters	1904
Wonders	Grand Forks	Red skirts, white sweaters with red letters, G.F. and white touques	1910

Appendix 9: Goal Leaders, Year by Year

In order to provide the most meaningful statistics possible, only games between senior teams in B.C. challenge or league matches have been counted. Intermediate, Junior, inner-city and city league games have not been counted. The challenge series by Rossland against Edmonton and Calgary in 1906, and the challenge series by Nelson against Edmonton in 1909 have not been counted, because Edmonton and Calgary did not compete against B.C. teams as part of the regular B.C. challenge process, and they considered these matches special events, which could not be counted as leading to any overall B.C. status. However, challenge matches against Coleman Alberta and Spokane Washington have been counted, because they considered themselves part of, or related to, the overall B.C. championship process. Some towns considered their teams to be Intermediate because they felt they were not as good as the usual powerhouses. However, where they used their best players against another town's best players, I have counted the results, because although they represent the weaker part of the spectrum, they still contribute to it in the same process. (Where a town had both senior and intermediate teams, the intermediate results have never been counted here.)

Unfortunately these stats were often reported intermittently or not at all, especially in the early years. There was never an overall goals champion compiled or annouced during this period. Thus, all of these results must be considered incomplete.

1895

No individual stats available.

1896

No individual stats available.

1897

		Goals	Games
Duncan, Tom, (or W.)	Nelson	3	1
Grierson, Andy	Sandon	2	1
McVichie, J. (?)	Sandon	1	1
Blackwood, Dudley	Sandon	1	1
Hunter, Sam	Kaslo	1	1
Smith, Frank	Nelson	1	1
Hipperson, Charles (?)	Nelson	1	1
Cameron	Sandon	1	1
Young, D.J.	Kaslo	1	1
Dill, B.	Kaslo	1	1

1898

Becher, A. Lorne	Rossland	6	2
Lahey, Mike (?)	Rossland	5	2
Chesterton, C.W. (?)	Rossland	3	2
McBride, C.R.	Rossland	2	1
O'Brien, Ed. M.	Rossland	2	2
Henderson, T.	Sandon	1	1
Rutherford, D (?)	Nelson	1	1

1899

Wetmore, M. (or A.)	Nelson	3	2
Chesterton, C.W.	Rosslands	3	2
Blackwood, Dudley	Nelson	2	1
Hunter, Sam	Kaslo	2	1
Davis, A.W.	Rosslands	2	2
Hammond, Bob	Sandon	1	1
Connelly	Kaslo	1	1
Smith, Frank - Daniel's Team,	Victoria	1	1
Campbell, Len - Langley's Team,	Victoria	1	1
McBride, C.R.	Rosslands	1	2
Chalmers, F.W.	Rossland Victorias	1	2

1900

Winn, Eldon H. S.	Rossland Victorias	3	1
Duncan, Tom	Nelson	1	1
McBride, C.R.	Rossland	1	1
Perry	Rosslands	1	1

1901

Thompson, Joe	Nelson	6	4
Perrier, Arthur	Nelson	6	4
Nace, O.	Nelson	5	4
Wetmore, M. (or A.)	Nelson	5	4
Carmichael, G.	Rossland	4	2
McDonald,	Revelstoke	3	2
Archibald, Cyril, (Barney)	Nelson	3	4
Neelands, P.N.	Rossland	2	1
O'Brien, E.M.	Rossland	2	2
Harris, W.S.	Rossland	1	1
Townshend, G.E. or J.	Rossland Victorias	1	1
Johnson, J.D.	Revelstoke	1	1
McLellan	Rossland	1	1
Niles, C.H.	Phoenix	1	1
Monk, E.W.	Phoenix	1	1
Winn, Eldon H.S.	Rossland Victorias	1	2
Birchell	Sandon	1	2
Grierson, Andy	Sandon	1	2
Howarth, W. or Grierson, A.	Sandon	1	2
Crawford, Jack	Sandon	1	2

1902

Hood(s), W.R.	Sandon	9	3
Howarth, William	Sandon	8	4
Monk, E.W.	Phoenix	5	3
McArthur, P.C. (?)	Phoenix	5	3
Thompson, Joe	Nelson	3	2
Grierson, Andy	Sandon	3	3

1902 cont.

Wetmore, M. or A.	Nelson	2	1
Nace, O.	Nelson	2	1
Carmichael, G.	Rossland	1	1
Pullen	Nelson	1	1
Perrier, Alf	Nelson	1	1
Coulton	Phoenix	1	1
Harris, Al (?)	Rossland Victorias	1	1

1903

Thompson, Joe	Nelson	7	4
Felion	Rossland	6	3
Hood(s), W.R.	Sandon	5	3
Elworthy, E.	Vernon	4	3
Crowell, T.E.	Vernon	4	3
Jackson, E.s.	Vernon	3	3
Howarth, William	Sandon	2	1
Mabee, C.	Vernon	2	1
Shatford, S.A.	Vernon	2	1
Niles, C.H.	Grand Forks	2	2
Robertson, R.W. (or H.)	Vernon	2	2
Clothier, George (?)	Rossland Victorias	2	3
Harris, A.(?)	Rossland Victorias	2	3
Hacker, A.	Nelson	2	3
Archibald, Cyril (Barney)	Nelson	2	4
Coulton	Grand Forks	1	1
Tier, J.	Sandon	1	1
McQueen	Grand Forks	1	2
Cliffe William (?)	Sandon	1	2
Carmichael, G.	Rossland	1	3
McPherson	Rossland	1	3
Blackwood, Dudley	Nelson	1	4
Baker, A. C. or T.	Nelson	1	4
Perrier, Arthur	Nelson	1	5

1904

Thompson, Joe	Nelson	9	5
Graham, C.	Revelstoke	2	1
Allan, J.	Revelstoke	2	1
Hood(s), W.R.	Rossland/Sandon	2	3
Mills, Billy	Silverton	2	1
McMillan	Slocan City	2	1
Sharp(e), Roy	Nelson	1	1
Bain	Silverton	1	1
Blomfield	Silverton	1	1
McKinnon	Silverton	1	1
Milne	Silverton	1	1
Robertson, I.G.	Nelson	1	2
Baker, A. (or C.)	Nelson	1	2
Barber, W.J.	Revelstoke	1	2
Perrier, Arthur	Nelson	1	2
Howarth, William	Rossland	1	2
Clothier, (George ?)	Rossland	1	2

1904 cont.

Guay, A.	Nelson	1	2
McLachlan, J.	Fernie	1	2

1905

Howarth, William	Rossland	9	6
Thompson, F.H.V.	Nelson	9	8
Thompson, Joe	Nelson	8	6
Hood(s), W. R.	Rossland	7	4
Armitage, A. or R.	Nelson	7	6
Bishop, Archie	Nelson	6	7
Wilson	Rossland	5	5
Guay, A.	Nelson	4	1
Baker, A. (or C.)	Nelson	4	4
Martin, W.	Fernie	3	2
Robertson, I.G.	Nelson	3	5
Smith, Y.	Fernie	2	2
Fraser, J.	Fernie	2	2
Cody, E.D.	Nelson	2	4
Deacon, W.H.	Nelson	2	6
McQueen, A.	Vernon	1	1
Moe, C.E.	Grand Forks	1	1
Birnie, W.J.	Grand Forks	1	1
Dalmage, F.	Fernie	1	2
Kastner, M.(?)	Fernie	1	2
Steel, L.	Fernie	1	3
Jamieson, H. (or A.)	Rossland	1	6

1906

Bishop, Archie	Nelson	14	7
Hood(s), R.	Sandon/Rossland	12	7
Howarth, William	Rossland	7	7
Thompson, Joe	Nelson	6	7
Crawford, (?)	Rossland	6	7
Thompson, F,H.V. (Frank)	Nelson	4	4
Steel(e), Les	Nelson	4	7
Jamieson, H. or A.	Rossland	4	7
Robertson, I.G.	Nelson	3	2
Lafferty,	Rossland	2	6
Guay, A.	Nelson	2	7
McQueen, A.	Boundary	1	1

1907

Bishop, Archie	Nelson	26	9
Keating, Al.	Rossland	13	7
Thompson, Joe	Nelson	13	9
Dixon, James (or S.)	Rossland	11	7
Howarth, William	Rossland	7	7
Clunis, M.	Nelson	7	7
McGaugherty, Ernest	Spokane	5	3

1907 cont.

Bishop, Ed.	Nelson	4	3
Bell, Ole	Nelson	4	4
Trainer, G.	Spokane	3	1
Niblett, J	Spokane	3	2
Bell, R.	Nelson	3	3
Lafferty, T.	Phoenix	3	4
Hood(s), R.	Phoenix	3	4
McQueen, A.	Phoenix	3	4
Donahue, Jack	Rossland	3	5
Neil(l), Herb	Rossland	3	7
Steel(e), Les	Nelson	3	8
Jeffs, C.	Nelson	2	2
Barber, W.J. (or Allen)	Revelstoke	2	2
Dunn, P.	Revelstoke	2	2
Sharp(e), Roy	Nelson	2	3
Robertson, R.H.	Phoenix	2	4
Deacon, W.H.	Rossland	2	5
Bellerose	Nelson	2	5
Jamieson, H.	Phoenix	1	2
Allen, J.	Revelstoke	1	2
Fraser, J.	Phoenix	1	3
Trezona, J.	Spokane	1	3

1908

McGaugherty, Tom	Spokane/Rossland	7	3
Keating, Al.	Rossland	5	4
Neil(l), Herb	Rossland	5	4
Dixon, J.(?)	Rossland	5	4
Bishop, Archie	Nelson	4	3
Trezona, J.	Spokane	3	2
Patrick, Lester	Nelson	3	3
Hood(s), W.R.	Nelson	2	1
Lewis	Coleman (Alberta)	2	1
Kemp	Nelson	2	1
Rillance	Rossland	2	4
Jamieson	Coleman (Alberta)	1	1
Baker	Coleman (Alberta)	1	1
Gresack, F.	Coleman (Alberta)	1	1
Cardiff	Spokane	1	2
Steel(e), Les	Nelson	1	3
Thompson, Joe	Nelson	1	3
Bellerose	Nelson	1	3

1909

Bishop, Archie	Nelson	24	6
Patrick, Lester	Nelson	22	6
Thompson, Joe	Nelson	10	6
Patrick, Frank	Nelson	9	5
Russell, C.	Greenwood	4	1
Dixon, J.	Rossland	4	1

1909 cont.

Steel(e), Les	Nelson	4	6
Neil(l), Herb	Rossland	3	5
Allen, K.C.	Rossland	3	5
Bawlf	Moyie	2	2
Keating, Al.	Rossland	2	5
Dunn(e), Tim	Nelson	2	6
McQueen, A.	Phoenix	1	1
McDonald, A.	Phoenix	1	1
Clothier, George (?)	Moyie	1	2
Sherman	Moyie	1	3

1910

Bishop, Archie	Nelson	15	6
Bishop, Harry	Nelson	15	6
Dimock, R.	Phoenix	9	4
Neil(l), Herb	Phoenix	9	4
McWha, P.C.	Moyie	6	4
Clark, R.	Phoenix	5	3
McQueen, A.	Phoenix	4	3
Cameron	Greenwood	4	3
Keating, Al	Rossland	3	1
Bloomfield	Greenwood	3	3
Treherne, w.	Rossland	2	3
Demuth	Rossland	2	3
Russell, Cliff	Greenwood	2	4
McKelvey	Phoenix	1	3
Bloomfield	Greenwood	1	3
Sheridan, H.	Moyie	1	3
Stanaway, Ed.	Rossland	1	3
McGaugherty Tom (?)	Rossland	1	3
Longfellow, Ed.	Rossland	1	3
Davison	Rossland	1	3
Dunne, Tim	Nelson	1	6
Hacking, e.	Nelson	1	6
Steel(e), Les	Nelson	1	6

1911

Bishop, Archie	Nelson	14	5
Patrick, Lester	Nelson	11	5
Bishop, Harry	Nelson	11	5
Lynn(e), Rusty	Phoenix	7	6
Dixon, J. (or S.)	Rossland	5	4
Miller	Rossland/Grand Forks	5	5
McWha, P.C.	Phoenix/Fernie/Cranbrook	5	6
Grubbe, E.H.	New Denver	4	2
Macdonald, D.J.	Greenwood	4	3
Thrasher	Phoenix/Fernie	4	5
Ames, F.	Rossland	3	4
Steel(e), Les	Nelson	3	5
Tier, J.	New Denver	2	2
Jewell, E.	Rossland	2	3

1911 cont.

Stanaway, Ed.	Missoula (Montana)	1	1
Dorman	Missoula (Montana)	1	1
Quinn, Barney	Grand Forks	1	1
Demuth	Grand Forks	1	1
Reid, Bert	Grand Forks	1	1
Dunlap	Fernie	1	1
McGregor	Cranbrook	1	1
Russell, Cliff	Greenwood	1	2
Blumenaur, R.	New Denver	1	2
Ferguson, W.A.	Nelson	1	2
Jenkins	Nelson	1	2
McGaugherty, E.	Greenwood	1	2
McCarthy, F.	Greenwood	1	2
Mercer	Grand Forks/Rossland	1	3
Donahue, Jack	Rossland	1	3
Saunders	Phoenix	1	4
Ouillett	Phoenix	1	4
Jopp, V.	Rossland	1	4

Appendix 10: Overall Goal Leaders (top 30 players)

(These results are, of course, unofficial only, since no official records were ever kept.)

* = Year's top goal leader
BC = BC Champion
K = Kootenay League Champion
I = International, or Open Champion at the Rossland Carnival
B = Boundary champion

				Goals	Games	AVG
Bishop, Archie	BC	Nelson	1905	6	7	
	*	Nelson	1906	14	7	
	*I	Nelson	1907	26	9	
		Nelson	1908	4	3	
	*BC I K	Nelson	1909	24	6	
	*(shared) BC	Nelson	1910	15	6	
	*	Nelson	1911	14	5	
	totals:			103	43	2.39

cont.

Thompson, Joe		Nelson	1898	goals not known		
		Nelson	1899	goals not known		
		Nelson	1900	goals not known		
*(shared) BC		Nelson	1901	6	4	
BC		Nelson	1902	3	2	
*BC		Nelson	1903	7	4	
*		Nelson	1904	9	5	
BC		Nelson	1905	8	6	
		Nelson	1906	6	7	
I		Nelson	1907	13	9	
		Nelson	1908	1	3	
BC I K		Nelson	1909	10	6	
totals:				63	46	1.369

Hood(s), W.R.	*	Sandon	1902	9	3	
(Robertson)		Sandon	1903	5	3	
		Rossland	1904	1	1	
		Rossland	1905	7	4	
BC (disputed)		Rossland	1906	12	7	
		Rossland/Phoenix	1907	3	4	
		Nelson	1908	2	1	
totals:				39	23	1.695

Patrick, Lester		Nelson	1908	3	3	
BC I K		Nelson	1909	22	6	
		Nelson	1911	11	5	
totals:				36	14	2.57

Howarth, William		Sandon	1901	1	2	
		Sandon	1902	8	4	
		Sandon	1903	2	1	
		Rossland	1904	1	2	
*		Rossland	1905	9	5	
BC (disputed)		Rossland	1906	7	7	
BC		Rossland	1907	7	7	
totals:				35	28	1.25

Bishop, Harry	*(shared) BC	Nelson	1910	15	6	
		Nelson	1911	11	5	
totals:				26	11	2.36

Name	League	Team	Year			
Dixon, James, (or S.)	BC	Rossland	1907	11	7	
	BC (disputed)	Rossland	1908	5	4	
		Rossland	1909	4	5	
		Rossland	1911	5	4	
	totals:			25	20	1.25
Keating, Al	BC	Rossland	1907	13	7	
	BC (disputed)	Rossland	1908	5	4	
		Rossland	1909	2	5	
		Rossland	1910	3	1	
	totals:			23	17	1.35
Neil(l), Herb	BC	Rossland	1907	3	7	
	BC (disputed)	Rossland	1908	5	4	
		Rossland	1909	3	5	
		Phoenix	1910	9	4	
	totals:			20	20	1.00
Steel(e), Les		Nelson	1906	4	7	
		Nelson	1907	3	8	
		Nelson	1908	1	3	
	BC	Nelson	1909	4	6	
	BC	Nelson	1910	1	6	
		Nelson	1911	3	5	
	totals:			16	35	0.457
Thompson, Frank H.V.	BC	Nelson	1905	9	8	
		Nelson	1906	4	4	
	totals:			13	12	1.08
McWha, P.C.		Moyie	1910	6	4	
	BC	Phoenix/Fernie/Cranbrook	1911	5	6	
	totals:			11	10	1.10

Player	Team	Location	Year	G	A	Ratio
Wetmore, M. or A.		Nelson	1899	3	2	
	BC	Nelson	1901	5	4	
	BC	Nelson	1902	2	1	
	totals:			10	7	1.43
McQueen, A.		Vernon	1905	1	1	
		Boundary	1906	1	1	
		Phoenix	1907	3	4	
		Phoenix	1909	1	1	
		Phoenix	1910	4	3	
	totals:			10	10	1.00
Dimmock, R.		Moyie	1909	0	3	
		Moyie	1910	9	4	
	totals:			9	7	1.28
Patrick, Frank	BC I K	Nelson	1909	9	5	
		Nelson	1911	0	3	
	totals:			9	8	1.13
Perrier, Arthur *(shared)	BC	Nelson	1901	6	4	
	BC	Nelson	1902	1	1	
	BC	Nelson	1903	1	5	
		Nelson	1904	1	2	
	totals:			9	12	0.75
McGaugherty, Tom	*	Spokane/Rossland	1908	7	3	
		Rossland	1910	1	3	
	totals:			8	6	1.33
Russell, Cliff		Greenwood	1909	4	1	
		Greenwood	1910	2	4	
		Greenwood	1911	1	2	
	totals:			7	7	1.00

Player		Team	Year	GP	G	Avg
Lynne, Rusty	BC I B	Phoenix	1911	7	6	
	totals:			7	6	1.17
Armitage		Nelson	1905	7	6	
	totals:			7	6	1.17
Clunis, M.		Nelson	1907	7	7	
	totals:			7	7	1.00
Robertson, I.G.		Nelson	1904	1	2	
	BC	Nelson	1905	3	5	
		Nelson	1906	3	2	
	totals:			7	9	0.78
Guay, A.		Nelson	1904	1	2	
		Nelson	1905	4	1	
		Nelson	1906	2	7	
	totals:			7	10	0.7
Jamieson, H. (or A.)		Rossland	1905	1	6	
	BC(disputed)	Rossland	1906	4	7	
		Phoenix	1907	1	2	
		Coleman	1908	1	1	
	totals:			7	16	0.44
Becher, A. Lorne		Rossland Victorias	1898	6	2	
	BC	Rossland Victorias	1899		unknown	
	totals:			6	2	3.00
Felion		Rossland Victorias	1903	6	3	
	totals:			6	3	2.00

Monk (possibly E. W.)	Phoenix	1901	1	1	
	Phoenix	1902	5	3	
totals:			6	4	1.50
Carmichael, G.	Rossland	1901	4	2	
	Rossland	1902	1	1	
	Rossland	1903	1	3	
totals:			6	6	1.00
Grierson, Andy BC	Sandon	1897	2	1	
	Sandon	1901	1	2	
	Sandon	1902	3	3	
totals:			6	6	1.00

Appendix 11:   Top goal scoring averages

(Only players with two seasons or more, who also appear in the top 30 goal scorers are counted here, and only goals from Senior challenge inter-city games are counted.)

	Goals	Games	Avg.	goal scoring leader (# of times)
Patrick, Lester	36	14	2.57	
Bishop, Archie	103	43	2.39	5 (1 shared)
Bishop, Harry	26	11	2.36	1 (shared)
Hood(s), W.R.	39	23	1.69	1
Wetmore, M.	10	7	1.43	1 (shared)
Monk, E.W. (?)	6	4	1.50	
Thompson, Joe	63	46	1.37	3 (1 shared)
Keating, Al	23	17	1.35	
McGaugherty, Tom	8	6	1.33	1
Dimmock, R.	9	7	1.29	
Howarth, William	35	28	1.25	1
Dixon, James	25	20	1.25	
Patrick, Frank	9	8	1.13	
McWha, P.C.	11	10	1.10	
Thompson, Frank H.V.	12	11	1.09	
Neil(l),	20	20	1.00	
McQueen, A.	10	10	1.00	
Carmichael, G.	6	6	1.00	
Grierson, Andy	6	6	1.00	
Russell, Cliff	7	7	1.00	
Robertson, I.G.	7	9	0.78	
Perrier, Arthur	9	12	0.75	1 (shared)
Guay, A.	7	10	0.70	
Steel(e), Les	16	35	0.46	
Jamieson, H.	7	16	0.44	

Appendix 12:   Multiple goal games

(Only Senior, inter-city challenge games are counted here)

Bishop, Archie	7 goals twice
	6 goals twice
	5 goals four times
	4 goals once
	3 goals four times
Patrick, Lester	7 goals once
	5 goals twice
	3 goals twice
Bishop, Harry	6 goals once
	3 goals three times
Thompson, Joe	5 goals once
	4 goals once
	3 goals five times
Hood(s), W.R.	5 goals twice
	3 goals twice
Dimmock, R.	5 goals once
McGaugherty, Tom	4 goals once
	3 goals twice
Keating, Al	4 goals once
	3 goals once
Thompson, Frank, H.V.	4 goals once
	3 goals once
Russell, Cliff	4 goals once
Dixon, James, or S.	4 goals once
Wetmore, M.	4 goals once
Becher, A. Lorne	4 goals once
Lahey, Mike	4 goals once
Lynne, Rusty	4 goals once
Howarth, William	3 goals twice
Neil(l), Herb	3 goals twice
McWha, P.C.	3 goals twice
Thrasher	3 goals once

Ames, F.	3 goals once
Grubbe, E.H.	3 goals once
Wurtele, Hunter	3 goals once
Perrier, Arthur	3 goals once
Winn, Eldon H. S.	3 goals once
Crawford (?)	3 goals once
Trainer	3 goals once
Clunis	3 goals once
Chesterton, C.	3 goals once
Carmichael, G.	3 goals once
McLennan	3 goals once
Felion	3 goals once
Martin, W.	3 goals once
Allen, K.C.	3 goals once

Appendix 13: Goalies Records Year by Year

* = B.C. Champion
Int. = International or Open champion at Rossland Carnival
Whelan = Whelan Cup winner
EC = Ellison Cup
SC = "The Silver Cup"
BD = Boundary Champion

Name	Town	W	L	T	GA	GP	SO	AVG.
1895								
Marshall, C.	Golden	0	1	0	9	1		9.0

1896 No results

cont.

1897

Name	Town	W	L	T	GA	GP	SO	AVG.
Hammond, Robert *	Sandon	4	0	0	9	4		2.25
Brown, Arthur Henry	Kaslo	0	2	0	10	2		5.00
Watson, J.	Rossland	0	2	0	11	2		5.50
McIntyre	Nelson	1	1	0	15	2		7.50
Smith, A.	Kaslo	1	1	0	15	2		7.50
Nash	Rossland	0	0	0	2	1		2.00
Egan	Rossland Bank	0	0	1	2	1		2.00
Nelson Goalie	Nelson	0	1	0	14	1		14.00

1898

Name	Town	W	L	T	GA	GP	SO	AVG.
McCreary, W.(?) *	Rossland	4	0	1	8	5	1	1.60
Harrington, C.	Nelson	1	0	1	8	2		4.00
Nunn, (George, ?)	Nelson	0	2	0	8	2		4.00
Burchell, S.	Sandon	2	2	0	20	4	1	5.00
Kane, C.	Kaslo	0	1	0	5	1		5.00
Jeffs, A. (Alf)	Nelson	0	1	0	6	1		6.00
Burchell	Kaslo	0	1	0	12	1		12.00

1899

Name	Team	W	L	T	GA	GP	SO	AVG
MacIntosh, E.C.*	Rossland Victorias	2	1	0	4	3		1.33
McCreary, J. or W.	Rosslands	3	1	0	6	4		1.50
Nunn, George	Nelson	1	1	0	8	2		4.00
Black	Banff	1	0	0	0	1	1	0.00
Schultz, Sam	Langley's Team, Victoria	0	0	1	1	1		1.00
Blain, C.	Daniel's Team, Victoria	0	0	1	1	1		1.00
Lacrosse Club goalie	Vancouver	1	0	0	1	1		1.00
McLellan, McFeely Co. goalie, Vancouver		1	0	0	1	1		1.00
Hammond, Robert	Sandon	1	0	0	2	1		2.00
Vancouver Picked Team goalie		0	1	0	2	1		2.00
Lovatt	Kaslo	0	1	0	3	1		3.00
B.C. Sugary Refinery goalie	Vancouver	0	1	0	3	1		3.00
Bell, G.	Nelson	0	1	0	4	1		4.00
Revelstoke goalie	Revelstoke	0	1	0	7	1		7.00
Field, (Clarence?)	Golden	0	1	0	8	1		8.00
Guest, H.	Slocan City	0	1	0	8	1		8.00

1900

Name	Team	W	L	T	GA	GP	SO	AVG.
McCreary, J.*(Jack/Jasper)	Rossland Victorias	4	0	0	6	4		1.50
Nunn, George	Nelson Lacrosse-Hockey	1	1	0	6	2		2.50

Name	Team	W	L	T	GA	GP	SO	AVG.
Goninan	Rosslands	2	0	0	8	3		2.66
Greenwood Goalie	Greenwood	0	3	0	7	3		2.50

1900 cont.

Name	Team	W	L	T	GA	GP	SO	AVG.
Becher, A. Lorne	Rosland Victorias	1	1	0	6	2		3.00
Stuart, J.	Kaslo	1	0	0	7	2		3.50
Neelands, Sam	Nelson City	0	2	0	11	2		5.50
Crowell, T.E.	Vernon	1	0	0	0	1	1	0.00
Revelstoke goalie	Revelstoke	0	1	0	8	1		8.00

1901

Name	Team	W	L	T	GA	GP	SO	AVG.
Cheyne	New Westminster	2	0	0	2	2		1.00
Neelands, Sam *	Nelson	5	0	0	15	5		3.00
Hogan, (or Hoggan), George	Sandon	1	1	0	6	2	1	3.00
Sandon goalie (Crawford ?)	Sandon	1	1	0	10	3		3.33
Brown, A.H.	Kaslo	1	1	0	7	2		3.50
Leighton, Art, G.	Rosslands	0	2	1	13	3		4.33
McCreary, John (Jack)	Victorias (Ross.)	1	2	1	26	4		6.25
Sawyer, W.	Revelstoke	1	1	0	8	2		4.00
Oliver, E.	Enderby	1	0	0	0	1		0.00
Oliver	Sandon	1	0	0	2	1		2.00
Jackson, E.R.	Vernon	0	1	0	2	1		2.00
CPR goalie	Vancouver	0	1	0	2	1		2.00
Dunn, N.	Vancouver	0	1	0	2	1		2.00
Mitchell	Phoenix	0	1	0	4	1		4.00
Silverton goalie	Silverton	0	1	0	6	1		6.00
Sandon goalie	Sandon	0	1	0	6	1		6.00
Slocan City goalie	Slocan City	0	1	0	8	1		8.00

1902

Name	Team	W	L	T	GA	GP	SO	AVG.
Leighton, Art	Victorias (Ross.)	4	0	0	18	4	1	4.50
Hogan, George (or Hoggan)	Sandon	2	1	0	13	3		4.33
Greyerbiehl, Paul (Flukie)*	Nelson	2	1	0	14	3		4.66
Mitchell	Phoenix	2	1	0	12	3		4.00
Stowe	Greenwood/Phoenix	1	1	0	10	2		5.00
Cochrane	Grand Forks	0	2	0	12	2		6.00
Conklin	Trail	0	4	0	29	4		7.25
McLaughlin, J.	Vernon	1	0	0	3	1		3.00
Dennings, T.	Kamloops	1	0	0	1	1		1.00
Revelstoke goalie	Revelstoke	0	1	0	5	1		5.00
Cropp, Rev.	Nicola lake	0	1	0	8	1		8.00

1903

Name	Team	W	L	T	GA	GP	SO	AVG.
Sawyer, W.	Vernon	4	0	1	5	5	3	1.00
McCeary, John (Jack)	Rossland Victorias	5	1	0	17	6		2.83
Hogan, George (or Hoggan)	Sandon	0	4	1	16	5		3.20

1903 cont.

Name	Team	W	L	T	GA	GP	SO	AVG
Cochrane, A.O.	Grand Forks	2	4	0	22	6	1	3.66
Bishop, Harry*	Nelson	4	0	0	18	4		4.50

1903 cont.

Name	Team	W	L	T	GA	GP	SO	AVG
Sharp	Pincher Creek	1	1	0	10	2		5.00
Cole	Phoenix	2	2	0	16	4		4.00
Blair, Clifford	Kamloops	0	2	0	10	2		5.00
Leighton, Art	Rossland Citizens	0	2	0	18	2		9.00
Greenwood's goalie	Greenwood	1	0	0	0	1	1	0.00
Medicine Hat goalie	Medicine hat (Alb)	1	0	0	3	1		3.00
York, L.	Slocan City	0	1	0	4	1		4.00
Allum, E.M.	Revelstoke	0	1	0	4	1		4.00
Hamberger	Slocan City	1	0	0	5	1		5.00
Bowes	Silverton	0	1	0	6	1		6.00

1904

Name	Team	W	L	T	GA	GP	SO	AVG
Sawyer, W. *	Vernon	2	0	0	5	2		2.50
Bishop, Harry	Nelson	4	1	0	15	5		3.00
Leighton, Art	Rossland	4	5	1	3	10		3.20
Rutherford	Fernie	0	2	0	9	2		4.50
Woods	Revelstoke	0	3	0	28	3		9.33
Haverty, John	Phoenix	1	1		3+	2		3.0+

(Only one game of Haverty's has complete score.)

1905

Name	Team	W	L	T	GA	GP	SO	AVG
Bishop, Harry*	Nelson	6	2	1	23	9		2.55
Sawyer, W.	Vernon	1	2	0	12	3		4.00
McCreary, John (Jack)	Rossland	4	1	2	36	8		4.50
McQuaig	Rossland	1	2	1	20	4		5.00
Miller, J.	Fernie	1	2	0	24	3		8.00
Woodland	Grand Forks	1	0	0	0	1	1	0.00
Hilliard	Phoenix	0	1	0	2	1		2.00
Smith	Fernie	0	1	0	4	1		4.00
Greyerbiehl, Paul, (Flukie)	Nelson	0	1	0	7	1		7.00
Nunn, George	Nelson	0	1	0	8	1		8.00
Woods	Revelstoke	0	1	0	11	1		11.00
Wilson	Grand Forks	0	1	0	12	1		12.00

1906

Name	Team	W	L	T	GA	GP	SO	AVG
McCreary, Jack or Jasper	Rossland	2	0	0	1	2	1	0.50
Bishop, Harry	Nelson	2	0	4	18	6		3.00
Greenwood's goalie	Greenwood	1	1	0	7	2		3.50
Leighton, Art* (disputed)	Rossland	4	1	4	33	9		3.55
Stewart, N.	Nelson	0	1	1	10	2		5.00

1906 cont.

Name	Team	W	L	T	GA	GP	SO	AVG
New Denver's goalie	New Denver	1	0	0	4	1		4.00
Phoenix's goalie	Phoenix	0	1	0	5	1		5.00
Grand Fork's goalie	Grand Forks	0	1	0	6	1		6.00
Wade, M.P. (or W.C.)	Boundary	0	1	0	7	1		7.00
Sandon's goalie	Sandon	0	1	0	8	1		8.00
Miller	Fernie	0	1	0	9	1		9.00

1907

Name	Team	W	L	T	GA	GP	SO	AVG
McQueen	Vancouver	3	0	0	3	3	2	1.00
Sawyer, W.	Vernon	2	0	0	5	2		2.50
McCreary, Jack*	Rossland	4	3	0	22	7	1	3.14
Bishop, Harry (Int)	Nelson	7	1	0	27	8		3.42
Robertson, Charles E.	Spokane	1	1	0	8	2		4.00
Kelly	Phoenix	0	2	0	13	2		6.50
Bush, W.	Revelstoke	0	2	0	15	2		7.50
Wade, M.P.	Boundary /Phoenix	0	2	0	2	2		10.00
Gifford, T. (?)	New Westminster	0	1	0	4	1		4.00
Fernie's goalie	Fernie	1	0	0	5	1		5.00
Egan, Charlie	New Westminster	0	1	0	5	1		5.00
Enderby's goalie	Enderby	0	1	0	6	1		6.00
Burnyeat, D.	Armstrong	0	1	0	6	1		6.00
Coleman's goalie	Coleman (Alberta)	0	1	0	6	1		6.00
Townley	Vancouver Bankers	0	1	0	7	1		7.00
Geyerbiehl, Paul	Nelson	0	1	0	8	1		8.00
Ferrier, Roy	Spokane	0	1	0	8	1		8.00

1908

Name	Team	W	L	T	GA	GP	SO	AVG
Summerland's goalie	Summerland	2	1	0	2	3	2	0.66
Nicola's goalie	Nicola	2	0	0	2	2		1.00
Sawyer, W. EC	Vernon	4	0	0	6	4		1.50
Brennan, W.	Kamloops	0	2	0	4	2		2.00
Fernie's goalie (Whelan)	Fernie	2	0	0	7	2		3.50
(Also had two more wins against Coleman, but score unknown)								
Bishop, Harry	Nelson	2	2	0	16	4		4.00
Maundrell, S.	Armstrong	1	4	0	20	5		4.00
Higgins	Coleman (Alb)	0	3	0	14	3		4.66
(Also had two more losses to Fernie, but score not known)								
McCreary, Jack *(disp) I	Rossland	2	2	0	16	4		4.75
Robertson, Charles E.	Spokane	1	1	0	12	2		6.00
Cowley's goalie	Cowley	1	0	0	0	1	1	0.00
Kelowna's goalie	Kelowna	1	0	0	0	1	1	0.00
Camborne's goalie SC	Camborne	1	0	0	1	1		1.00
Peachland's goalie	Peachland	0	1	0	2	1		2.00
Penticton's goalie	Penticton	0	1	0	2	1		2.00
Ferguson's goalie	Ferguson	0	0	1	3	1		3.00
Spencer, H.(?)	Vernon	0	1	0	7	1		7.00

1909

Name	Team	W	L	T	GA	GP	SO	AVG
Fuller	Kelowna	1	1	0	3	2	1	1.50
Bishop, Harry */I/K	Nelson	6	0	0	12	6	1	2.00
Rutherford	Summerland	1	1	0	4	2		2.00
Woodland BD	Grand Forks	2	1	0	9	3		3.00
Spencer, H.	Vernon	2	0	1	12	4		3.00
Sawyer, W.	Armstrong	1	2	1	14	4		3.50
McCreary, J.	Rossland	1	3	0	27	4		6.75
Grady	Moyie	0	3	0	33	3		11.00
Lackey, S.	Phoenix	1	2	0	20	3		6.67
Carruthers	Rossland	0	1	0	14	1		14.00
Watson, W.G.	Greenwood	2	6	0	not known			
Laires and Tomes	Slocan City	results not complete						
Jacobssen, C.	NewnDenver	results not complete						

1910

Name	Team	W	L	T	GA	GP	SO	AVG
Cummings	Ferguson	1	1	0	5	2		2.50
Gorrell	Trout Lake	1	2	0	8	3		2.66
Lang, Bert I	Grand Forks/Greenwood	4	5	0	32	9		3.55
Watson BD	Greenwood	5	3	0	34	8		4.25
McCreary, J.	Phoenix	5	6	0	64	11		5.82
Grady, H.	Moyie	2	2	2	28	6		4.66
Bishop, Ed *	Nelson	4	1	1	29	6		4.83
Cosgriff	Rossland	0	2	0	16	2		8.00
Rennan, William	Kamloops	1	0	0	1	1		1.00
Revelstoke goalie	Revelstoke	1	0	0	1	1		1.00
McKaskill, J.	Cody	0	0	1	1	1		1.00
Kelson, J.	Sandon	0	0	1	1	1		1.00
Madden, Bob	Gerrard	1	0	0	2	1		2.00
Coleman's goalie	Coleman	0	0	1	2	1		2.00
Doc Curtin	Nicola	0	1	0	2	1		2.00
CPR Vancouver goalie	Vancouver	0	1	0	3	1		3.00
Greyerbiehl, Paul	Nelson	0	0	1	5	1		5.00
Fernie's goalie	Fernie	0	1	0	12	1		12.00

1911

Name	Team	W	L	T	GA	GP	SO	AVG
Tams, C.F.	Sandon	1	1	0	5	2		2.50
Slaatebreck, C.		1	1	0	6	2		3.00
Lang, Bert */ I /BD	Phoenix	6	3	1	38	10		3.80
McCarthy, C.	Greenwood	1	6	0	27	7		3.87
Bishop, Eddie	Nelson	4	0	0	20	5		4.00
Boland, "Baby Doll"	Rossland/Grand Forks	2	5	1	42	7		6.00
McManus	Cranbrook	0	2	0	13	2		6.50
Cosgriff, F.	Rossland	0	3	0	27	3		9.00
Brown	Nelson	1	0	0	4	1		4.00

1911 cont.

		Win	Loss	Tie	GA	GP	Avg.
Murphy	Fernie	0	1	0	9	1	9.00
Bliss	Missoula (Mont)	1	0	0	13	1	13.00

Appendix 14: Goaltender's Records Individual

Only goalies who played goal for more than one year are counted here. They are listed in order of goals against average.

Legend:
- * = B.C. Champion
- I = International or Open Champion at Rossland Carnival
- K = Kootenay League Champion
- B = Boundary Champion

			Win	Loss	Tie	GA	GP	SO	Avg.
Hammond, Robert *		Sandon 1897	4	0	0	9	4		2.25
"		Sandon 1899	1	0	0	2	1		2.00

win %: 1.000   overall average: 2.20

			Win	Loss	Tie	GA	GP	SO	Avg.
Sawyer, W.		Revelstoke 1901	1	1	0	8	2		4.00
" "		Vernon 1903	4	0	1	5	5	3	1.00
" "	*	Vernon 1904	2	0	0	5	2		2.50
" "		Vernon 1905	1	2	0	12	3		4.00
" "		Vernon 1907	2	0	0	5	2		2.50
" "		Vernon 1908	4	0	0	6	4		1.50
" "		Armstrong 1909	1	2	1	14	4		3.50

win%: .682   overall average: 2.50

Goaltenders Records Individual continued

			Win	Loss	Tie	GA	GP	Avg.
Bishop, Harry	*	Nelson 1903	4	0	0	18	4	4.50
" "		Nelson 1904	4	1	0	15	5	3.00
" "	*	Nelson 1905	6	2	1	23	9	2.55
" "		Nelson 1906	2	0	4	18	6	3.00
" "	I	Nelson 1907	7	1	0	27	8	3.42
" "		Nelson 1908	2	2	0	16	4	4.00
" "	*/I/K	Nelson 1909	6	0	0	12	6	2.00

win%: .738   overall average: 3.07

cont.

Goaltenders Records Individual continued

Hogan, (or Hoggan), George

			Team	Year	W	L	T	GF	GA	SO	GAA
"	"	"	Sandon	1900	1	0	0	0	1	1	0.00
"	"	"	Sandon	1901	1	1	0	7	2		3.50
"	"	"	Sandon	1902	2	1	0	13	3		4.33
"	"	"	Sandon	1903	0	4	1	16	5		3.20

win% .364   overall average: 3.27

Lang, Bert

			Team	Year	W	L	T	GF	GA	SO	GAA
	I		Grand Forks/Greenwood	1910	4	5	0	32	9		3.55
"	"	*/I	Phoenix	1911	6	3	1	38	10		3.80

win%: .526   overall average: 3.68

Neelands, Sam

		Team	Year	W	L	T	GF	GA	SO	GAA
		Nelson	1900	0	2	0	11	2		5.50
"	*	Nelson	1901	5	0	0	15	5		3.00

win%: .714   overall average: 3.71

McCreary, John (Jack or Jasper)

			Team	Year	W	L	T	GF	GA	SO	GAA
"	"	*	Rossland	1898	4	0	1	8	5	1	1.60
"	"		Rossland	1899	3	0	1	6	4		1.50
"	"	*	Rossland	1900	4	0	0	6	4		1.50
"	"		Rossland	1901	1	2	1	20	4		6.25
"	"		Rossland	1902	0	1	0	14	1		14.00
"	"		Rossland	1903	5	1	0	17	6		2.83
"	"		Rossland	1905	4	1	1	26	6		4.30
"	"		Rossland	1906	2	0	0	1	2	1	0.50
"	"	*	Rossland	1907	4	3	0	22	7	1	3.14
"	"	*(disputed)	Rossland	1908	2	2	0	19	4		4.75
"	"		Rossland	1909	1	3	0	27	4		6.75
"	"		Phoenix	1910	5	6	0	64	11		5.81

win%: .603   overall average: 3.96

Mitchell

	Team	Year	W	L	T	GF	GA	SO	GAA
	Phoenix	1901	0	1	0	4	1		4.00
"	Phoenix	1902	2	1	0	12	3		4.00

win%: .500   overall average: 4.00

Leighton, Art G.

		Team	Year	W	L	T	GF	GA	SO	GAA
		Rossland	1901	0	2	1	13	3		4.33
"	"	Rossland Victorias	1902	4	0	0	18	4	1	4.50
"	"	Rossland	1903	0	2	0	18	2		9.00
"	"	Rossland	1904	4	5	1	32	10		3.20
"	*(disputed)	Rossland	1906	4	1	4	33	9		3.55

win%: .571   overall average: 4.10

Goaltenders Records Individual continued

Nunn, George	Nelson 1898	0	2	0	8	2	4.00
" "	Nelson 1899	1	1	0	8	2	4.00
" "	Nelson 1900	1	1	0	5	2	2.50
" "	Nelson 1902	1	0	0	4	1	4.00
" "	Nelson 1905	0	1	0	8	1	8.00

win%: .375   overall average: 4.12

Watson, W.G.	Greenwood 1909	2	6	rest not known			
" " B	Greenwood 1910	5	3	0	34	8	4.25

win%: .466   overall average: 4.25?

Cochrane, A.O.							
" "	Grand Forks 1902	0	0	0	12	2	6.00
" "	Grand Forks 1903	2	4	0	22	6	3.66

win%: .250   overall average: 4.25

Bishop, Eddie	Nelson 1910	4	1	1	29	6	4.83
" "	Nelson 1911	4	0	0	20	5	4.00

win%: .727   overall average: 4.45

Robertson, Charles E.							
" "	Spokane 1907	1	1	0	8	2	4.00
" "	Spokane 1907	1	1	0	12	2	6.00

win%: .500   overall average: 5.00

Greyerbiehl, Charles("Flukie")							
" "	Nelson 1902	2	1	0	14	3	4.66
" "	Nelson 1905	0	0	1	7	1	7.00
" "	Nelson 1907	0	1	0	8	1	8.00
" "	Nelson 1910	0	0	1	5	1	5.00

win%: .333   overall average: 5.67

Grady, H.	Moyie 1909	0	3	0	33	3	11.00
"	Moyie 1910	2	2	2	28	6	4.66

win% .222   overall average: 6.77

Goaltenders Records Individual continued

Miller, J.	Fernie 1905	1	2	0	24	3	8.00
"	Fernie 1906	0	0	1	9	1	9.00
	win% .250				overall average: 8.25		
Cosgriff, F.	Rossland 1910	0	2	0	16	2	8.00
"	Rossland 1911	0	3	0	27	3	9.00
	win%: .000				overall average: 8.60		
Woods	Revelstoke 1904	0	3	0	28	3	9.33
"	Revelstoke 1905	0	1	0	11	1	11.00
	win%: .000				overall average: 9.75		

APPENDIX 15   Trophy Winners

B.C. Championships: The first championship was unofficially held at the first tournament in B.C. at Sandon. A silver cup was offered, but it was not named. It was clear that the four towns which had competitive teams considered it a kind of B.C. Championship. In Rossland, at the first Rossland Carnival in 1898, it was announced that all teams would be playing for the B.C. Championships, to which they agreed. Provided for this event was a silver cup, reportedly 19 inches tall, on a base of onyx. Later, however, it was reported to be 27 inches tall, on a base of ebony. It had a pair of miniature sticks and a puck at the bottom of the cup, just before the base, with a "facing off" sketch on one side of the cup itself, and an inscription on the other side. These sides were often switched in photos, according to the preferences of the teams. The cup was open at the top, with two flanges, and had two handles. There were two hockey players standing on either side of the base, upright, holding their sticks straight down. In 1904 the Giant Powder Cup was provided, when Nelson won the previous silver cup three times in a row. This new cup was closed at the top, with one hockey player standing on the top, with his stick down and one foot in the air. It had two handles, and in the middle were two hockey sticks crossed, with the base underneath. In 1908 this cup was then kept by Rossland, after winning it three times in a row. Then the Giant Powder Company replaced this cup in 1909 with the Giant Powder Shield, which was silver on an oak frame. (It was also referred to as the Hamilton Shield). The original B.C. Championship cup was also called the Rossland Citizen's Cup, or the Citizen's Cup, or the Carnival Cup.

In 1909 the Nelson team won the B.C. Championships and the Open competition at the Rossland Carnival. When they had their picture taken they confused the issue by including not only the Giant Powder Shield, and Fraser trophy, but also the Daily News Cup, which they did not win, and the original B.C. Championship Cup, which they also technically did not win. The Daily News Cup was supposed to be awarded to the Thistles or the Victorias, both Nelson city teams, but the result was left open, as the teams had tied, and it was never played off. The Nelson team also displayed the previous Carnival Cup in their 1904 and 1907 team photos, so it seems this became a tradition.

B.C. Championships

1895 not offered
1896 not offered
1897 Sandon (Sandon Carnival)
1898 Rossland
1899 Rossland Victorias
1900 Rossland Victorias
1901 Nelson
1902 Nelson
1903 Nelson
1904 Vernon
1905 Nelson
1906 Rossland (Disputed. Rossland actually tied with Nelson)
1907 Rossland
1908 Rossland (Disputed)
1909 Nelson
1910 Nelson
1911 Phoenix

Later B.C. championship Winners
1912 Greenwood
1913 Fernie
1914 Rossland
1915 Trail
1916 Rossland
1917 Rossland
1918 - onward, no longer offered. (See Epilogue)

Fraser Cup for International or Open Competition at the Rossland Carnival

1907 Nelson
1908 Rossland
1909 Nelson
1910 Greenwood
1911 Phoenix

B.C. Hockey League Trophy
Initially offered as a continuing trophy for each year's overall champion, the organization broke down after its first year and was never played for officially again. Instead, a series of informal challenge matches prevailed. Finally, in 1913, the Kootenay and Boundary hockey association managed to form a more stable organization for a yearly challenge cup, using the Daily News Cup, among others.

1900 Rossland Victorias

Junior B.C. Championship (at Rossland Carnival)

In 1899 a cup was offered by Ross Thompson, of Rossland, called the Ross Thompson Cup, to be played for the Junior Championship of B.C. at the Rossland Carnival. (The cup was thin, with a hockey player standing erect at the top, with his stick straight down at his feet, and two hockey sticks crossed in the middle of the stand, with a small base beneath it.) It was not always stated, however, that the Cup was being played for.

Junior Championship cont.

1897 Not known
1898 Not known
1899 Sandon
1900 Sandon
1901 Sandon
1902 Rossland
1903 Not known - possibly not played
1904 Rossland (The Rossland team beat Trail, but it might have been only an exhibition)
1905 Rossland
1906 Rossland
1907 Rossland
1908 Rossland
1909 Nelson
1910 not known
1911 not known - not played at Rossland Carnival

B.C. Juvenile championship

In 1905 a Juvenile championship was offered at the Rossland Carnival. But this was not played for regularly. It's not known exactly what the age limit was.

1905 Rossland
1907 Nelson
1908 Rossland and Trail tied. (Not indicated as a championship game)

Intermediate B.C. Championship (At the Rossland Carnival)

1906 Rossland
1907 Rossland
1908 Phoenix
1909 Rossland
1910 Rossland
1911 Missoula Montana or Nelson. (Nelson beat Rossland, and Missoula beat Nelson, but the Missoula game was not officially recognized, with no reason given.)

Ladies Championship
Only once was a Ladies game at the Rossland Carnival considered the B.C. Championship, and that was in 1900. All other games were only challenge matches.

1900 Rossland Ladies
1906 Rossland Ladies (unofficial)
1911 Rossland Ladies (unofficial)

cont.

Ellison Cup, for the champions of the Okanagan
(Donated by MP Price Ellison)
1907 Not known – probably Vernon
1908 Vernon
1909 Vernon (Won a challenge series against Armstrong, but not named specifically as winner of Ellison cup)
1910 not known, possibly not played for.
1911 not known, possibly not played for.

Rossland-Trail Industrial League

1904 was the first year they played in an official league, for an official trophy, and all teams were from Rossland. In 1905 Trail was asked to join. Other cities were also asked, but none fielded teams. In 1905 the League was also referred to as the Kootenay Industrial League.

1904 Le Roi Mine
1905 Le Roi and Hunter Brothers. (These teams were supposed to play off, but due to delays and mild weather, the final game never took place.)
1906 Centre Star Mine
1907 Le Roi Mine
1908 Le Roi Mine
1909 not known - appears to have been abandoned

Boundary League championship

1903 Grand Forks (the total results are not known, but Grand Forks claimed the championship)
1904 not known at this time. It might not have been played for.
1905 not known at this time. It might not have been played for.
1906 not known at this time. It might not have been played for.
1907 not known at this time. It might not have been played for.
1908 not known at this time. It might not have been played for.
1909 Grand Forks
1910 Greenwood
1911 Phoenix

Crow's Nest Pass League championship and Whelan Cup

1903 Medicine Hat Alberta
1904 Fernie
1905 Not known at this time.
1906 Not known at this time.
1907 Coleman Alberta
1908 Fernie
1909 not claimed in newspaper reports. Moyie appeared to have best record.
1910 Moyie(?)
1911 Cranbrook

cont.

Daily News Cup

The first year it was offered, in 1908, it was played for only by Nelson inner city teams. Later, in 1913, it became a trophy representing the best team in the Kootenays as a challenge cup.)

1908 Mountains (Nelson)
1909 Victorias or Thistles - they were tied, and the winner was not played off.
1910 Victorias and Thistles tied.
1911 not played for

Member's cup

This was ostensibly a challenge cup for Kootenay Intermediate teams

1910 Kaslo and Rossland tied
1911 not played for.

C.F. Nelson Cup

This was a challenge cup for the New Denver city League.

1911 New Denver A's (?)

Haddad Trophy

This was a challenge cup in the Kamloops area.

1909 Nicola
1910 not known
1911 not known

Cornwall Cup

This was a challenge cup in the Slocan Valley. It was donated by T.E. Cornwall, a resident of New Denver, who then moved to Spokane.

1909 Slocan City
1910 not known
1911 not known

Championship of the Pacific Coast

This was only played for once, and was called this after a Vancouver team defeated two rivals, one from New Westminster, and another from Vancouver. Generally there weren't enough ice days to have any kind of true championship. However, in this case it appears that medals and a trophy were actually manufactured for the winning team.

1907 Herman's Champions (also called the Vancouver Terminals)

Appendix 16:   Illustrations

Plate 01. Bandy illustration from Badminton Library, Skating, 1892, page:	9.
Plate 02. John Toole's painting of Skating On the Ice, circa 1835, page:	13.
Plate 03. Currier and Ives Lithograph, 1855, Winter Pastime, page:	13.
Plate 04. William Armstrong's painting, Toronto Bay, 1852, page:	16.
Plate 05. Thames Skating engraving 1855, page:	17.
Plate 06. Map of South-Eastern British Columbia, page:	21.
Plate 07. Rossland Ladies Team circa 1900, page:	61.
Plate 08. Sandon Senior Hockey Team 1901 photograph, page:	78.
Plate 09. Sandon Junior Hockey Team 1901 photograph, page:	79.
Plate 10. Nelson Hockey Team 1901, photograph, page:	80.
Plate 11. Nelson Hockey Team 1903, photograph, page:	106.
Plate 12. Nelson Hockey Team 1904, photograph, page:	124.
Plate 13. Revelstoke Hockey Team 1904, photograph, page:	125.
Plate 14. Vernon Hockey Team, 1904, photograph, page:	126.
Plate 15. Silverton Men's Team, 1904, photograph, page:	127.
Plate 15(a). Silverton Ladies's Team, 1904, photograph, page:	128.
Plate 16. Centre Star, Industrial League Team, Rossland, 1906, photo, page:	165.
Plate 17. Rossland Ladies Team 1906, photo, page:	166.
Plate 18. Hunter Wurtele, Spokane's Star, Newspaper, 1906, page:	166.
Plate 19. Nelson Senior Men's Hockey Team, 1907, photo, page:	186.
Plate 20. Rossland Senior Men's Hockey Team, 1907, photo, page:	187.
Plate 21. Le Roi Industrial League Team, Rossland, 1907, photo, page:	188.
Plate 22. Spokane Senior Hockey Team, 1907, newspaper, page:	189.
Plate 23. Vancouver Team, Herman's Champions, 1907, photo, page:	190.
Plate 24. Nelson Senior Men's Team, 1908, newspaper, page:	212.
Plate 25. Rossland Senior Men's Team, 1908, photo, page:	213.
Plate 26. Rossland Senior Men's Team, 2nd 1908, photo, page:	214.
Plate 27. Vernon Hockey Team, 1908, photograph, page:	215.
Plate 28. Nelson Senior Men's Team, 1909, photo, page:	238.
Plate 29. Nelson Intermediates, 1909, photo, page:	239.
Plate 30. Nelson Rink, 1909, newspaper, page:	240.
Plate 31. Nelson Ladies, 1910, photo, page:	263.
Plate 32. Rossland Senior Men's Team, in Arena, 1910, photo, page:	264.
Plate 33. Moyie Senior Team, 1910, photo, page:	265.
Plate 34. Grand Forks Senior Team, 1910, photo, page:	266.
Plate 35. Nelson Rovers Junior Team, 1911, photo, page:	293.
Plate 36. Rossland Ladies 1912, photo, page:	297.
Plate 37. Greenwood Senior Team, 1912, photo, page:	298.

Appendix 17:   Source Material

(Sources which yielded no related hockey information, although voluminous, are not listed.)

Newspapers

The Sandon Paystreak
The Nelson Miner
The Nelson Daily News

The Golden Star
The Golden Era
Victoria Daily Colonist
Vancouver World
Vancouver Daily Province
New Westminster Daily Columbian
Fort George Herald
Fort George Weekly Tribune
Grand Forks Gazette
Grand Forks News Gazette
Grand Forks Miner Gazette
Ashcroft Journal
Kamloops Sentinel
Trail Creek News
Rossland Miner
Rossland Weekly Miner
Greenwood Miner
Vernon News
Kaslo Kootenian
Calgary Daily Herald
Edmonton Bulletin
Vancouver News Advertiser
Spokane Spokesman Review
Toronto Patriot

Other:

"Hockey, Canada's Royal Winter Game," by Arthur Farrell, C.R. Corneil, Montreal, 1899.

Henderson British Columbia Directories

Wrigley British Columbia Directories

"Saint Nicholas magazine," January 1929, article by Thomas K. Fischer, New York, 1929.

"Kinbasket Country," the story of Golden and the Columbia Valley, the Golden district and Historical Society, 1972.

"Old Silverton," John Norris, Silverton Historical Society, 1985.

"The Year Book of British Columbia," R.E. Gosnell, Government of B.C. Victoria, 1903.

"The Year Book of British Columbia," 1898
Other Sources cont.

Wikipedia, the free encyclopedia, World Wide Web, 2006.

"The Puck Starts Here," Garth Vaughn, Goose Lane Editions, Fredericton NB, 1996.

"Ice Age Memoirs," A Bibliography and Compendium of Early hockey publications, Craig Bowlsby, Ice Age Publications, Vancouver 1996.

"Hockey's Captains, Colonels and Kings," J. W. (Bill) Fitsell, Boston Mills Press, Erin Ontario, 1987.

The Society of North American Hockey Historians and Researchers, or SONAHHR, web site on the world wide web, 2006.

Society for International Hockey Research (SIHR)

"The Trail of the Stanley Cup," Volume 1, Charles L. Coleman, National Hockey League, Toronto, 1966.

"Trail On Ice," Murray Grieg, Trail City Archives, 1999.

"Alberta on Ice," Gary W. Zeman, GMS Ventures inc. Edmonton, 1985-86.

"Wind and Ice," (one hundred years of Kamloops hockey), Glen Cowley, rockface books, Kamloops, 1999.

"Manitoba Hockey," A History, Vince Leah, Manitoba Hockey Player's Foundation, 1970-71.

"Halifax, Warden of the North," by Raddall, Thomas H., McClelland and Stewart, Toronto,1948., (also revised edition below).

"Halifax, Warden of the North," by Raddall, Thomas H. McClelland and Stewart, Toronto, 1971, revised edition.

The History of Nova Scotia Web Site, world wide web 2006

"The History of Hockey in B.C.," by Denny Boyd, an historical supplement to the Vancouver Canucks Hockey Magazine, Vancouver Canucks, Circa 1970.

"A History of the British Columbia Amateur Hockey Association," Leo Atwell, Privately Printed (?), 1989.

"The Patricks," by Eric Whitehead, Doubleday, Toronto, 1980.
    Eric Whitehead gives no bibliography. He explains in his preface that he had the support of many people around the hockey community, and Lester Patrick's family, and an, "access," to historical material by a fan named Boyd Robinson, to which Lester Patrick had contributed. [According to Boyd Robinson's widow, G. Irene, this historical material consisted of a trunk of clippings given to Boyd by Stan Patrick, Lester's brother, which he had collected over the early years. Boyd eventually gave this trunk to the Patrick family, and its whereabouts are now apparently unknown.] Although Whitehead does not specifically mention this, there was apparently some kind of Lester Patrick diary, or memoir, which was lent him by Lester Patrick's family. As Lester and Frank were both deceased, Whitehead apparently followed this diary, or other writings of Lester Patrick, very closely in following Lester's early career, without delving very far, (if any) into B.C. newspaper reports. (Many B.C. newspaper reports are quoted, but it appears these are clippings from the Boyd Robinson material, or the Patrick family's scrapbooks.) The diary, scrapbooks, etc., are no longer available. Some have been distributed to various family members, and the rest were destroyed.
    Eric Whitehead is deceased.

"Cyclone Taylor," by Eric Whitehead, Doubleday, Toronto, 1977.

"Hockey Heritage, 88 years of puck chasing in Saskatchewan," by Brenda Zeman, & others, 1983, Saskatchewan Sports Hall of Fame.

"My Strange Rescue, and other Stories of Sport and Adventure in Canada," by J. Macdonald Oxley, 1895, Thomas Nelson and Sons. New York, London and Edinburgh. The book was reprinted at least until 1903. Oxley gives an eight page chapter called, "The Game of Rink Hockey," which was probably published earlier in a Youth Magazine, but had to be between 1887 and 1895. Oxley did actually play the game. He was born in 1855 in Halifax and died in Toronto in 1907. His early life and schooling took place in Halifax, and he practiced law there until about 1883, when he moved variously to Ottawa, Montreal and Toronto. Joseph Strutt, referred to by Oxley, lived from 1749-1802, but the earliest copy of his book, The Sports and Pastimes of the English People, I could find listed, was 1810.

"Hockey's Home, Halifax-Dartmouth," by Martin Jones, Nimbus Publishing, Halifax. 2002.

"The Macmillan Dictionary of Canadian Biography," edited by Stewart Wallace and W.A. McKay, Macmillan of Canada, Toronto, 1978.

"Alberta On Ice," by Gary Zeman, published by Gary Zeman, Edmonton, 1985.

"The Badminton Library of sports and Pastimes, Skating," by J.M. Heathcote and C.G. Tebbutt. London, 1892. Tebbutt has written here a 16 page treatise entitled, Bandy.

"Fifty Years of My Life In the World of Sport, At Home and Abroad," by Sir John Dugdale, Astley, Bart., London, Hurst and Blackett, 1895.

"Silver Lead and Hell," by Veronica Pellowski, Prospector Pick Publishing, New Denver, 1992

"The Renfrew Millionaires," by Frank Cosentino, the General Store Publishing House, Burnstown Ontario, 1990.

Donald M. Black, M.D. Typewritten Memoir, "Boyhood days in Nelson 1902-1909." Located now in Nelson Museum.

Douglas Jerome, typewritten memoir on the Bishop Brothers, submitted in 1980's (?) Located now in Nelson Museum.

"The Story of South Africa," World Publishing company, Guelph Ontario, 1899, List of First Canadian contingent.

Historical Atlas of Canada, Thomas Nelson and sons, Don Mills Ontario, 2nd ed. 1966

Mrs. Sheelah Castle's memories, through telephone conversations. (Sheelah Castle is Guy Patrick's daughter).

"Hockey in Canada" by William McLennan, Illustrated by Arthur Hemming. Harper's Weekly, New York NY, January 12, 1895, page 45.

The Ridout Letters, or "Ten Years of Upper Canada in Peace and War, 1805-1815," and edited portion of letters by Thomas Ridout et al.

"New Voyages and Travels," or "Travels Through the Canadas," by George Heriot. London, 1807.

This is number

221

of 500 copies

signed